My Neighbor Seki

no Seki-kun

2

Takuma Morishige

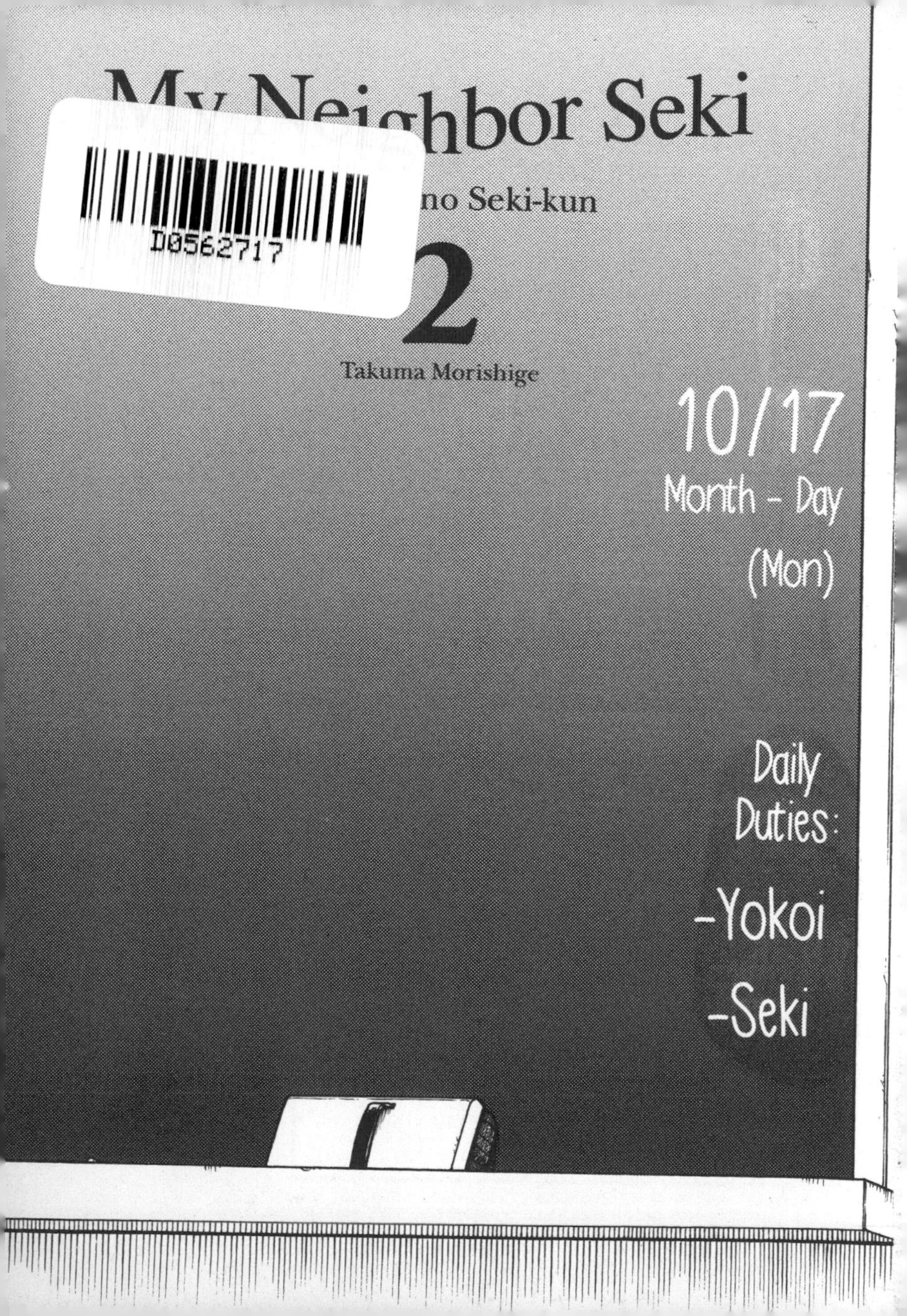
10/17
Month - Day
(Mon)
Daily Duties:
-Yokoi
-Seki

My Neighbor Seki

2

Schedule

16th Period ③	17th Period ⑬	18th Period ㉓	19th Period ㉟
20th Period ㊺	21st Period (55)	22nd Period (77)	23rd Period (101)
24th Period (111)	25th Period (121)	26th Period (133)	27th Period (143)
28th Period (153)	Bonus ① (166)	Bonus ② (170)	

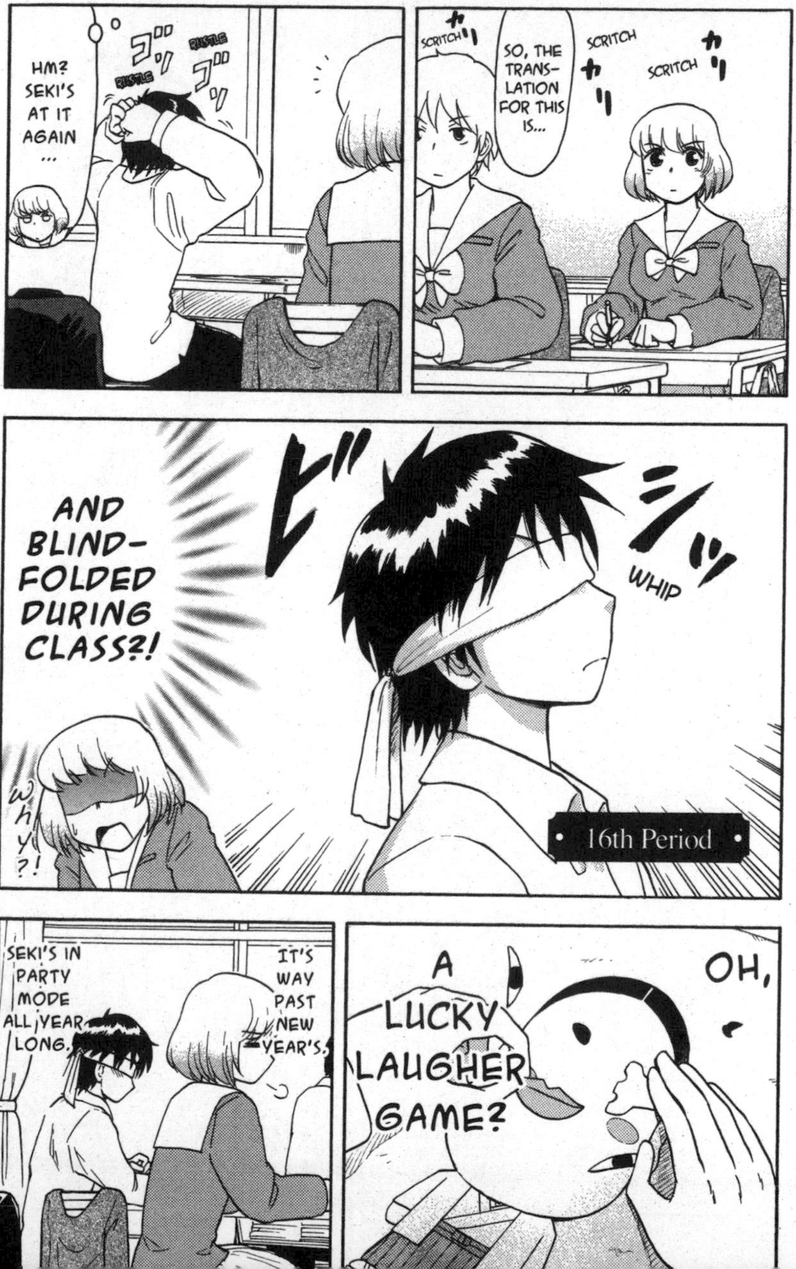
SCRITCH
SO, THE TRANS-LATION FOR THIS IS...
SCRITCH
SCRITCH
HM? SEKI'S AT IT AGAIN...
RUSTLE
RUSTLE
AND BLIND-FOLDED DURING CLASS?!
WHIP
why?!
16th Period
OH,
A LUCKY LAUGHER GAME?
IT'S WAY PAST NEW YEAR'S.
SEKI'S IN PARTY MODE ALL YEAR LONG.

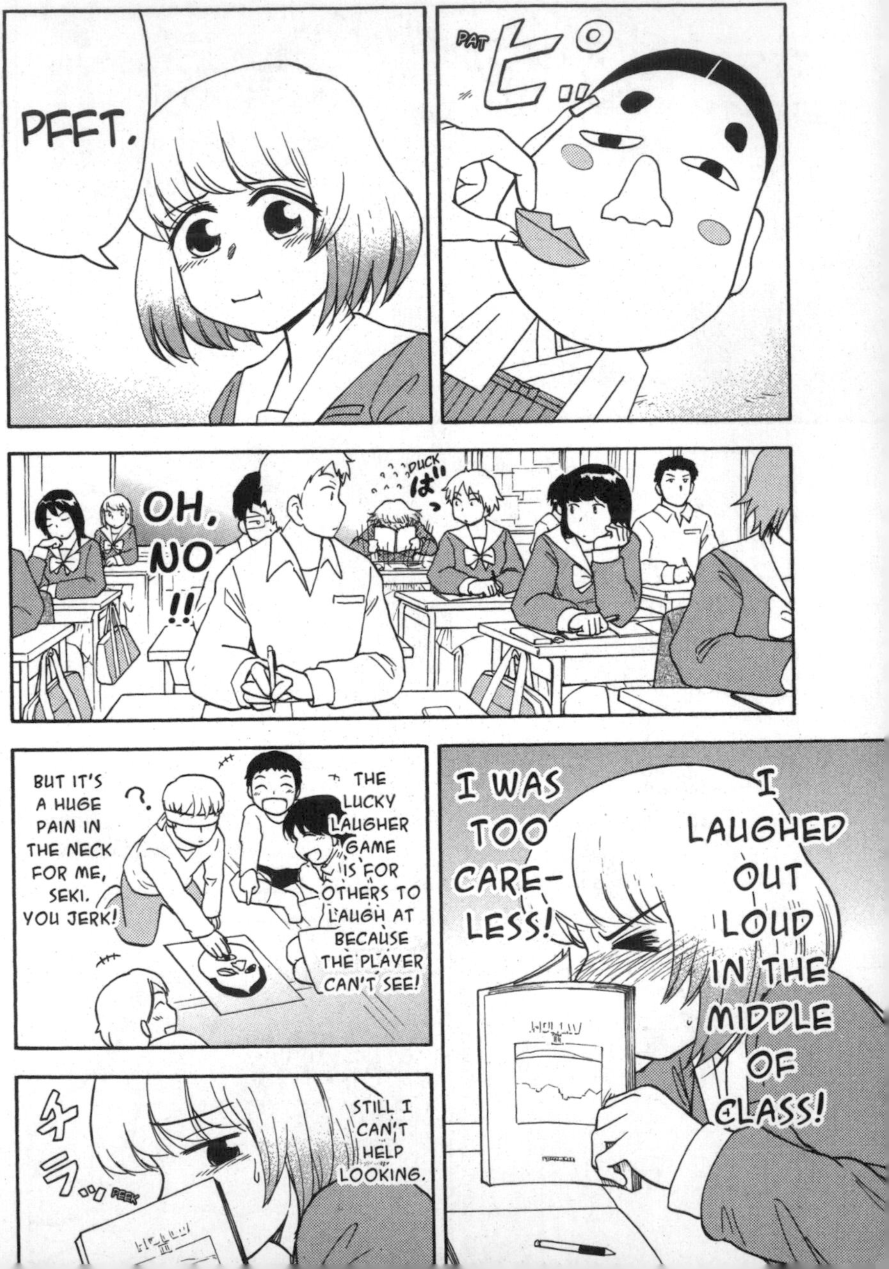
PAT
ピッ
PFFT.
DUCK
ばっ
OH, NO!!
I LAUGHED OUT LOUD IN THE MIDDLE OF CLASS!
I WAS TOO CARELESS!
THE LUCKY LAUGHER GAME IS FOR OTHERS TO LAUGH AT BECAUSE THE PLAYER CAN'T SEE!
BUT IT'S A HUGE PAIN IN THE NECK FOR ME, SEKI. YOU JERK!
STILL I CAN'T HELP LOOKING.
チラッ
PEEK

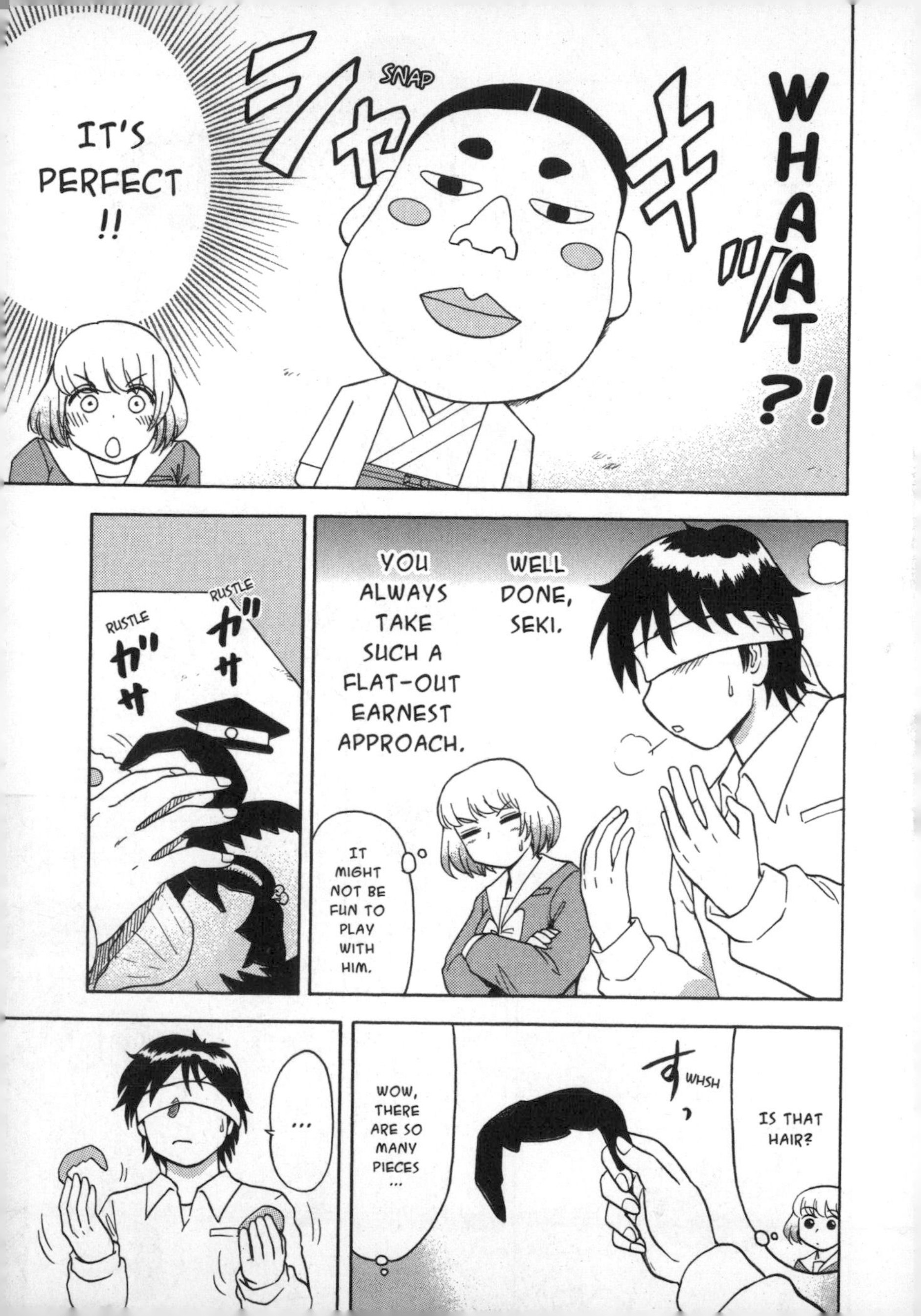
WHAT?!
シャキ
SNAP
IT'S PERFECT!!
WELL DONE, SEKI.
YOU ALWAYS TAKE SUCH A FLAT-OUT EARNEST APPROACH.
IT MIGHT NOT BE FUN TO PLAY WITH HIM.
ガサ
RUSTLE
ガサ
RUSTLE
IS THAT HAIR?
す
WHSH
WOW, THERE ARE SO MANY PIECES...
...

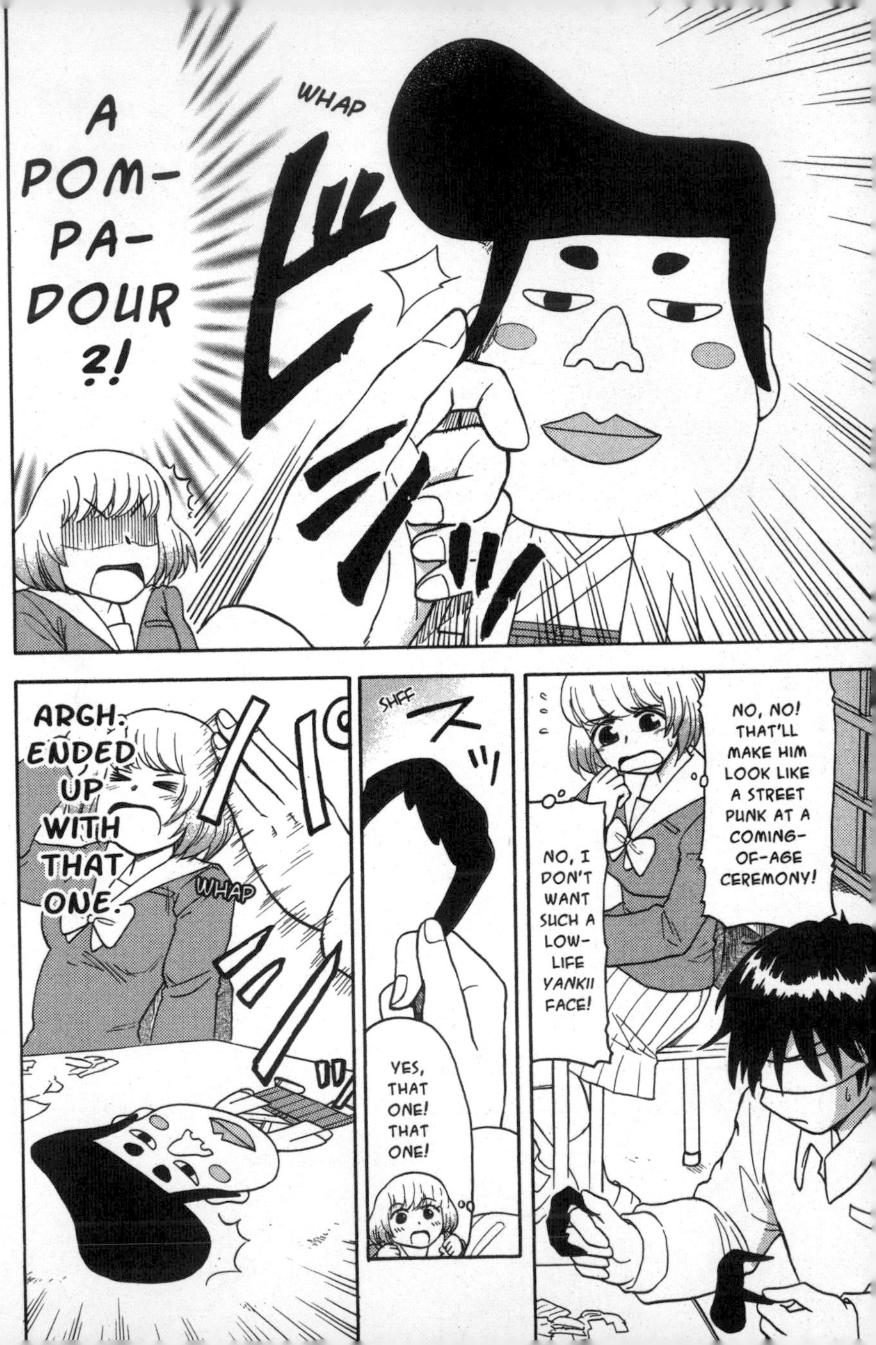
WHAP
A POM-PA-DOUR?!
NO, NO! THAT'LL MAKE HIM LOOK LIKE A STREET PUNK AT A COMING-OF-AGE CEREMONY!
NO, I DON'T WANT SUCH A LOW-LIFE YANKII FACE!
SHFF
YES, THAT ONE! THAT ONE!
ARGH. ENDED UP WITH THAT ONE.
WHAP

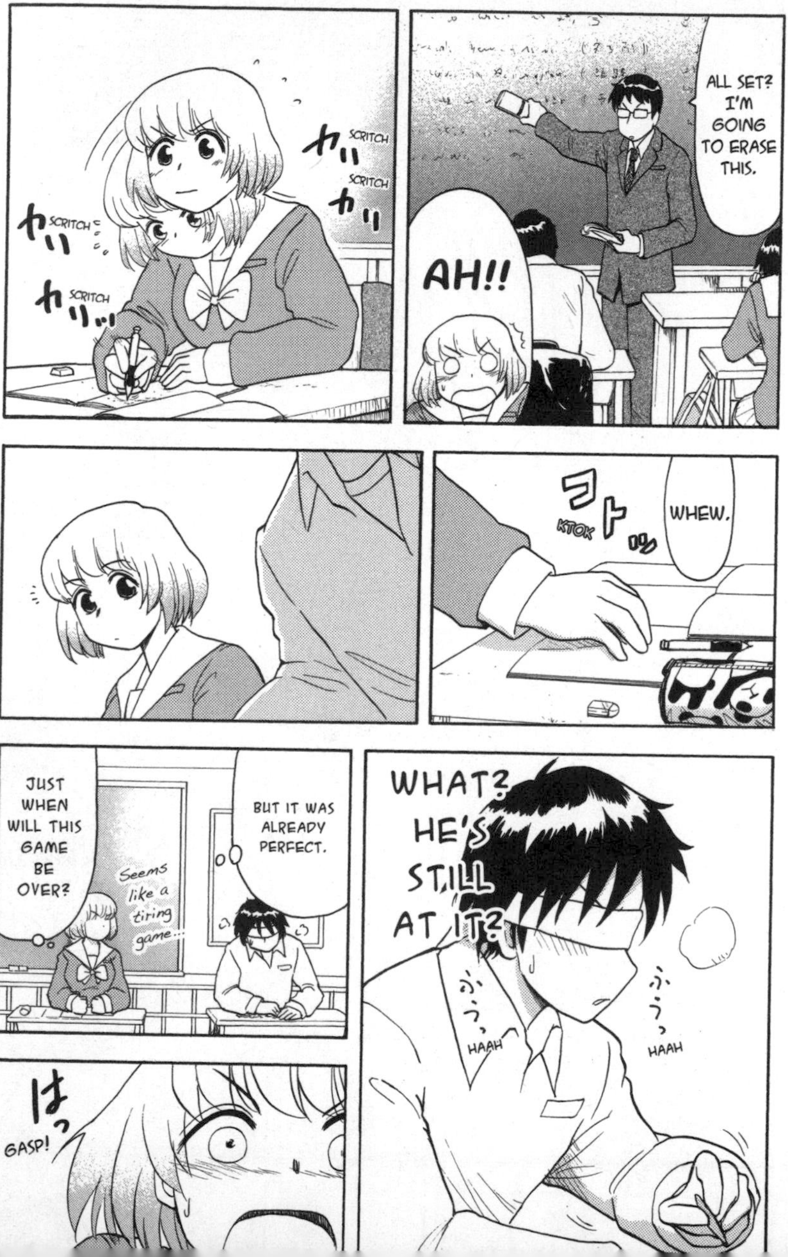
ALL SET? I'M GOING TO ERASE THIS.
AH!!
SCRITCH
SCRITCH
SCRITCH
SCRITCH
コトッ
KTOK
WHEW.
WHAT? HE'S STILL AT IT?
ふうっ
HAAH
ふうっ
HAAH
BUT IT WAS ALREADY PERFECT.
JUST WHEN WILL THIS GAME BE OVER?
Seems like a tiring game...
はっ
GASP!

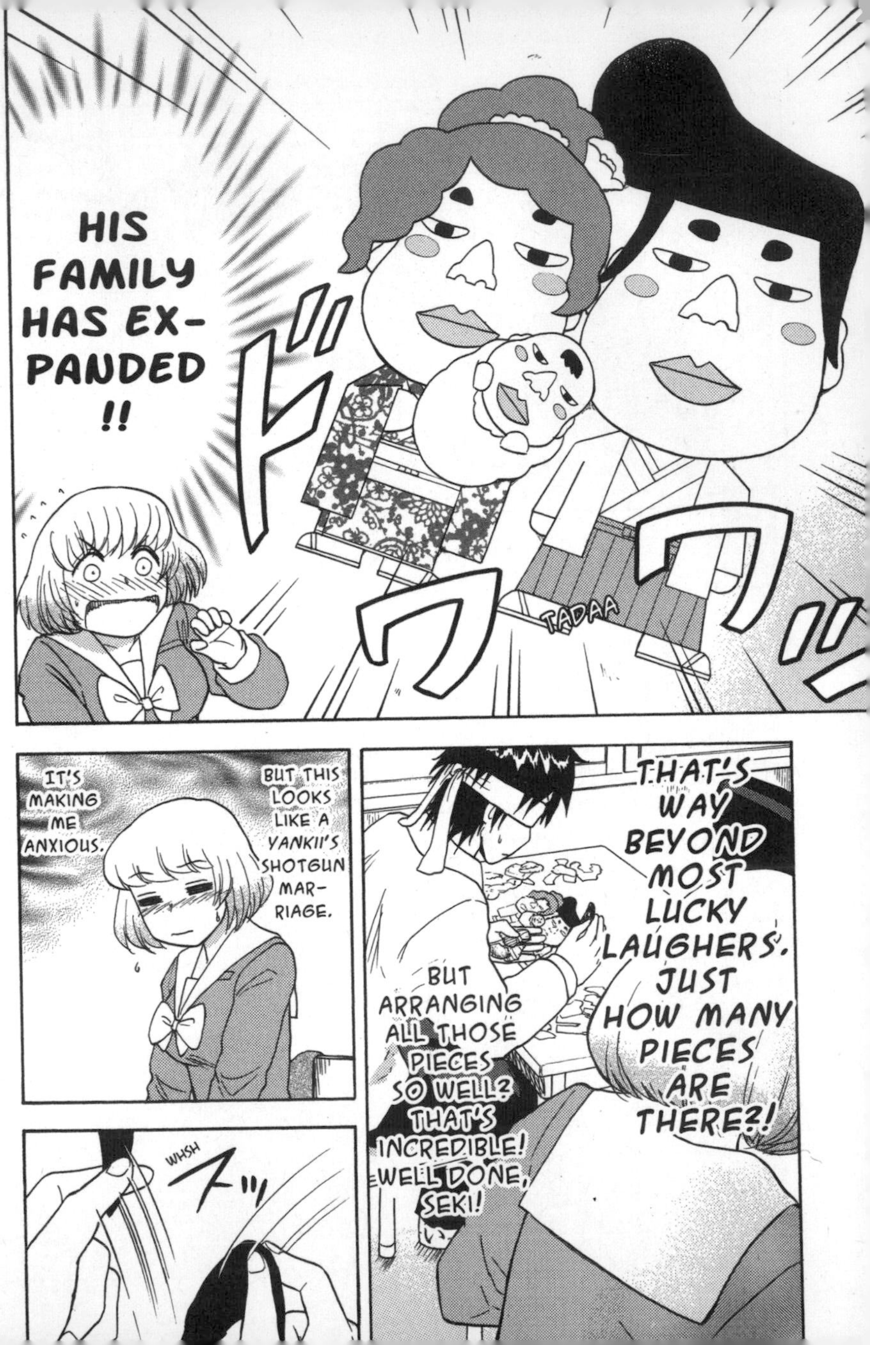
HIS FAMILY HAS EX-PANDED!!
TADAA
THAT'S WAY BEYOND MOST LUCKY LAUGHERS. JUST HOW MANY PIECES ARE THERE?!
BUT ARRANGING ALL THOSE PIECES SO WELL? THAT'S INCREDIBLE! WELL DONE, SEKI!
BUT THIS LOOKS LIKE A YANKII'S SHOTGUN MAR-RIAGE.
IT'S MAKING ME ANXIOUS.
WHSH

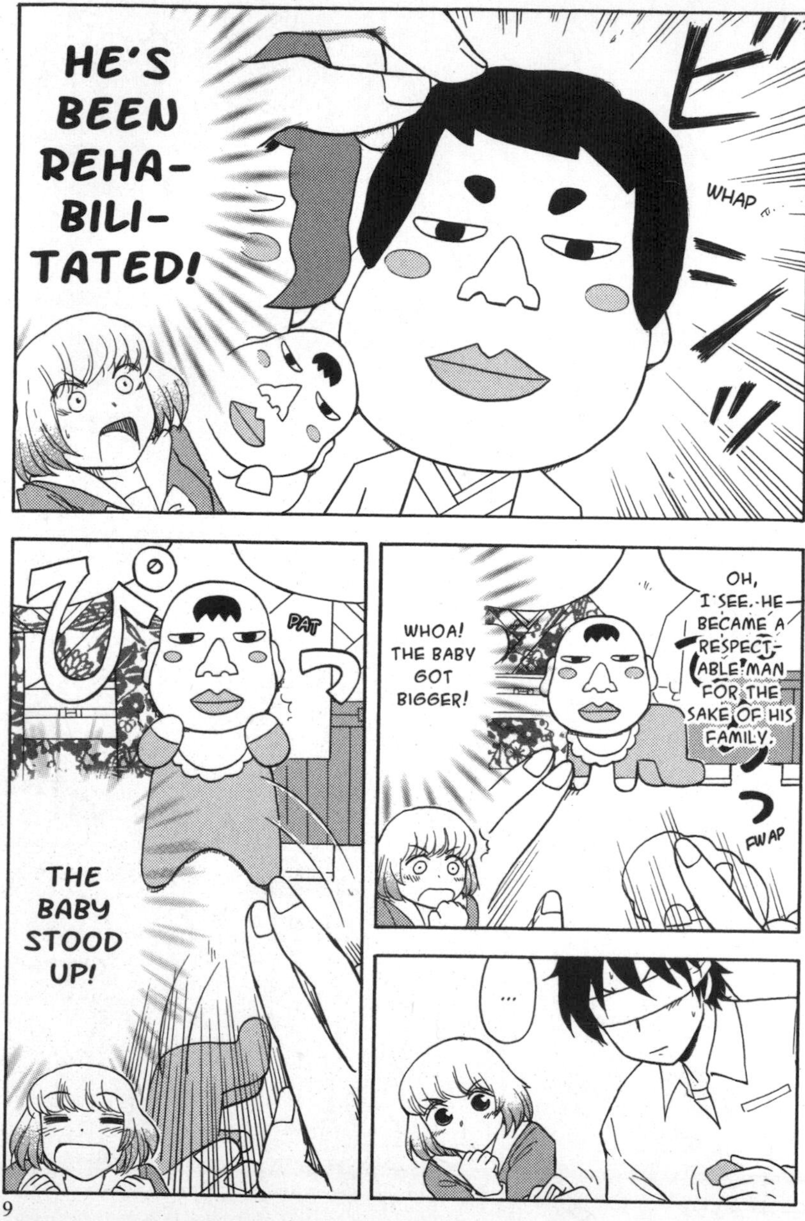
HE'S BEEN REHA-BILI-TATED!
WHAP
OH, I SEE. HE BECAME A RESPECT-ABLE MAN FOR THE SAKE OF HIS FAMILY.
WHOA! THE BABY GOT BIGGER!
FWAP
...
PAT
THE BABY STOOD UP!

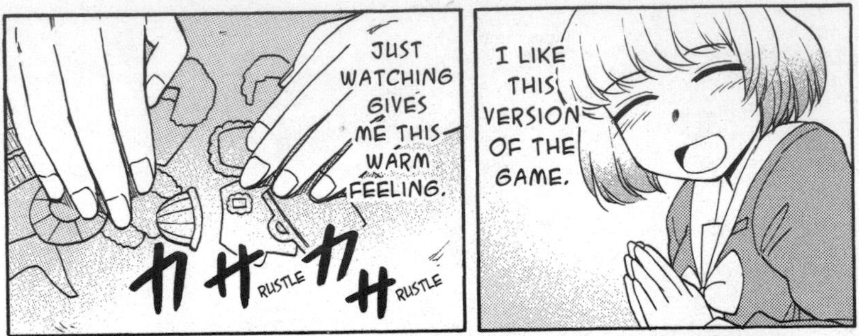
I LIKE THIS VERSION OF THE GAME.
JUST WATCHING GIVES ME THIS WARM FEELING.
カサ RUSTLE カサ RUSTLE

※ 7-5-3 is a rite of passage celebrated by kids aged five, seven and three in November.

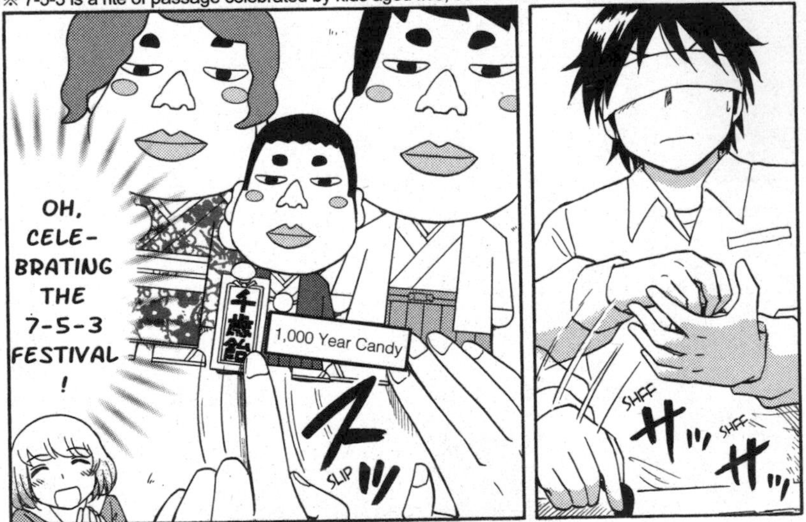
SHFF サッ SHFF サッ
OH, CELEBRATING THE 7-5-3 FESTIVAL!
1,000 Year Candy
スッ SLIP

※ 1000 Year Candy is given to kids on 7-5-3 for health and longevity.

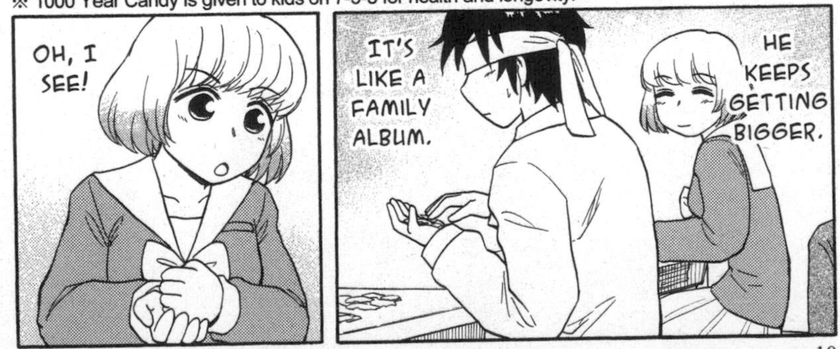
HE KEEPS GETTING BIGGER.
IT'S LIKE A FAMILY ALBUM.
OH, I SEE!

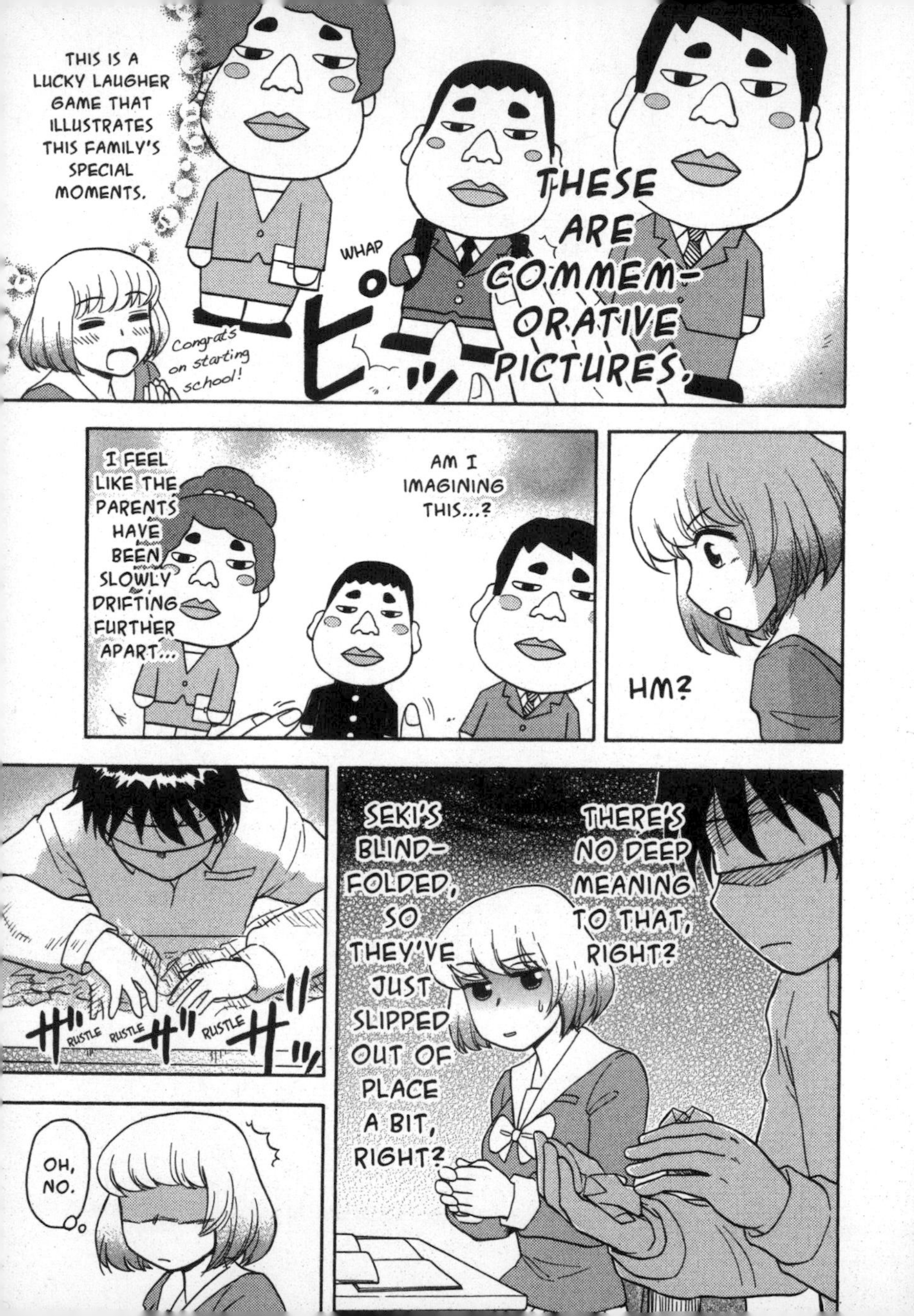
THESE ARE COMMEM-ORATIVE PICTURES.
THIS IS A LUCKY LAUGHER GAME THAT ILLUSTRATES THIS FAMILY'S SPECIAL MOMENTS.
WHAP
ピッ
Congrats on starting school!
HM?
AM I IMAGINING THIS...?
I FEEL LIKE THE PARENTS HAVE BEEN SLOWLY DRIFTING FURTHER APART...
THERE'S NO DEEP MEANING TO THAT, RIGHT?
SEKI'S BLIND-FOLDED, SO THEY'VE JUST SLIPPED OUT OF PLACE A BIT, RIGHT?
ザ RUSTLE ザ RUSTLE ザ RUSTLE ザーッ
OH, NO.

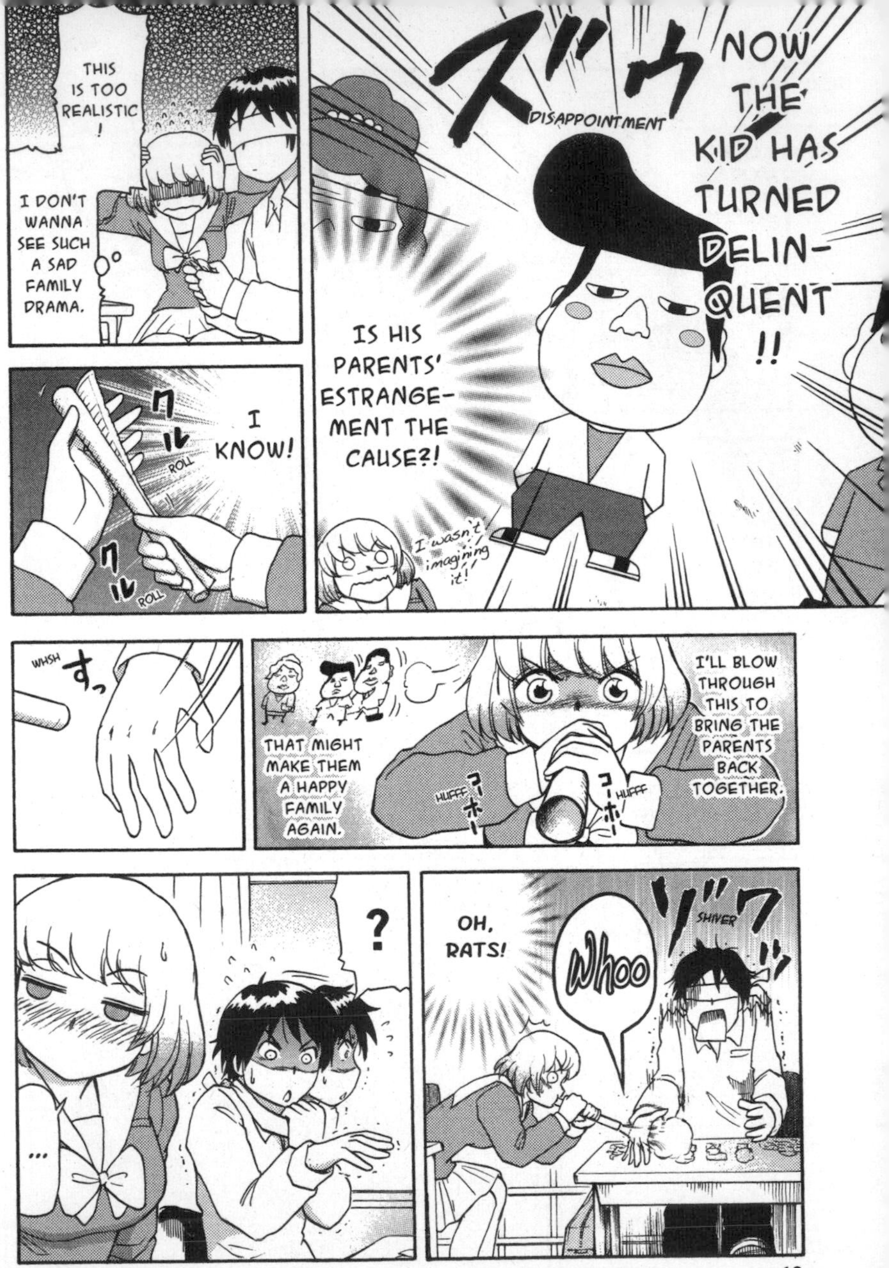
ズウ
DISAPPOINTMENT
NOW THE KID HAS TURNED DELIN-QUENT!!
IS HIS PARENTS' ESTRANGE-MENT THE CAUSE?!
I wasn't imagining it!
THIS IS TOO REALISTIC!
I DON'T WANNA SEE SUCH A SAD FAMILY DRAMA.
クル
ROLL
I KNOW!
クル
ROLL
I'LL BLOW THROUGH THIS TO BRING THE PARENTS BACK TOGETHER.
THAT MIGHT MAKE THEM A HAPPY FAMILY AGAIN.
コーホー
HUFFF
コーホー
HUFFF
すっ
WHSH
ゾワッ
SHIVER
Whoo
OH, RATS!
?
...

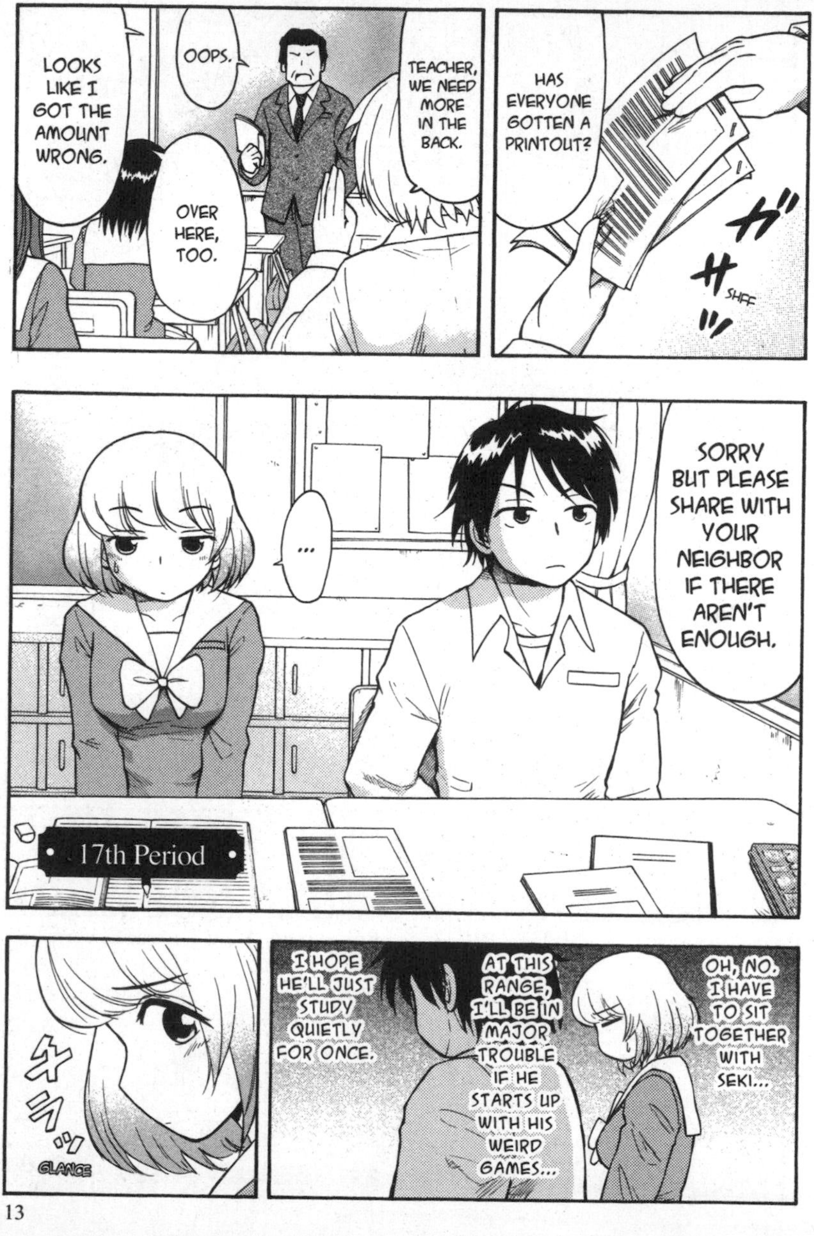
HAS EVERYONE GOTTEN A PRINTOUT?
SHFF
TEACHER, WE NEED MORE IN THE BACK.
OVER HERE, TOO.
OOPS.
LOOKS LIKE I GOT THE AMOUNT WRONG.
SORRY BUT PLEASE SHARE WITH YOUR NEIGHBOR IF THERE AREN'T ENOUGH.
...
17th Period
OH, NO. I HAVE TO SIT TOGETHER WITH SEKI...
AT THIS RANGE, I'LL BE IN MAJOR TROUBLE IF HE STARTS UP WITH HIS WEIRD GAMES...
I HOPE HE'LL JUST STUDY QUIETLY FOR ONCE.
GLANCE

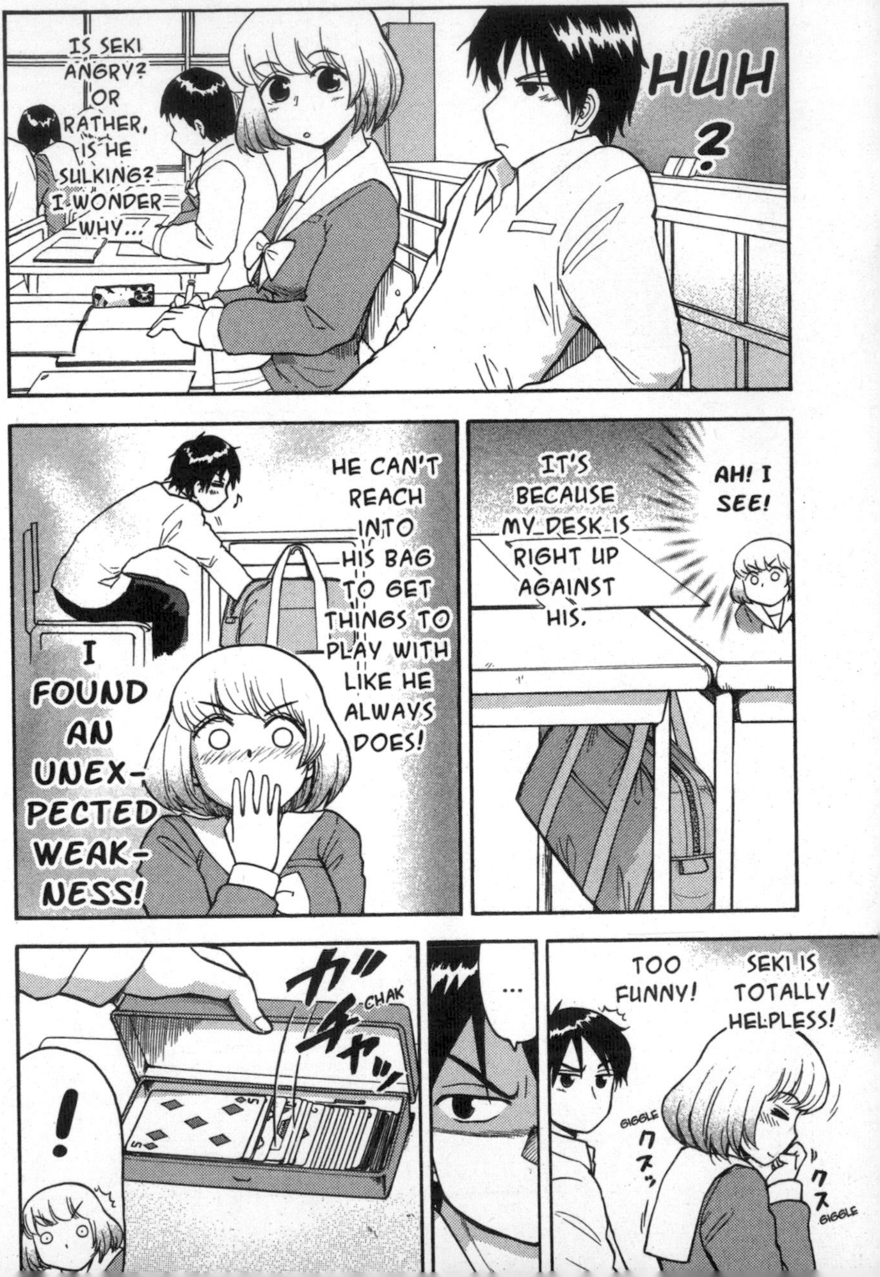

HUH ?
IS SEKI ANGRY? OR RATHER, IS HE SULKING? I WONDER WHY...
AH! I SEE!
IT'S BECAUSE MY DESK IS RIGHT UP AGAINST HIS.
HE CAN'T REACH INTO HIS BAG TO GET THINGS TO PLAY WITH LIKE HE ALWAYS DOES!
I FOUND AN UNEX-PECTED WEAK-NESS!
SEKI IS TOTALLY HELPLESS!
TOO FUNNY!
GIGGLE
GIGGLE
...
CHAK
!

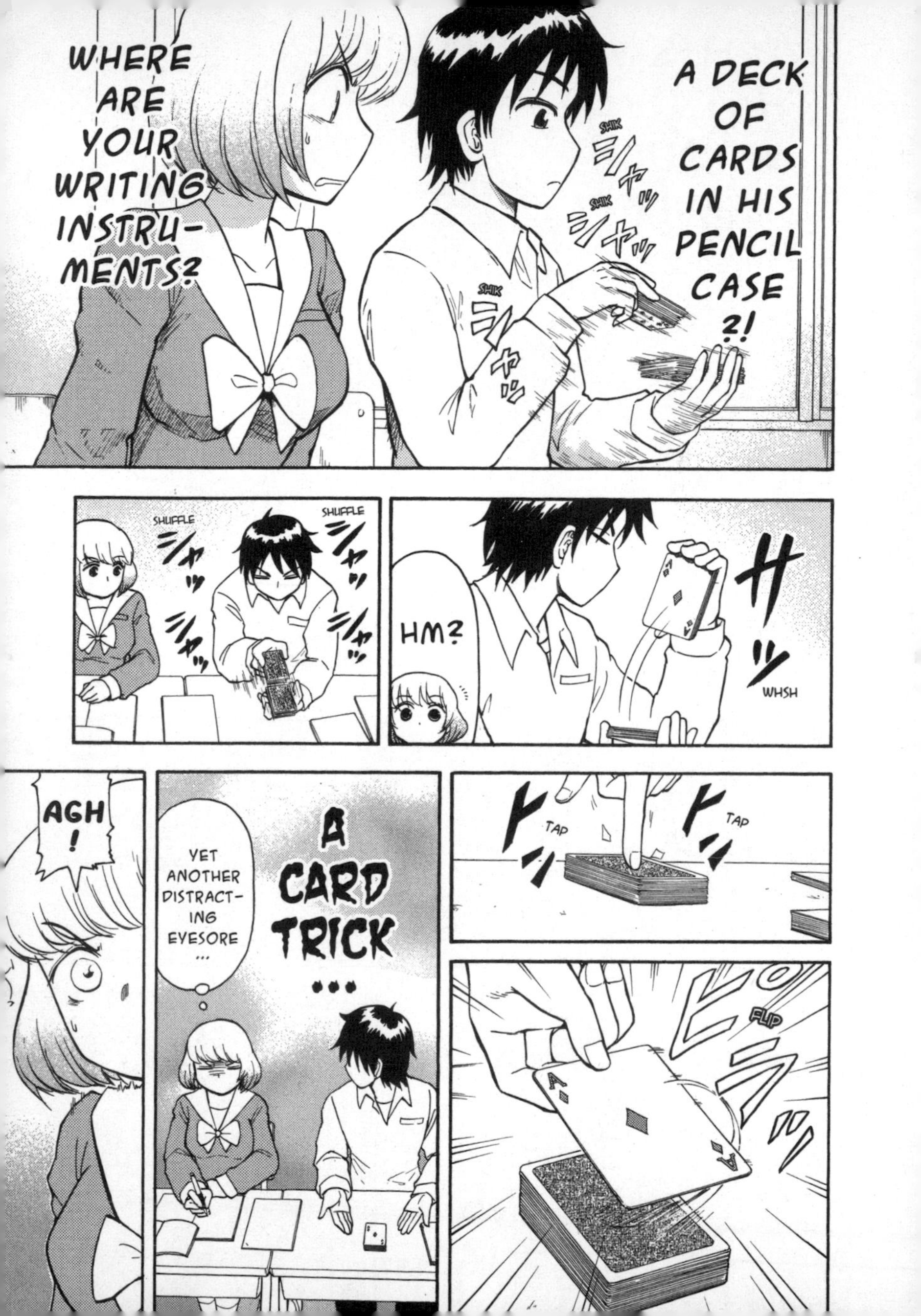

A DECK OF CARDS IN HIS PENCIL CASE ?!
SHIK
SHIK
SHIK
WHERE ARE YOUR WRITING INSTRU- MENTS?
WHSH
HM?
SHUFFLE
SHUFFLE
TAP
TAP
FLIP
A CARD TRICK...
YET ANOTHER DISTRACT- ING EYESORE ...
AGH !

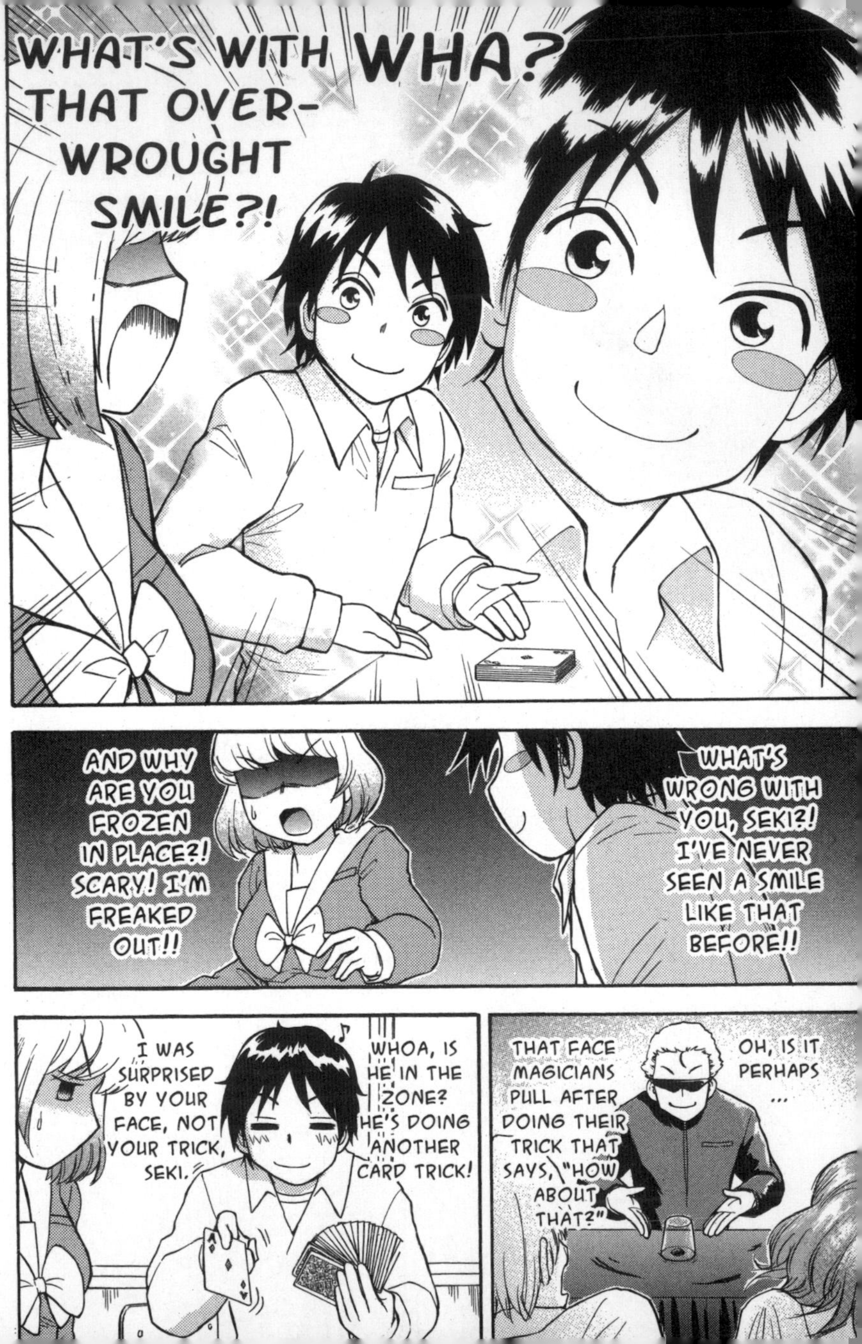
WHA?
WHAT'S WITH THAT OVER-WROUGHT SMILE?!
WHAT'S WRONG WITH YOU, SEKI?! I'VE NEVER SEEN A SMILE LIKE THAT BEFORE!!
AND WHY ARE YOU FROZEN IN PLACE?! SCARY! I'M FREAKED OUT!!
OH, IS IT PERHAPS ...
THAT FACE MAGICIANS PULL AFTER DOING THEIR TRICK THAT SAYS, "HOW ABOUT THAT?"
WHOA, IS HE IN THE ZONE? HE'S DOING ANOTHER CARD TRICK!
I WAS SURPRISED BY YOUR FACE, NOT YOUR TRICK, SEKI.

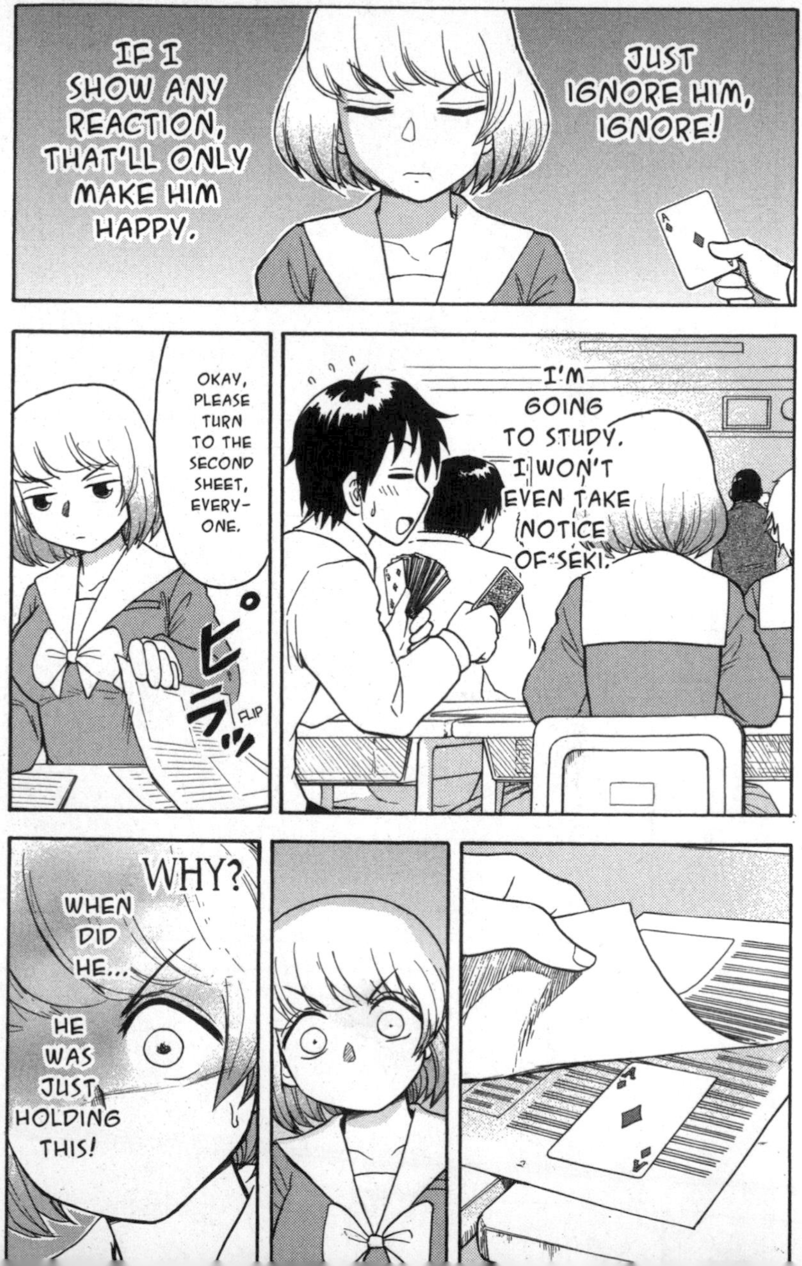
JUST IGNORE HIM, IGNORE!
IF I SHOW ANY REACTION, THAT'LL ONLY MAKE HIM HAPPY.
I'M GOING TO STUDY. I WON'T EVEN TAKE NOTICE OF SEKI.
OKAY, PLEASE TURN TO THE SECOND SHEET, EVERY-ONE.
FLIP
WHY?
WHEN DID HE...
HE WAS JUST HOLDING THIS!

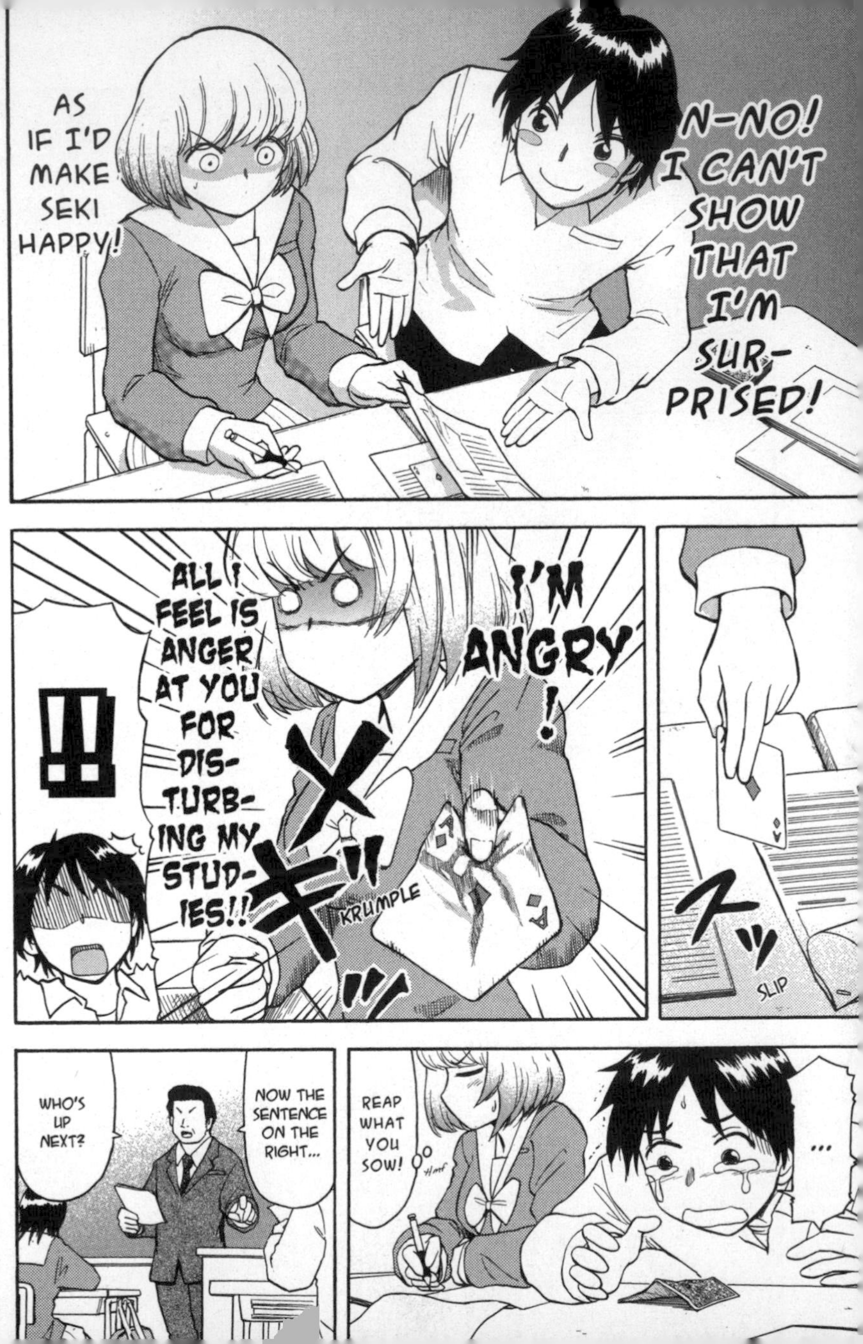
N-NO! I CAN'T SHOW THAT I'M SUR-PRISED!
AS IF I'D MAKE SEKI HAPPY!
SLIP
I'M ANGRY!
ALL I FEEL IS ANGER AT YOU FOR DIS-TURB-ING MY STUD-IES!!
KRUMPLE
!!
...
REAP WHAT YOU SOW!
NOW THE SENTENCE ON THE RIGHT...
WHO'S UP NEXT?

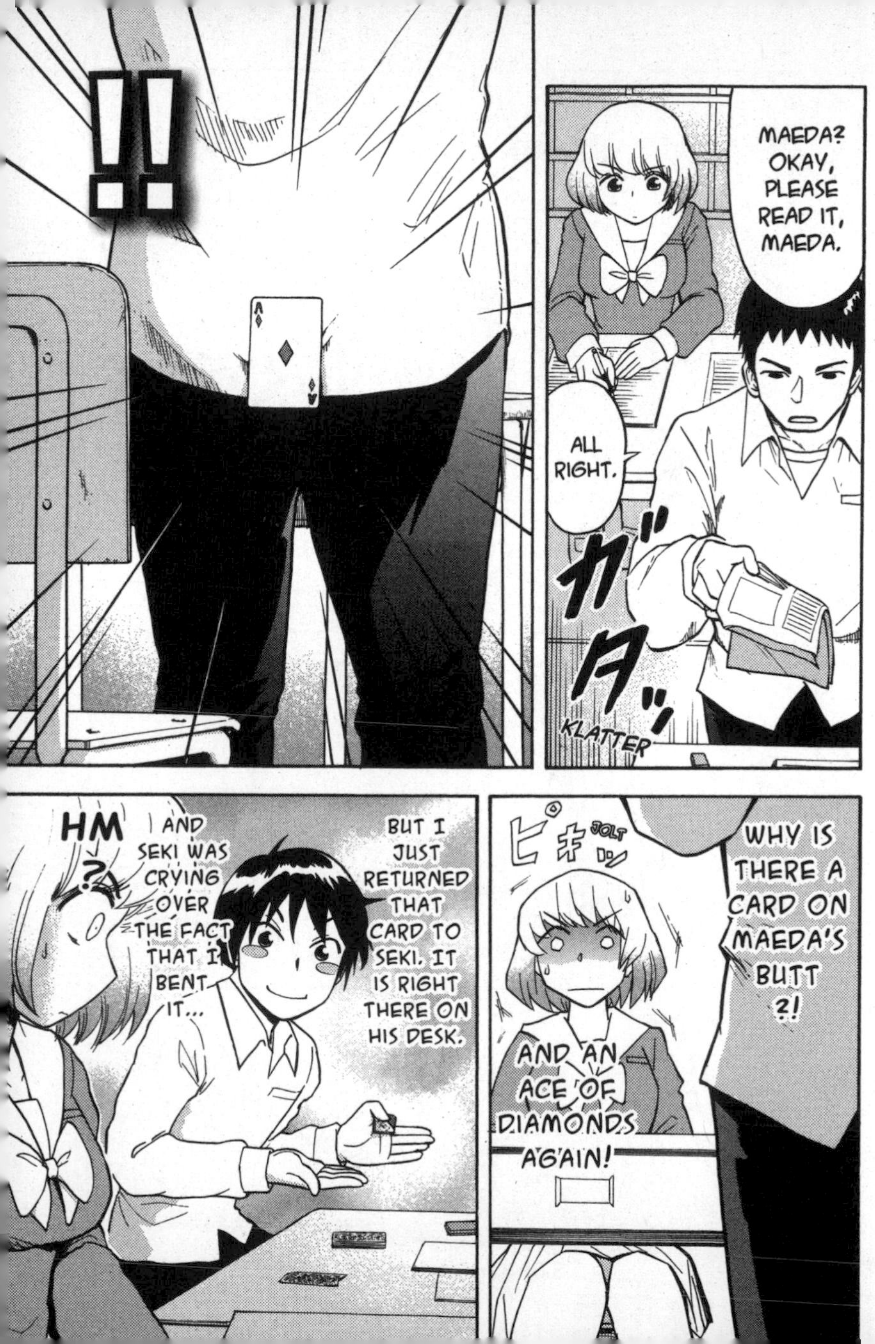
MAEDA? OKAY, PLEASE READ IT, MAEDA.
ALL RIGHT.
ガタッ
KLATTER
!!
WHY IS THERE A CARD ON MAEDA'S BUTT ?!
JOLT
AND AN ACE OF DIAMONDS AGAIN!
BUT I JUST RETURNED THAT CARD TO SEKI. IT IS RIGHT THERE ON HIS DESK.
AND SEKI WAS CRYING OVER THE FACT THAT I BENT IT...
HM
?

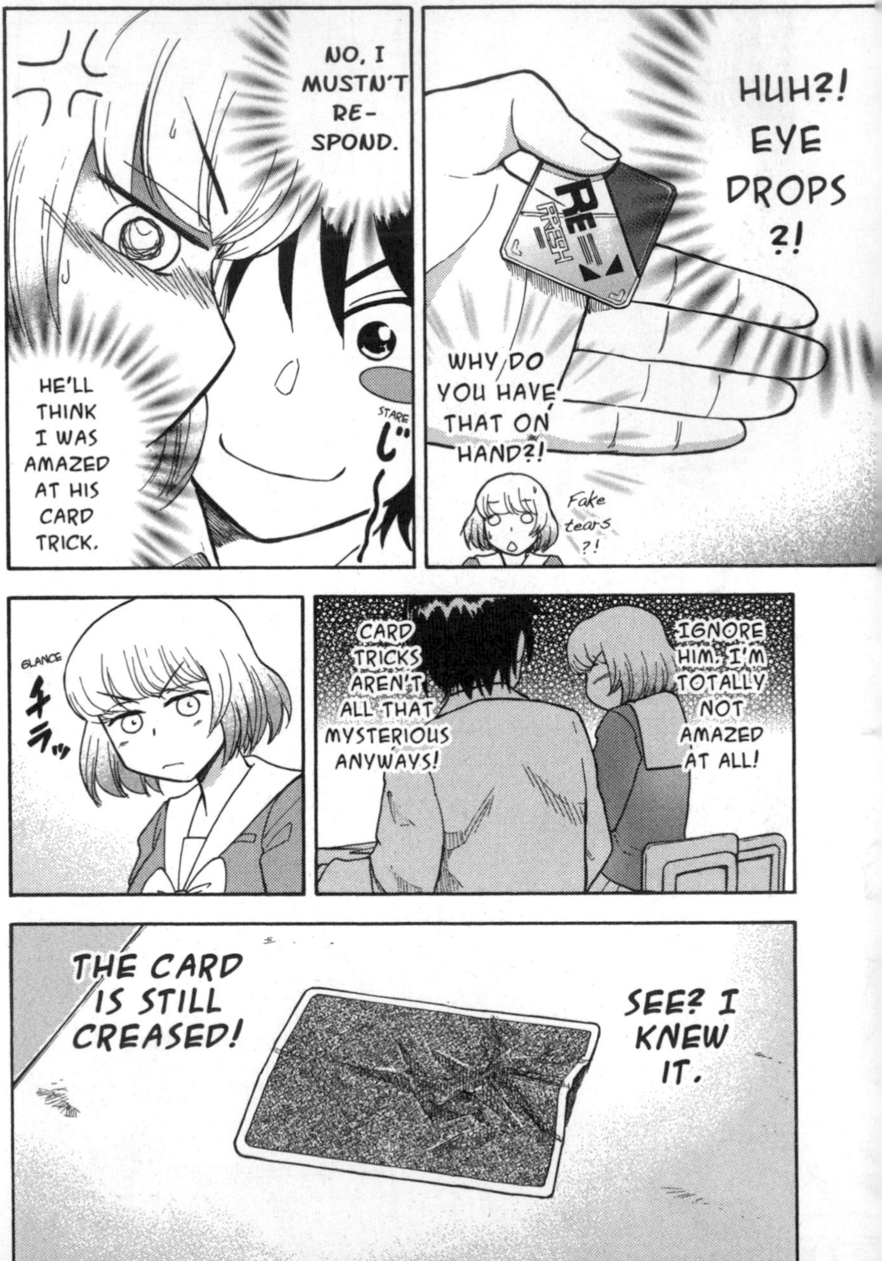
HUH?! EYE DROPS ?!
RE FRESH
WHY DO YOU HAVE THAT ON HAND?!
Fake tears ?!
NO, I MUSTN'T RE-SPOND.
STARE
HE'LL THINK I WAS AMAZED AT HIS CARD TRICK.
IGNORE HIM. I'M TOTALLY NOT AMAZED AT ALL!
CARD TRICKS AREN'T ALL THAT MYSTERIOUS ANYWAYS!
GLANCE
SEE? I KNEW IT.
THE CARD IS STILL CREASED!

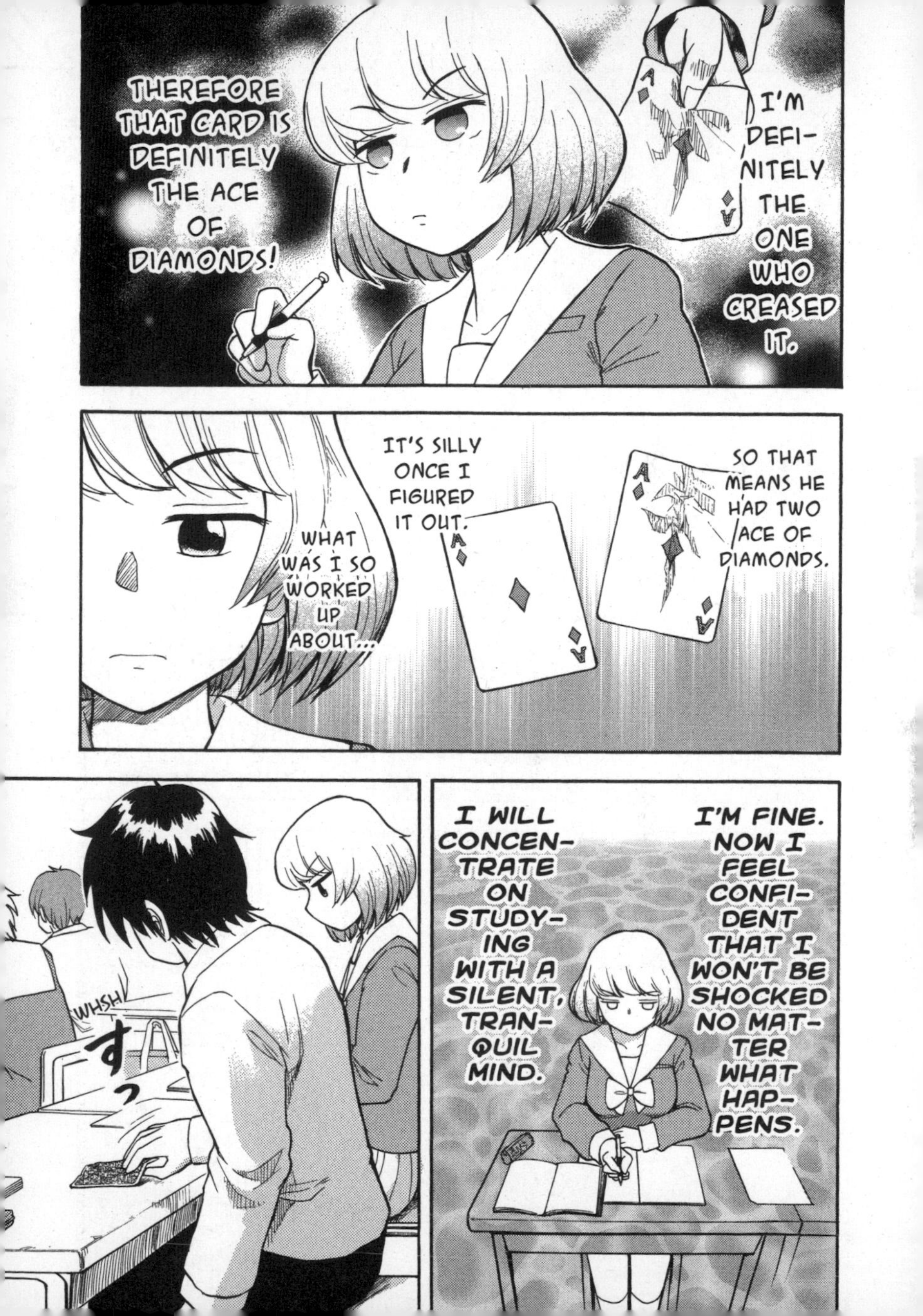
I'M DEFINITELY THE ONE WHO CREASED IT.
THEREFORE THAT CARD IS DEFINITELY THE ACE OF DIAMONDS!
SO THAT MEANS HE HAD TWO ACE OF DIAMONDS.
IT'S SILLY ONCE I FIGURED IT OUT.
WHAT WAS I SO WORKED UP ABOUT...
I'M FINE. NOW I FEEL CONFIDENT THAT I WON'T BE SHOCKED NO MATTER WHAT HAPPENS.
I WILL CONCENTRATE ON STUDYING WITH A SILENT, TRANQUIL MIND.
WHSH
すっ

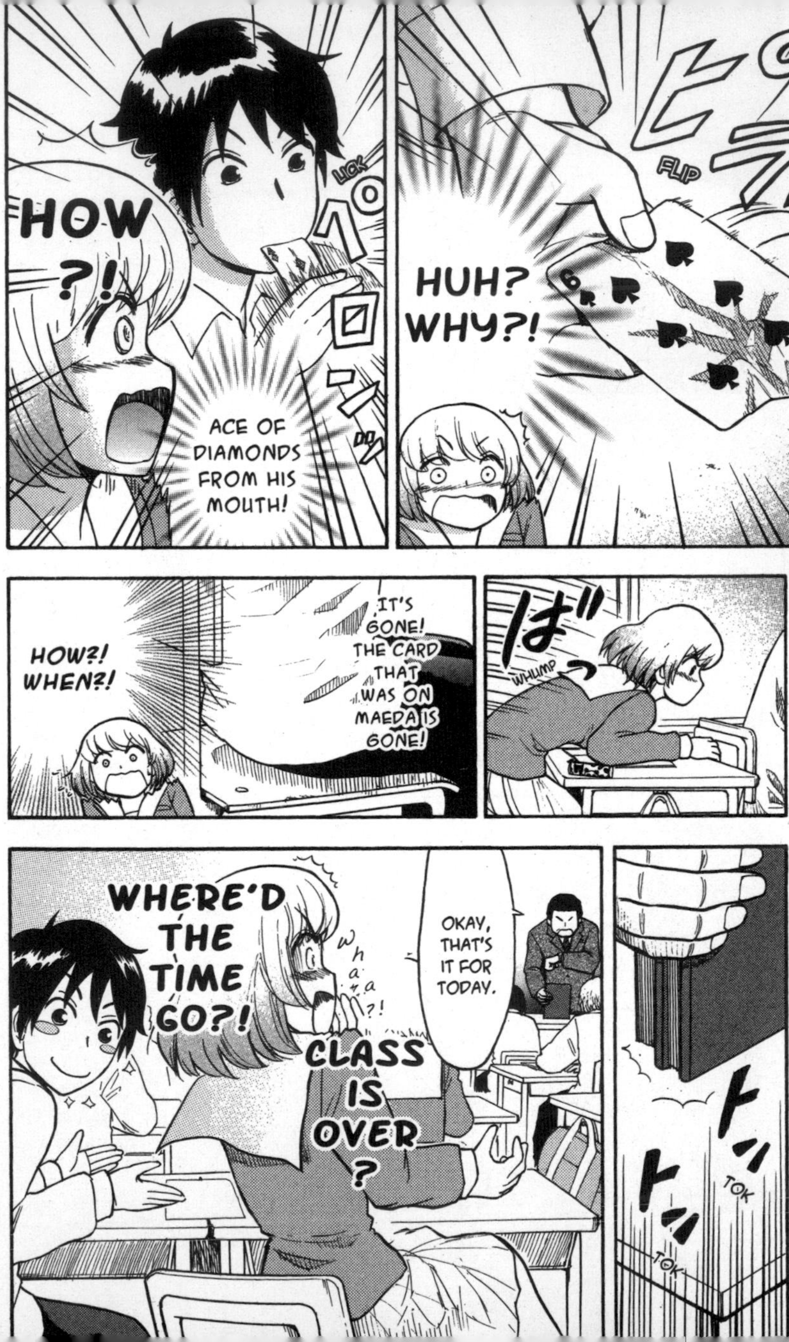
FLIP
HUH? WHY?!
LICK
HOW ?!
ACE OF DIAMONDS FROM HIS MOUTH!
WHUMP
IT'S GONE! THE CARD THAT WAS ON MAEDA IS GONE!
HOW?! WHEN?!
TOK
TOK
OKAY, THAT'S IT FOR TODAY.
CLASS IS OVER ?
WHERE'D THE TIME GO?!

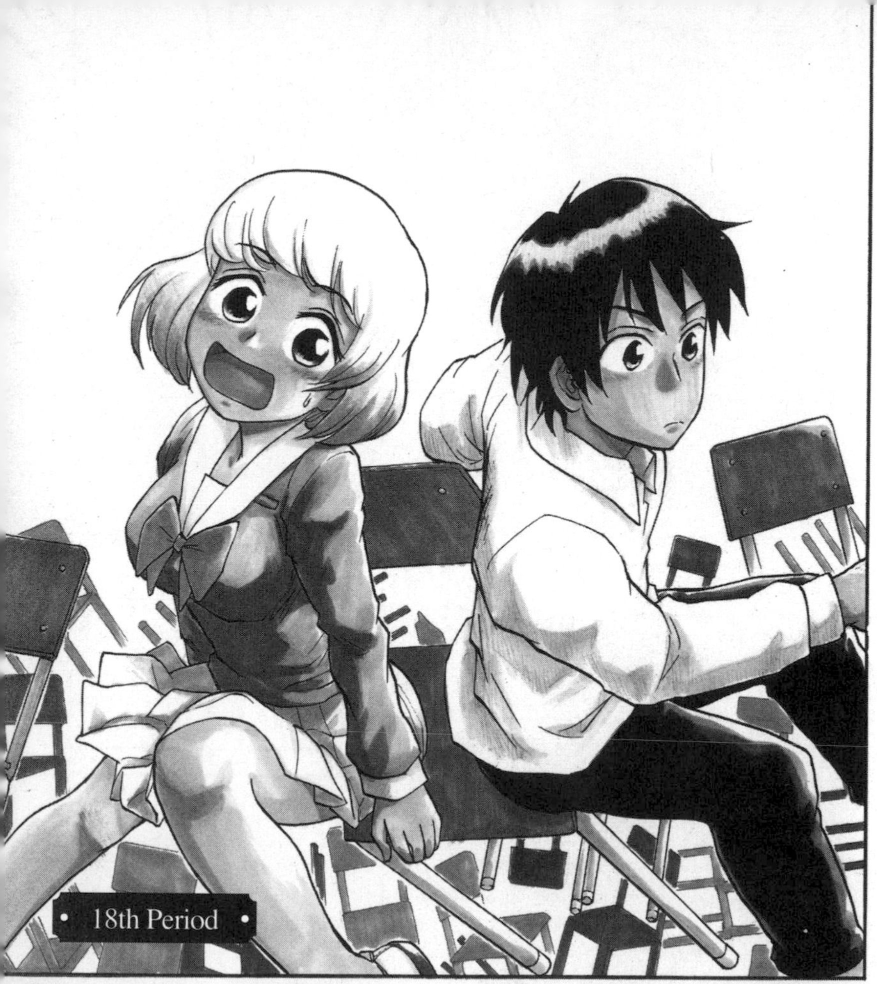
18th Period

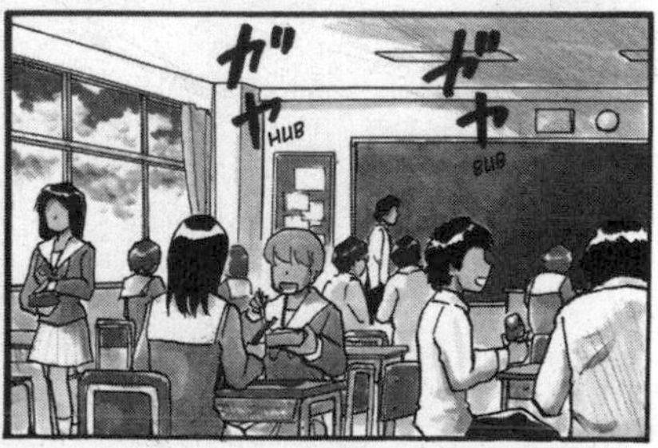
ガヤ
HUB
ガヤ
BUB

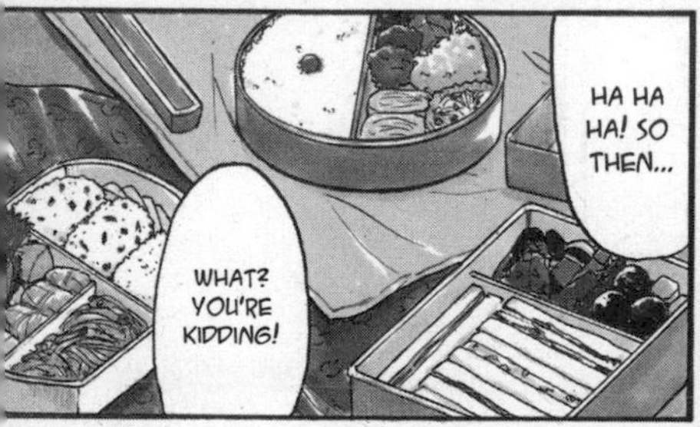
HA HA HA! SO THEN...
WHAT? YOU'RE KIDDING!

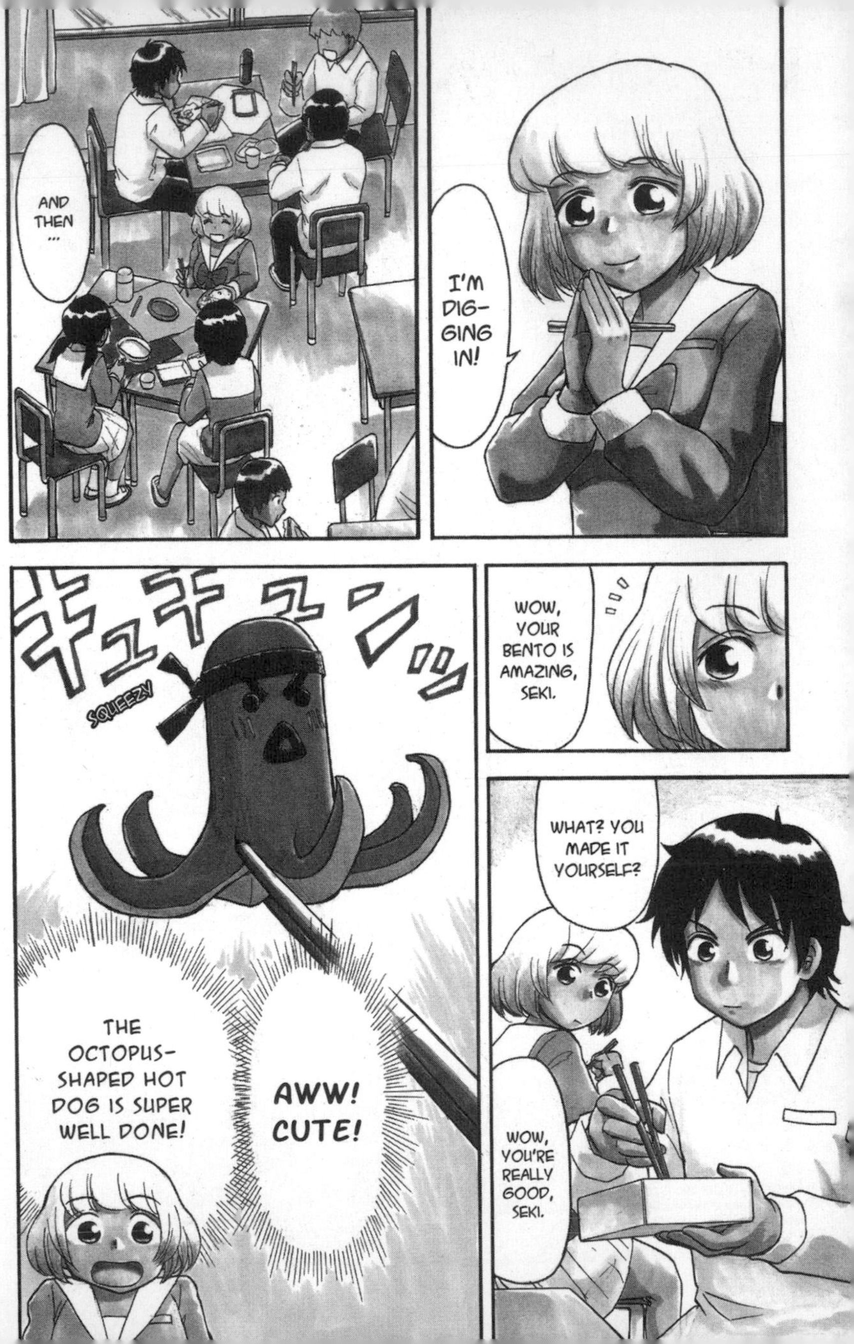
I'M DIG-GING IN!
AND THEN ...
WOW, YOUR BENTO IS AMAZING, SEKI.
WHAT? YOU MADE IT YOURSELF?
WOW, YOU'RE REALLY GOOD, SEKI.
SQUEEZY!
AWW! CUTE!
THE OCTOPUS-SHAPED HOT DOG IS SUPER WELL DONE!

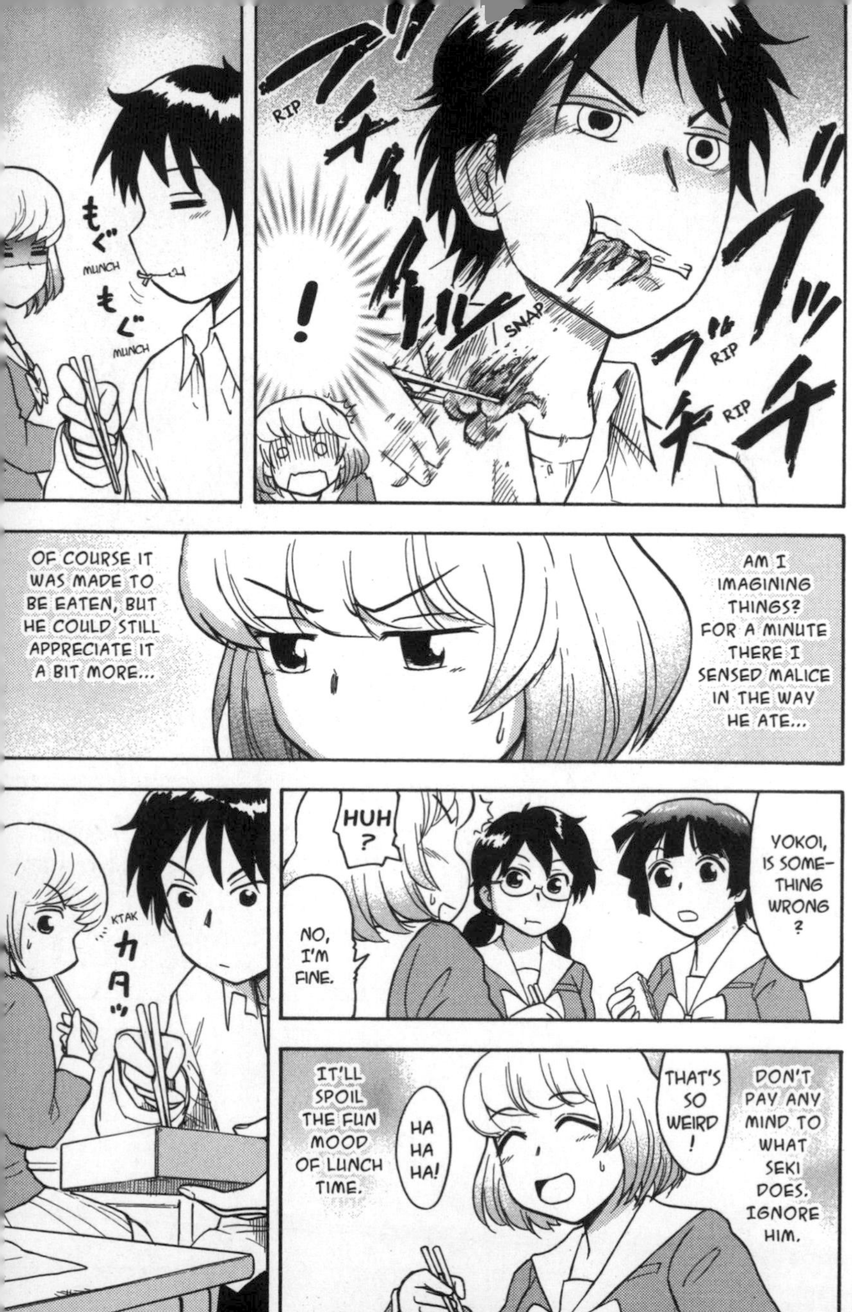

ブッチ
RIP
ブチ
RIP
SNAP
RIP
!
もぐ
MUNCH
もぐ
MUNCH
AM I IMAGINING THINGS? FOR A MINUTE THERE I SENSED MALICE IN THE WAY HE ATE...
OF COURSE IT WAS MADE TO BE EATEN, BUT HE COULD STILL APPRECIATE IT A BIT MORE...
YOKOI, IS SOME-THING WRONG?
HUH?
NO, I'M FINE.
DON'T PAY ANY MIND TO WHAT SEKI DOES. IGNORE HIM.
THAT'S SO WEIRD!
HA HA HA!
IT'LL SPOIL THE FUN MOOD OF LUNCH TIME.
カタッ
KTAK

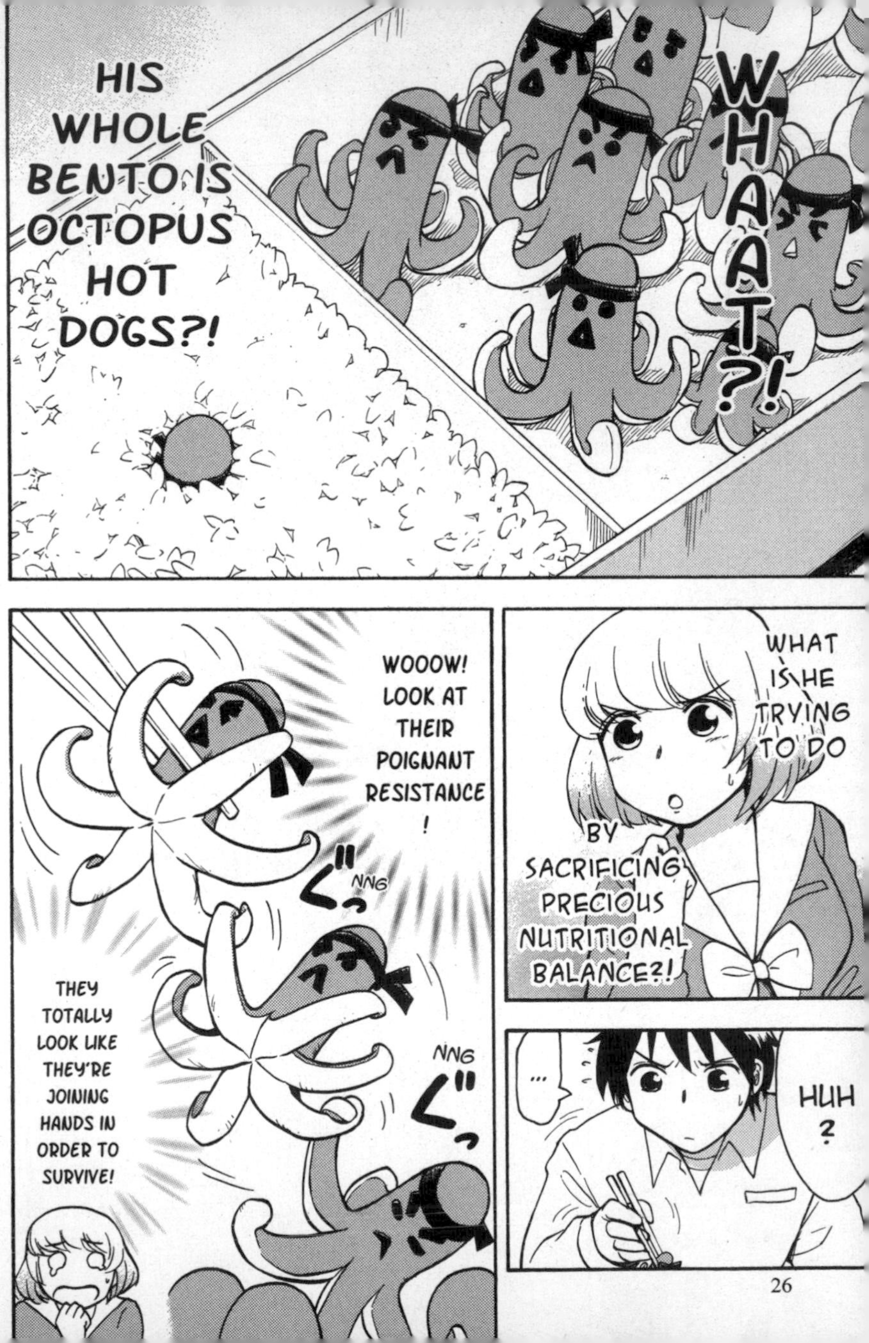
WHAT?!
HIS WHOLE BENTO IS OCTOPUS HOT DOGS?!
WHAT IS HE TRYING TO DO
BY SACRIFICING PRECIOUS NUTRITIONAL BALANCE?!
HUH?
...
WOOOW! LOOK AT THEIR POIGNANT RESISTANCE!
NNG
NNG
THEY TOTALLY LOOK LIKE THEY'RE JOINING HANDS IN ORDER TO SURVIVE!

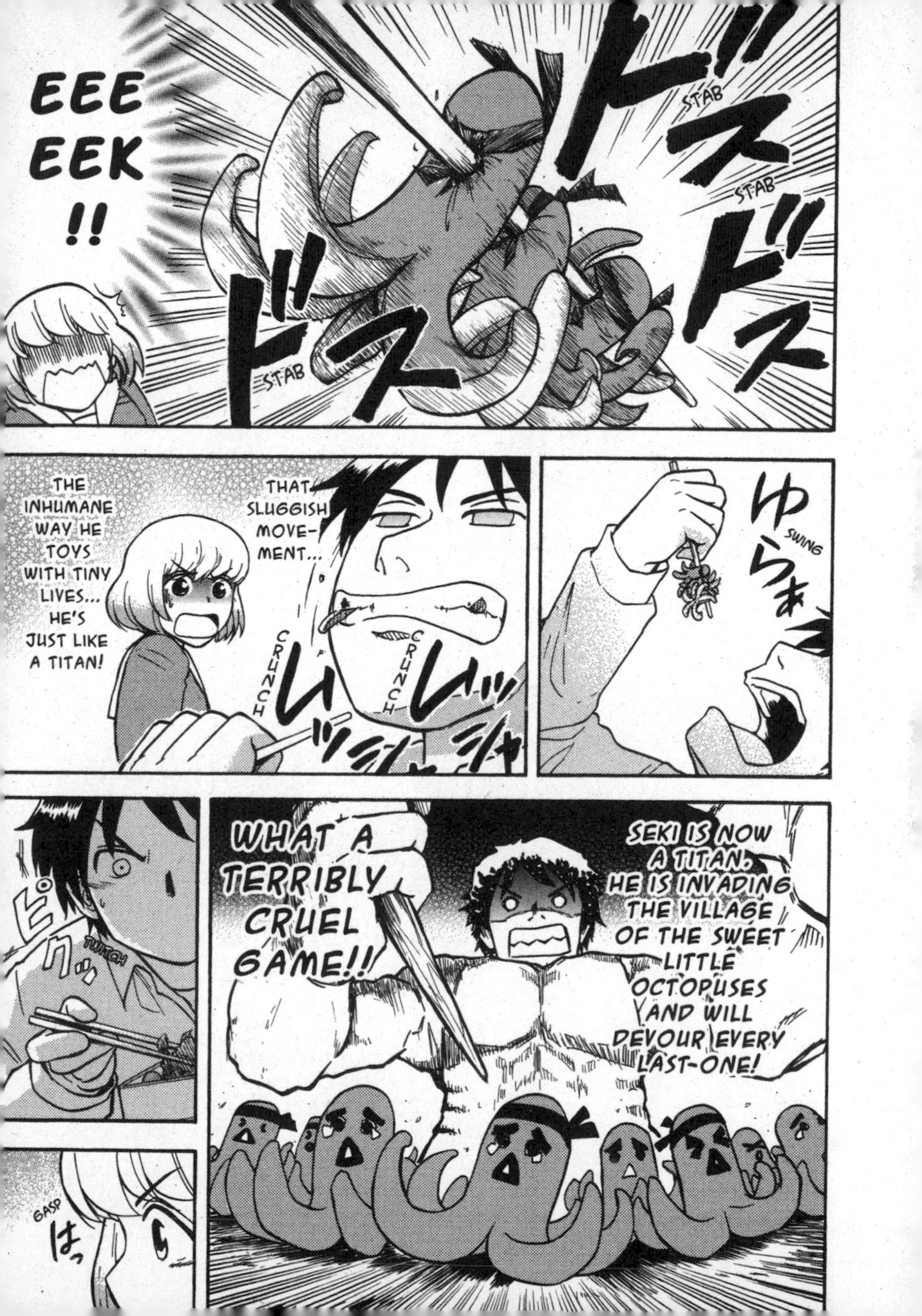

STAB
STAB
EEEEEK!!
STAB
THAT SLUGGISH MOVEMENT...
THE INHUMANE WAY HE TOYS WITH TINY LIVES... HE'S JUST LIKE A TITAN!
CRUNCH
CRUNCH
SWING
SEKI IS NOW A TITAN. HE IS INVADING THE VILLAGE OF THE SWEET LITTLE OCTOPUSES AND WILL DEVOUR EVERY LAST-ONE!
WHAT A TERRIBLY CRUEL GAME!!
TWITCH
GASP

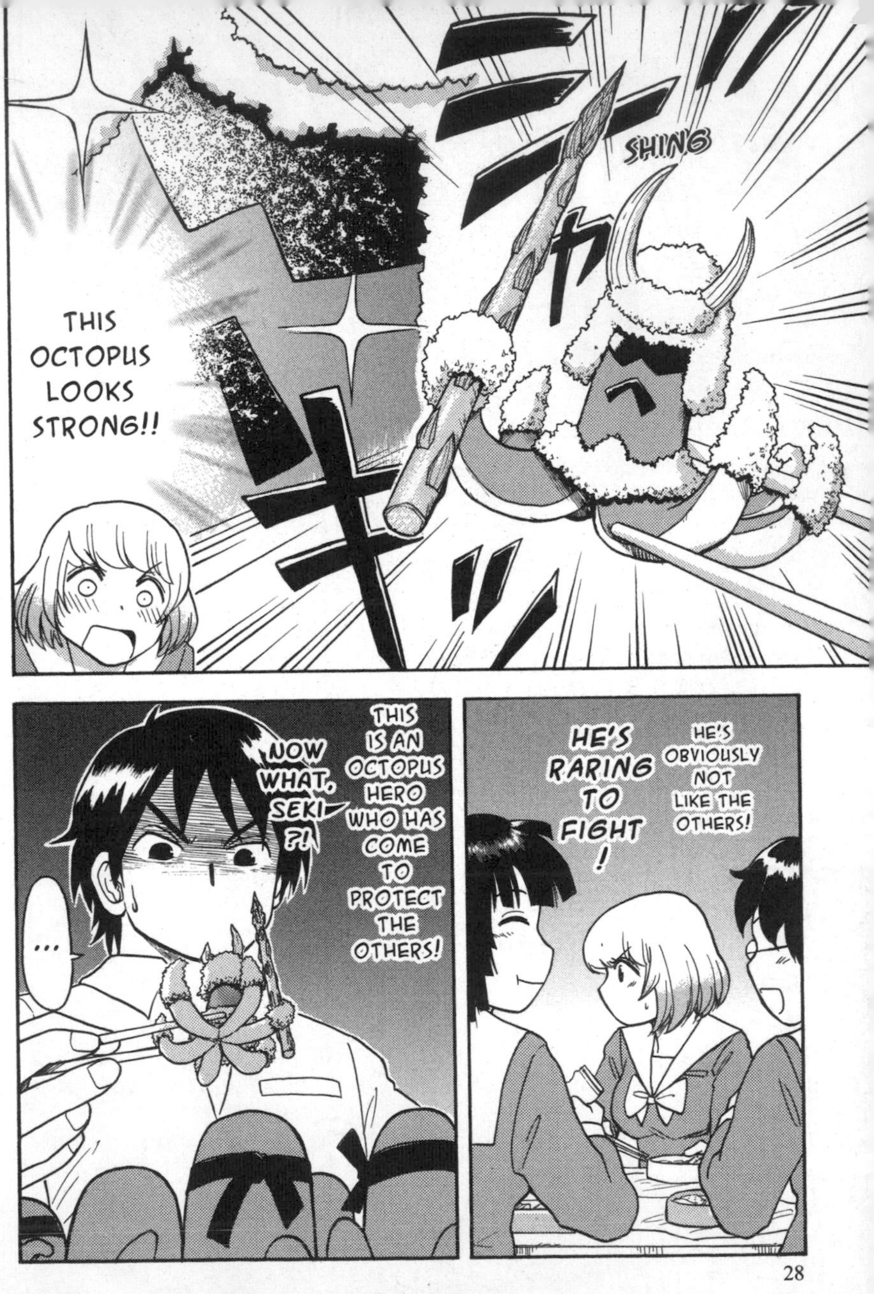
SHING
THIS OCTOPUS LOOKS STRONG!!
HE'S OBVIOUSLY NOT LIKE THE OTHERS!
HE'S RARING TO FIGHT!
THIS IS AN OCTOPUS HERO WHO HAS COME TO PROTECT THE OTHERS!
NOW WHAT, SEKI?!
...

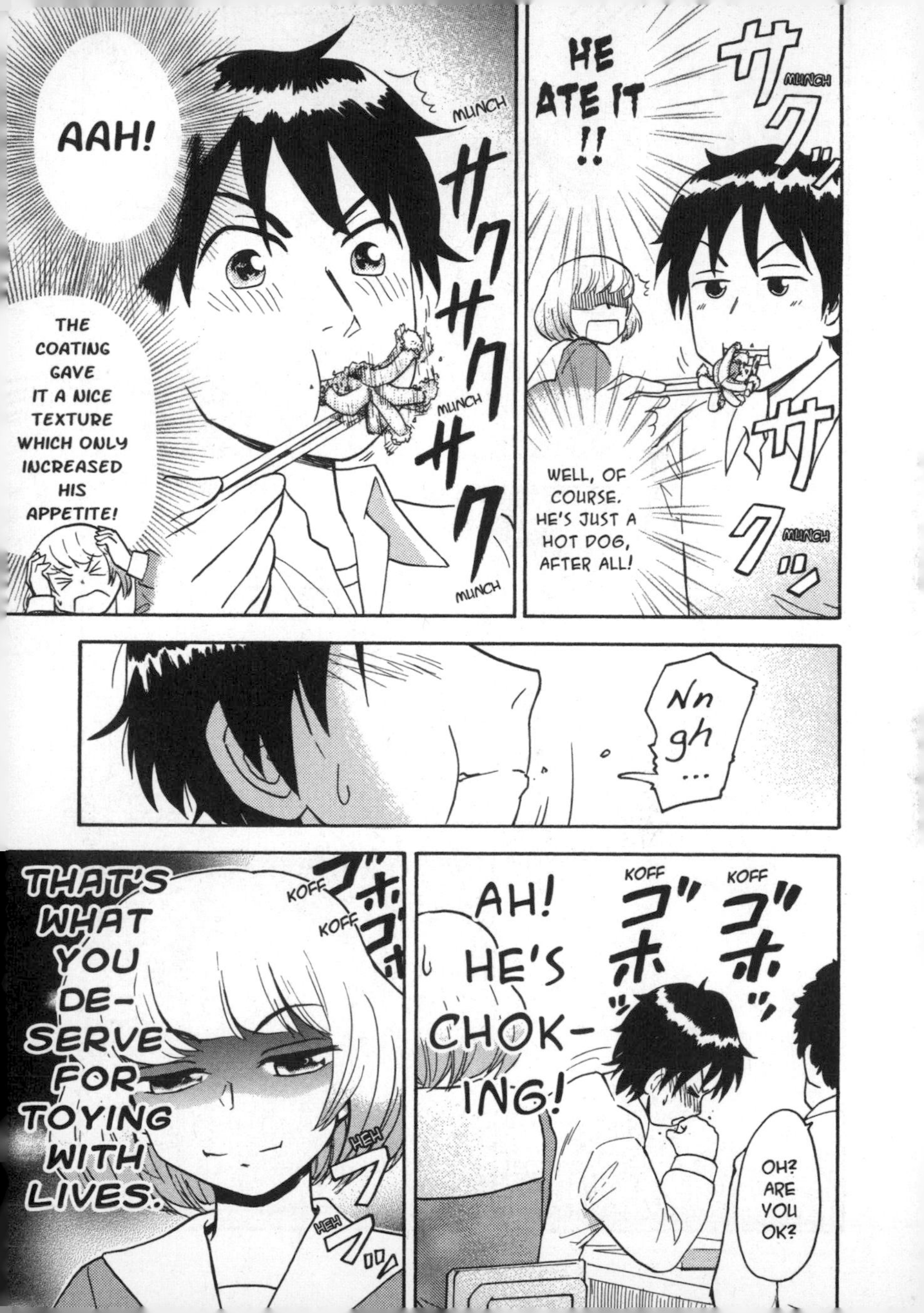
HE ATE IT !!
サクッ
MUNCH
サクッ
MUNCH
WELL, OF COURSE. HE'S JUST A HOT DOG, AFTER ALL!
AAH!
MUNCH
サクサクサク
MUNCH
MUNCH
THE COATING GAVE IT A NICE TEXTURE WHICH ONLY INCREASED HIS APPETITE!
Nngh...
ゴホッ
KOFF
ゴホッ
KOFF
AH! HE'S CHOK-ING!
OH? ARE YOU OK?
ゴホッ
KOFF
KOFF
THAT'S WHAT YOU DE-SERVE FOR TOYING WITH LIVES.
フ
HEH
ハッ
HEH

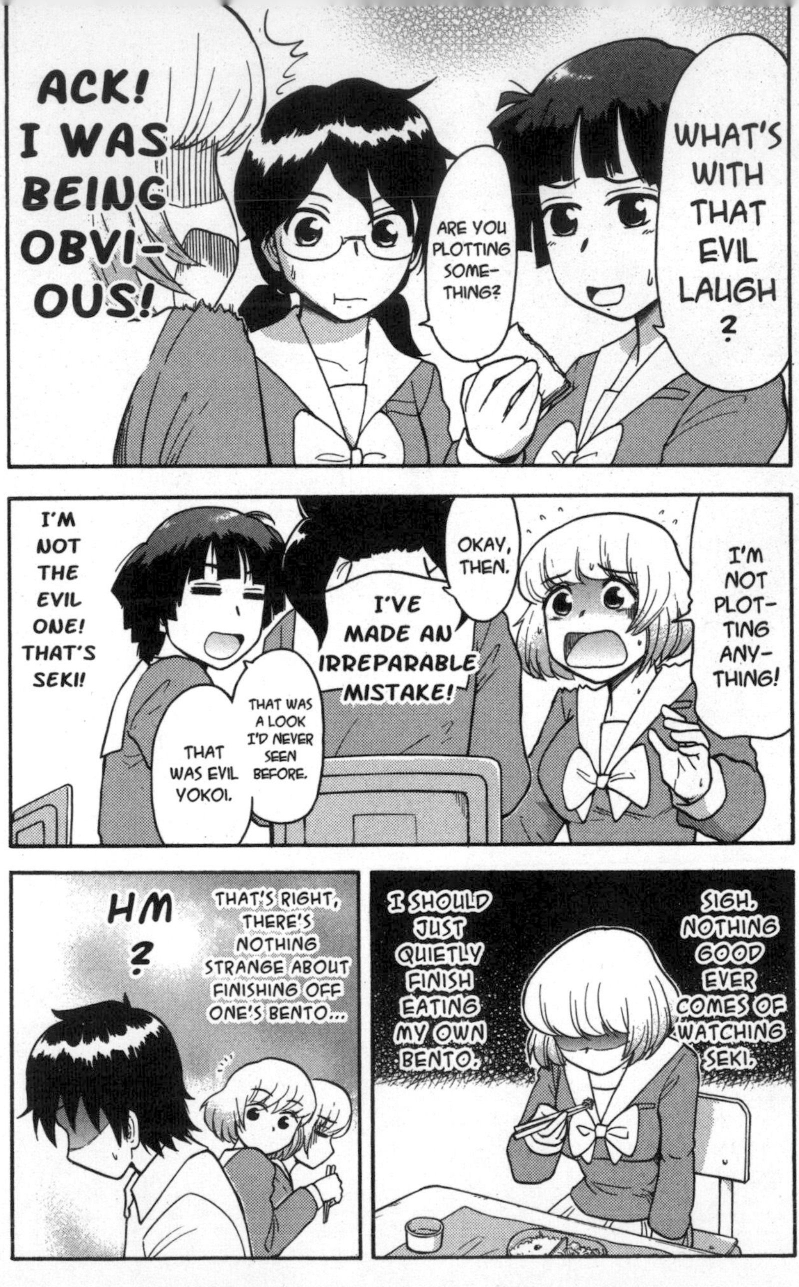
WHAT'S WITH THAT EVIL LAUGH?
ARE YOU PLOTTING SOMETHING?
ACK! I WAS BEING OBVIOUS!
I'M NOT PLOTTING ANYTHING!
OKAY, THEN.
I'VE MADE AN IRREPARABLE MISTAKE!
THAT WAS A LOOK I'D NEVER SEEN BEFORE.
THAT WAS EVIL YOKOI.
I'M NOT THE EVIL ONE! THAT'S SEKI!
SIGH. NOTHING GOOD EVER COMES OF WATCHING SEKI.
I SHOULD JUST QUIETLY FINISH EATING MY OWN BENTO.
THAT'S RIGHT, THERE'S NOTHING STRANGE ABOUT FINISHING OFF ONE'S BENTO...
HM?

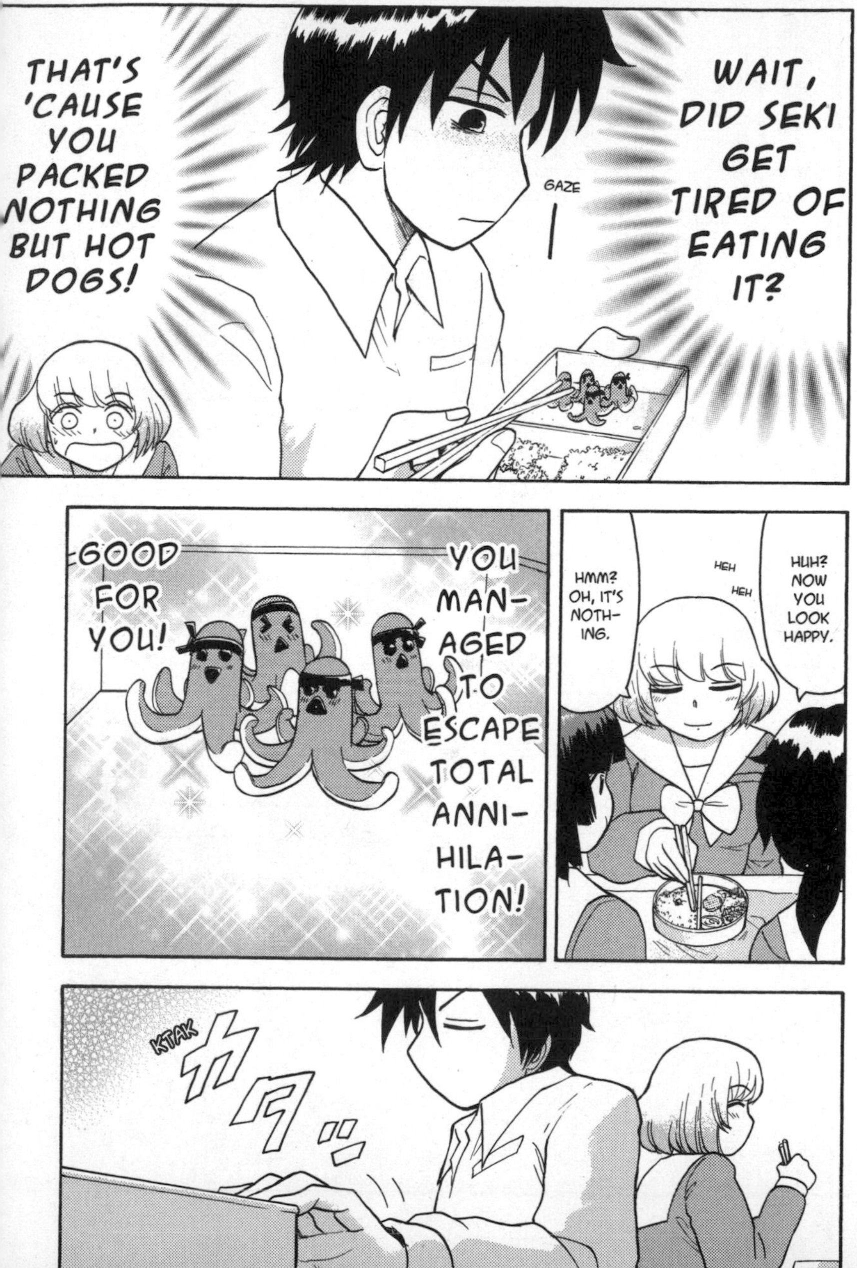
WAIT, DID SEKI GET TIRED OF EATING IT?
GAZE
THAT'S 'CAUSE YOU PACKED NOTHING BUT HOT DOGS!
HUH? NOW YOU LOOK HAPPY.
HEH HEH
HMM? OH, IT'S NOTH-ING.
YOU MAN-AGED TO ESCAPE TOTAL ANNI-HILA-TION!
GOOD FOR YOU!
KTAK
カタッ

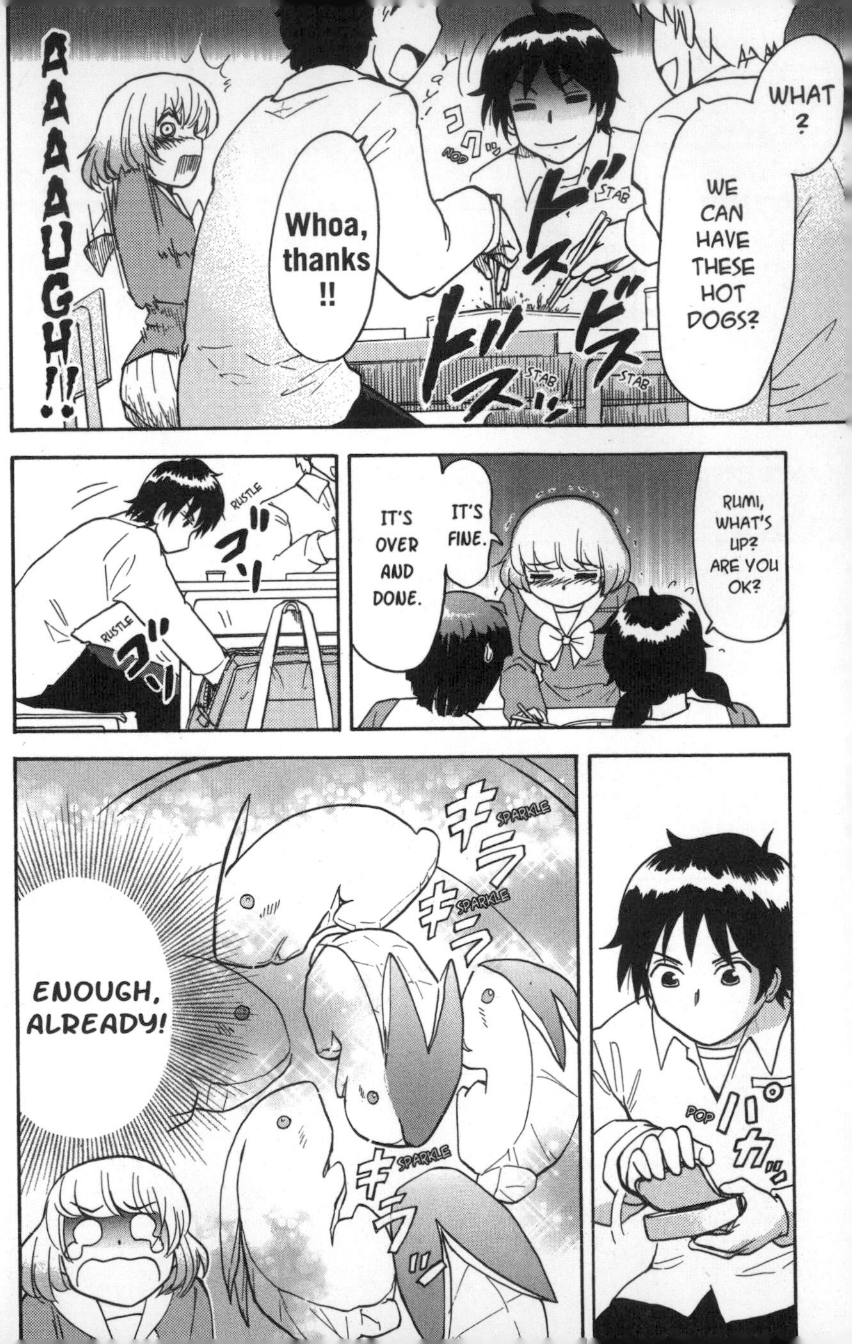
WHAT?
WE CAN HAVE THESE HOT DOGS?
STAB
STAB
STAB
NOD
Whoa, thanks!!
AAAAAUGH!!
RUMI, WHAT'S UP? ARE YOU OK?
IT'S FINE.
IT'S OVER AND DONE.
RUSTLE
RUSTLE
POP
SPARKLE
SPARKLE
SPARKLE
ENOUGH, ALREADY!

My Neighbor Seki

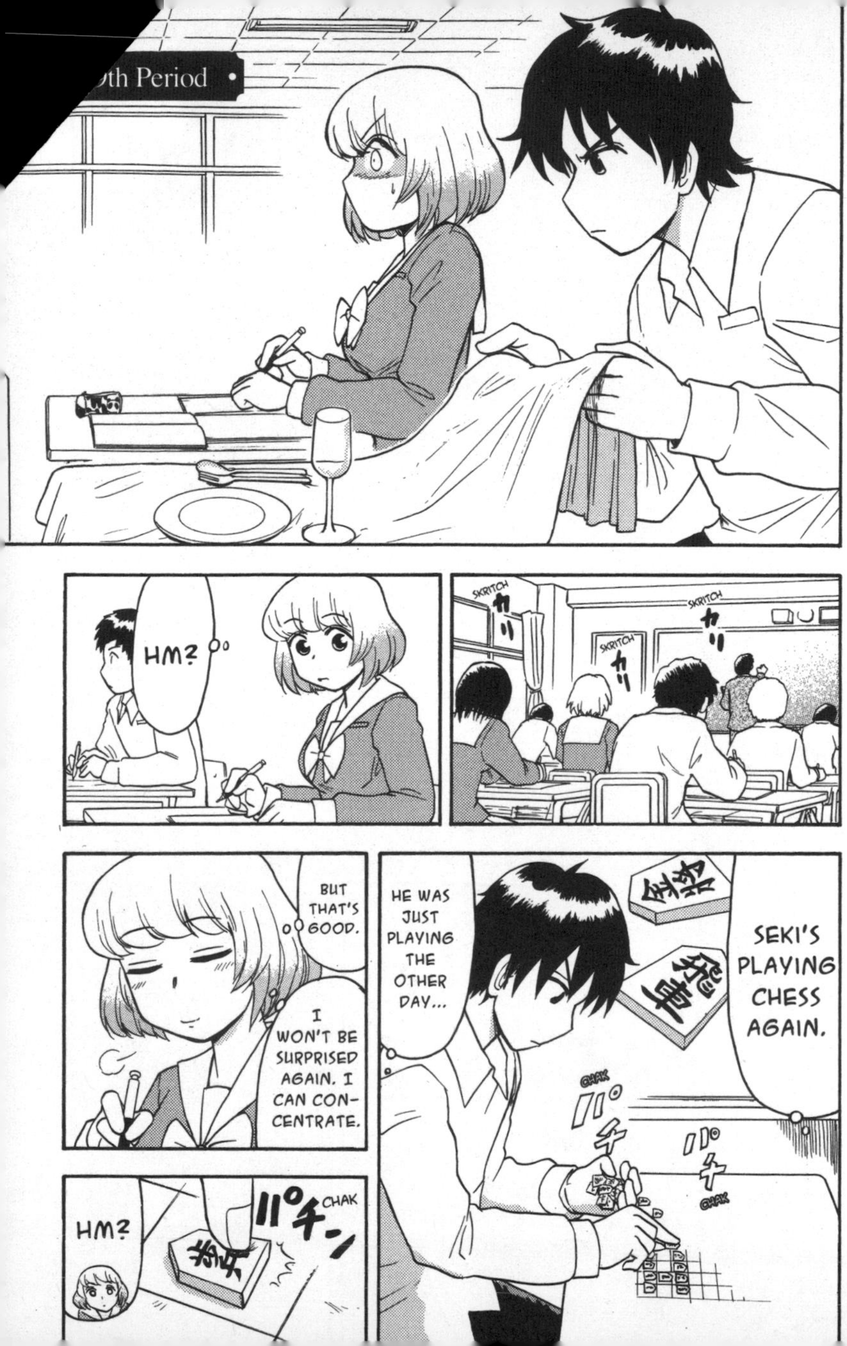
0th Period
SKRITCH
SKRITCH
SKRITCH
HM?
SEKI'S PLAYING CHESS AGAIN.
HE WAS JUST PLAYING THE OTHER DAY...
CHAK
CHAK
BUT THAT'S GOOD.
I WON'T BE SURPRISED AGAIN. I CAN CONCENTRATE.
CHAK
HM?

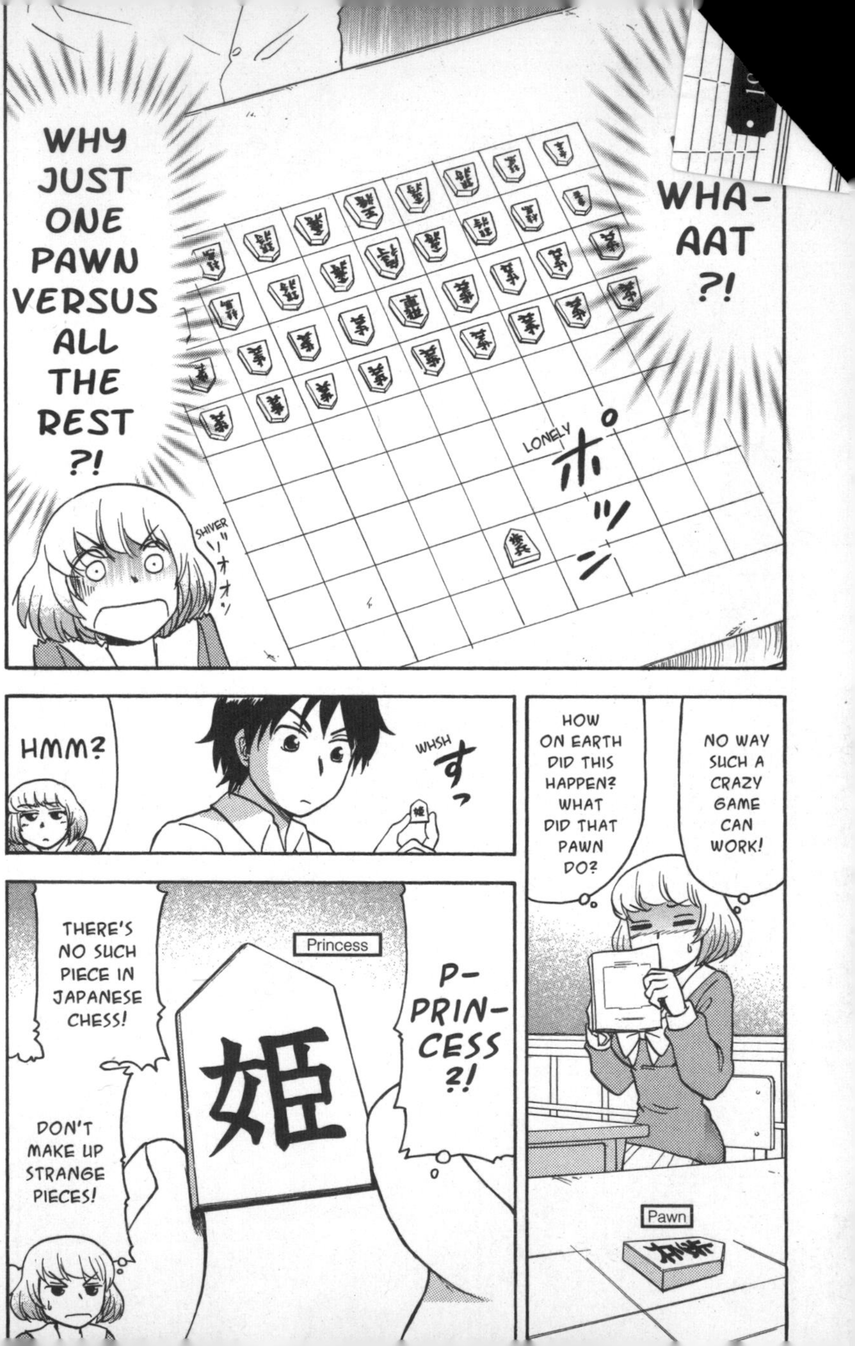
WHA-AAT ?!
LONELY
WHY JUST ONE PAWN VERSUS ALL THE REST ?!
SHIVER
NO WAY SUCH A CRAZY GAME CAN WORK!
HOW ON EARTH DID THIS HAPPEN? WHAT DID THAT PAWN DO?
Pawn
WHSH
HMM?
P-PRINCESS ?!
Princess
THERE'S NO SUCH PIECE IN JAPANESE CHESS!
DON'T MAKE UP STRANGE PIECES!

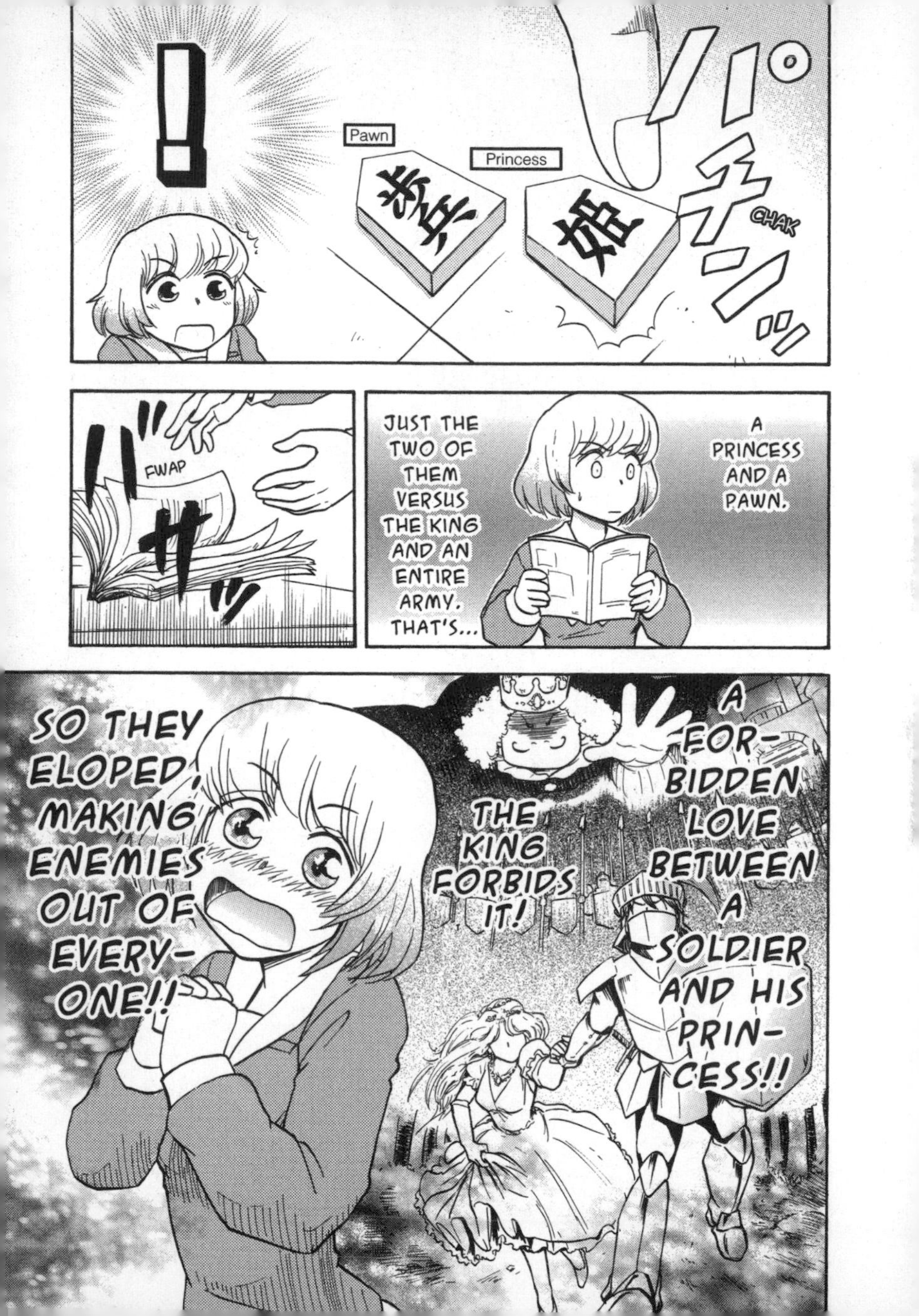
パチッ
CHAK
Princess
姫
Pawn
歩兵
!
A PRINCESS AND A PAWN.
JUST THE TWO OF THEM VERSUS THE KING AND AN ENTIRE ARMY. THAT'S...
バサッ
FWAP
A FORBIDDEN LOVE BETWEEN A SOLDIER AND HIS PRINCESS!!
THE KING FORBIDS IT!
SO THEY ELOPED, MAKING ENEMIES OUT OF EVERYONE!!

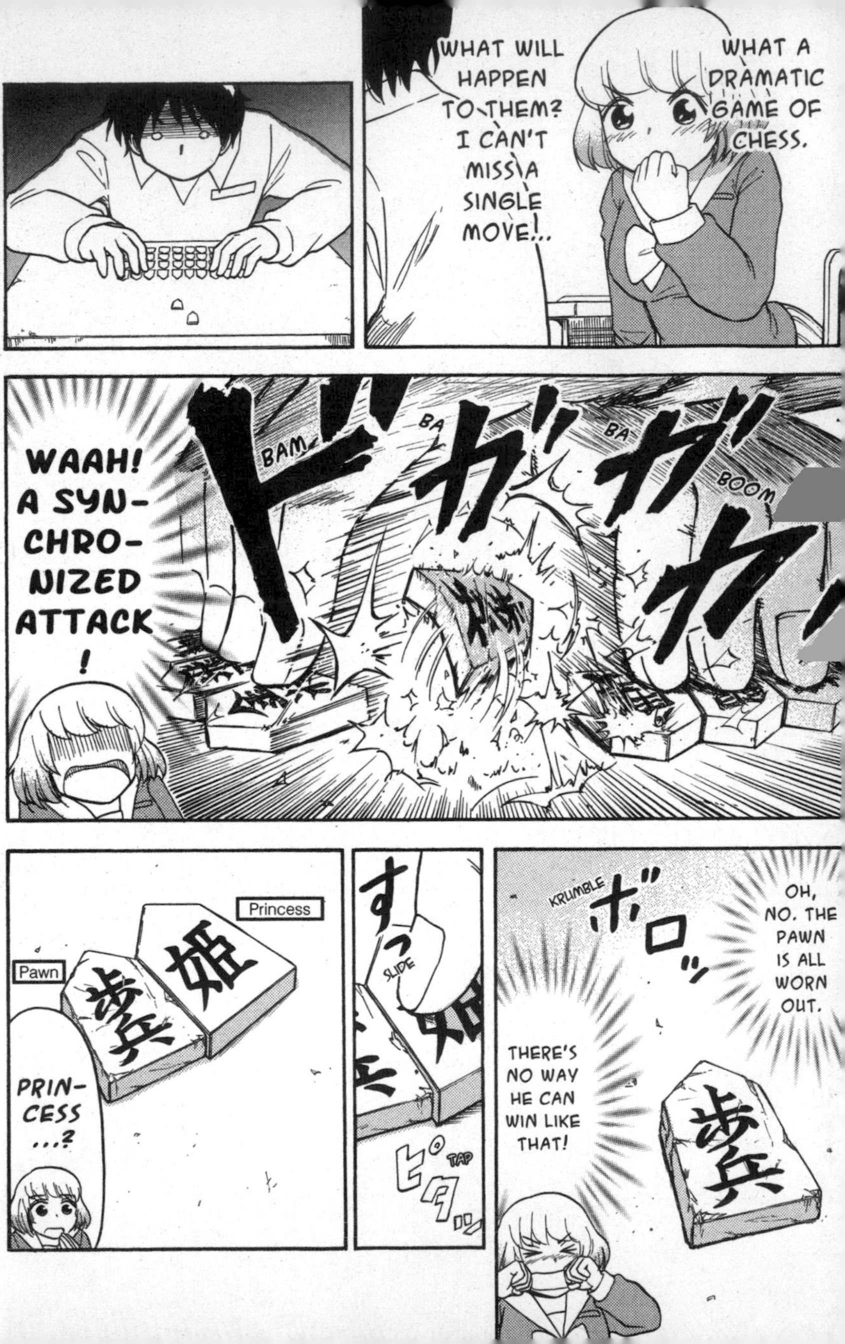
WHAT A DRAMATIC GAME OF CHESS.
WHAT WILL HAPPEN TO THEM? I CAN'T MISS A SINGLE MOVE!...
BOOM
BA
BA
ドガガガッ
BAM
WAAH! A SYN-CHRO-NIZED ATTACK!
OH, NO. THE PAWN IS ALL WORN OUT.
ボロッ
KRUMBLE
THERE'S NO WAY HE CAN WIN LIKE THAT!
歩兵
すっ
SLIDE
ピタッ
TAP
Princess
姫
Pawn
歩兵
PRIN-CESS ...?

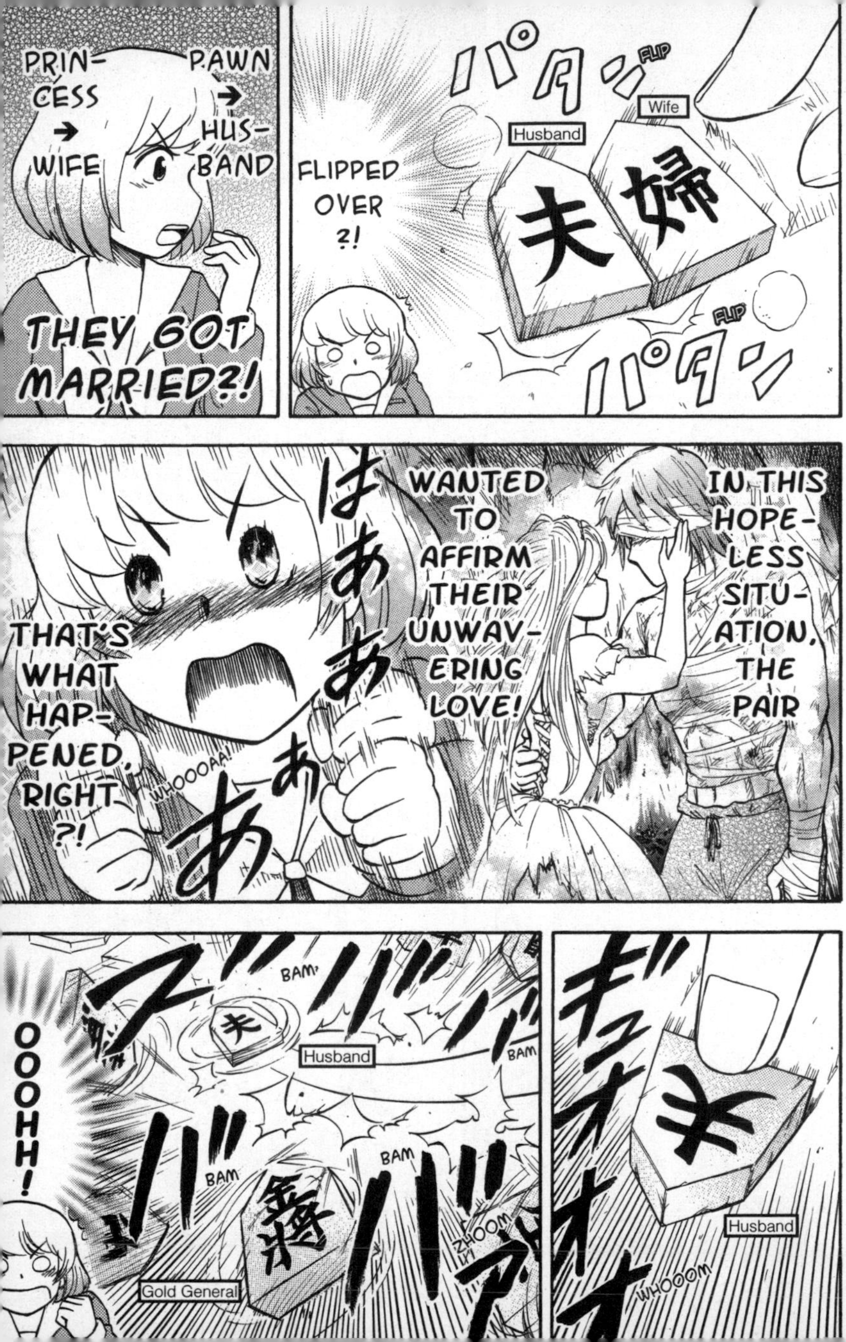
パタン
FLIP
Wife
Husband
夫
婦
FLIPPED OVER ?!
FLIP
パタン
PRIN-CESS → WIFE
PAWN → HUS-BAND
THEY GOT MARRIED?!
IN THIS HOPE-LESS SITU-ATION, THE PAIR
WANTED TO AFFIRM THEIR UNWAV-ERING LOVE!
はあああああ
WHOOOAA!
THAT'S WHAT HAP-PENED, RIGHT ?!
Husband
WHOOOM
BAM
Husband
BAM
BAM
BAM
ZHOOM
Gold General
OOOOHH!

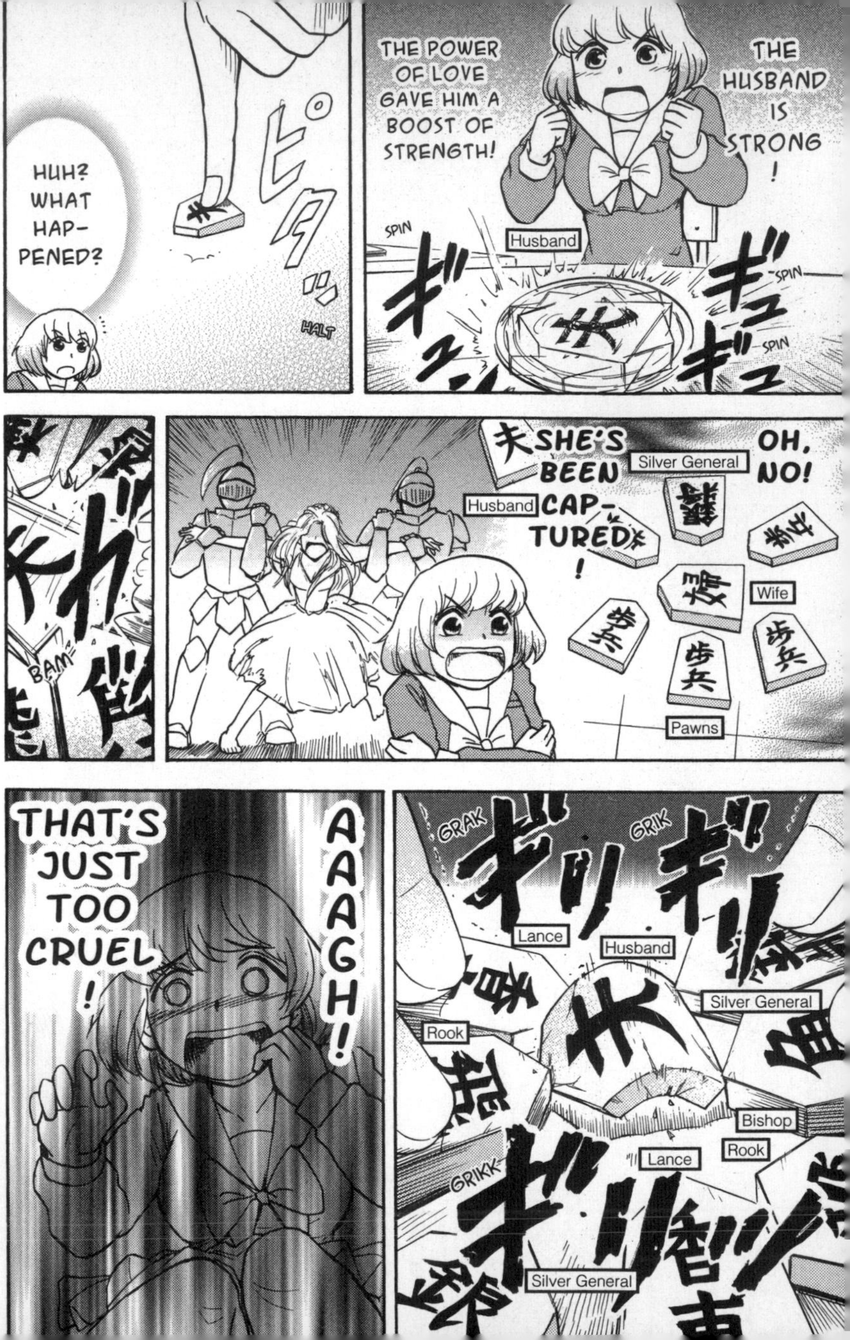
THE HUSBAND IS STRONG!
THE POWER OF LOVE GAVE HIM A BOOST OF STRENGTH!
SPIN
Husband
SPIN
SPIN
HALT
HUH? WHAT HAPPENED?
OH, NO!
SHE'S BEEN CAPTURED!
Silver General
Husband
Wife
Pawns
BAM
GRIK
GRAK
Lance
Husband
Silver General
Rook
Bishop
Rook
Lance
GRIKK
Silver General
AAAAGH!
THAT'S JUST TOO CRUEL!

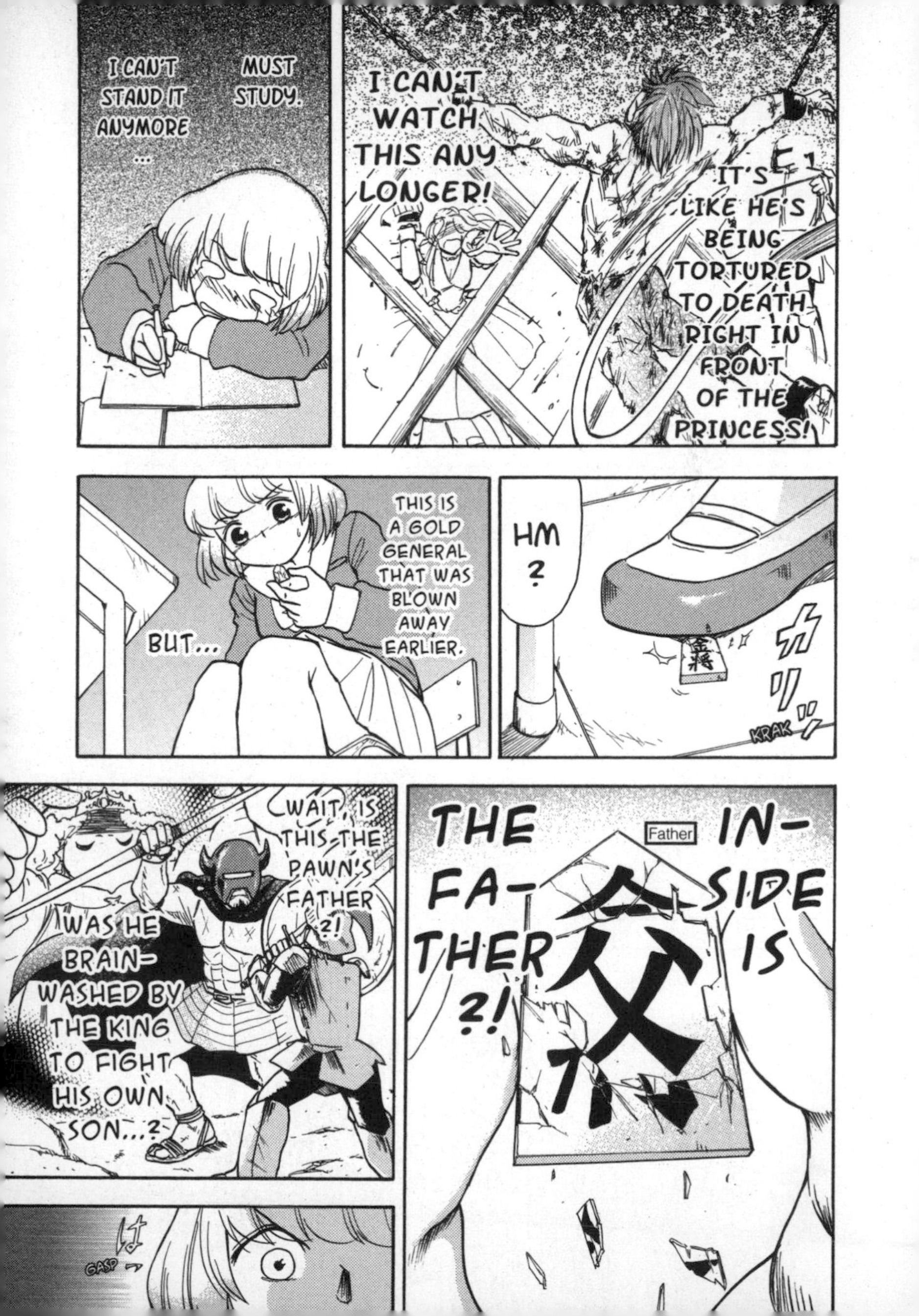
I CAN'T WATCH THIS ANY LONGER!
IT'S LIKE HE'S BEING TORTURED TO DEATH RIGHT IN FRONT OF THE PRINCESS!
MUST STUDY.
I CAN'T STAND IT ANYMORE ...
HM ?
KRAK
THIS IS A GOLD GENERAL THAT WAS BLOWN AWAY EARLIER.
BUT...
IN-SIDE IS
THE FA-THER ?!
Father
WAIT, IS THIS THE PAWN'S FATHER ?!
WAS HE BRAIN-WASHED BY THE KING TO FIGHT HIS OWN SON...?
GASP

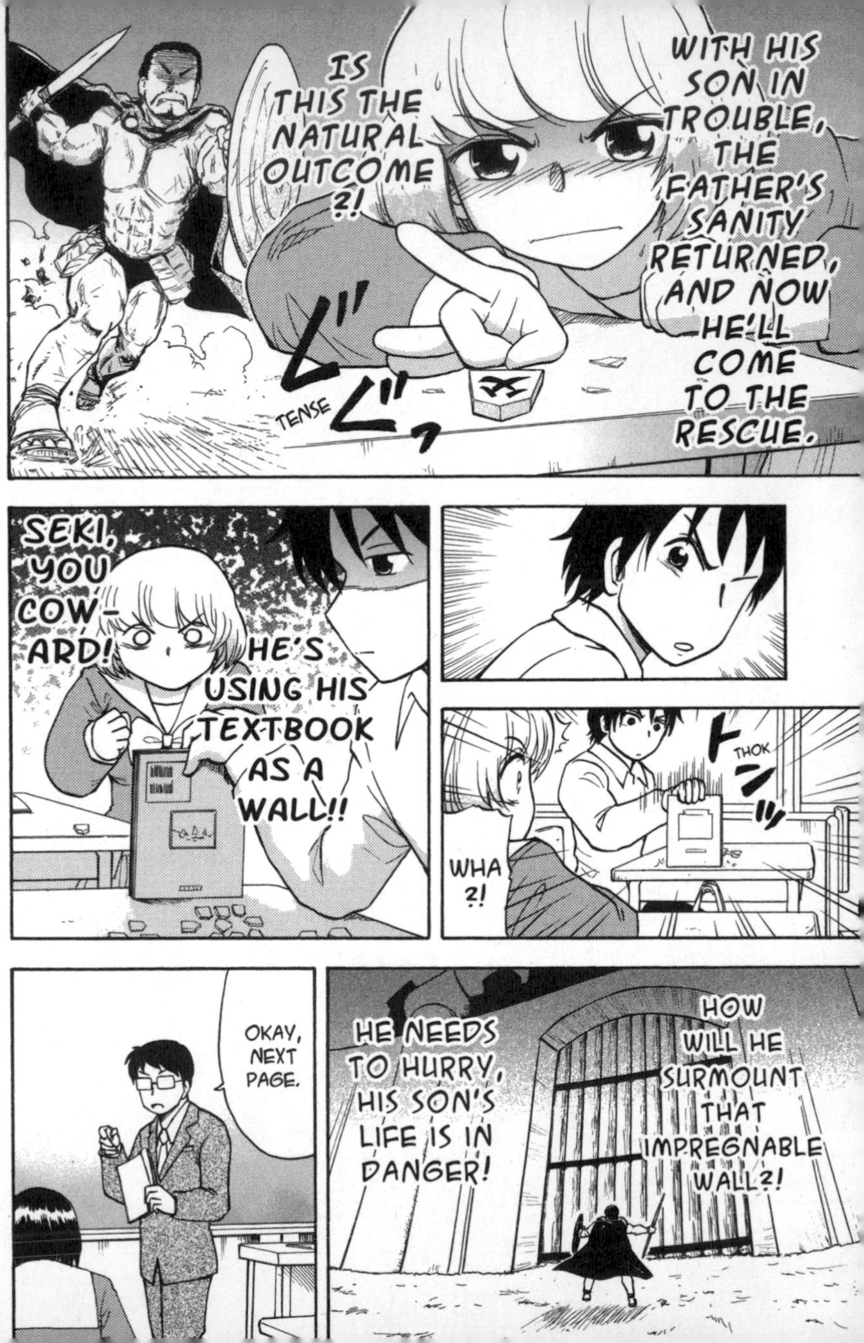
WITH HIS SON IN TROUBLE, THE FATHER'S SANITY RETURNED, AND NOW HE'LL COME TO THE RESCUE.
IS THIS THE NATURAL OUTCOME?!
TENSE
THOK
WHA?!
SEKI, YOU COW-ARD!
HE'S USING HIS TEXTBOOK AS A WALL!!
HOW WILL HE SURMOUNT THAT IMPREGNABLE WALL?!
HE NEEDS TO HURRY, HIS SON'S LIFE IS IN DANGER!
OKAY, NEXT PAGE.

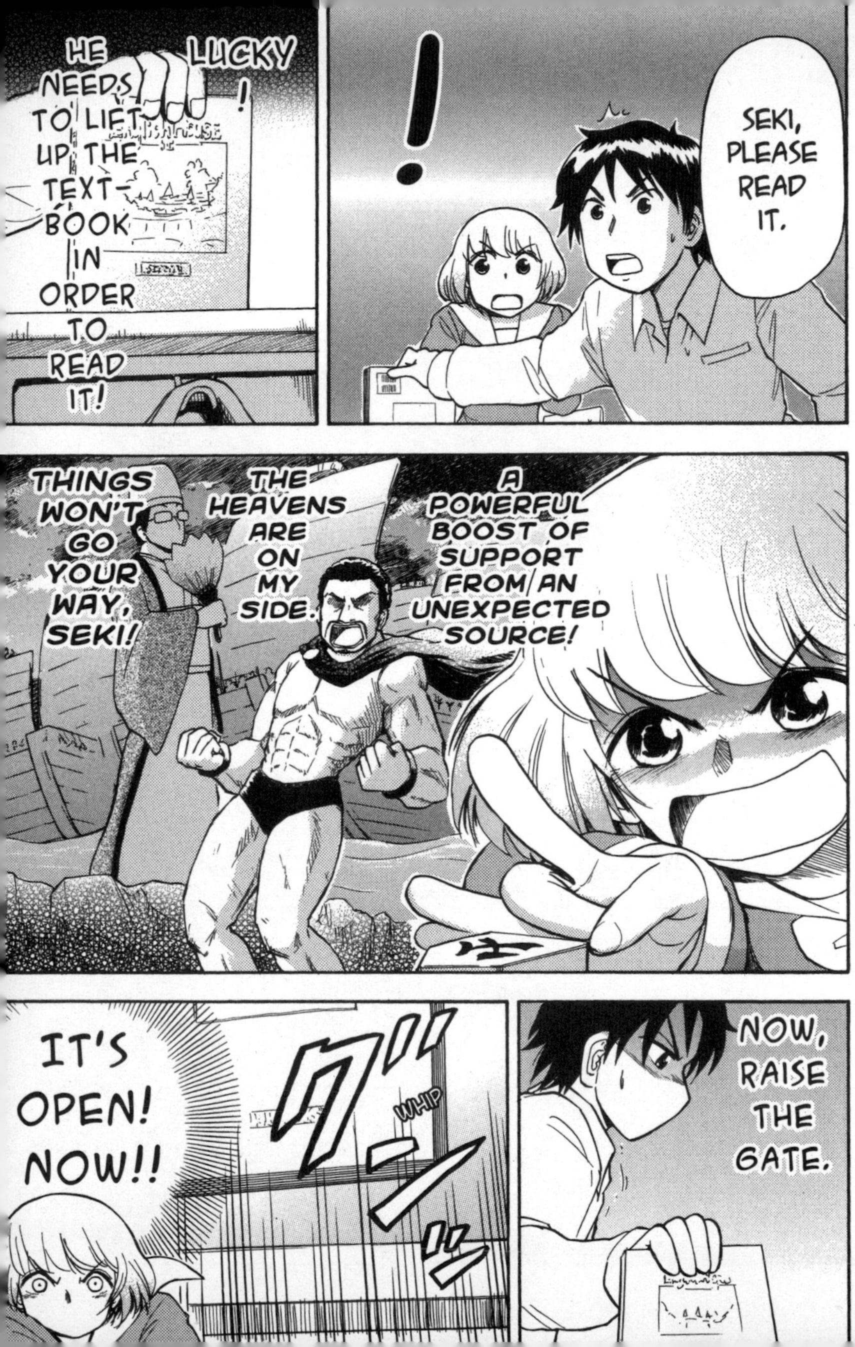
!
SEKI, PLEASE READ IT.
LUCKY!
HE NEEDS TO LIFT UP THE TEXTBOOK IN ORDER TO READ IT!
A POWERFUL BOOST OF SUPPORT FROM AN UNEXPECTED SOURCE!
THE HEAVENS ARE ON MY SIDE.
THINGS WON'T GO YOUR WAY, SEKI!
NOW, RAISE THE GATE.
WHIP
IT'S OPEN! NOW!!

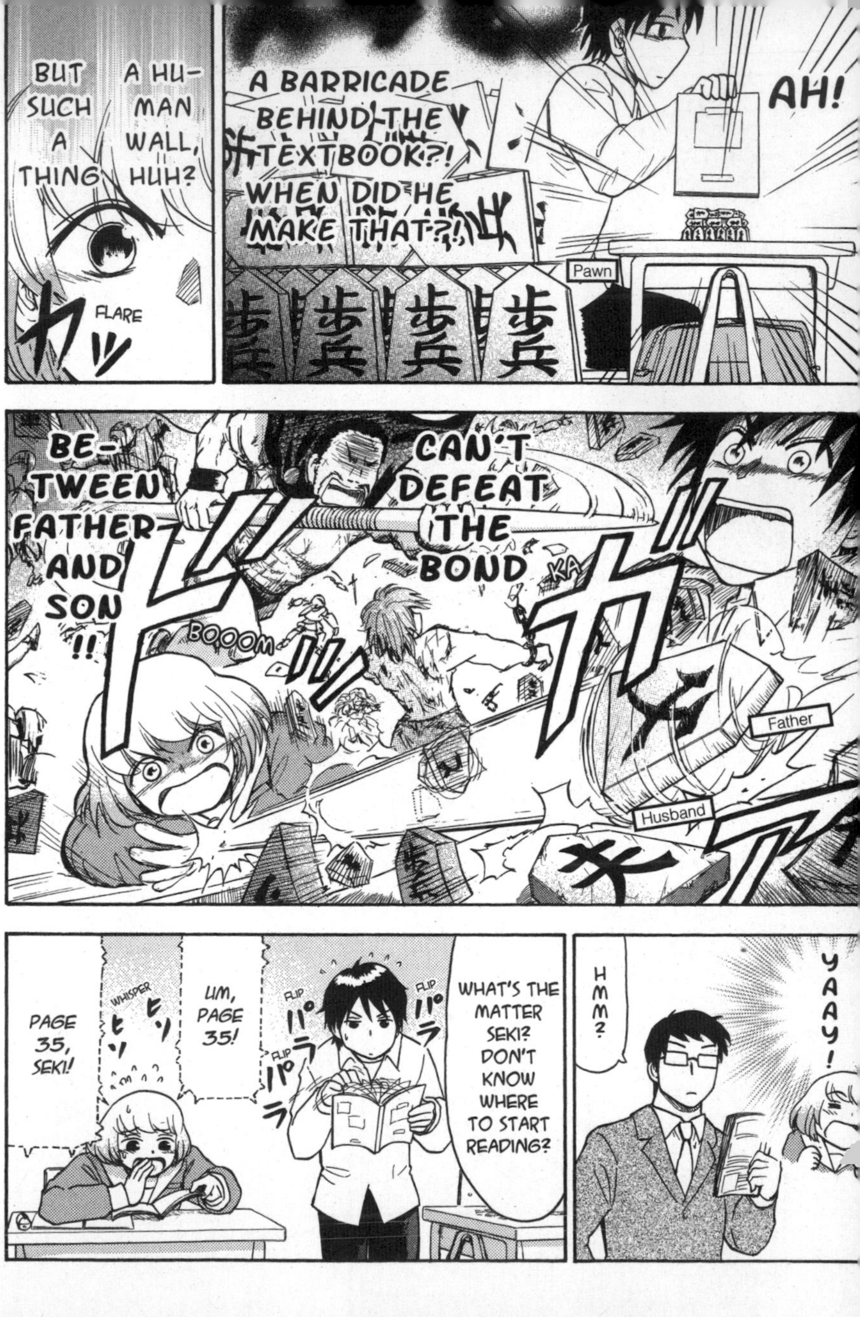
AH!
A BARRICADE BEHIND THE TEXTBOOK?! WHEN DID HE MAKE THAT?!
Pawn
A HU-MAN WALL, HUH?
BUT SUCH A THING
FLARE
CAN'T DEFEAT THE BOND
BE-TWEEN FATHER AND SON!!
KA
BOOOM
Father
Husband
YAAAY!
HMM?
WHAT'S THE MATTER SEKI? DON'T KNOW WHERE TO START READING?
FLIP
FLIP
FLIP
UM, PAGE 35!
WHISPER
PAGE 35, SEKI!

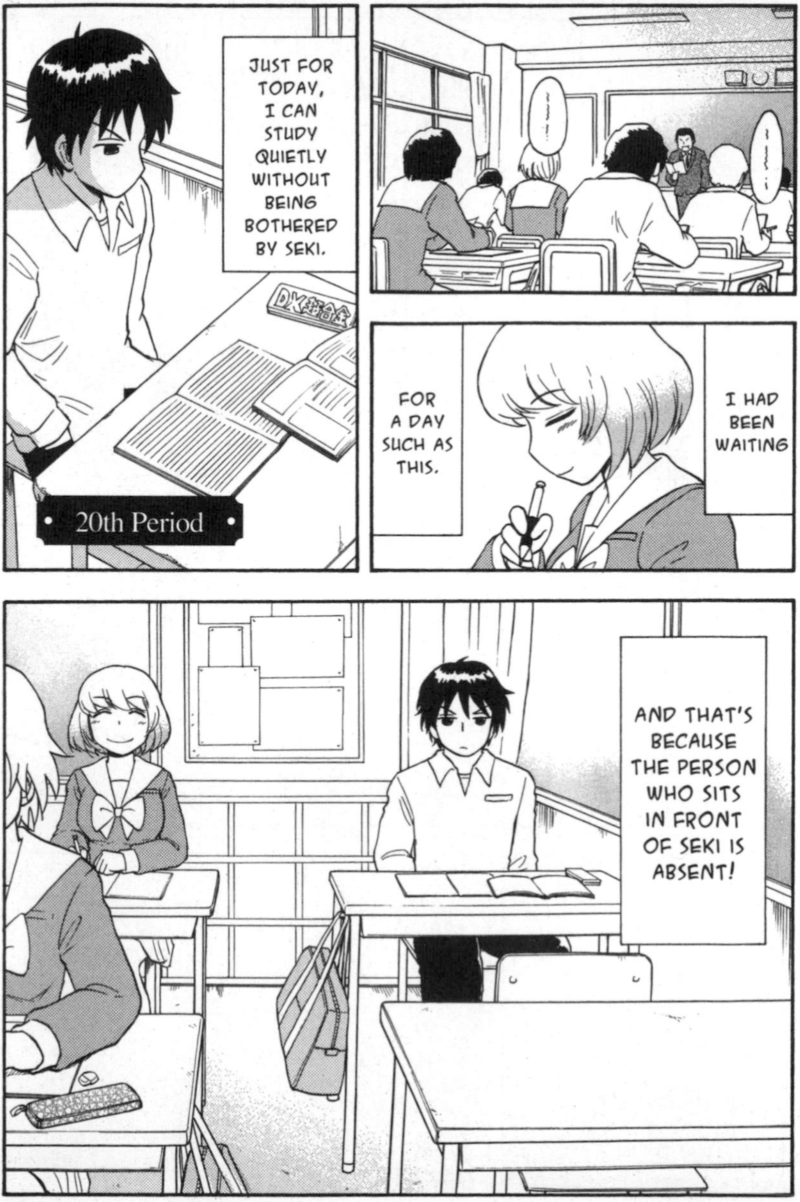
I HAD BEEN WAITING
FOR A DAY SUCH AS THIS.
JUST FOR TODAY, I CAN STUDY QUIETLY WITHOUT BEING BOTHERED BY SEKI.
20th Period
AND THAT'S BECAUSE THE PERSON WHO SITS IN FRONT OF SEKI IS ABSENT!

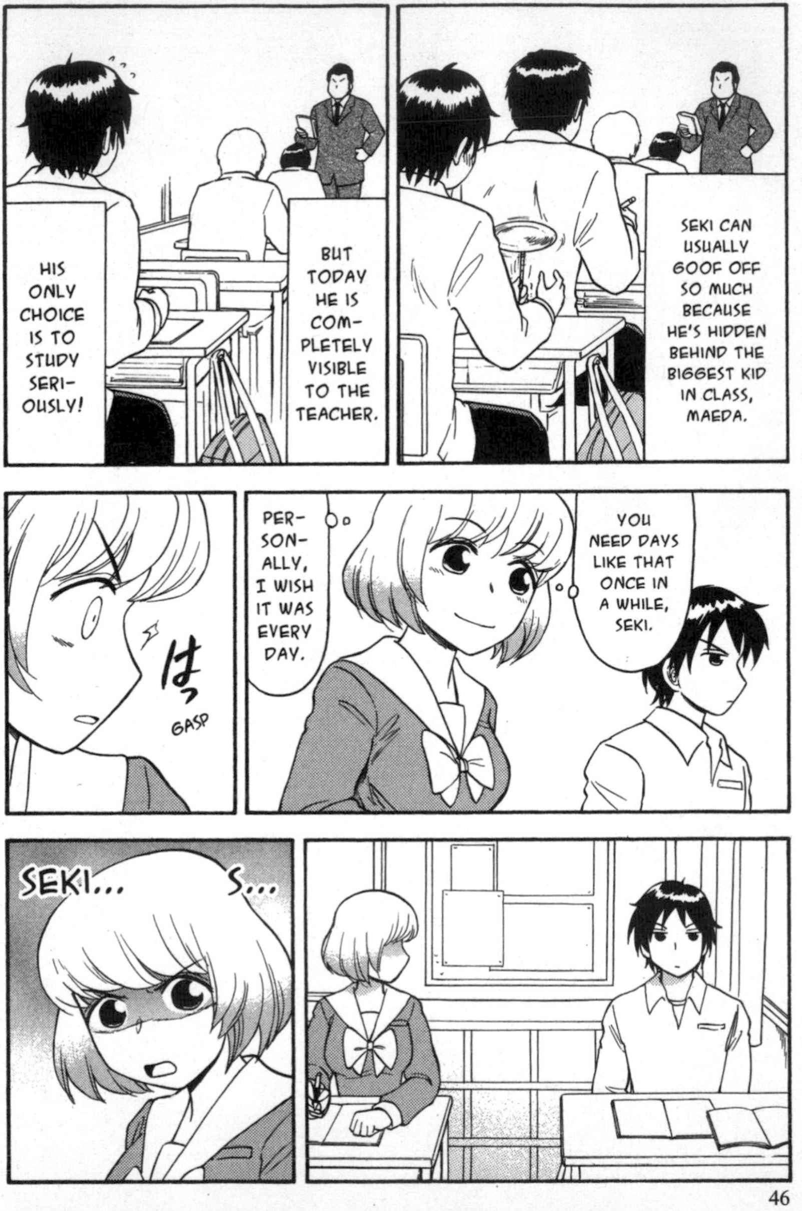
SEKI CAN USUALLY GOOF OFF SO MUCH BECAUSE HE'S HIDDEN BEHIND THE BIGGEST KID IN CLASS, MAEDA.
BUT TODAY HE IS COMPLETELY VISIBLE TO THE TEACHER.
HIS ONLY CHOICE IS TO STUDY SERIOUSLY!
YOU NEED DAYS LIKE THAT ONCE IN A WHILE, SEKI.
PERSONALLY, I WISH IT WAS EVERY DAY.
はっ
GASP
SEKI...
S...

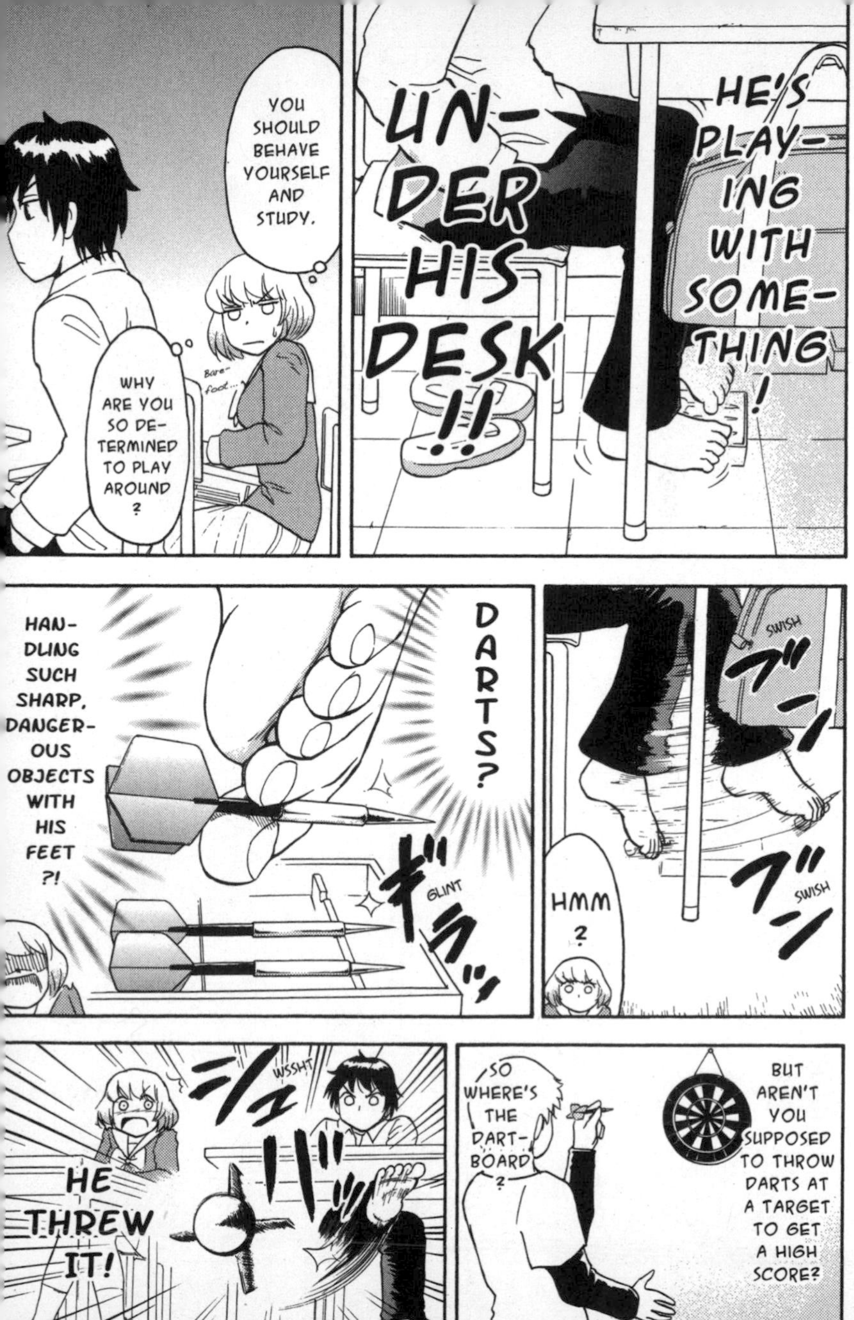
HE'S PLAYING WITH SOMETHING!
UNDER HIS DESK!!
YOU SHOULD BEHAVE YOURSELF AND STUDY.
Barefoot...
WHY ARE YOU SO DETERMINED TO PLAY AROUND?
SWISH
SWISH
HMM?
DARTS?
GLINT
HANDLING SUCH SHARP, DANGEROUS OBJECTS WITH HIS FEET?!
SO WHERE'S THE DARTBOARD?
BUT AREN'T YOU SUPPOSED TO THROW DARTS AT A TARGET TO GET A HIGH SCORE?
WSSHT
HE THREW IT!

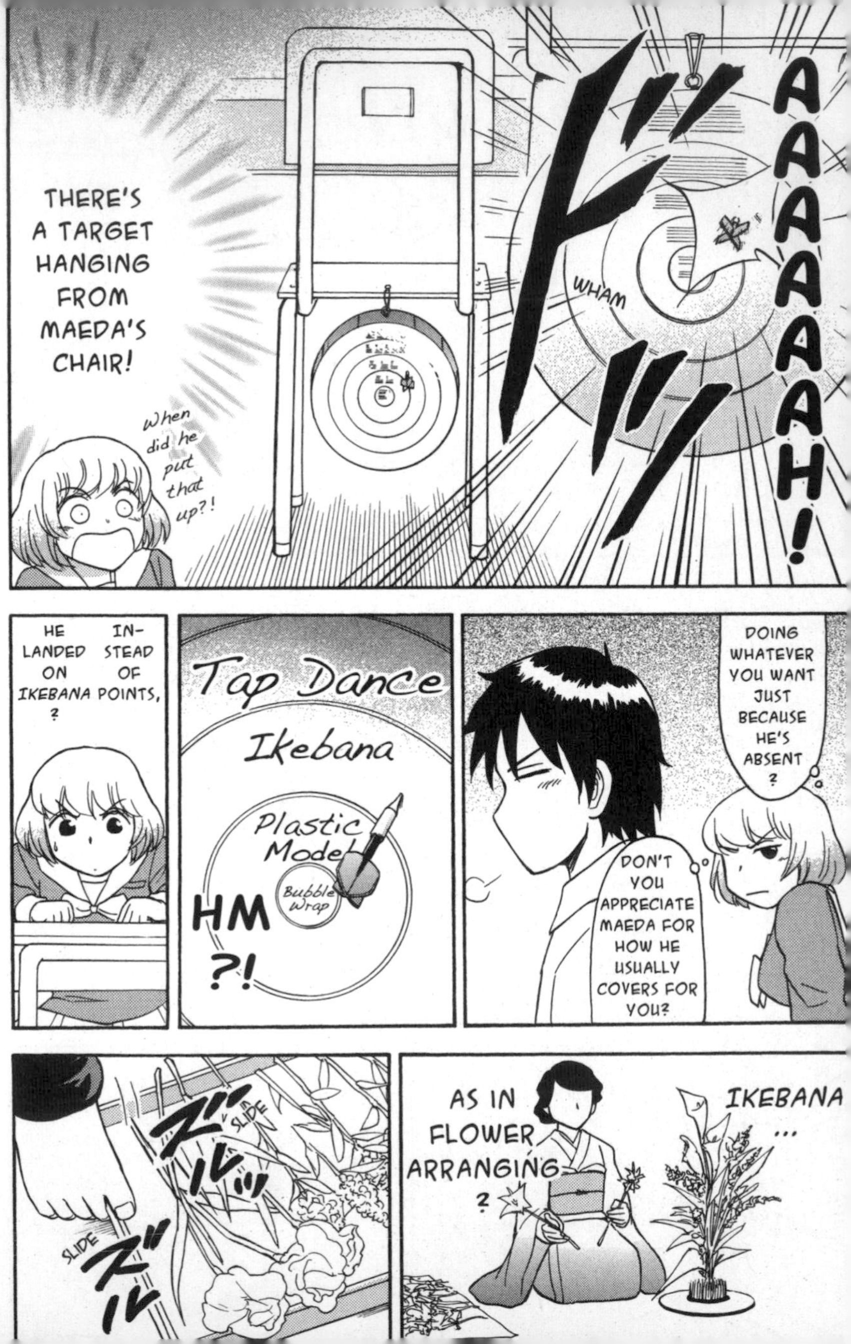
AAAAAAAH!
WHAM
THERE'S A TARGET HANGING FROM MAEDA'S CHAIR!
When did he put that up?!
DOING WHATEVER YOU WANT JUST BECAUSE HE'S ABSENT?
DON'T YOU APPRECIATE MAEDA FOR HOW HE USUALLY COVERS FOR YOU?
Tap Dance
Ikebana
Plastic Model
Bubble Wrap
HM?!
HE LANDED ON IKEBANA?
INSTEAD OF POINTS,
IKEBANA...
AS IN FLOWER ARRANGING?
SLIDE
SLIDE

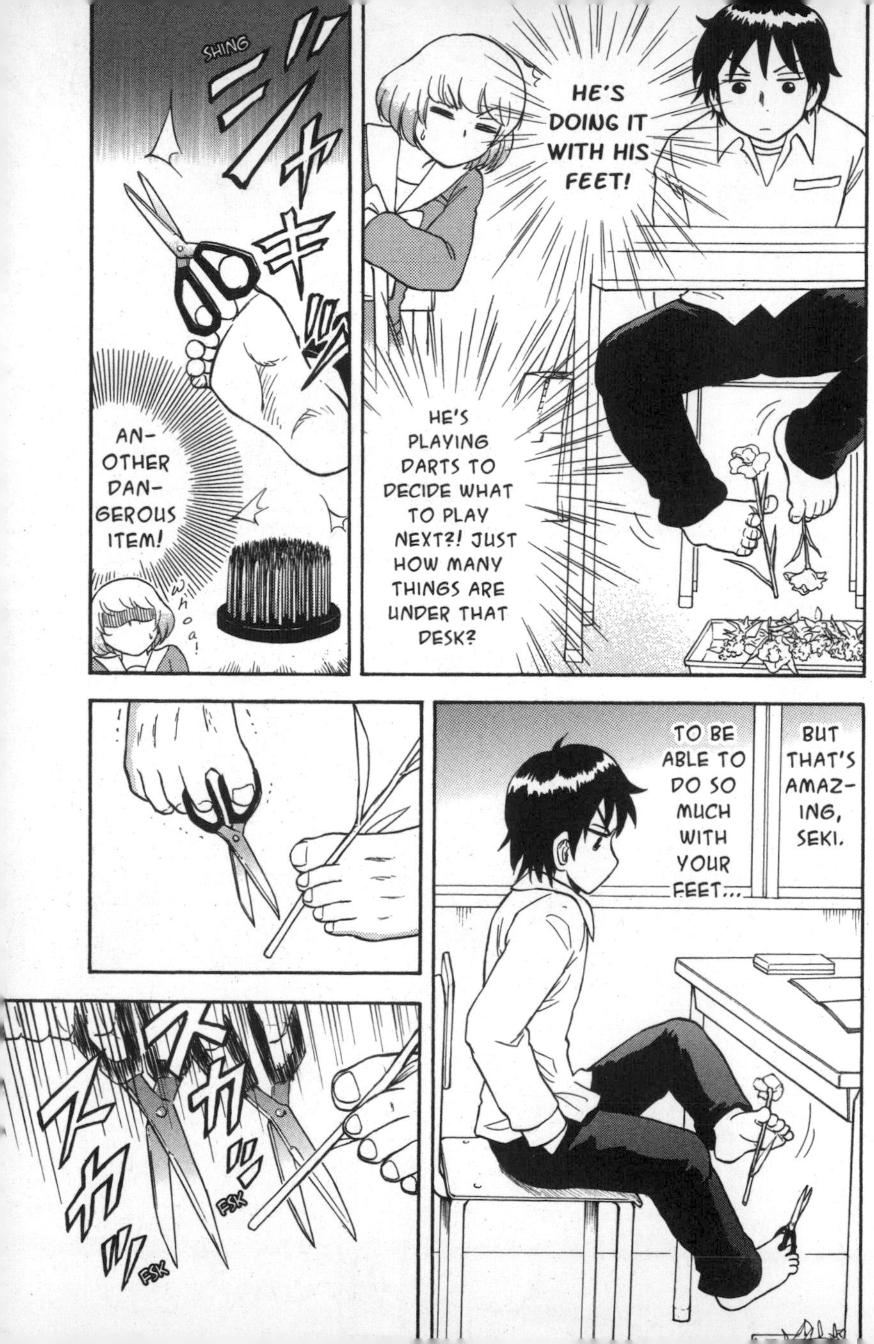
HE'S DOING IT WITH HIS FEET!
HE'S PLAYING DARTS TO DECIDE WHAT TO PLAY NEXT?! JUST HOW MANY THINGS ARE UNDER THAT DESK?
SHING
AN-OTHER DAN-GEROUS ITEM!
Whoa!
BUT THAT'S AMAZ-ING, SEKI.
TO BE ABLE TO DO SO MUCH WITH YOUR FEET...
FSK
FSK

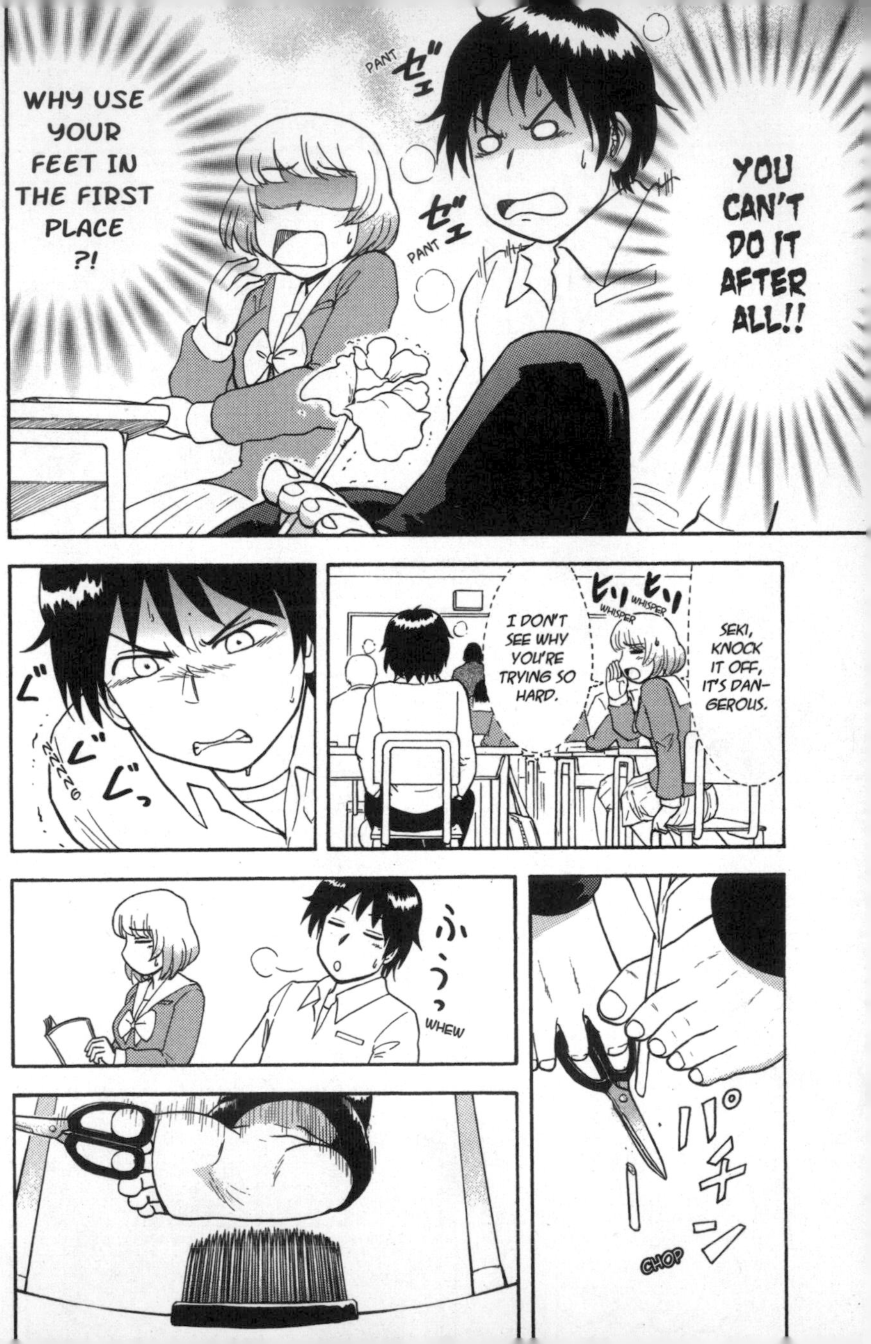
YOU CAN'T DO IT AFTER ALL!!
ゼェ PANT
ゼェ PANT
WHY USE YOUR FEET IN THE FIRST PLACE ?!
SEKI, KNOCK IT OFF, IT'S DANGEROUS.
ヒソ ヒソ WHISPER WHISPER
I DON'T SEE WHY YOU'RE TRYING SO HARD.
ぐ ぐぐっ
ZZZZG
パチーン
CHOP
ふうっ
WHEW

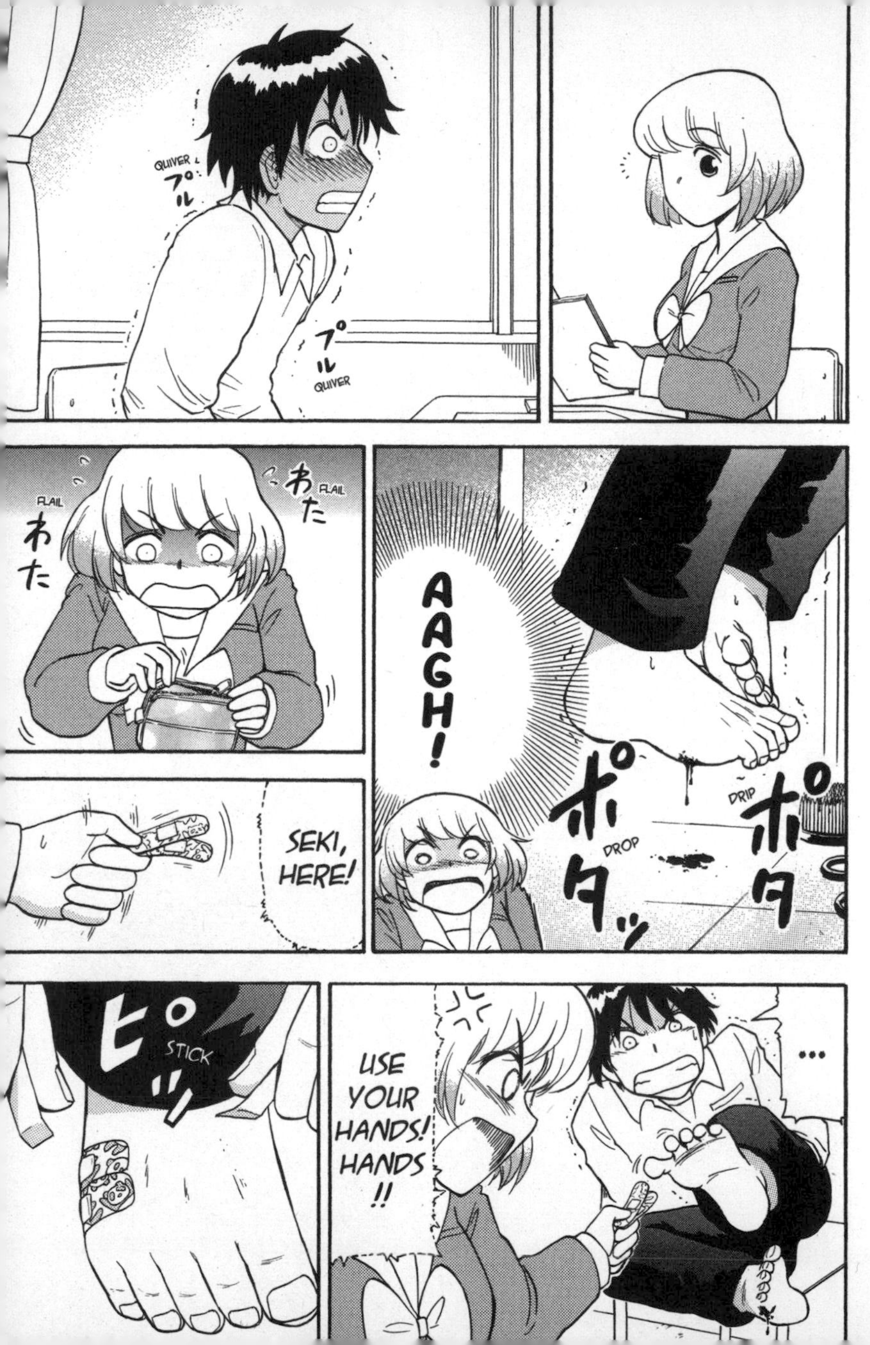
QUIVER
プル
プル
QUIVER
AAGH!
ポタ
DRIP
ポタッ
DROP
わた
FLAIL
わた
FLAIL
SEKI, HERE!
...
USE YOUR HANDS! HANDS !!
ピッ
STICK

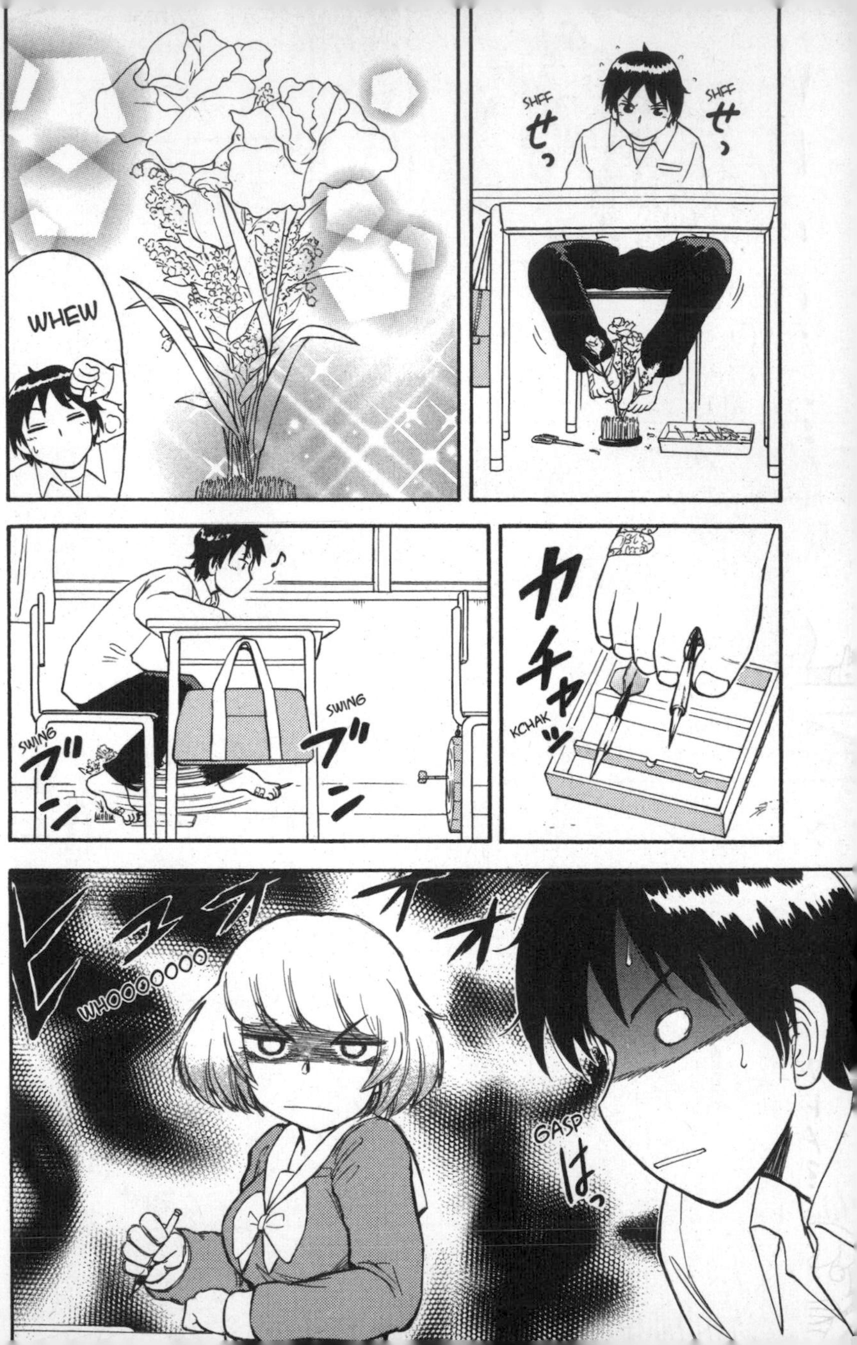
SHFF
せっ
SHFF
せっ
WHEW
カチャッ
KCHAK
SWING
ブン
SWING
ブン
ヒュオオオ
WHOOOOOOO
GASP
はっ

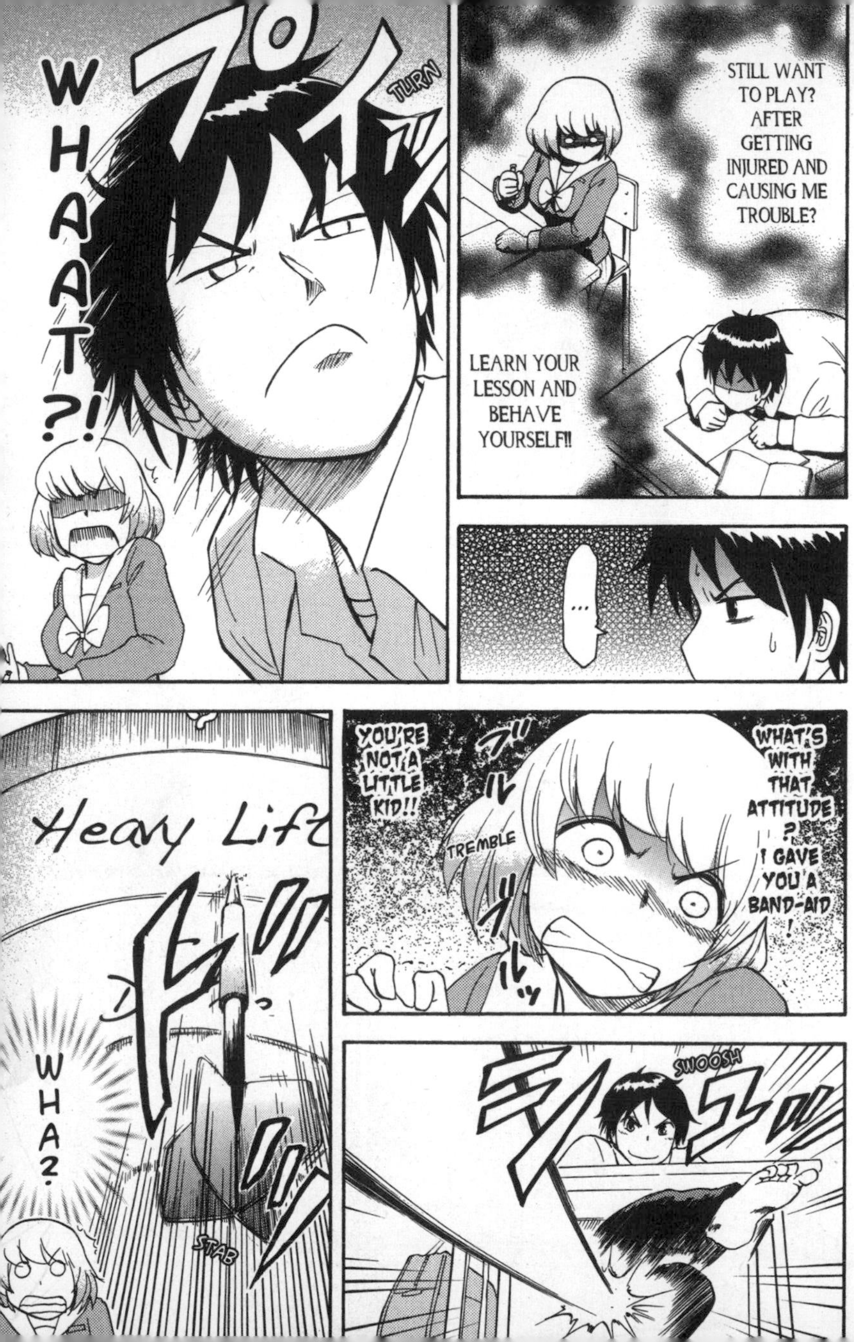
STILL WANT TO PLAY? AFTER GETTING INJURED AND CAUSING ME TROUBLE?
LEARN YOUR LESSON AND BEHAVE YOURSELF!!
...
TURN
WHAAT?!
WHAT'S WITH THAT ATTITUDE? I GAVE YOU A BAND-AID!
YOU'RE NOT A LITTLE KID!!
TREMBLE
SWOOSH
Heavy Lift
STAB
WHA?

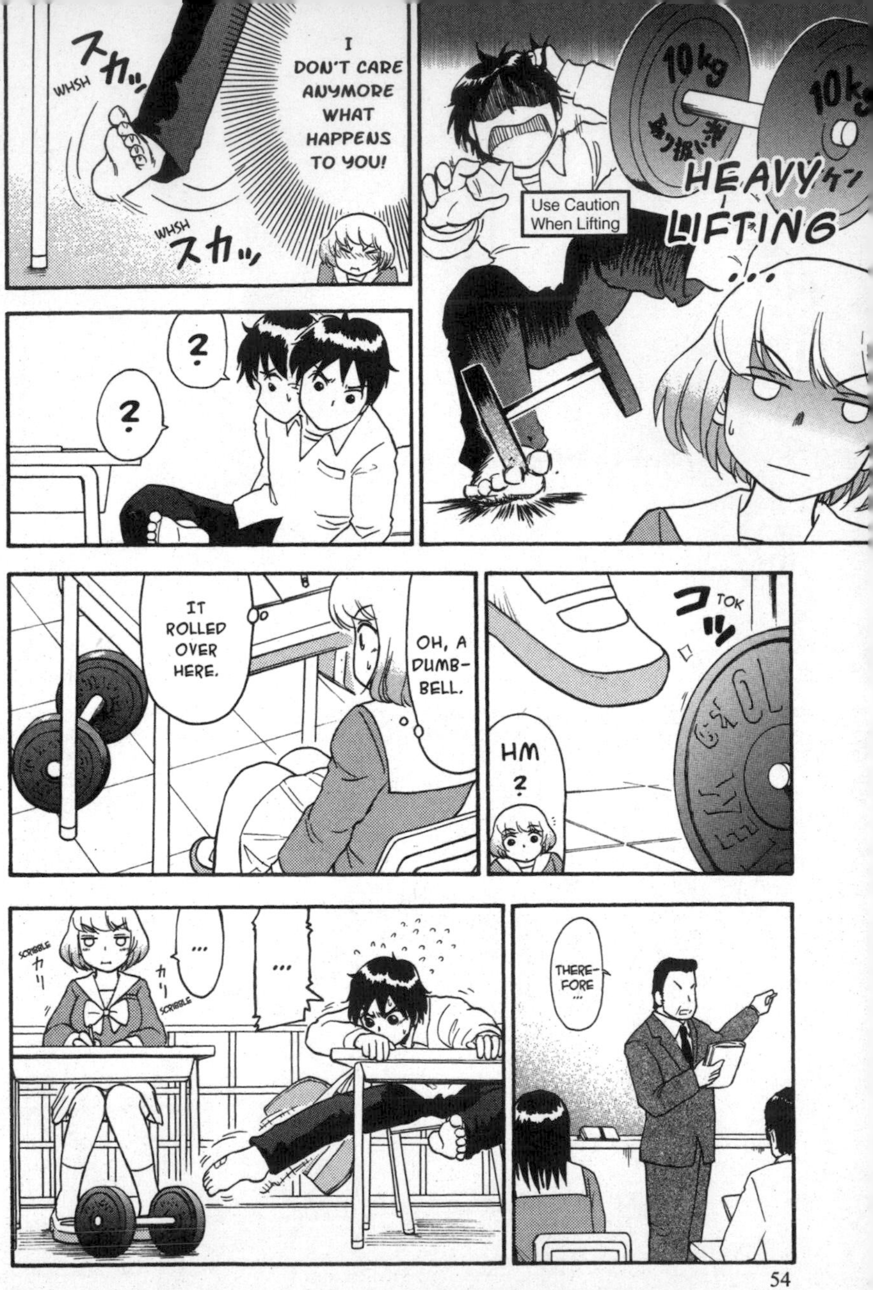

10kg
10kg
Use Caution When Lifting
HEAVY ケン LIFTING
...
I DON'T CARE ANYMORE WHAT HAPPENS TO YOU!
WHSH スカッ
WHSH スカッ
?
?
コッ TOK
HM ?
OH, A DUMBBELL.
IT ROLLED OVER HERE.
THERE-FORE ...
...
...
SCRIBBLE カリ
カリ SCRIBBLE

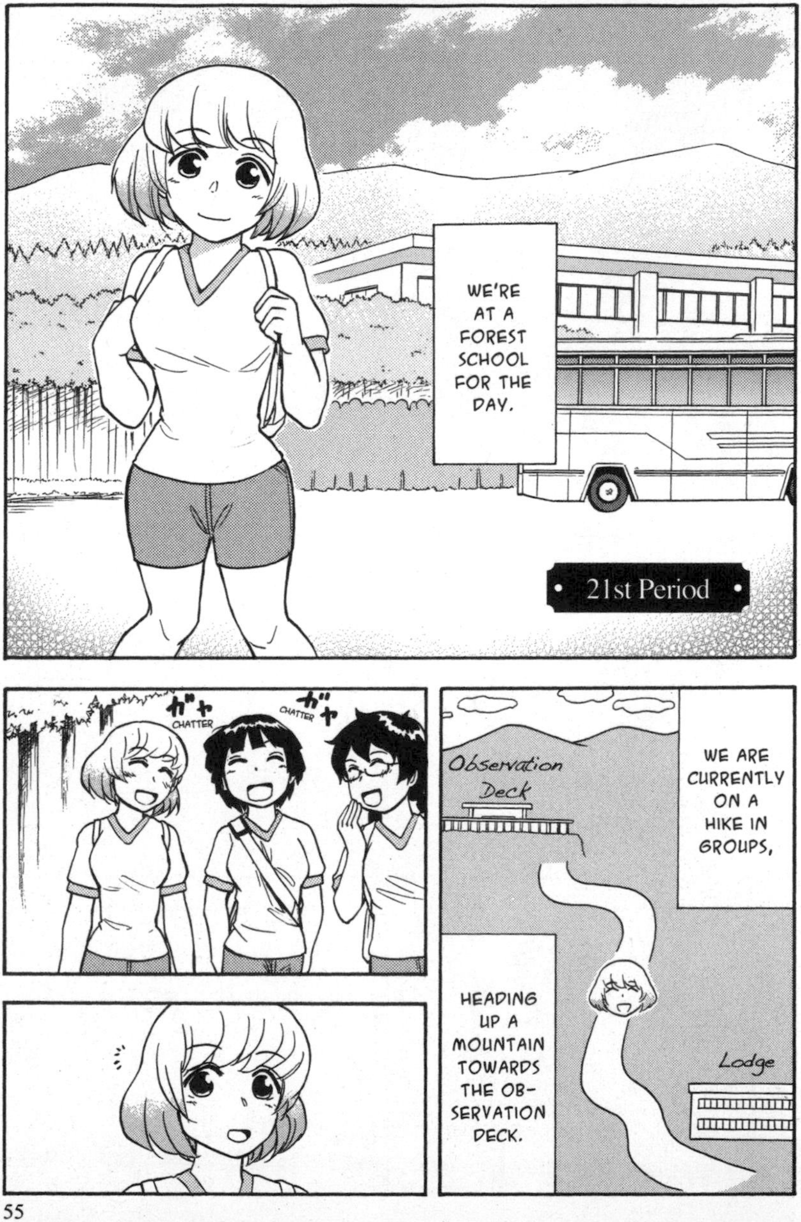
WE'RE AT A FOREST SCHOOL FOR THE DAY.
21st Period
WE ARE CURRENTLY ON A HIKE IN GROUPS,
Observation Deck
HEADING UP A MOUNTAIN TOWARDS THE OB-SERVATION DECK.
Lodge
ガヤ
CHATTER
ガヤ
CHATTER

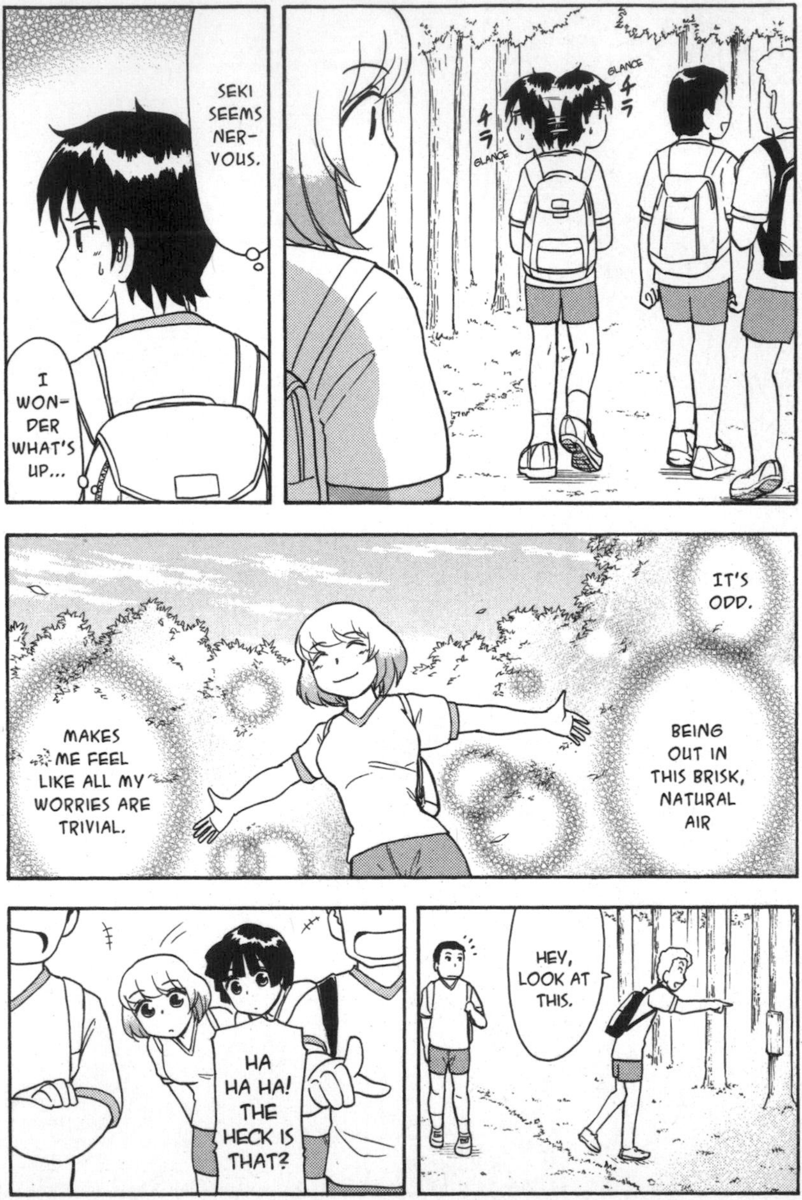
GLANCE
チラ
チラ
GLANCE
SEKI SEEMS NERVOUS.
I WONDER WHAT'S UP...
IT'S ODD.
BEING OUT IN THIS BRISK, NATURAL AIR
MAKES ME FEEL LIKE ALL MY WORRIES ARE TRIVIAL.
HEY, LOOK AT THIS.
HA HA HA! THE HECK IS THAT?

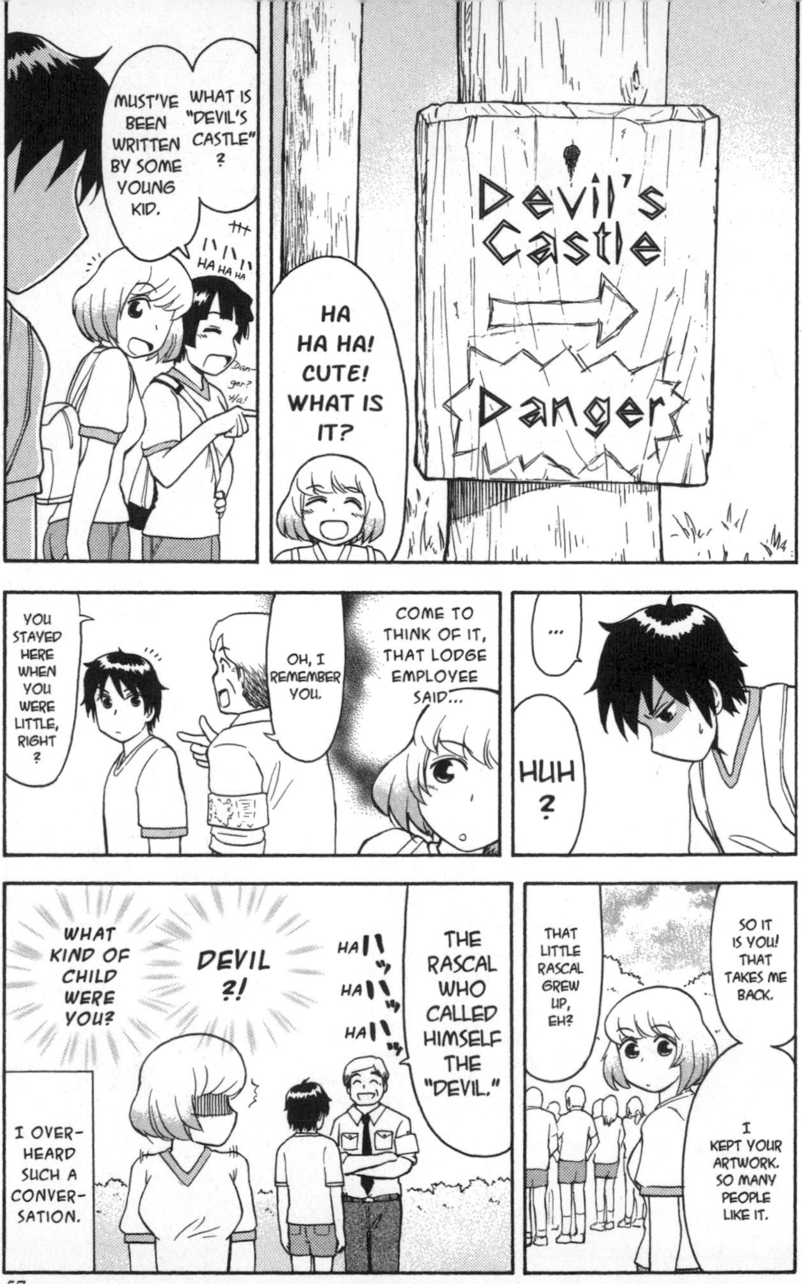
Devil's Castle
Danger
HA HA HA! CUTE! WHAT IS IT?
WHAT IS "DEVIL'S CASTLE"?
MUST'VE BEEN WRITTEN BY SOME YOUNG KID.
HA HA HA
Danger? Ha!
...
HUH?
COME TO THINK OF IT, THAT LODGE EMPLOYEE SAID...
OH, I REMEMBER YOU.
YOU STAYED HERE WHEN YOU WERE LITTLE, RIGHT?
SO IT IS YOU! THAT TAKES ME BACK.
THAT LITTLE RASCAL GREW UP, EH?
I KEPT YOUR ARTWORK. SO MANY PEOPLE LIKE IT.
THE RASCAL WHO CALLED HIMSELF THE "DEVIL."
HA HA HA
DEVIL?!
WHAT KIND OF CHILD WERE YOU?
I OVER-HEARD SUCH A CONVER-SATION.

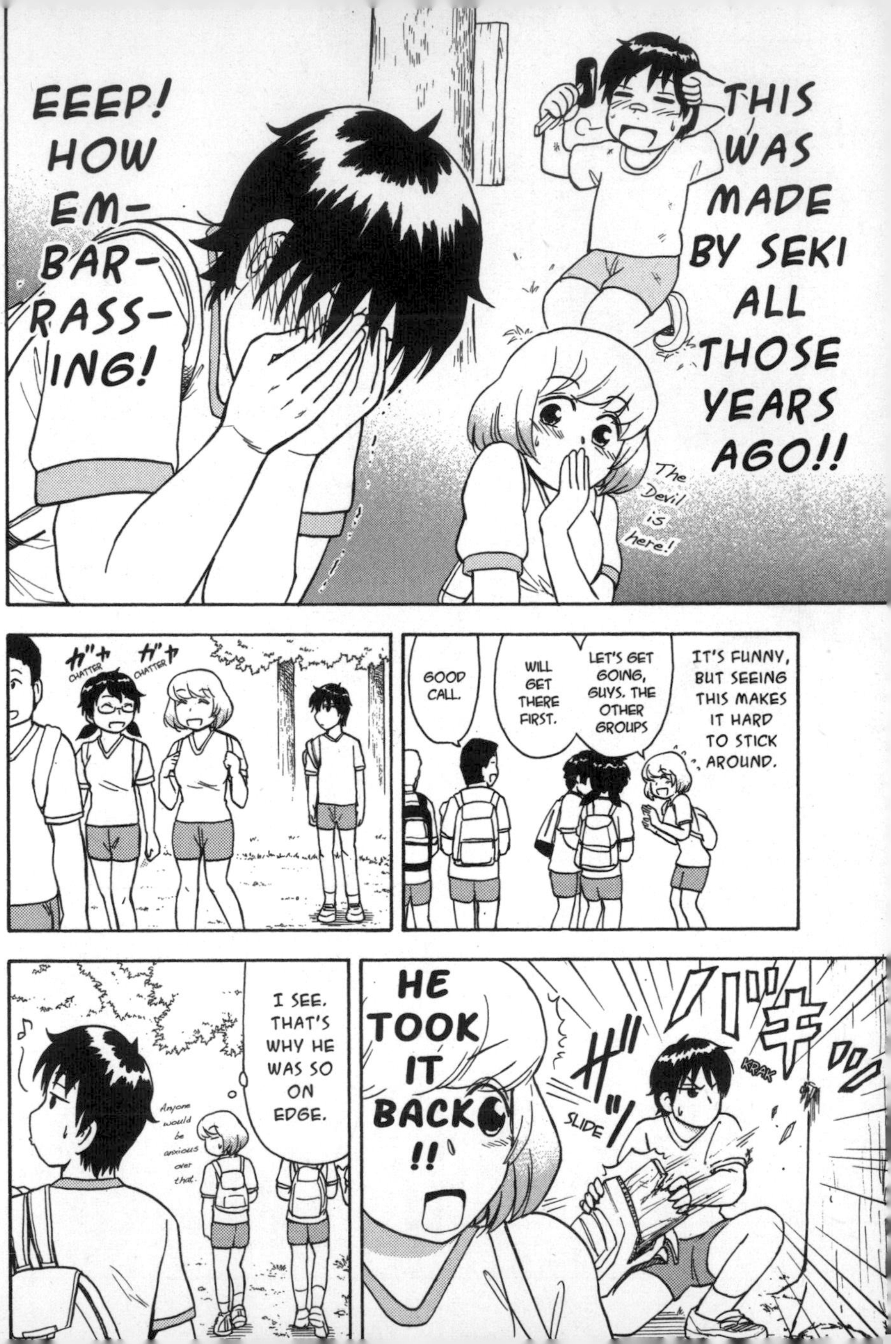
THIS WAS MADE BY SEKI ALL THOSE YEARS AGO!!
The Devil is here!
EEEP! HOW EM-BAR-RASS-ING!
IT'S FUNNY, BUT SEEING THIS MAKES IT HARD TO STICK AROUND.
LET'S GET GOING, GUYS. THE OTHER GROUPS
WILL GET THERE FIRST.
GOOD CALL.
ガヤ CHATTER
ガヤ CHATTER
バギ
KRAK
ザ
SLIDE
HE TOOK IT BACK!!
I SEE. THAT'S WHY HE WAS SO ON EDGE.
Anyone would be anxious over that.

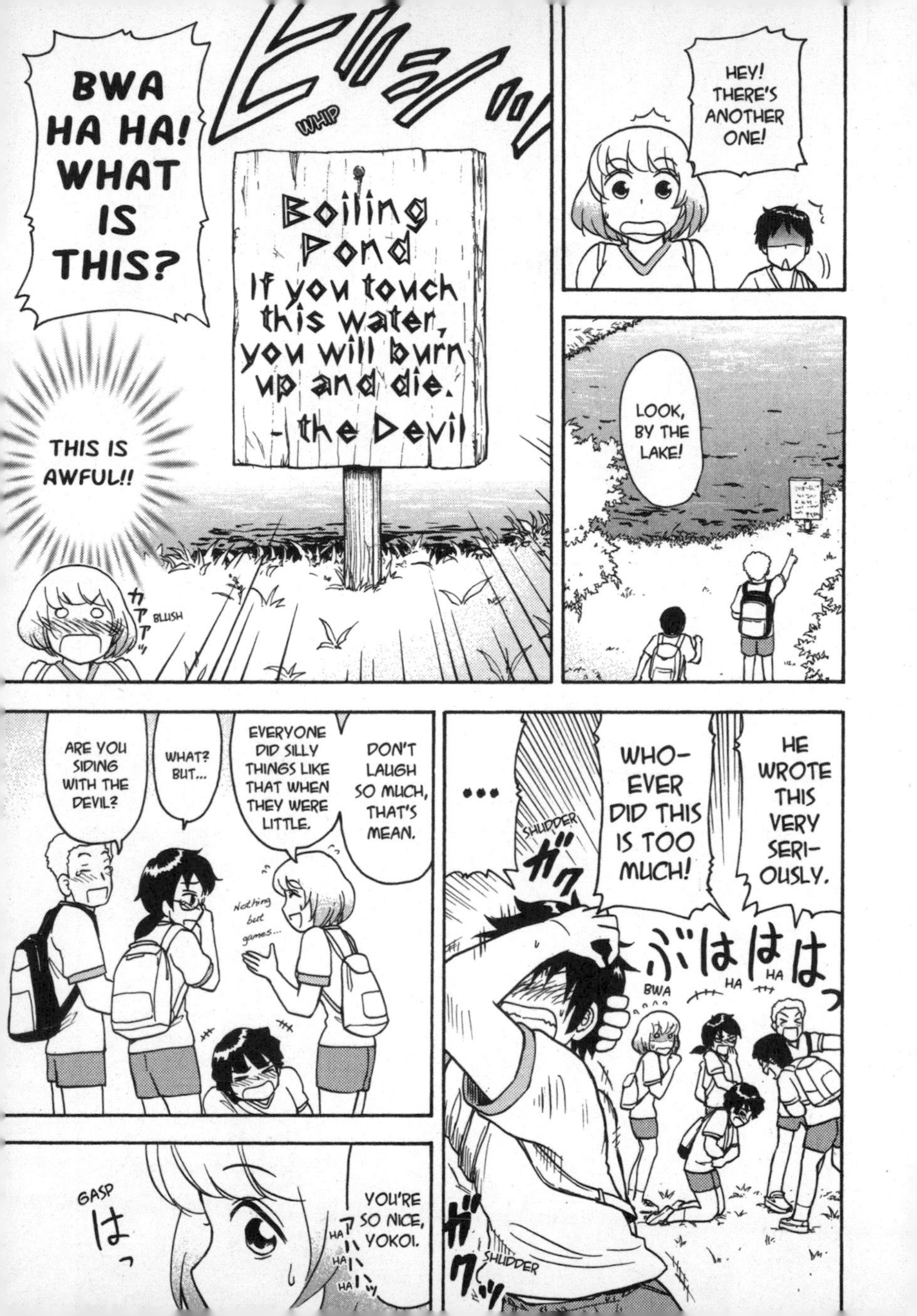
HEY! THERE'S ANOTHER ONE!
LOOK, BY THE LAKE!
WHIP
BWA HA HA! WHAT IS THIS?
Boiling Pond
If you touch this water, you will burn up and die.
- the Devil
THIS IS AWFUL!!
BLUSH
HE WROTE THIS VERY SERI-OUSLY.
WHO-EVER DID THIS IS TOO MUCH!
...
SHUDDER
ぶははは
BWA HA HA
SHUDDER
DON'T LAUGH SO MUCH, THAT'S MEAN.
EVERYONE DID SILLY THINGS LIKE THAT WHEN THEY WERE LITTLE.
WHAT? BUT...
ARE YOU SIDING WITH THE DEVIL?
Nothing but games...
YOU'RE SO NICE, YOKOI.
HA HA HA HA
GASP

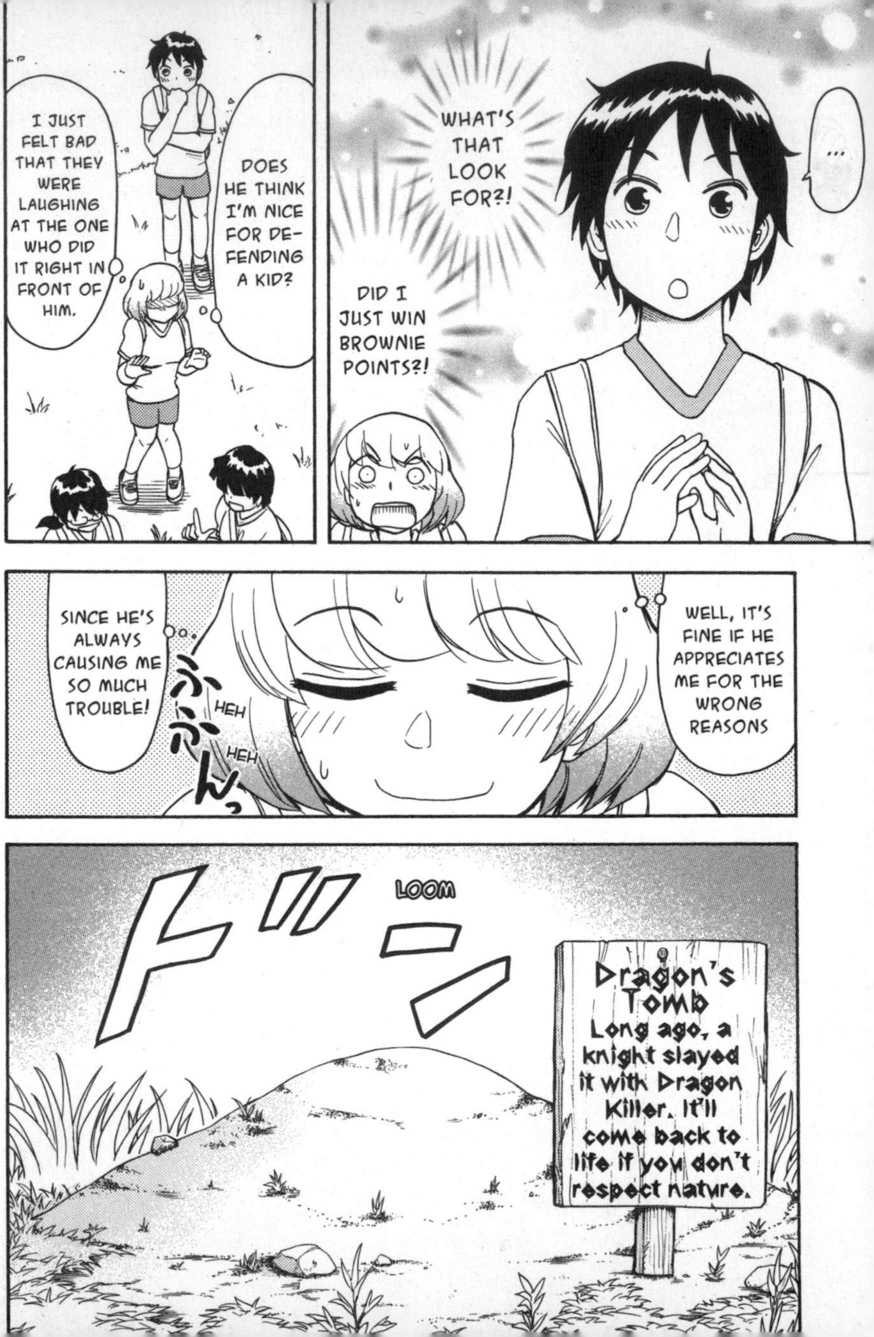
...
WHAT'S THAT LOOK FOR?!
DID I JUST WIN BROWNIE POINTS?!
DOES HE THINK I'M NICE FOR DE-FENDING A KID?
I JUST FELT BAD THAT THEY WERE LAUGHING AT THE ONE WHO DID IT RIGHT IN FRONT OF HIM.
WELL, IT'S FINE IF HE APPRECIATES ME FOR THE WRONG REASONS
HEH
HEH
SINCE HE'S ALWAYS CAUSING ME SO MUCH TROUBLE!
LOOM
Dragon's Tomb
Long ago, a knight slayed it with Dragon Killer. It'll come back to life if you don't respect nature.

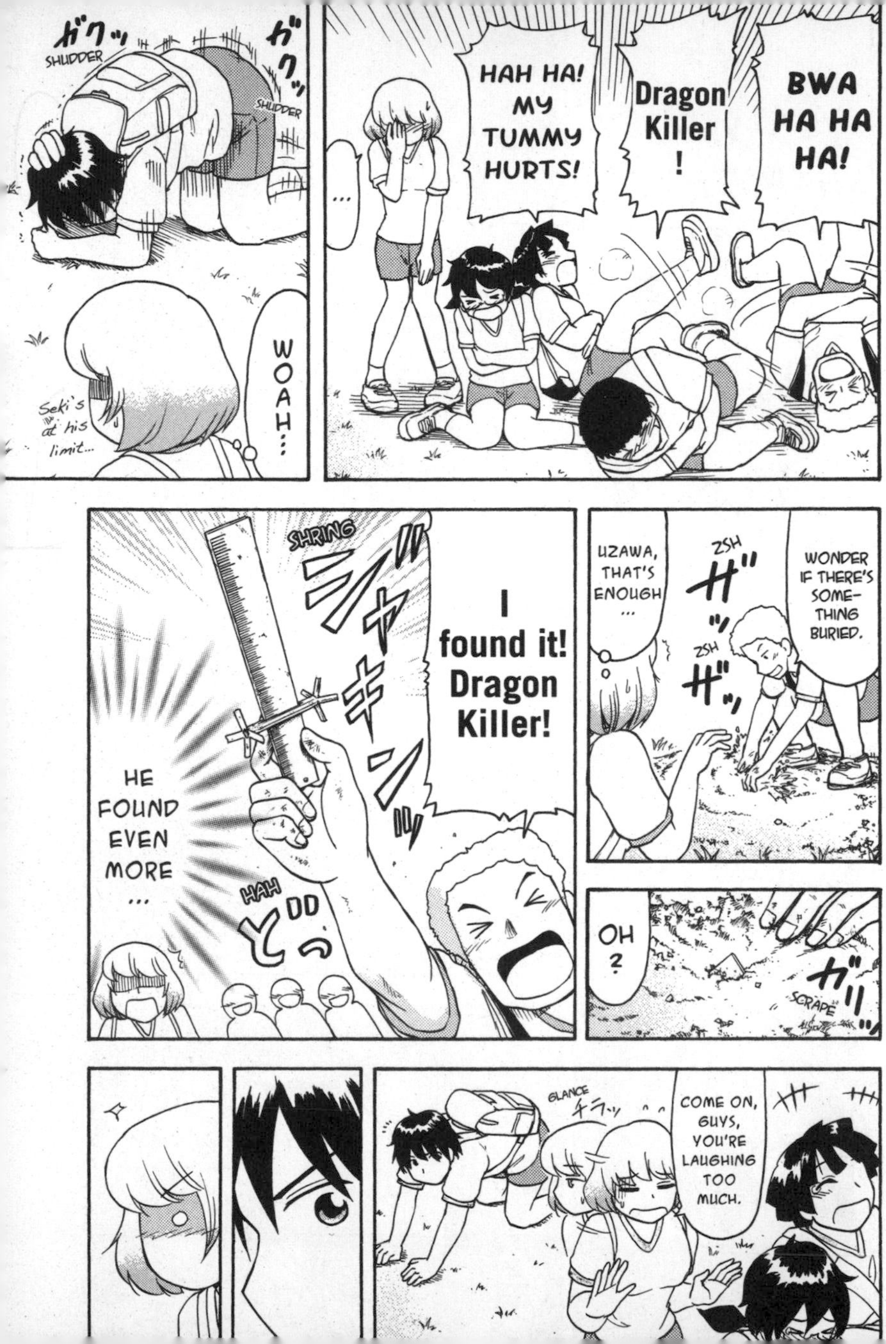

BWA HA HA HA!
Dragon Killer!
HAH HA! MY TUMMY HURTS!
...
ガクッ
SHUDDER
ガクッ
SHUDDER
WOAH...
Seki's at his limit...
WONDER IF THERE'S SOME-THING BURIED.
ZSH
ザッ
ZSH
ザッ
UZAWA, THAT'S ENOUGH...
ガリッ
SCRAPE
OH?
SHRING
シャキーン
I found it! Dragon Killer!
HAH
どっ
DD
HE FOUND EVEN MORE...
COME ON, GUYS, YOU'RE LAUGHING TOO MUCH.
GLANCE
チラッ

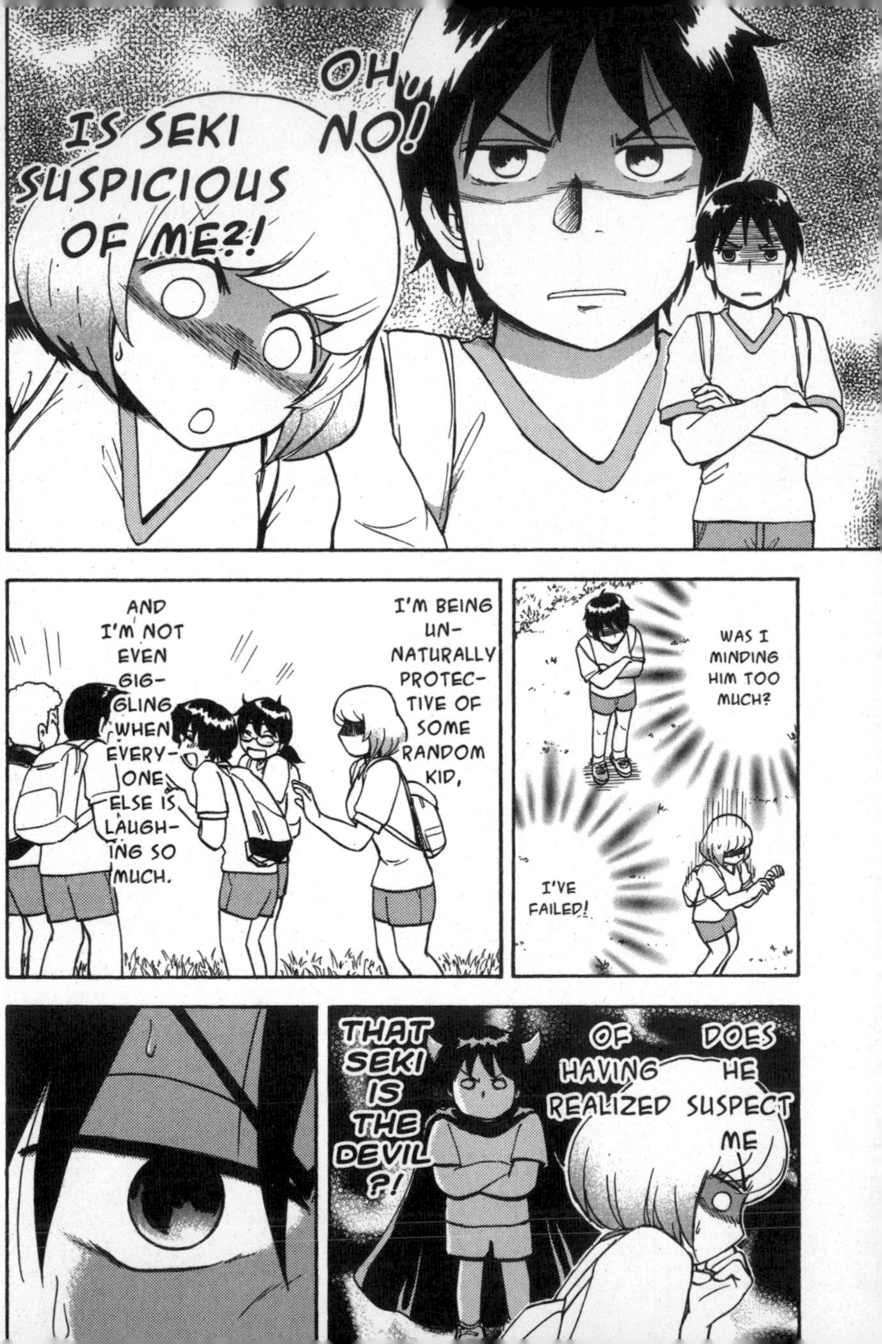
OH, NO!
IS SEKI SUSPICIOUS OF ME?!
WAS I MINDING HIM TOO MUCH?
I'VE FAILED!
I'M BEING UNNATURALLY PROTECTIVE OF SOME RANDOM KID,
AND I'M NOT EVEN GIGGLING WHEN EVERYONE ELSE IS LAUGHING SO MUCH.
DOES HE SUSPECT ME
OF HAVING REALIZED
THAT SEKI IS THE DEVIL?!

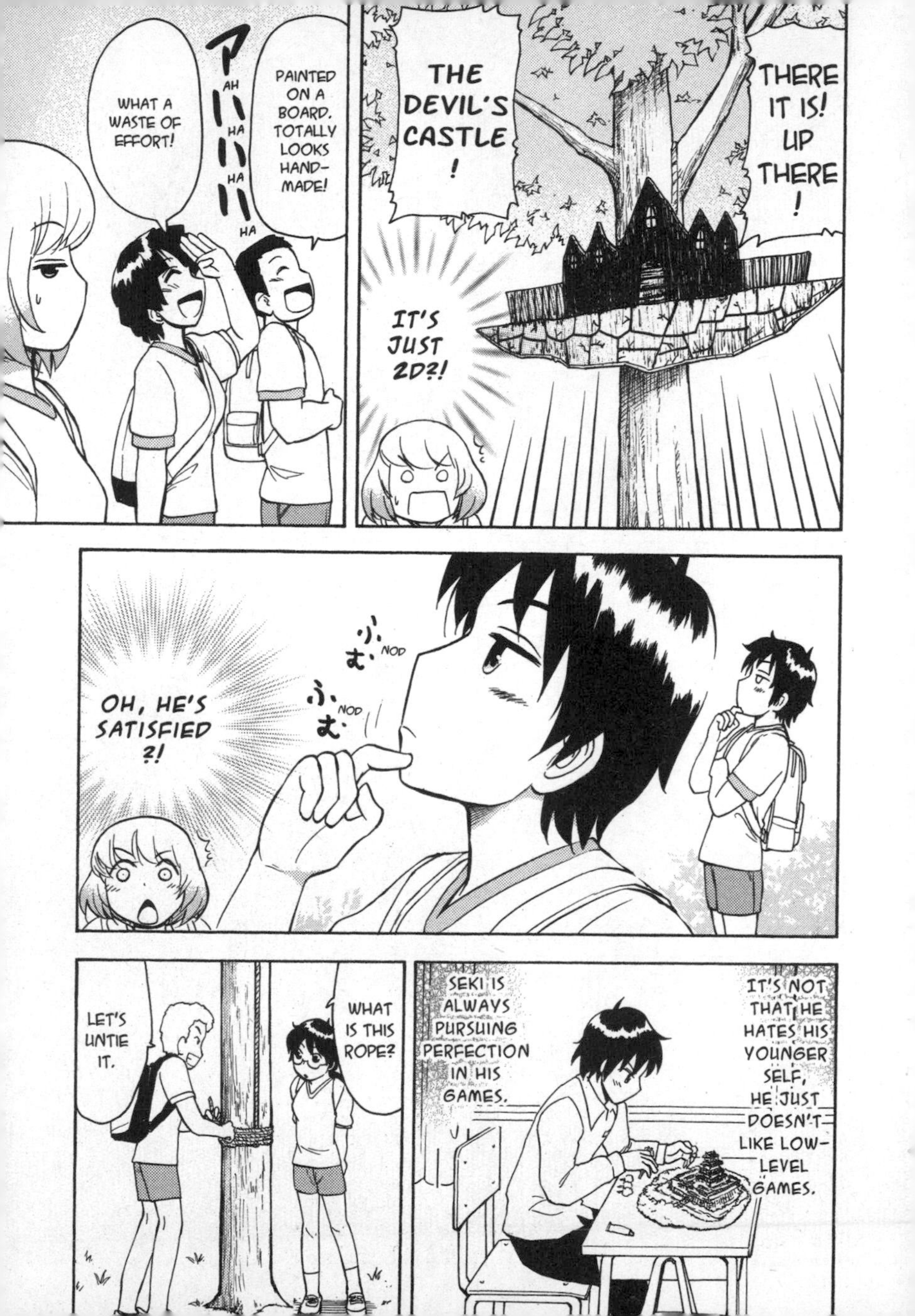

THERE IT IS! UP THERE!
THE DEVIL'S CASTLE!
IT'S JUST 2D?!
PAINTED ON A BOARD. TOTALLY LOOKS HAND-MADE!
アハハハ AH HA HA HA
WHAT A WASTE OF EFFORT!
ふむ NOD
ふむ NOD
OH, HE'S SATISFIED?!
IT'S NOT THAT HE HATES HIS YOUNGER SELF, HE JUST DOESN'T LIKE LOW-LEVEL GAMES.
SEKI IS ALWAYS PURSUING PERFECTION IN HIS GAMES.
WHAT IS THIS ROPE?
LET'S UNTIE IT.

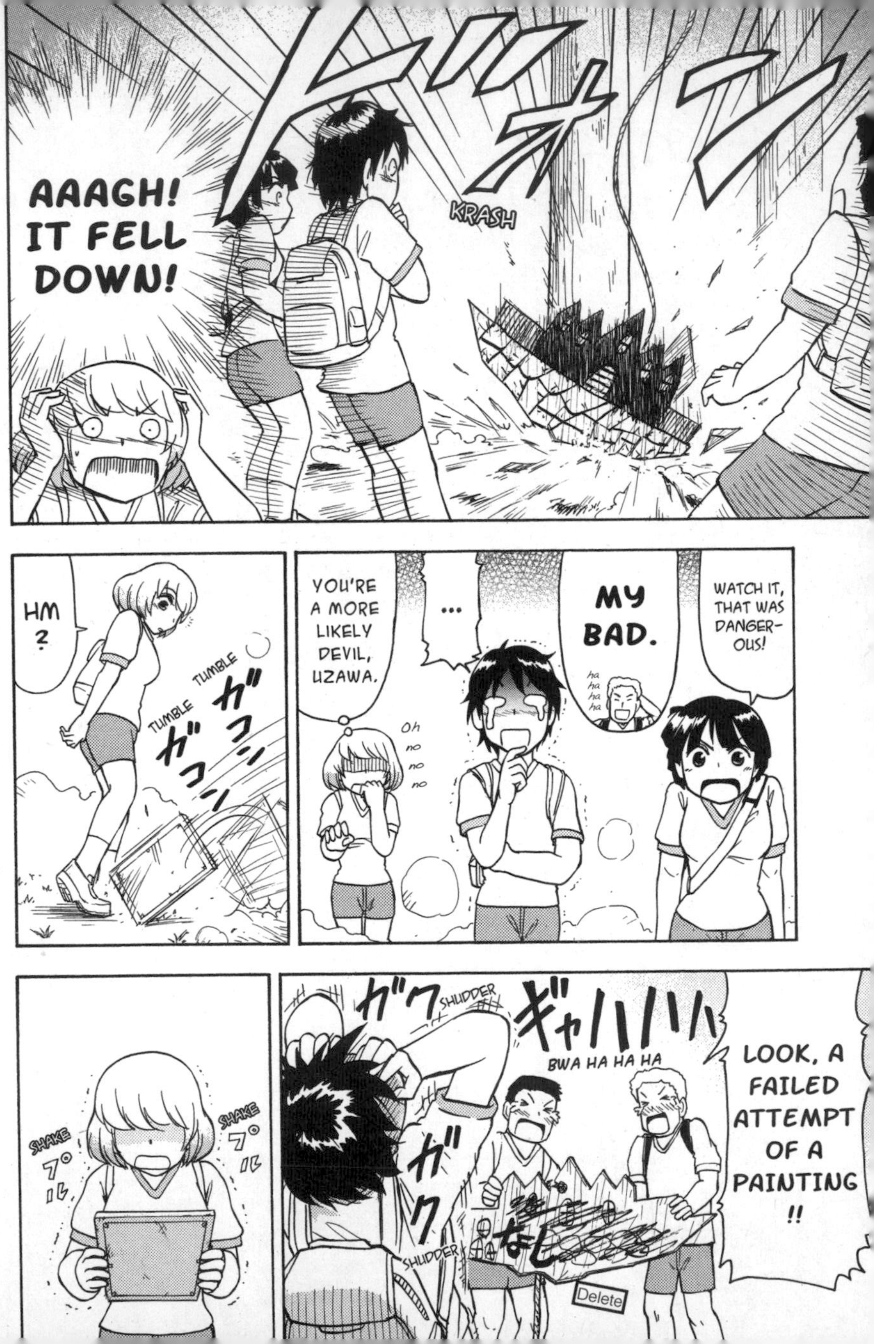
KRASH
AAAGH! IT FELL DOWN!
WATCH IT, THAT WAS DANGER-OUS!
MY BAD.
ha ha ha ha
...
YOU'RE A MORE LIKELY DEVIL, UZAWA.
Oh no no no
HM?
TUMBLE TUMBLE
LOOK, A FAILED ATTEMPT OF A PAINTING!!
BWA HA HA HA
SHUDDER
SHUDDER
Delete
SHAKE
SHAKE

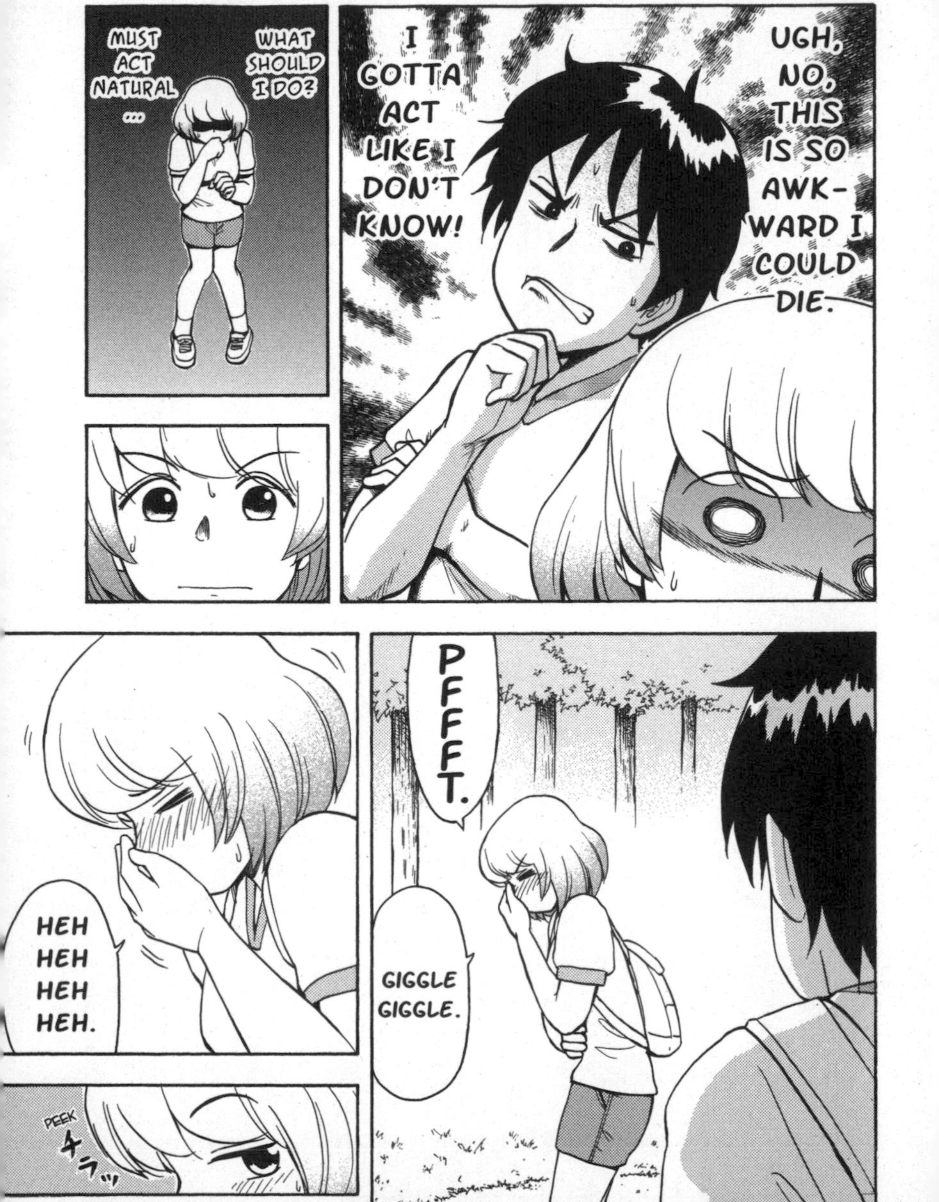
UGH, NO, THIS IS SO AWK-WARD I COULD DIE.
I GOTTA ACT LIKE I DON'T KNOW!
WHAT SHOULD I DO?
MUST ACT NATURAL ...
PFFFT.
GIGGLE GIGGLE.
HEH HEH HEH HEH.
PEEK

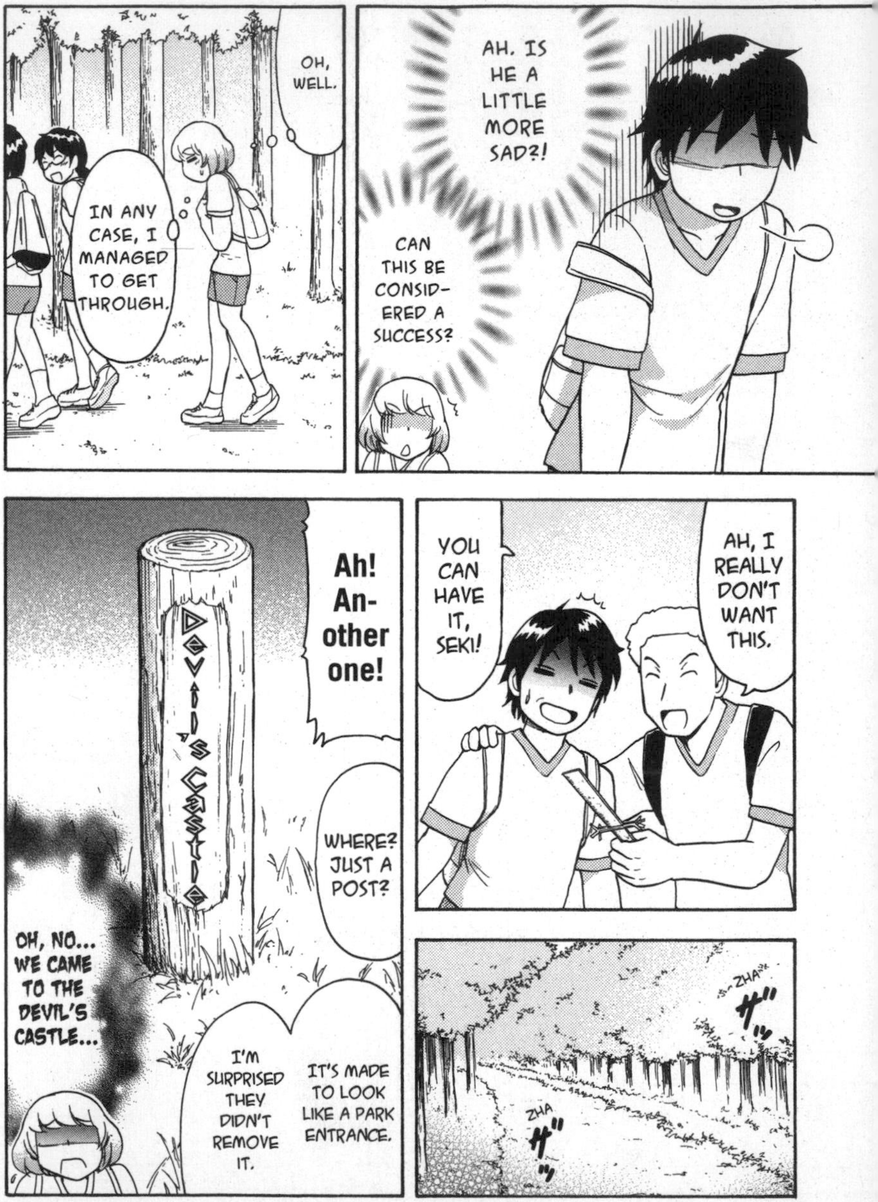
AH. IS HE A LITTLE MORE SAD?!
CAN THIS BE CONSID-ERED A SUCCESS?
OH, WELL.
IN ANY CASE, I MANAGED TO GET THROUGH.
AH, I REALLY DON'T WANT THIS.
YOU CAN HAVE IT, SEKI!
ZHA
ZHA
Ah! An-other one!
Devil's Castle
WHERE? JUST A POST?
IT'S MADE TO LOOK LIKE A PARK ENTRANCE.
I'M SURPRISED THEY DIDN'T REMOVE IT.
OH, NO... WE CAME TO THE DEVIL'S CASTLE...

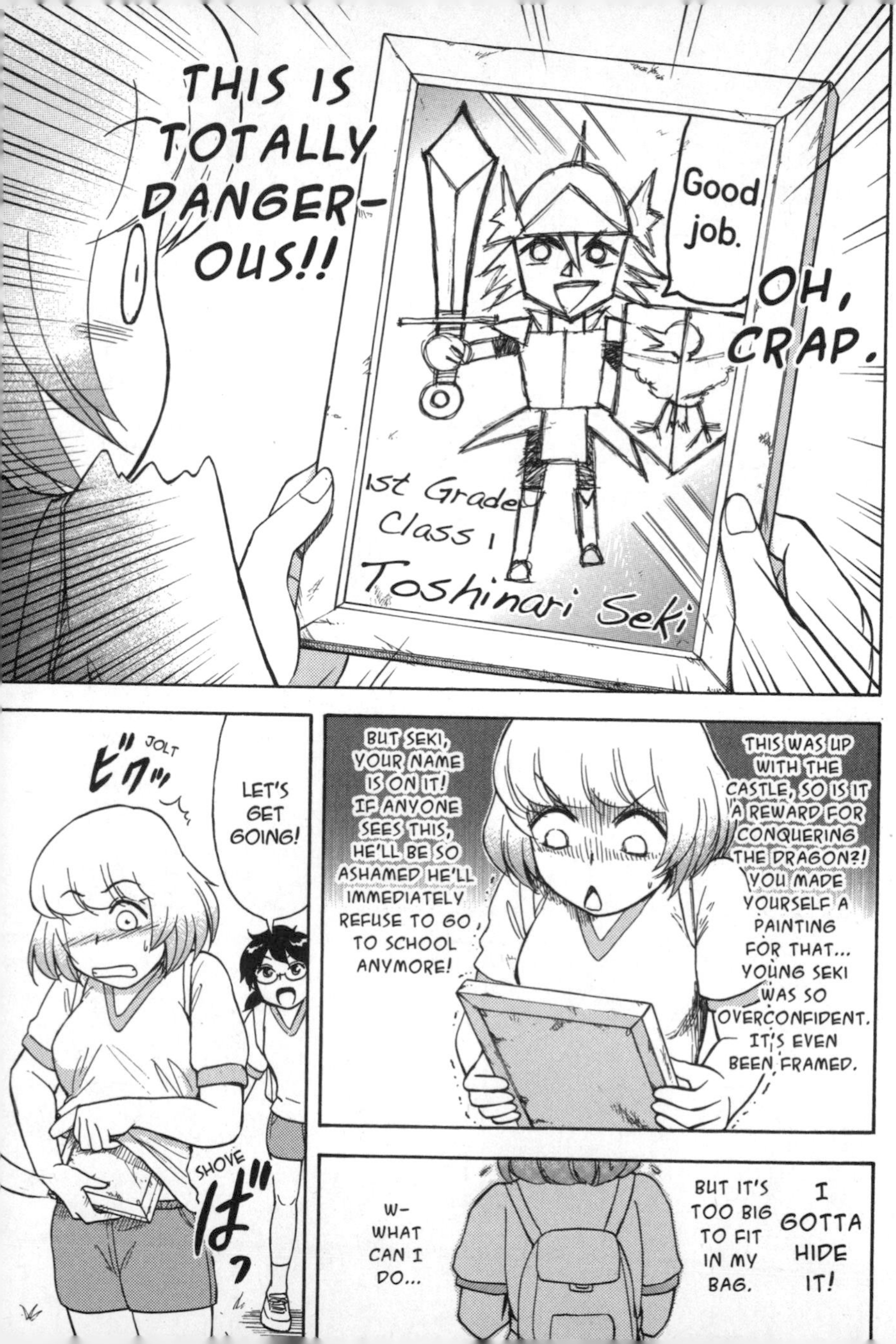
Good job.
OH, CRAP.
THIS IS TOTALLY DANGER-OUS!!
1st Grade Class 1 Toshinari Seki
THIS WAS UP WITH THE CASTLE, SO IS IT A REWARD FOR CONQUERING THE DRAGON?! YOU MADE YOURSELF A PAINTING FOR THAT... YOUNG SEKI WAS SO OVERCONFIDENT. IT'S EVEN BEEN FRAMED.
BUT SEKI, YOUR NAME IS ON IT! IF ANYONE SEES THIS, HE'LL BE SO ASHAMED HE'LL IMMEDIATELY REFUSE TO GO TO SCHOOL ANYMORE!
I GOTTA HIDE IT!
BUT IT'S TOO BIG TO FIT IN MY BAG.
W-WHAT CAN I DO...
ビクッ
JOLT
LET'S GET GOING!
SHOVE
ばっ

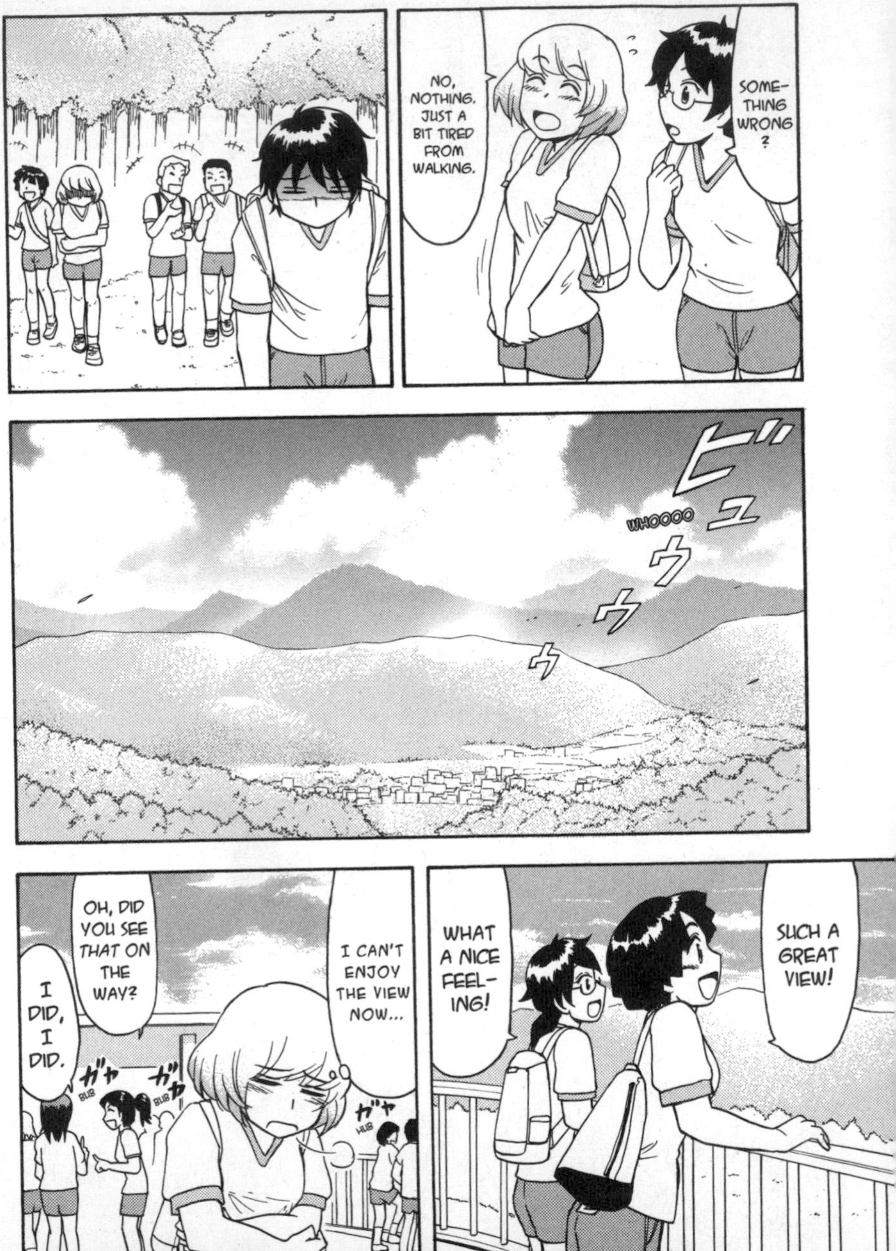
SOME-THING WRONG?
NO, NOTHING. JUST A BIT TIRED FROM WALKING.
ビュウウウ
WHOOOO
SUCH A GREAT VIEW!
WHAT A NICE FEEL-ING!
I CAN'T ENJOY THE VIEW NOW...
OH, DID YOU SEE THAT ON THE WAY?
I DID, I DID.
ガヤ
BUB
ガヤ
BUB
ガヤ
HUB

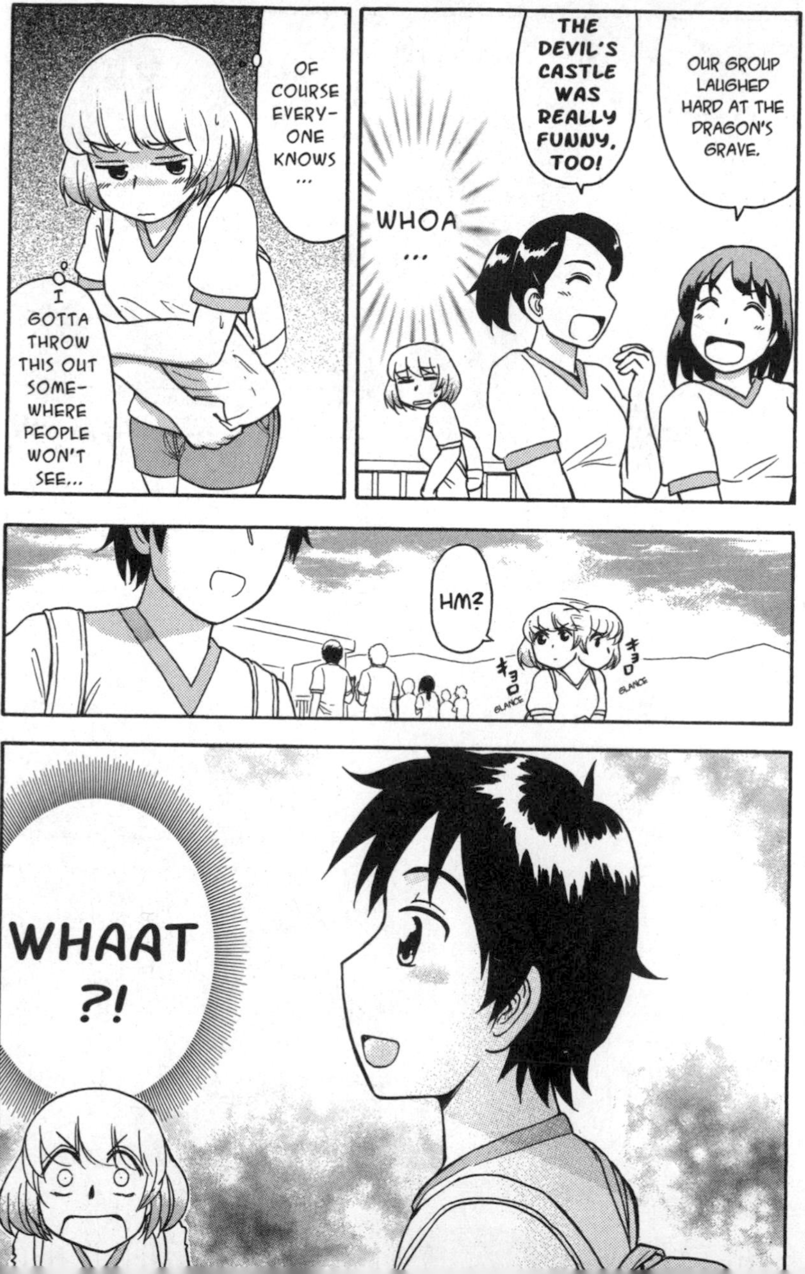
OUR GROUP LAUGHED HARD AT THE DRAGON'S GRAVE.
THE DEVIL'S CASTLE WAS REALLY FUNNY, TOO!
WHOA ...
OF COURSE EVERY-ONE KNOWS ...
I GOTTA THROW THIS OUT SOME-WHERE PEOPLE WON'T SEE...
HM?
キョロ GLANCE
キョロ GLANCE
WHAAT ?!

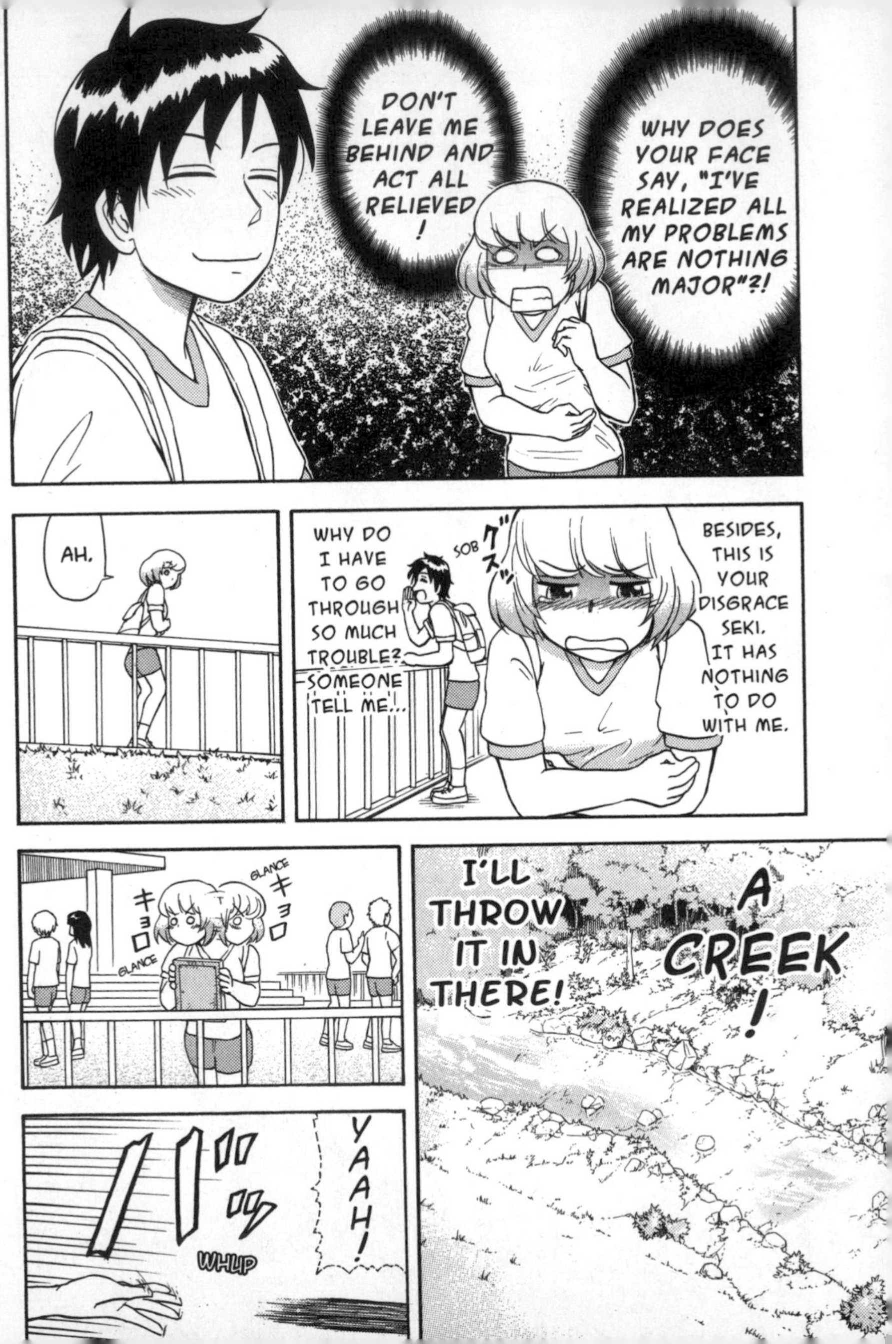
WHY DOES YOUR FACE SAY, "I'VE REALIZED ALL MY PROBLEMS ARE NOTHING MAJOR"?!
DON'T LEAVE ME BEHIND AND ACT ALL RELIEVED!
BESIDES, THIS IS YOUR DISGRACE SEKI. IT HAS NOTHING TO DO WITH ME.
SOB グズ
WHY DO I HAVE TO GO THROUGH SO MUCH TROUBLE? SOMEONE TELL ME...
AH.
A CREEK!
I'LL THROW IT IN THERE!
GLANCE キョロ
GLANCE キョロ
YAAAH!
WHUP

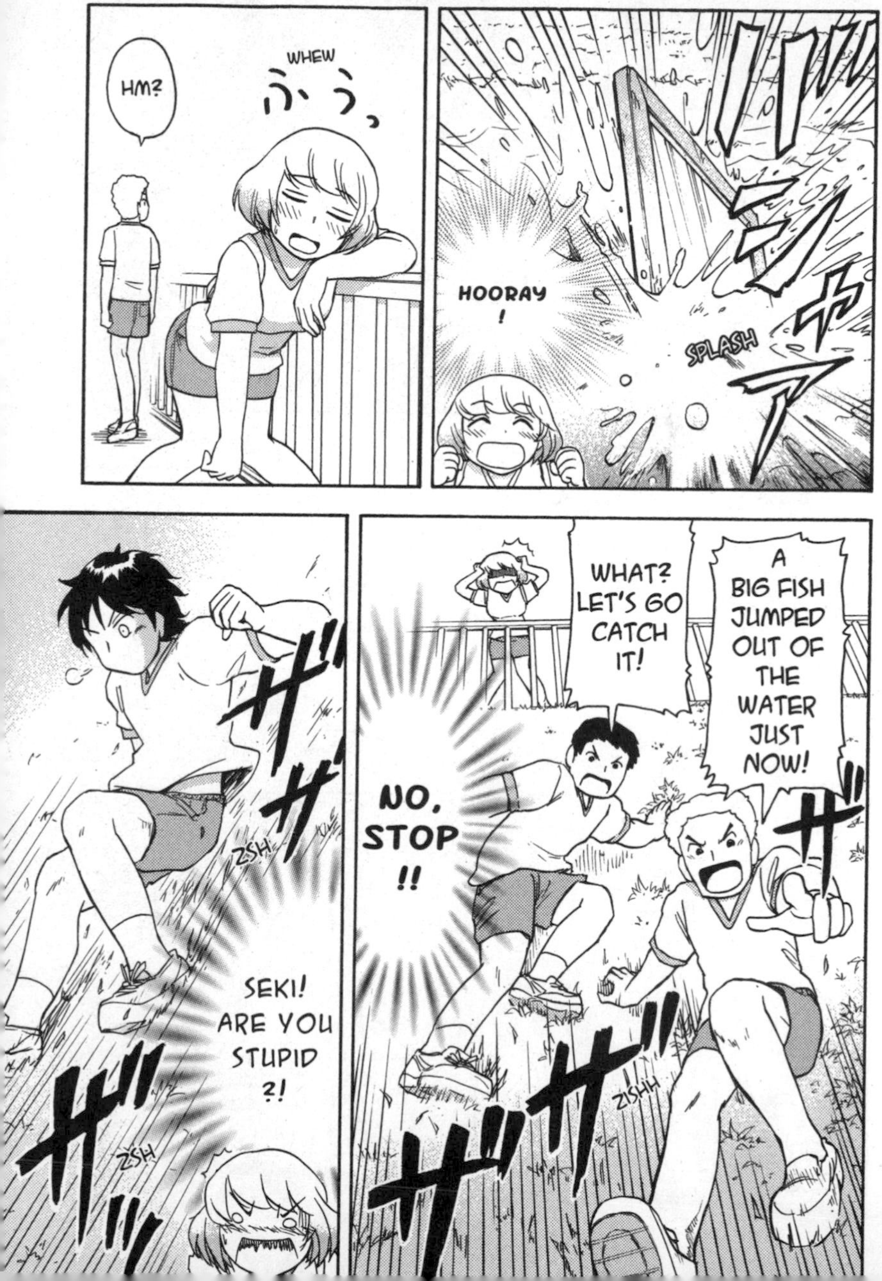
SPLASH
HOORAY!
WHEW
ふう
HM?
A BIG FISH JUMPED OUT OF THE WATER JUST NOW!
WHAT? LET'S GO CATCH IT!
ZISHH
NO, STOP!!
ZSH
SEKI! ARE YOU STUPID?!
ZSH

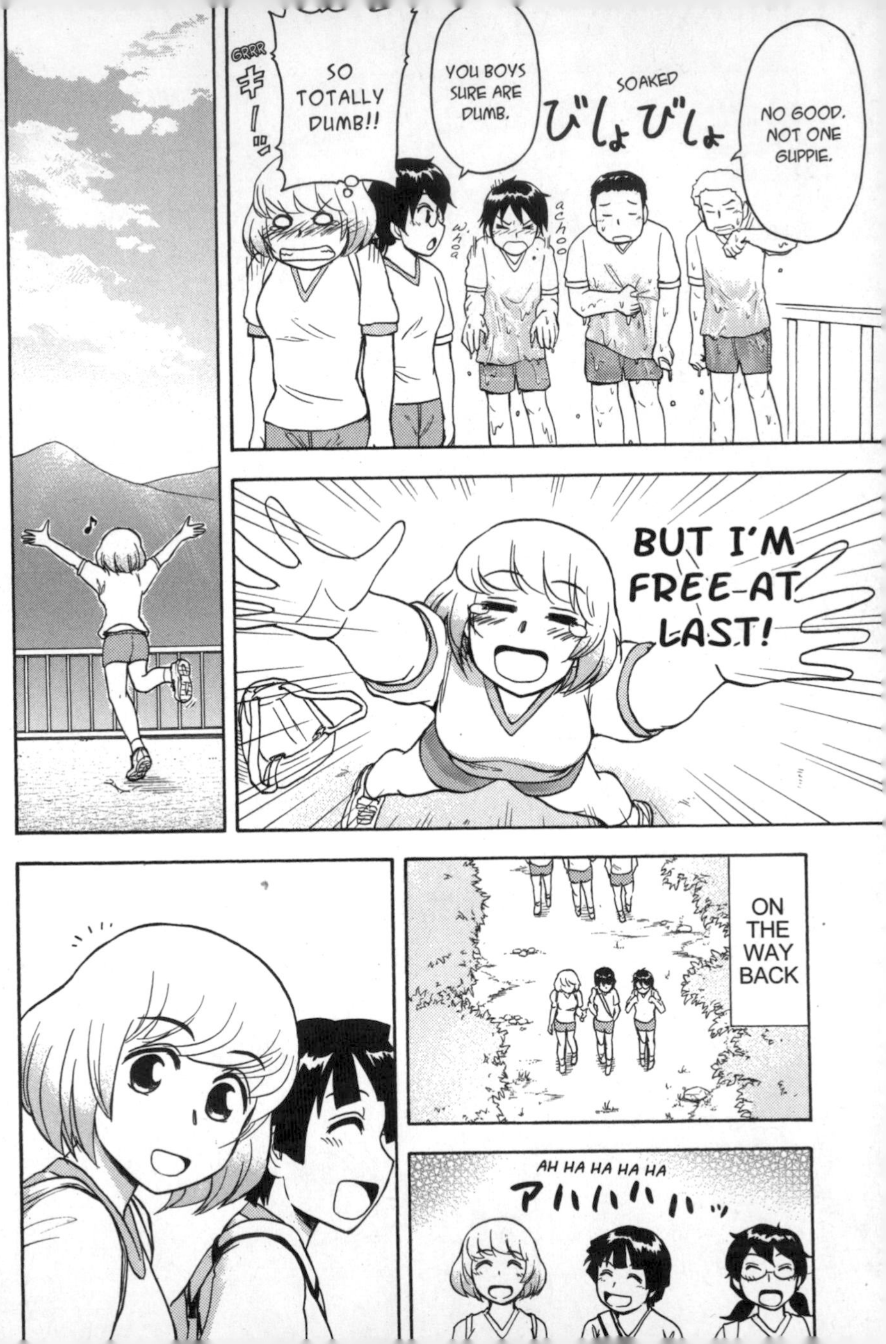
NO GOOD. NOT ONE GUPPIE.
SOAKED
びしょびしょ
achoo
whoa
YOU BOYS SURE ARE DUMB.
SO TOTALLY DUMB!!
GRRR
キーッ
BUT I'M FREE AT LAST!
ON THE WAY BACK
AH HA HA HA HA
アハハハハッ

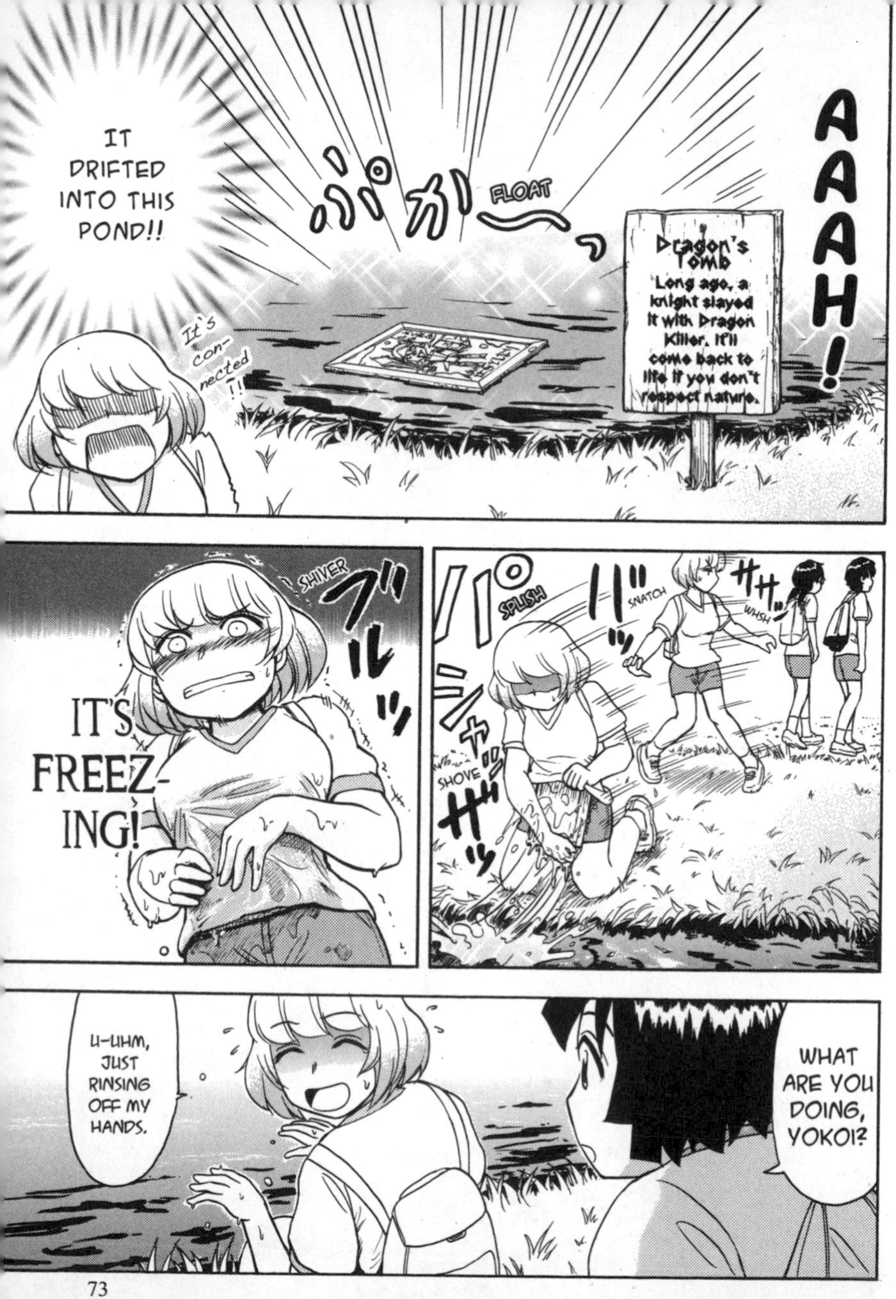
AAAAH!
Dragon's Tomb
Long ago, a knight slayed it with Dragon Killer. It'll come back to life if you don't respect nature.
FLOAT
IT DRIFTED INTO THIS POND!!
It's connected!!
SPLISH
SNATCH
WHSH
SHOVE
SHIVER
IT'S FREEZING!
WHAT ARE YOU DOING, YOKOI!?
U-UHM, JUST RINSING OFF MY HANDS.

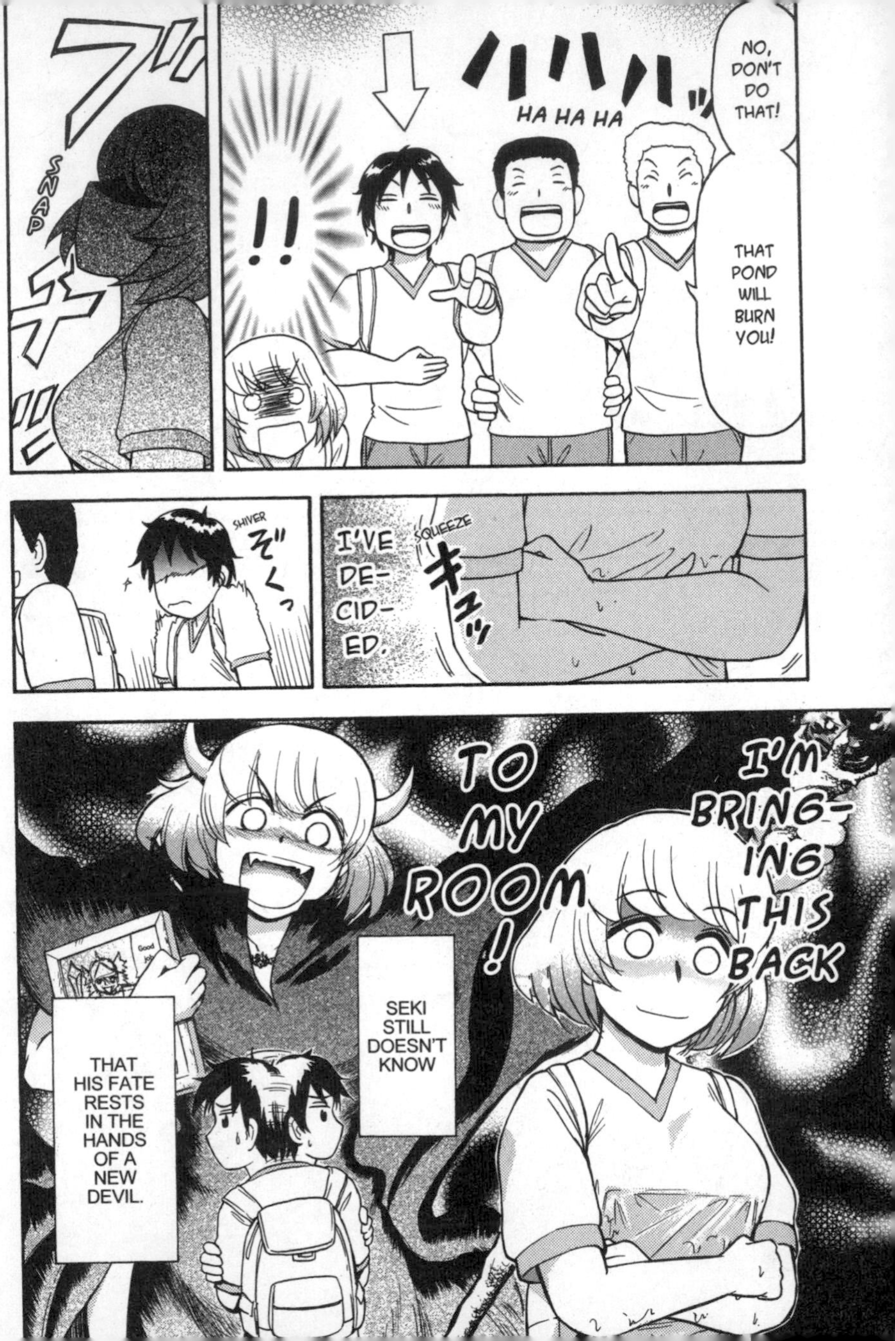
NO, DON'T DO THAT!
THAT POND WILL BURN YOU!
ハハハッ
HA HA HA
!!
ブチッ
SNAP
I'VE DE-CID-ED.
SQUEEZE
キュッ
SHIVER
ぞくっ
I'M BRING-ING THIS BACK
TO MY ROOM!
SEKI STILL DOESN'T KNOW
THAT HIS FATE RESTS IN THE HANDS OF A NEW DEVIL.

My Neighbor Seki

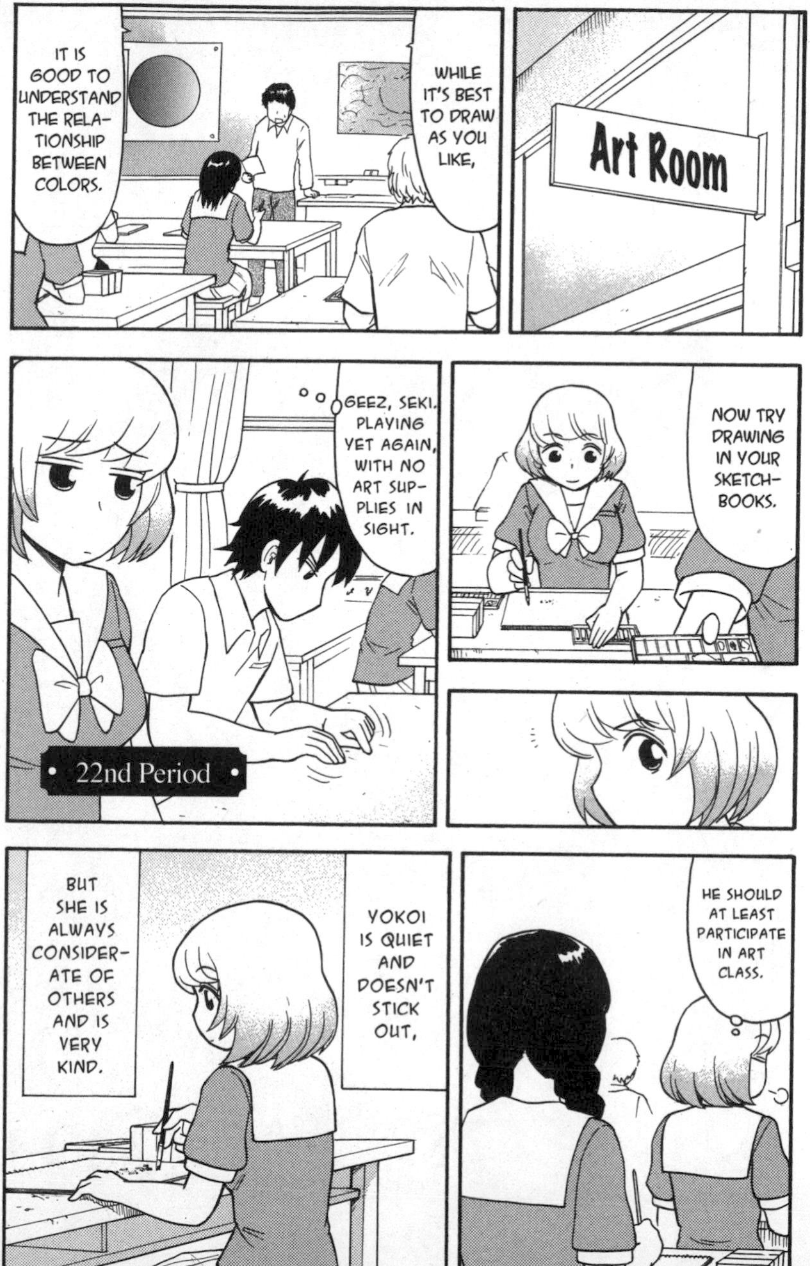
Art Room
WHILE IT'S BEST TO DRAW AS YOU LIKE,
IT IS GOOD TO UNDERSTAND THE RELA-TIONSHIP BETWEEN COLORS.
NOW TRY DRAWING IN YOUR SKETCH-BOOKS.
GEEZ, SEKI. PLAYING YET AGAIN, WITH NO ART SUP-PLIES IN SIGHT.
22nd Period
HE SHOULD AT LEAST PARTICIPATE IN ART CLASS.
YOKOI IS QUIET AND DOESN'T STICK OUT,
BUT SHE IS ALWAYS CONSIDER-ATE OF OTHERS AND IS VERY KIND.

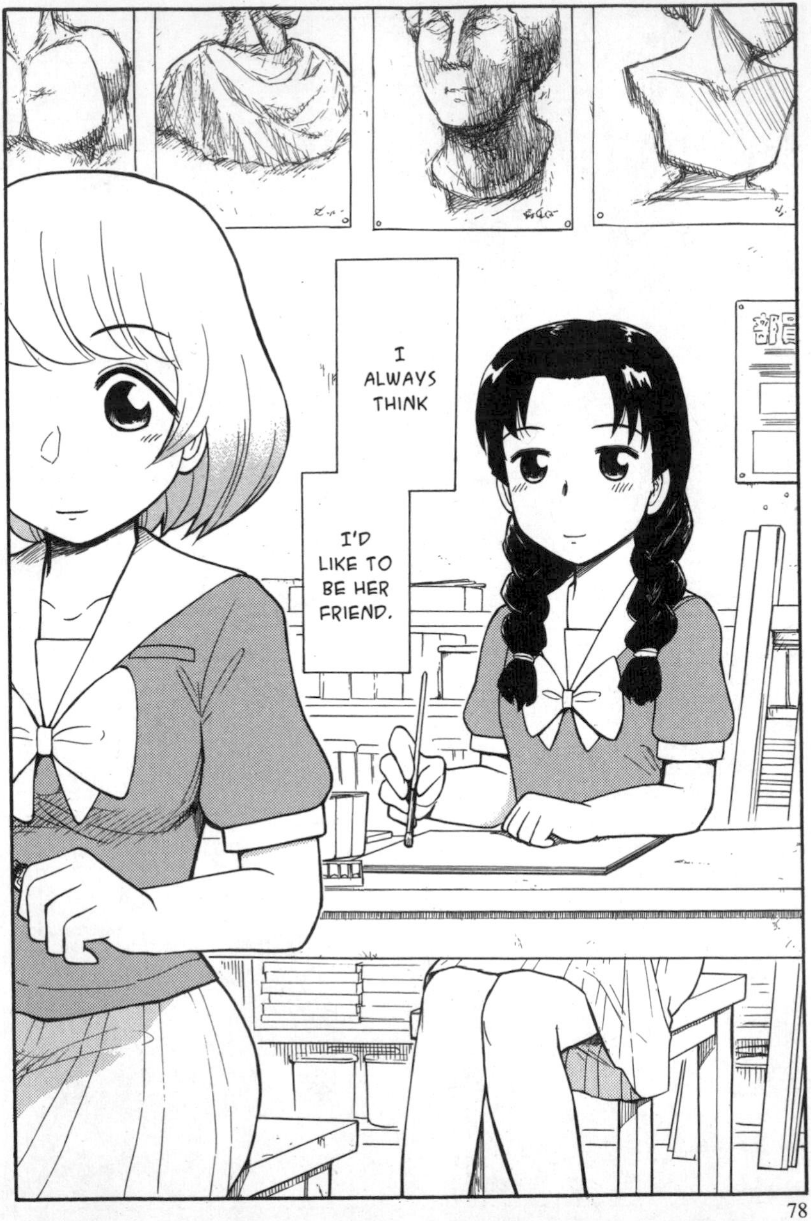
I ALWAYS THINK
I'D LIKE TO BE HER FRIEND.

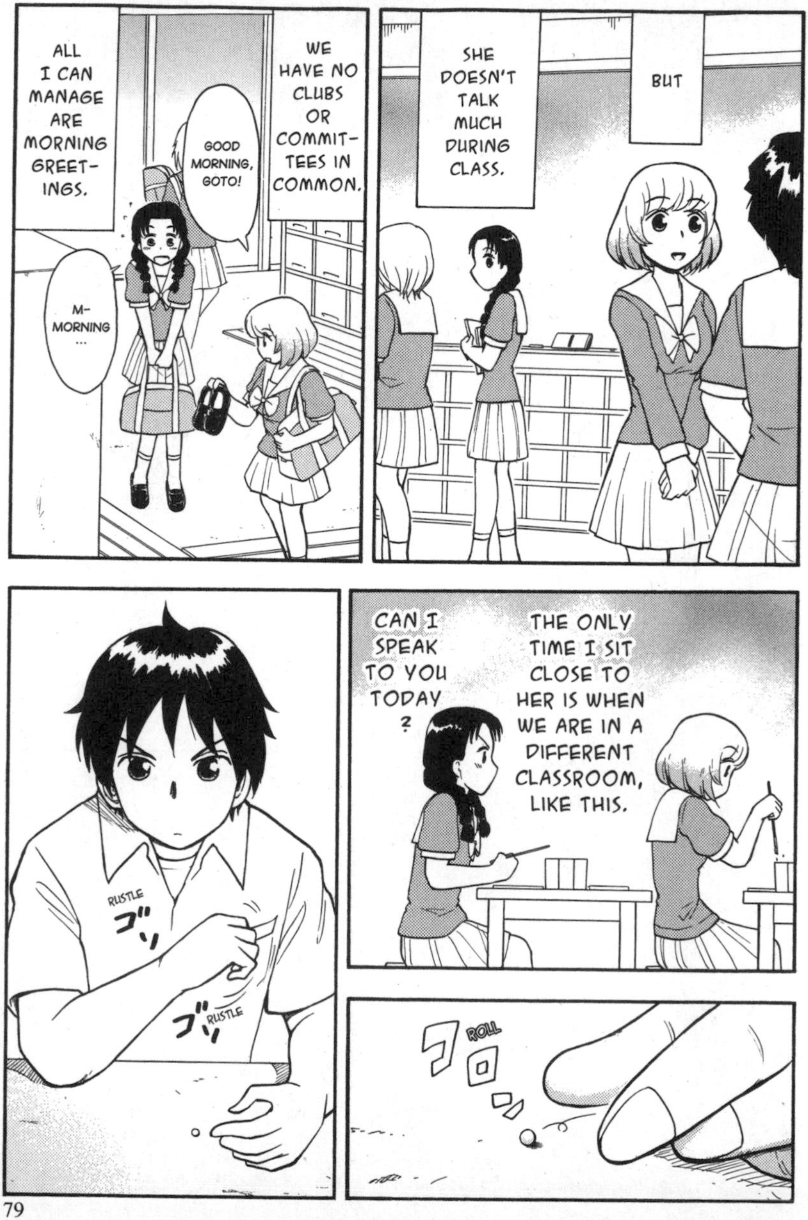
BUT
SHE DOESN'T TALK MUCH DURING CLASS.
WE HAVE NO CLUBS OR COMMITTEES IN COMMON.
GOOD MORNING, GOTO!
ALL I CAN MANAGE ARE MORNING GREETINGS.
M-MORNING...
THE ONLY TIME I SIT CLOSE TO HER IS WHEN WE ARE IN A DIFFERENT CLASSROOM, LIKE THIS.
CAN I SPEAK TO YOU TODAY?
ROLL
RUSTLE
RUSTLE

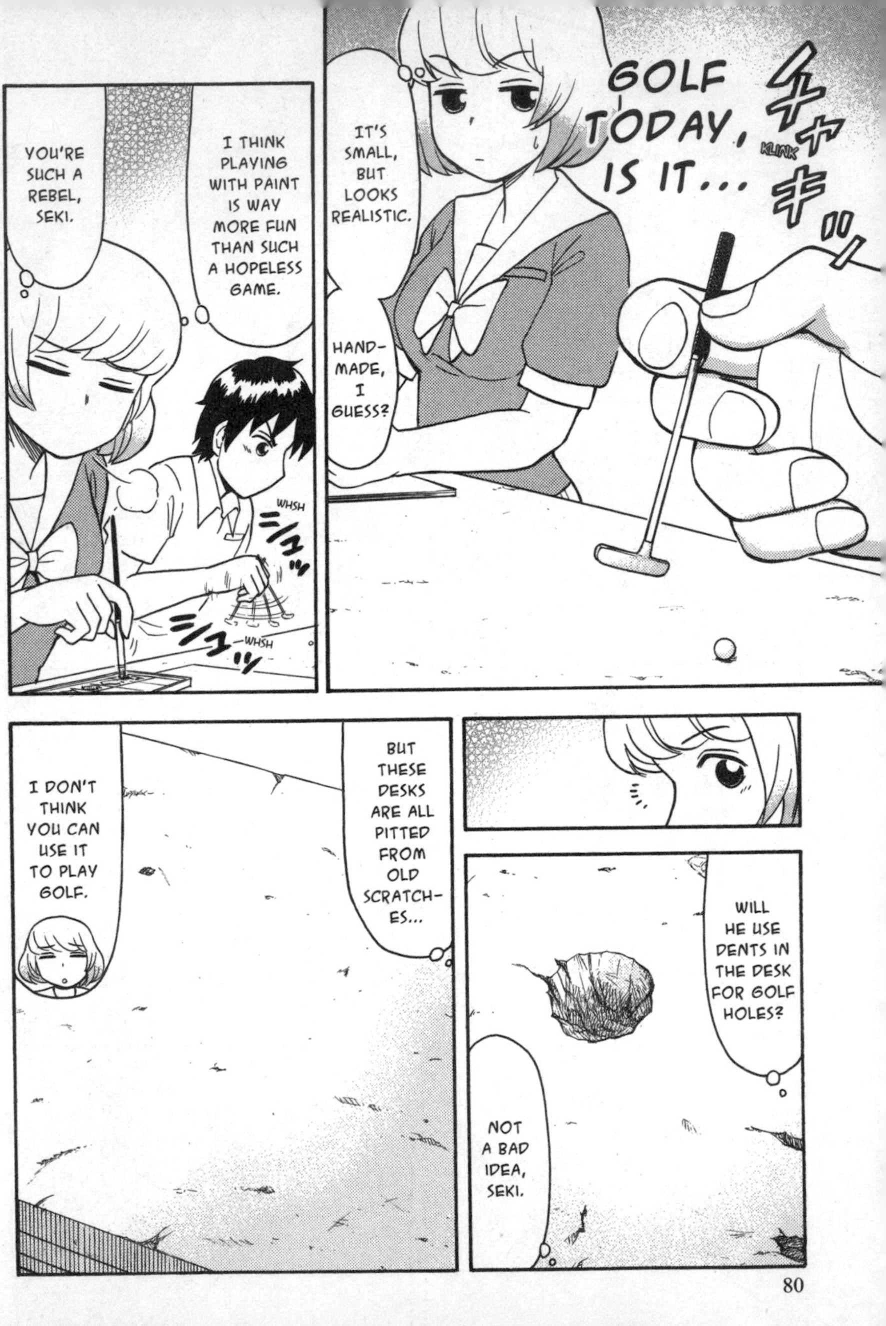
GOLF TODAY, IS IT...
KLINK
IT'S SMALL, BUT LOOKS REALISTIC.
HAND-MADE, I GUESS?
I THINK PLAYING WITH PAINT IS WAY MORE FUN THAN SUCH A HOPELESS GAME.
YOU'RE SUCH A REBEL, SEKI.
WHSH
WHSH
WILL HE USE DENTS IN THE DESK FOR GOLF HOLES?
NOT A BAD IDEA, SEKI.
BUT THESE DESKS ARE ALL PITTED FROM OLD SCRATCH-ES...
I DON'T THINK YOU CAN USE IT TO PLAY GOLF.

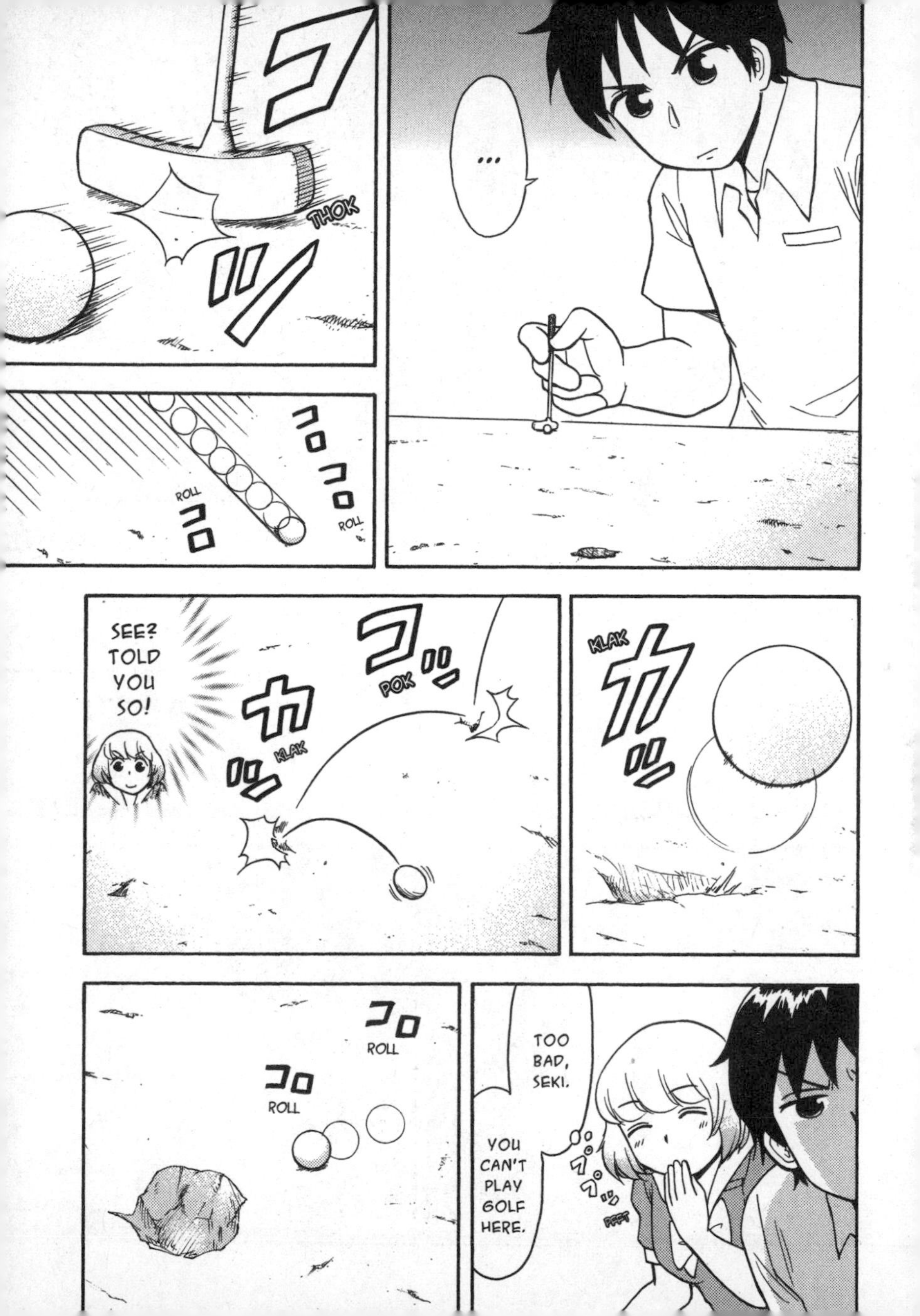
...
THOK
ROLL
ROLL
KLAK
POK
KLAK
SEE? TOLD YOU SO!
TOO BAD, SEKI.
YOU CAN'T PLAY GOLF HERE.
PFFT
ROLL
ROLL

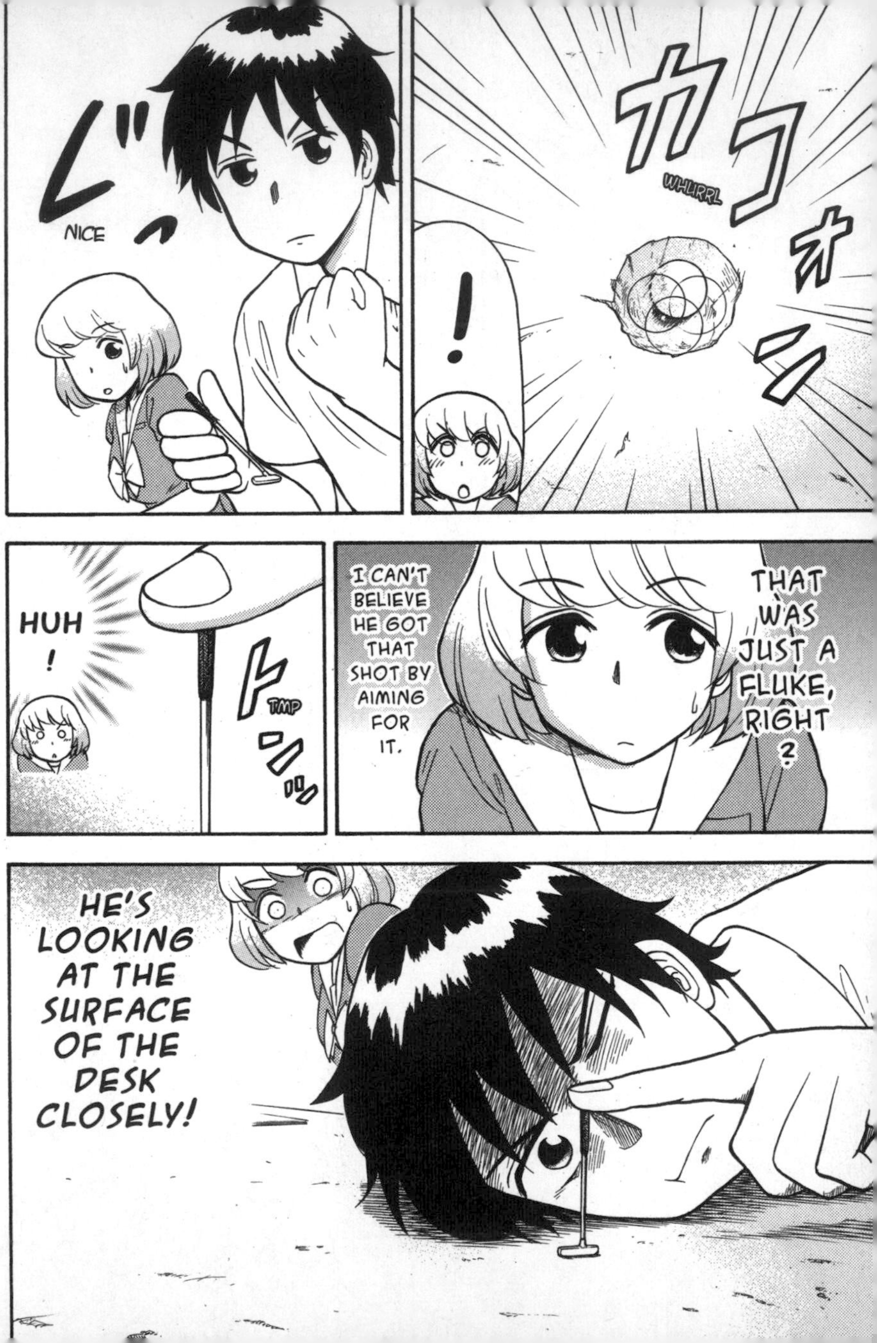
WHLRRL
!
NICE
THAT WAS JUST A FLUKE, RIGHT?
I CAN'T BELIEVE HE GOT THAT SHOT BY AIMING FOR IT.
TMP
HUH!
HE'S LOOKING AT THE SURFACE OF THE DESK CLOSELY!

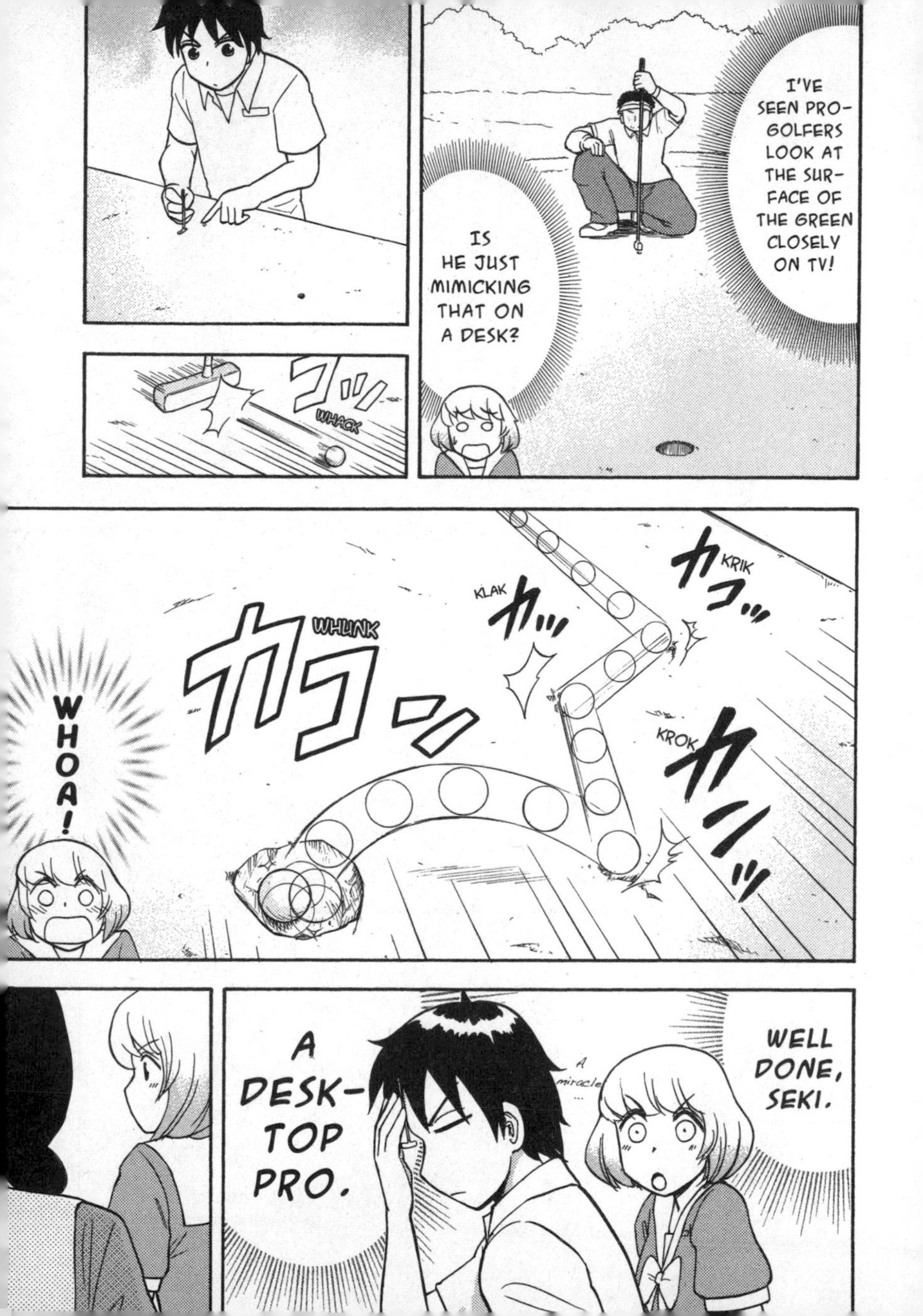
I'VE SEEN PRO-GOLFERS LOOK AT THE SURFACE OF THE GREEN CLOSELY ON TV!
IS HE JUST MIMICKING THAT ON A DESK?
コッ
WHACK
カコッ
KRIK
カッ
KLAK
カコッ
WHLINK
カンッ
KROK
WHOA!
WELL DONE, SEKI.
A miracle...
A DESK-TOP PRO.

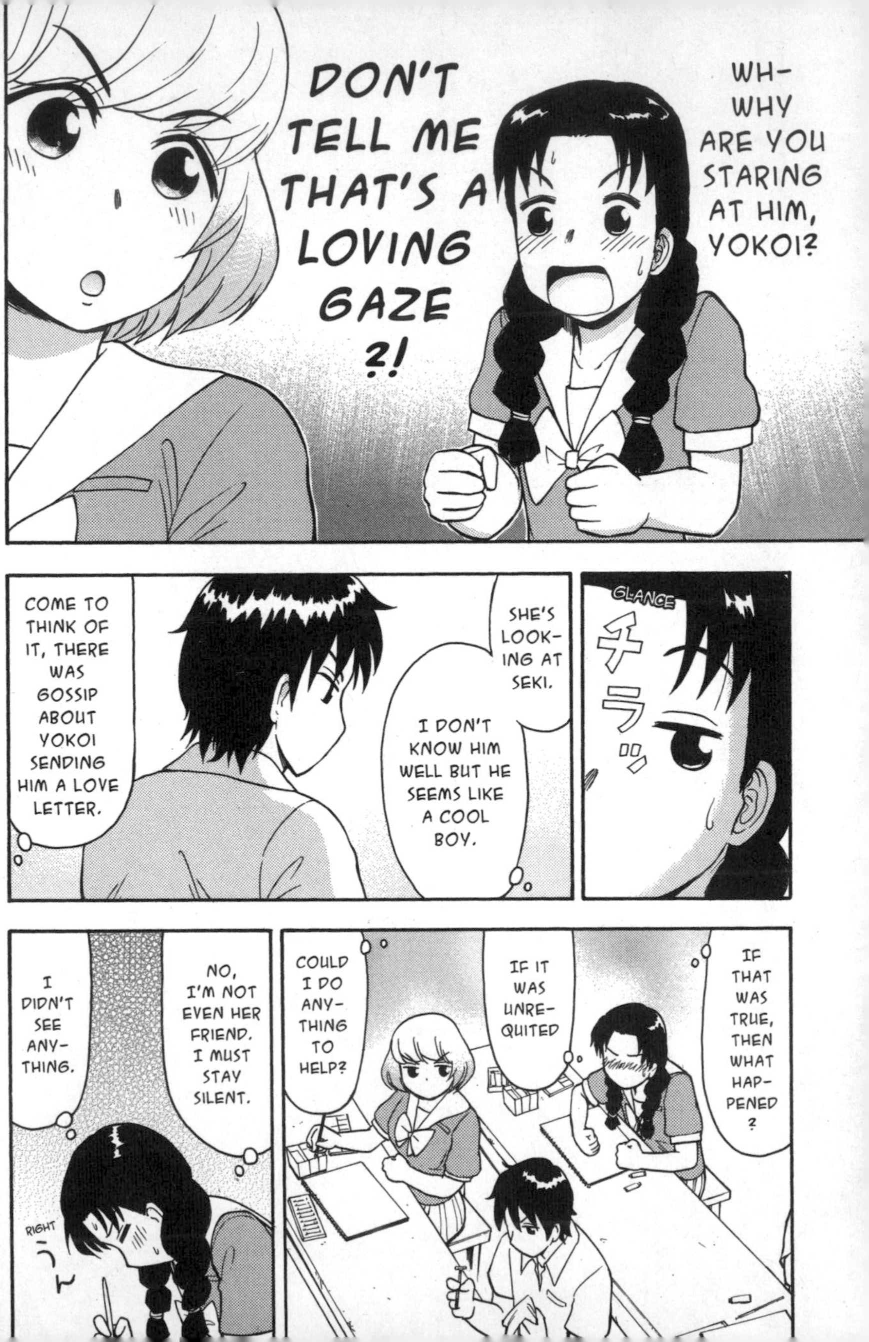
WH- WHY ARE YOU STARING AT HIM, YOKOI?
DON'T TELL ME THAT'S A LOVING GAZE ?!
GLANCE
チラッ
SHE'S LOOKING AT SEKI.
I DON'T KNOW HIM WELL BUT HE SEEMS LIKE A COOL BOY.
COME TO THINK OF IT, THERE WAS GOSSIP ABOUT YOKOI SENDING HIM A LOVE LETTER.
IF THAT WAS TRUE, THEN WHAT HAPPENED?
IF IT WAS UNREQUITED
COULD I DO ANYTHING TO HELP?
NO, I'M NOT EVEN HER FRIEND. I MUST STAY SILENT.
I DIDN'T SEE ANYTHING.
RIGHT

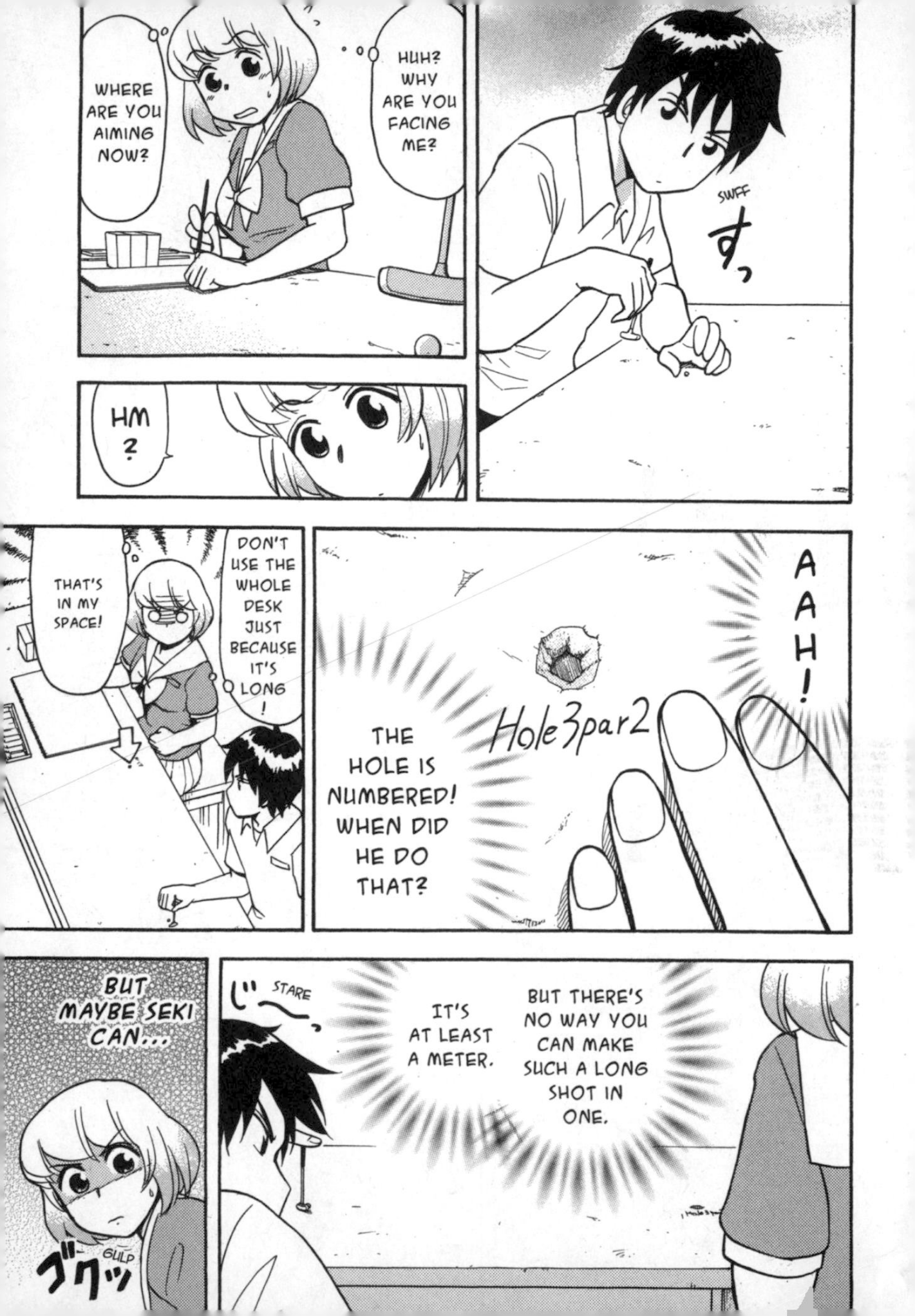
SWFF
すっ
HUH? WHY ARE YOU FACING ME?
WHERE ARE YOU AIMING NOW?
HM?
AAH!
Hole3par2
THE HOLE IS NUMBERED! WHEN DID HE DO THAT?
DON'T USE THE WHOLE DESK JUST BECAUSE IT'S LONG!
THAT'S IN MY SPACE!
BUT THERE'S NO WAY YOU CAN MAKE SUCH A LONG SHOT IN ONE.
IT'S AT LEAST A METER.
じ〜
STARE
BUT MAYBE SEKI CAN...
ゴクッ
GULP

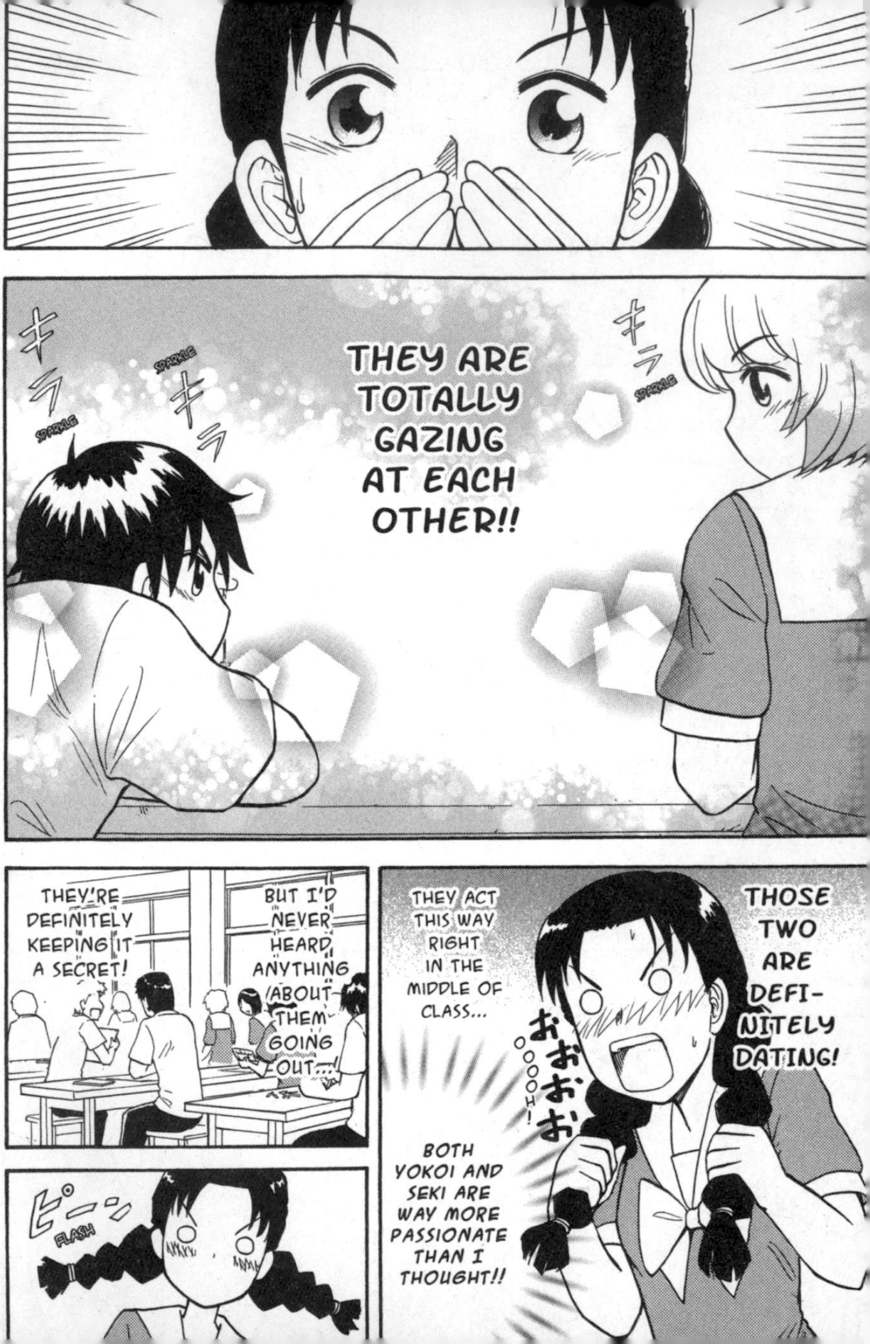
キラ
SPARKLE
THEY ARE TOTALLY GAZING AT EACH OTHER!!
キラ
SPARKLE
キラ
SPARKLE
THOSE TWO ARE DEFI-NITELY DATING!
THEY ACT THIS WAY RIGHT IN THE MIDDLE OF CLASS...
おおおお
OOOOH!
BOTH YOKOI AND SEKI ARE WAY MORE PASSIONATE THAN I THOUGHT!!
BUT I'D NEVER HEARD ANYTHING ABOUT THEM GOING OUT...
THEY'RE DEFINITELY KEEPING IT A SECRET!
ピーン
FLASH

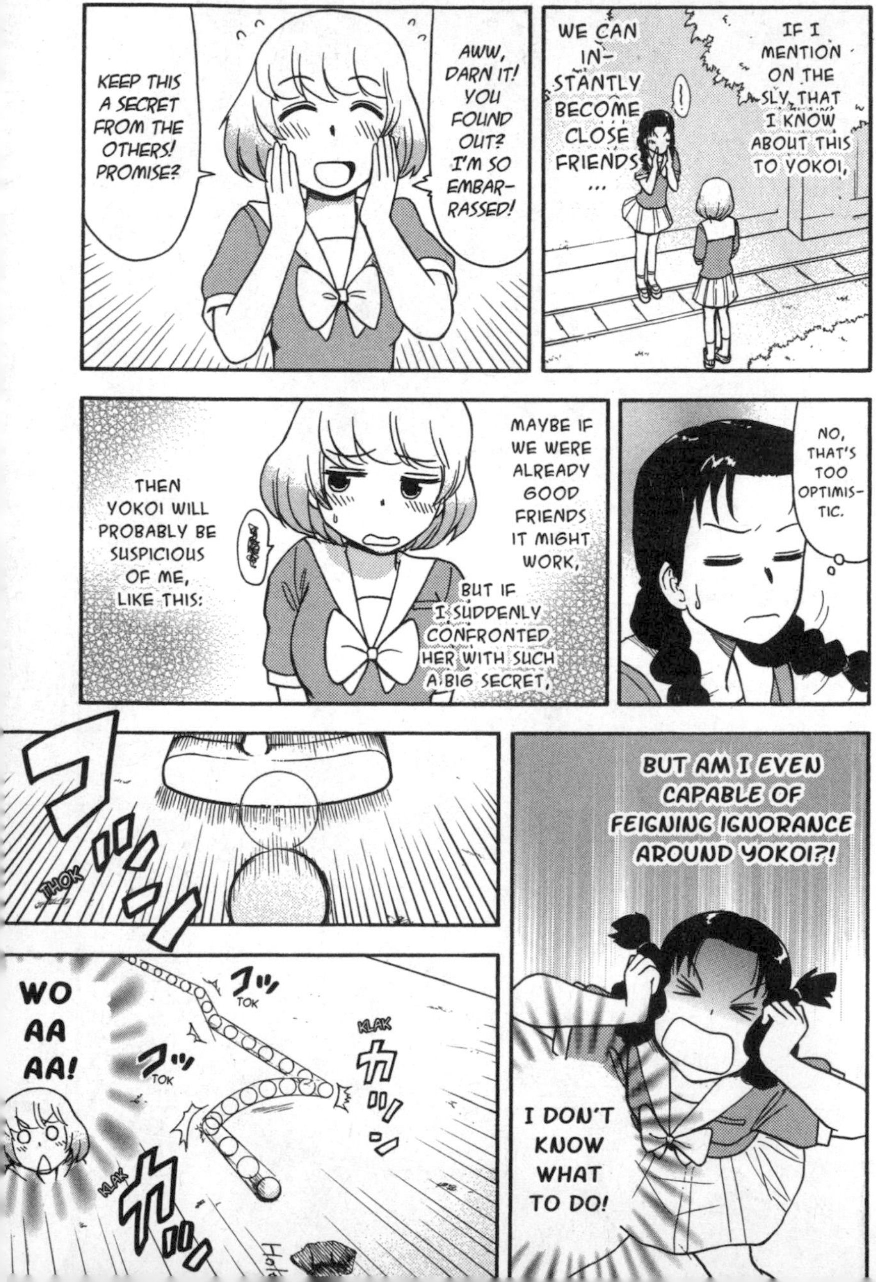
IF I MENTION ON THE SLY THAT I KNOW ABOUT THIS TO YOKOI,
WE CAN IN-STANTLY BECOME CLOSE FRIENDS...
!
AWW, DARN IT! YOU FOUND OUT? I'M SO EMBAR-RASSED!
KEEP THIS A SECRET FROM THE OTHERS! PROMISE?
NO, THAT'S TOO OPTIMIS-TIC.
MAYBE IF WE WERE ALREADY GOOD FRIENDS IT MIGHT WORK,
BUT IF I SUDDENLY CONFRONTED HER WITH SUCH A BIG SECRET,
THEN YOKOI WILL PROBABLY BE SUSPICIOUS OF ME, LIKE THIS:
BUT AM I EVEN CAPABLE OF FEIGNING IGNORANCE AROUND YOKOI?!
I DON'T KNOW WHAT TO DO!
THOK
TOK
TOK
KLAK
KLAK
WO AA AA AA!

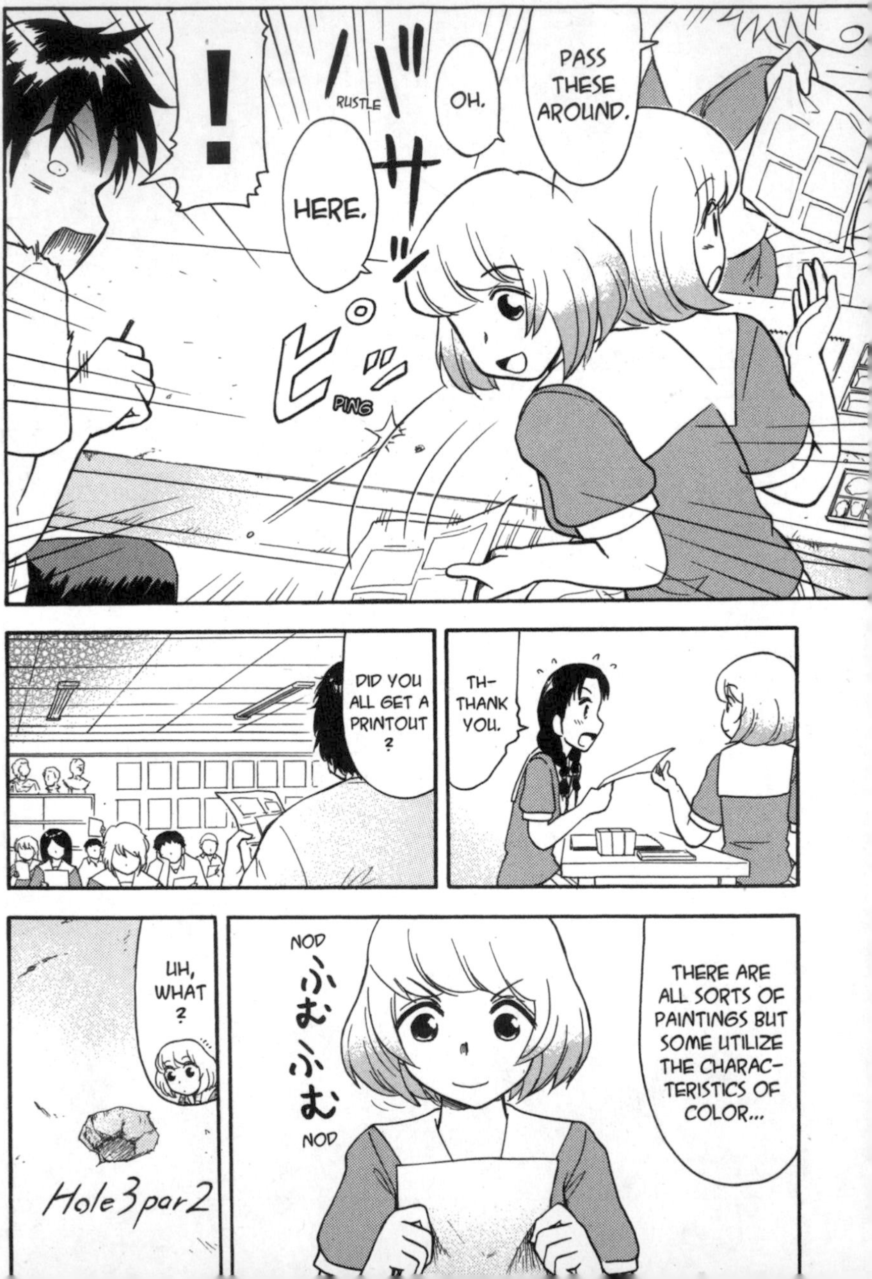
PASS THESE AROUND.
OH.
バサッ
RUSTLE
HERE.
!
ピッ
PING
TH- THANK YOU.
DID YOU ALL GET A PRINTOUT?
THERE ARE ALL SORTS OF PAINTINGS BUT SOME UTILIZE THE CHARAC-TERISTICS OF COLOR...
NOD
ふむふむ
NOD
UH, WHAT?
Hole3par2

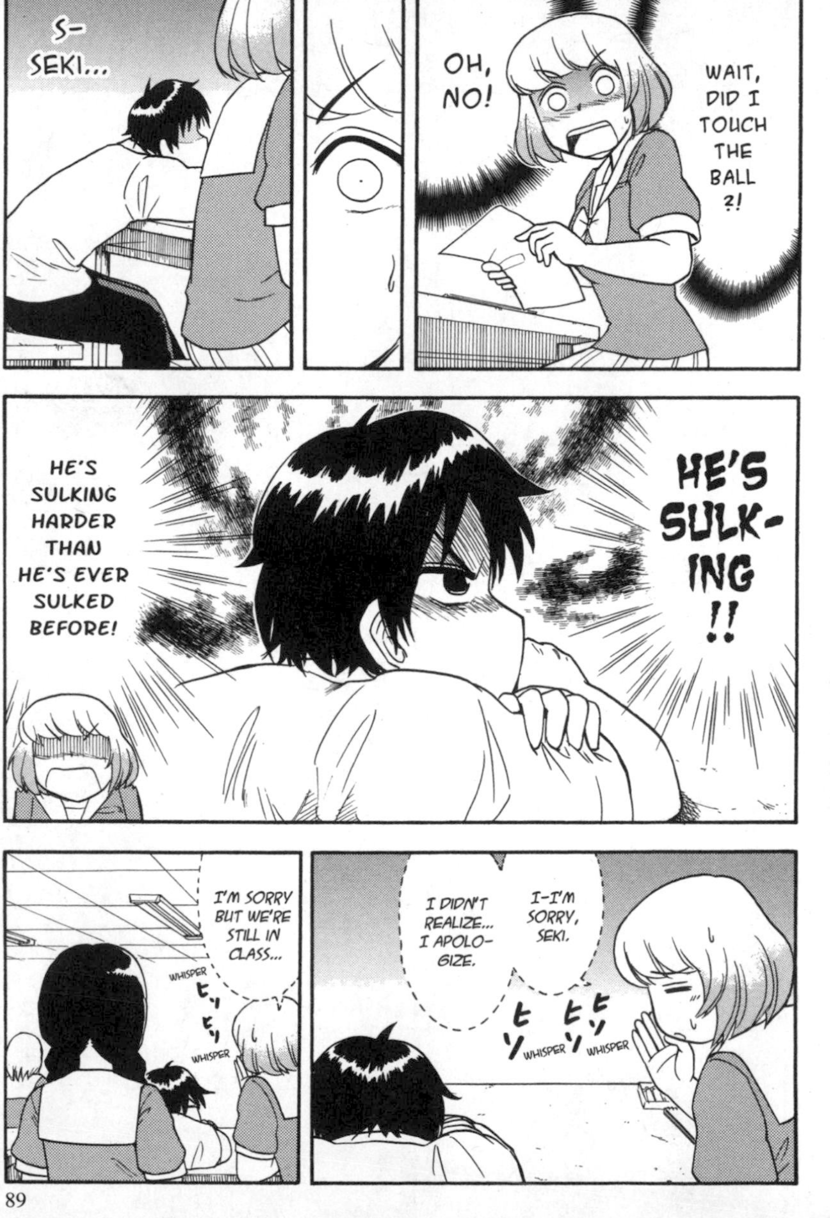
WAIT, DID I TOUCH THE BALL ?!
OH, NO!
S-SEKI...
HE'S SULK-ING!!
HE'S SULKING HARDER THAN HE'S EVER SULKED BEFORE!
I-I'M SORRY, SEKI.
I DIDN'T REALIZE... I APOLO-GIZE.
ヒソ WHISPER
ヒソ WHISPER
I'M SORRY BUT WE'RE STILL IN CLASS...
WHISPER ヒソ
ヒソ WHISPER

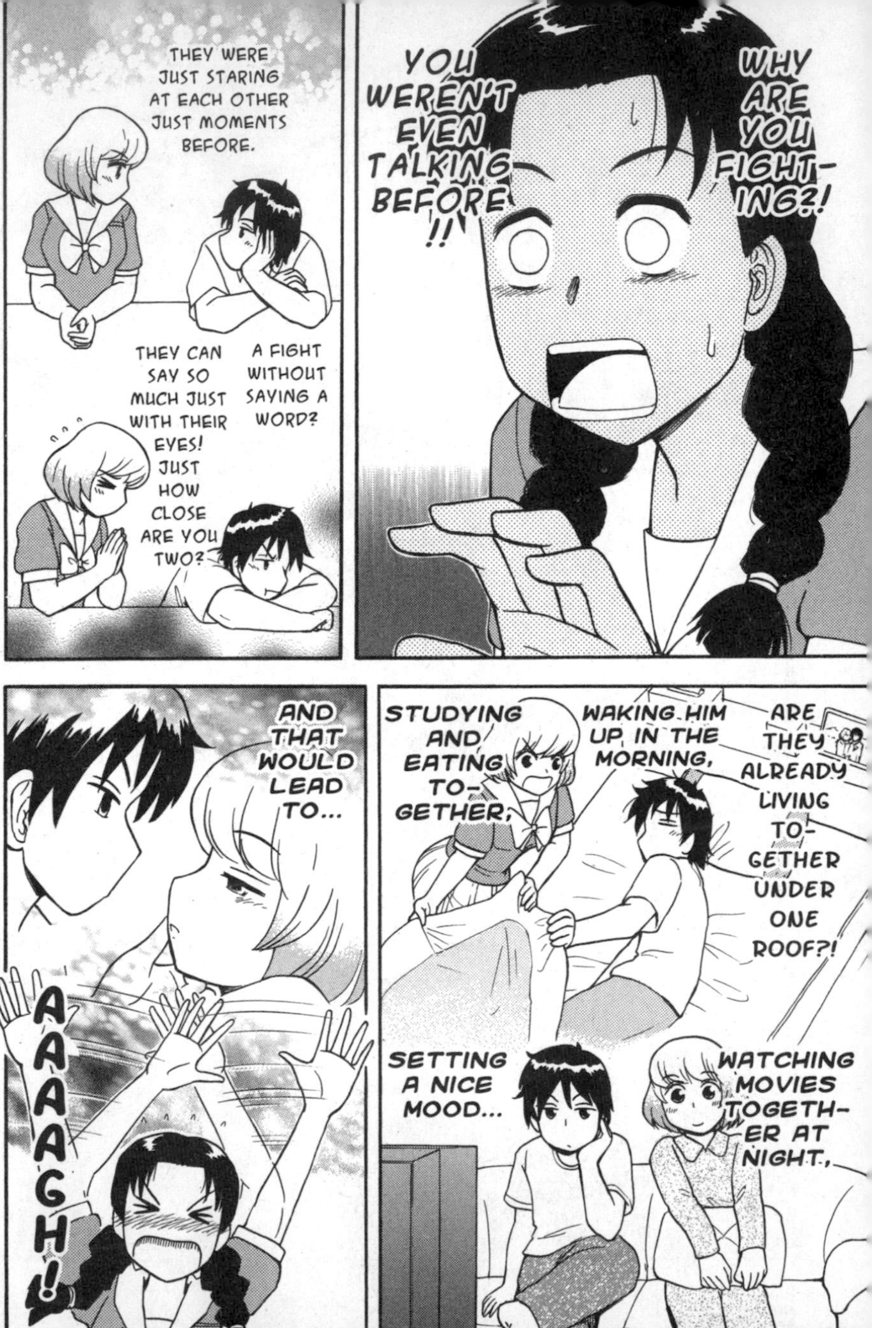
WHY ARE YOU FIGHT-ING?!
YOU WEREN'T EVEN TALKING BEFORE!!
THEY WERE JUST STARING AT EACH OTHER JUST MOMENTS BEFORE.
A FIGHT WITHOUT SAYING A WORD?
THEY CAN SAY SO MUCH JUST WITH THEIR EYES! JUST HOW CLOSE ARE YOU TWO?
ARE THEY ALREADY LIVING TO-GETHER UNDER ONE ROOF?!
WAKING HIM UP IN THE MORNING,
STUDYING AND EATING TO-GETHER,
WATCHING MOVIES TOGETH-ER AT NIGHT,
SETTING A NICE MOOD...
AND THAT WOULD LEAD TO...
AAAAAGH!

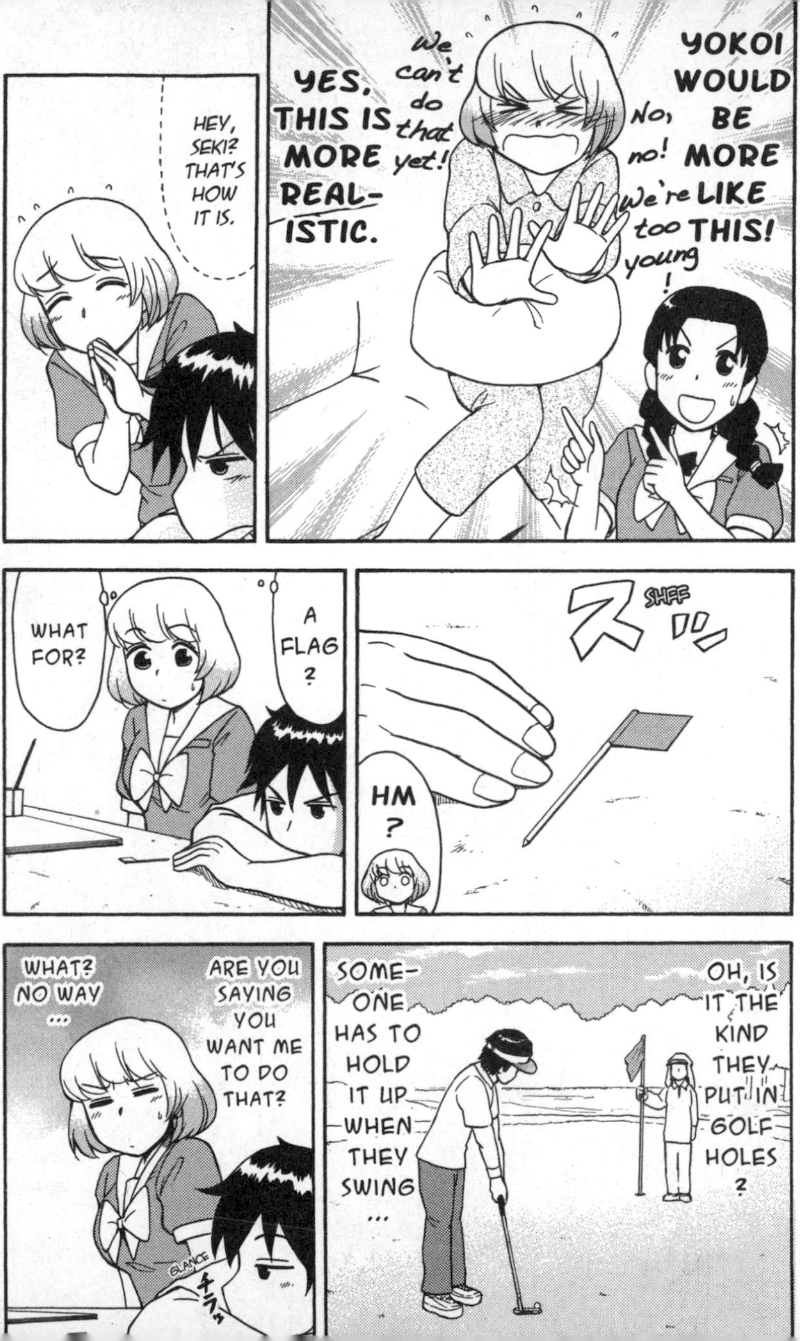
YOKOI WOULD BE MORE LIKE THIS!
No, no! We're too young!
We can't do that yet!
YES, THIS IS MORE REALISTIC.
HEY, SEKI? THAT'S HOW IT IS.
ス SHFF
HM?
A FLAG?
WHAT FOR?
OH, IS IT THE KIND THEY PUT IN GOLF HOLES?
SOMEONE HAS TO HOLD IT UP WHEN THEY SWING...
ARE YOU SAYING YOU WANT ME TO DO THAT?
WHAT? NO WAY...
チラッ GLANCE

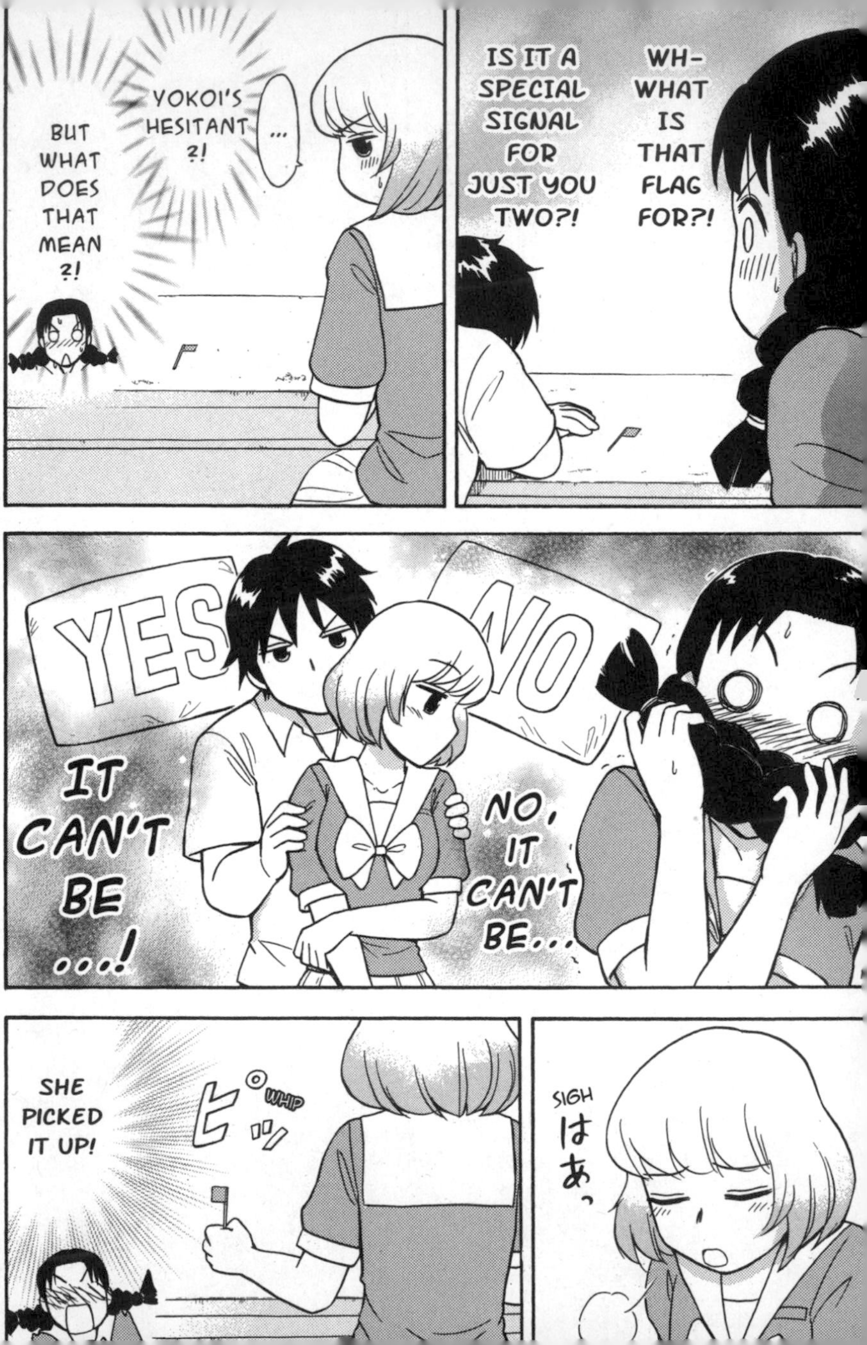
WH- WHAT IS THAT FLAG FOR?!
IS IT A SPECIAL SIGNAL FOR JUST YOU TWO?!
...
YOKOI'S HESITANT?!
BUT WHAT DOES THAT MEAN?!
NO
YES
NO, IT CAN'T BE...
IT CAN'T BE...!
SIGH
はあ
WHIP
ピッ
SHE PICKED IT UP!

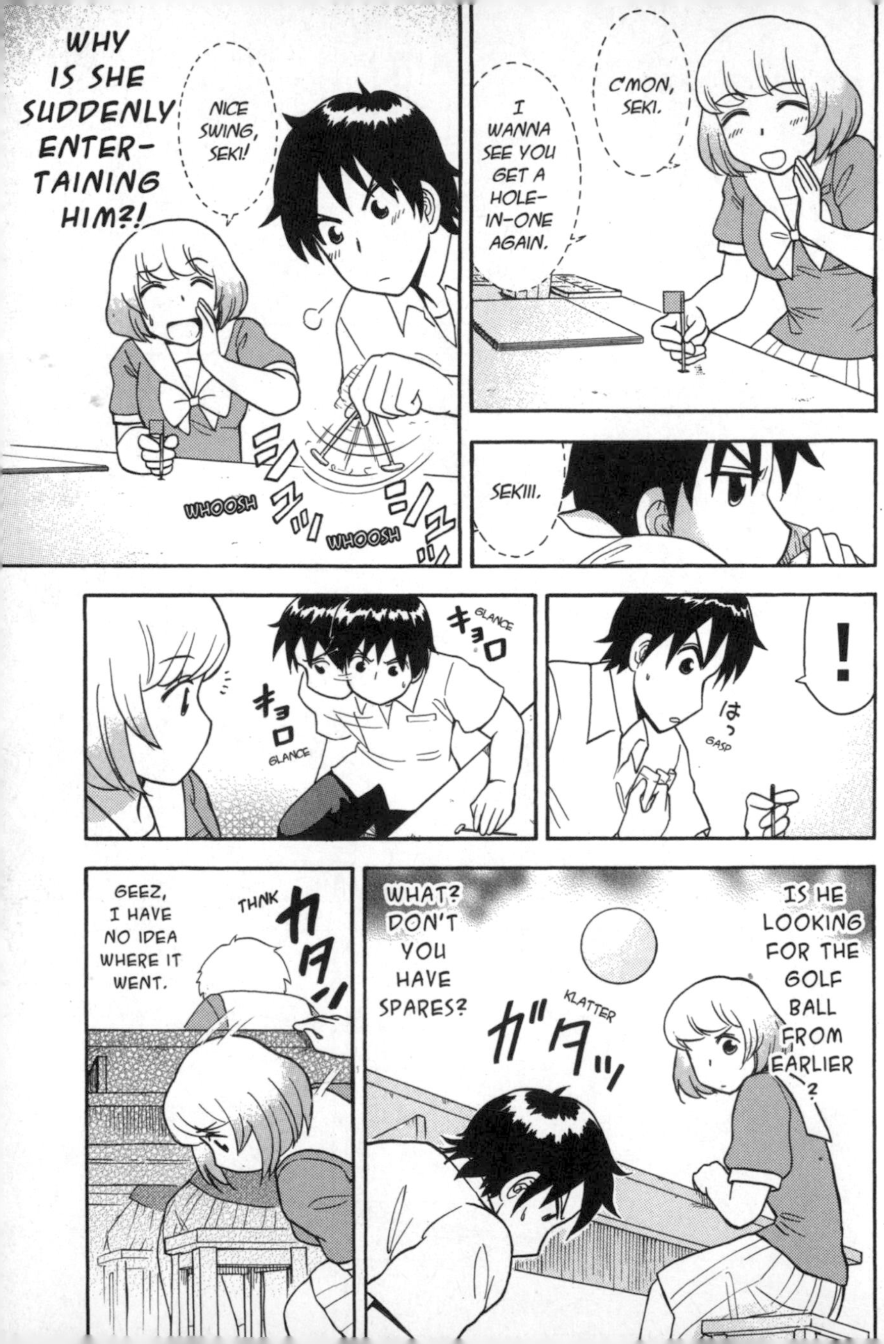
C'MON, SEKI.
I WANNA SEE YOU GET A HOLE-IN-ONE AGAIN.
SEKIII.
NICE SWING, SEKI!
WHY IS SHE SUDDENLY ENTERTAINING HIM?!
WHOOSH
WHOOSH
!
はっ
GASP
キョロ
GLANCE
キョロ
GLANCE
IS HE LOOKING FOR THE GOLF BALL FROM EARLIER?
ガタッ
KLATTER
WHAT? DON'T YOU HAVE SPARES?
カタン
THNK
GEEZ, I HAVE NO IDEA WHERE IT WENT.

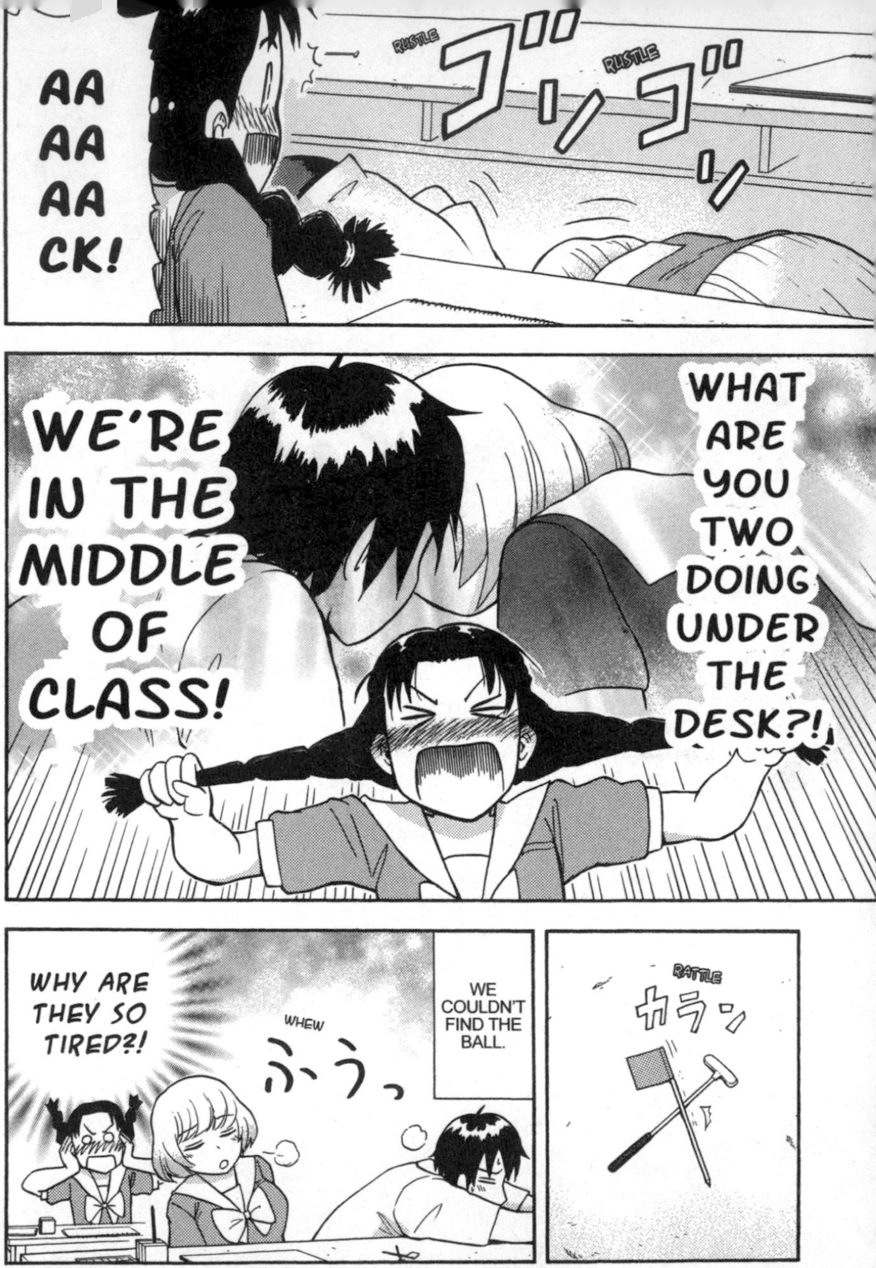
RUSTLE
ゴソ
RUSTLE
ゴソ
AA AA AA CK!
WHAT ARE YOU TWO DOING UNDER THE DESK?!
WE'RE IN THE MIDDLE OF CLASS!
RATTLE
カラン
WE COULDN'T FIND THE BALL.
WHEW
ふうっ
WHY ARE THEY SO TIRED?!

RECESS

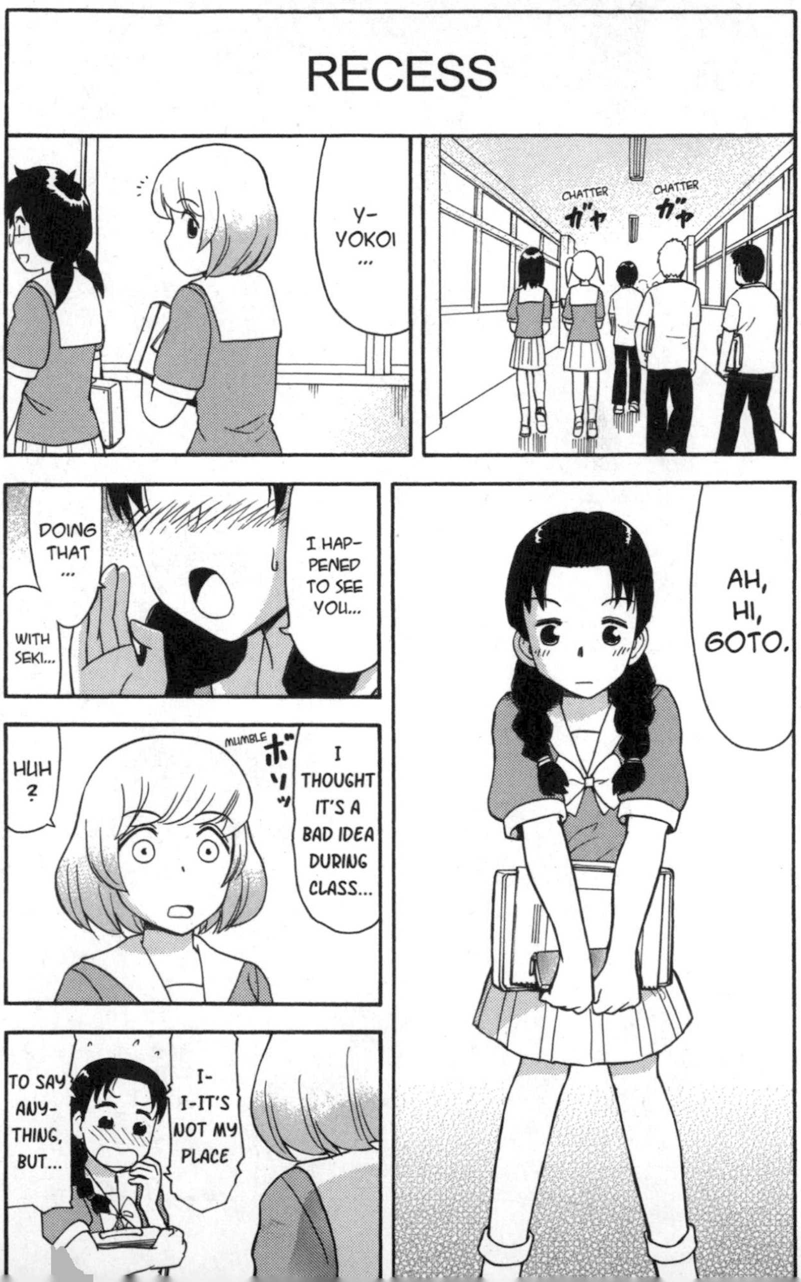

CHATTER ガヤ
CHATTER ガヤ
Y-YOKOI ...
AH, HI, GOTO.
I HAP-PENED TO SEE YOU...
DOING THAT ...
WITH SEKI...
MUMBLE ボソッ
I THOUGHT IT'S A BAD IDEA DURING CLASS...
HUH ?
I- I-IT'S NOT MY PLACE
TO SAY ANY-THING, BUT...

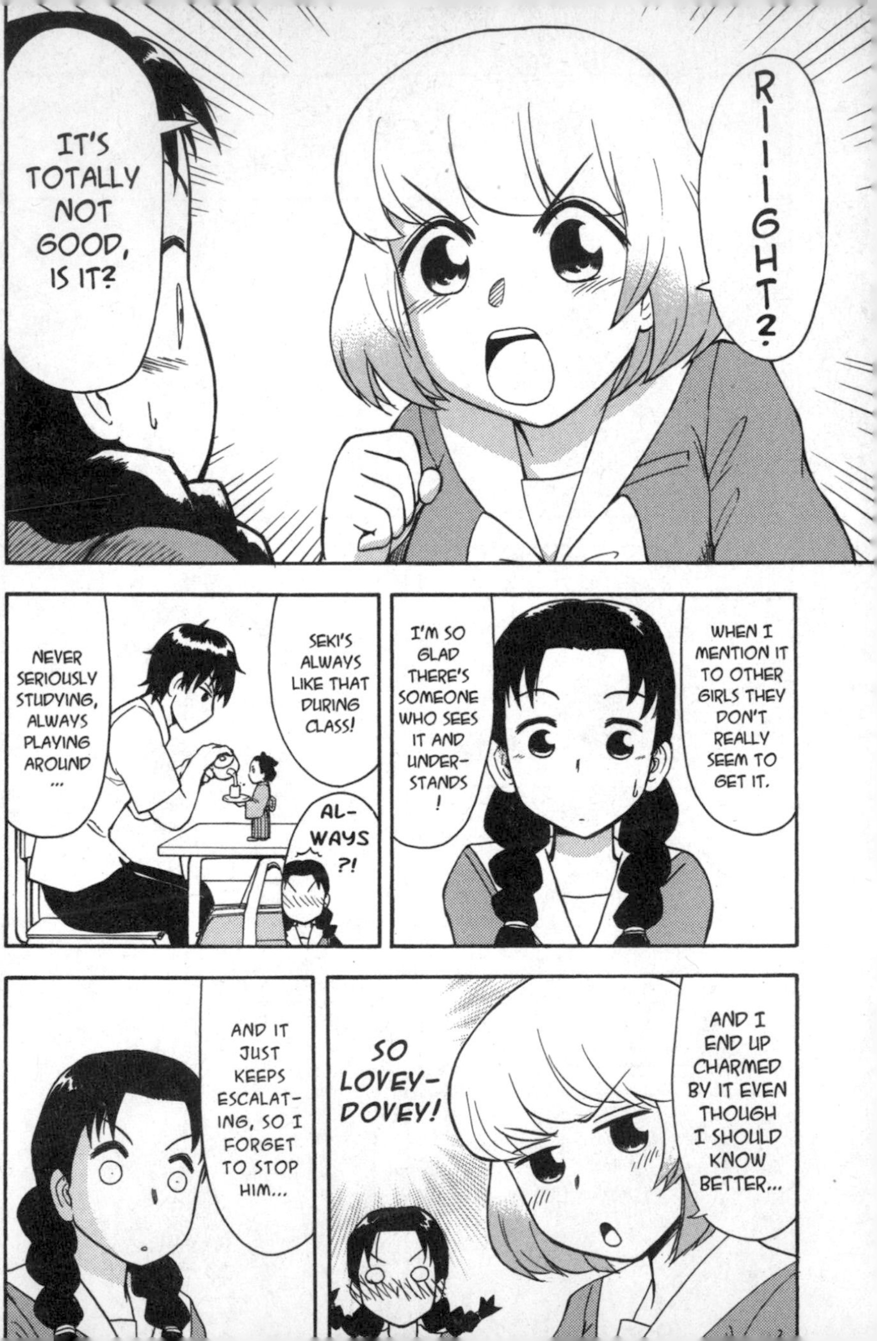
RIIIGHT?
IT'S TOTALLY NOT GOOD, IS IT?
WHEN I MENTION IT TO OTHER GIRLS THEY DON'T REALLY SEEM TO GET IT.
I'M SO GLAD THERE'S SOMEONE WHO SEES IT AND UNDER-STANDS!
SEKI'S ALWAYS LIKE THAT DURING CLASS!
NEVER SERIOUSLY STUDYING, ALWAYS PLAYING AROUND...
AL-WAYS?!
AND I END UP CHARMED BY IT EVEN THOUGH I SHOULD KNOW BETTER...
SO LOVEY-DOVEY!
AND IT JUST KEEPS ESCALAT-ING, SO I FORGET TO STOP HIM...

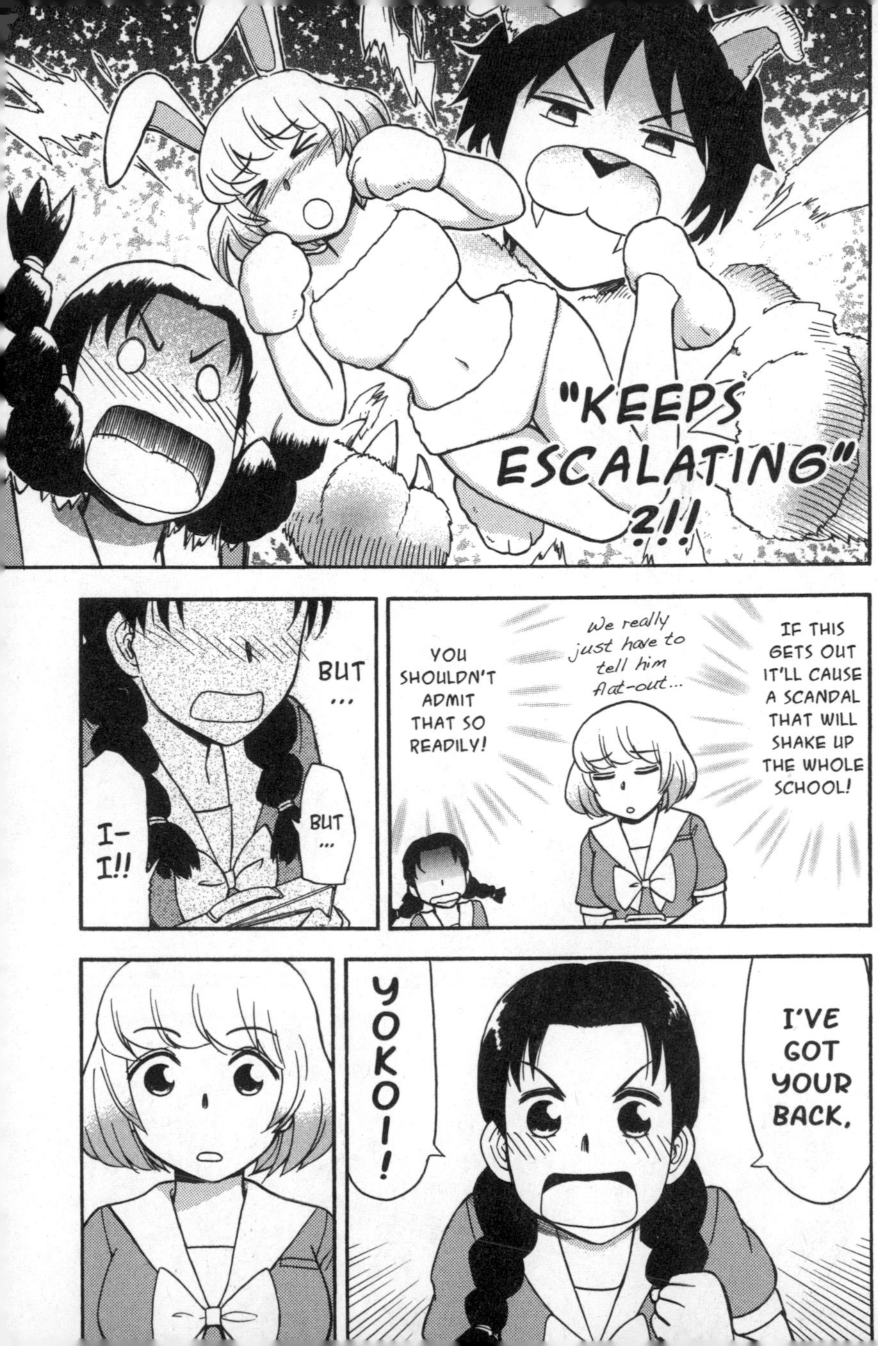
"KEEPS ESCALATING" ?!!
IF THIS GETS OUT IT'LL CAUSE A SCANDAL THAT WILL SHAKE UP THE WHOLE SCHOOL!
We really just have to tell him flat-out...
YOU SHOULDN'T ADMIT THAT SO READILY!
BUT ...
BUT ...
I- I!!
I'VE GOT YOUR BACK.
YOKO!!

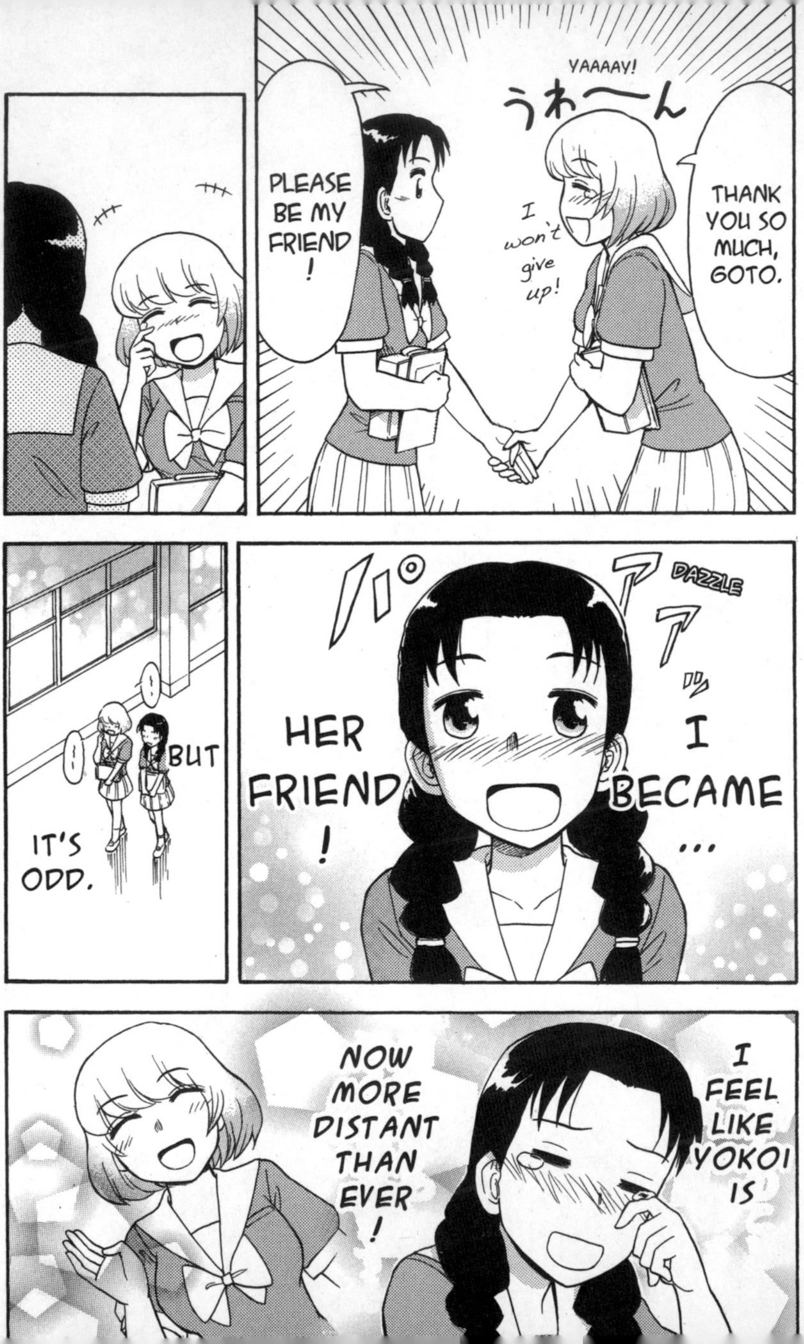

YAAAAY!
うわ〜ん
THANK YOU SO MUCH, GOTO.
I won't give up!
PLEASE BE MY FRIEND!
DAZZLE
パアアッ
I BECAME...
HER FRIEND!
BUT
IT'S ODD.
I FEEL LIKE YOKOI IS
NOW MORE DISTANT THAN EVER!

My Neighbor Seki

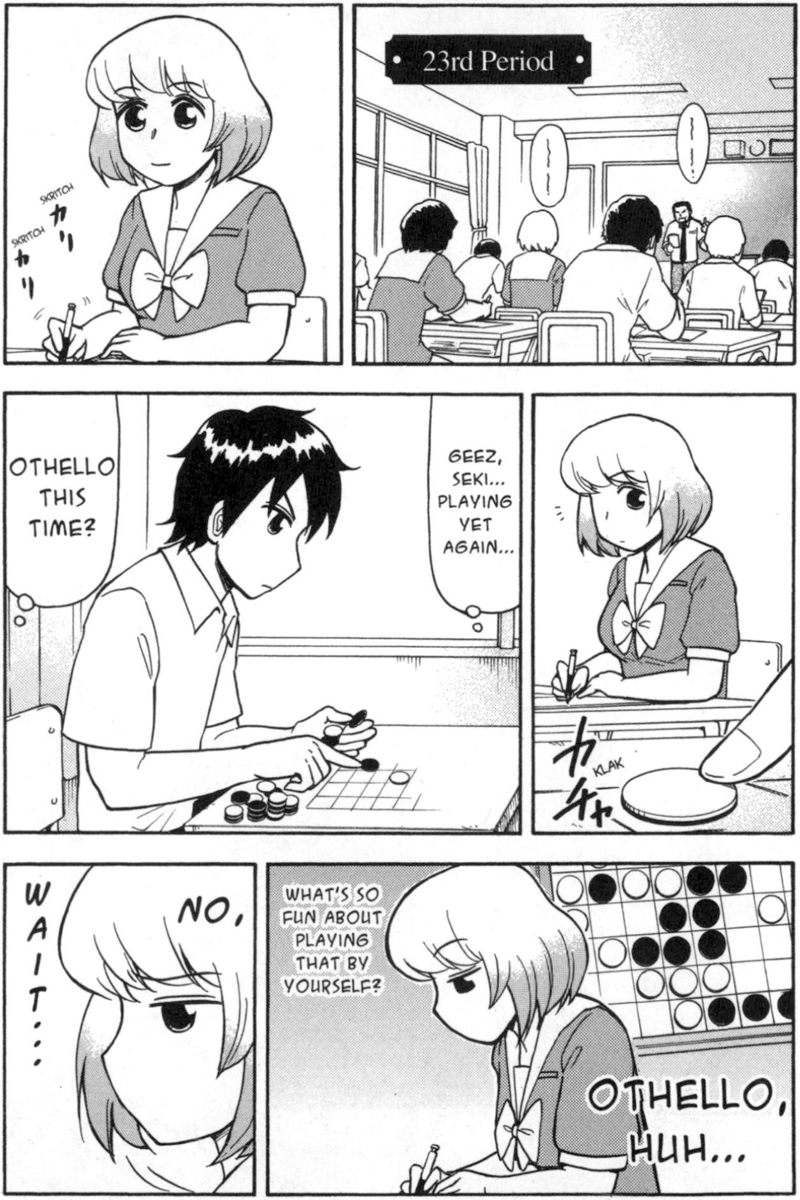

23rd Period
~~!
~~~
SKRITCH
SKRITCH
KLAK
GEEZ, SEKI... PLAYING YET AGAIN...
OTHELLO THIS TIME?
WHAT'S SO FUN ABOUT PLAYING THAT BY YOURSELF?
OTHELLO, HUH...
NO,
WAIT...
~~~

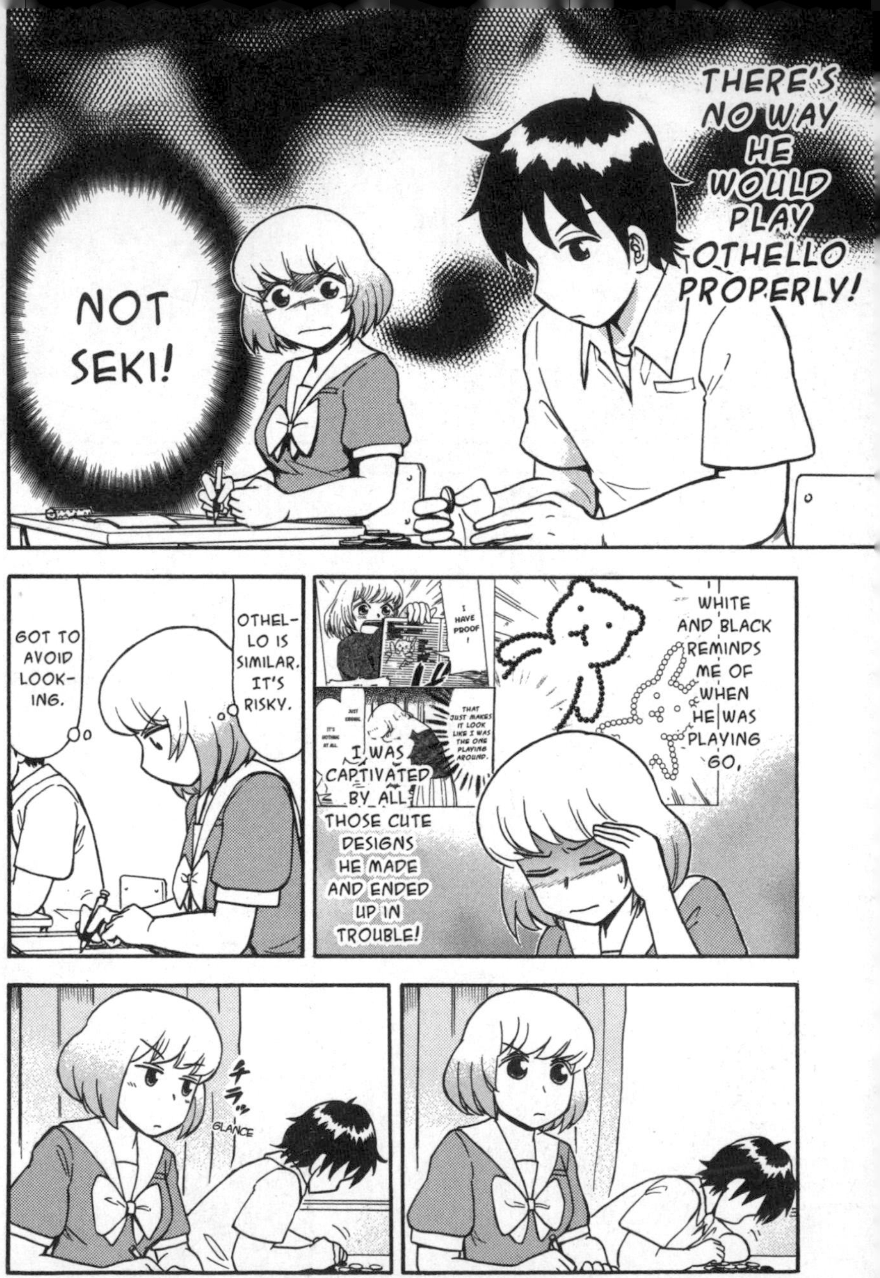
THERE'S NO WAY HE WOULD PLAY OTHELLO PROPERLY!
NOT SEKI!
WHITE AND BLACK REMINDS ME OF WHEN HE WAS PLAYING GO,
I HAVE PROOF!
THAT JUST MAKES IT LOOK LIKE I WAS THE ONE PLAYING AROUND.
IT'S NOTHING AT ALL
I WAS CAPTIVATED BY ALL THOSE CUTE DESIGNS HE MADE AND ENDED UP IN TROUBLE!
OTHELLO IS SIMILAR. IT'S RISKY.
GOT TO AVOID LOOKING.
チラッ
GLANCE

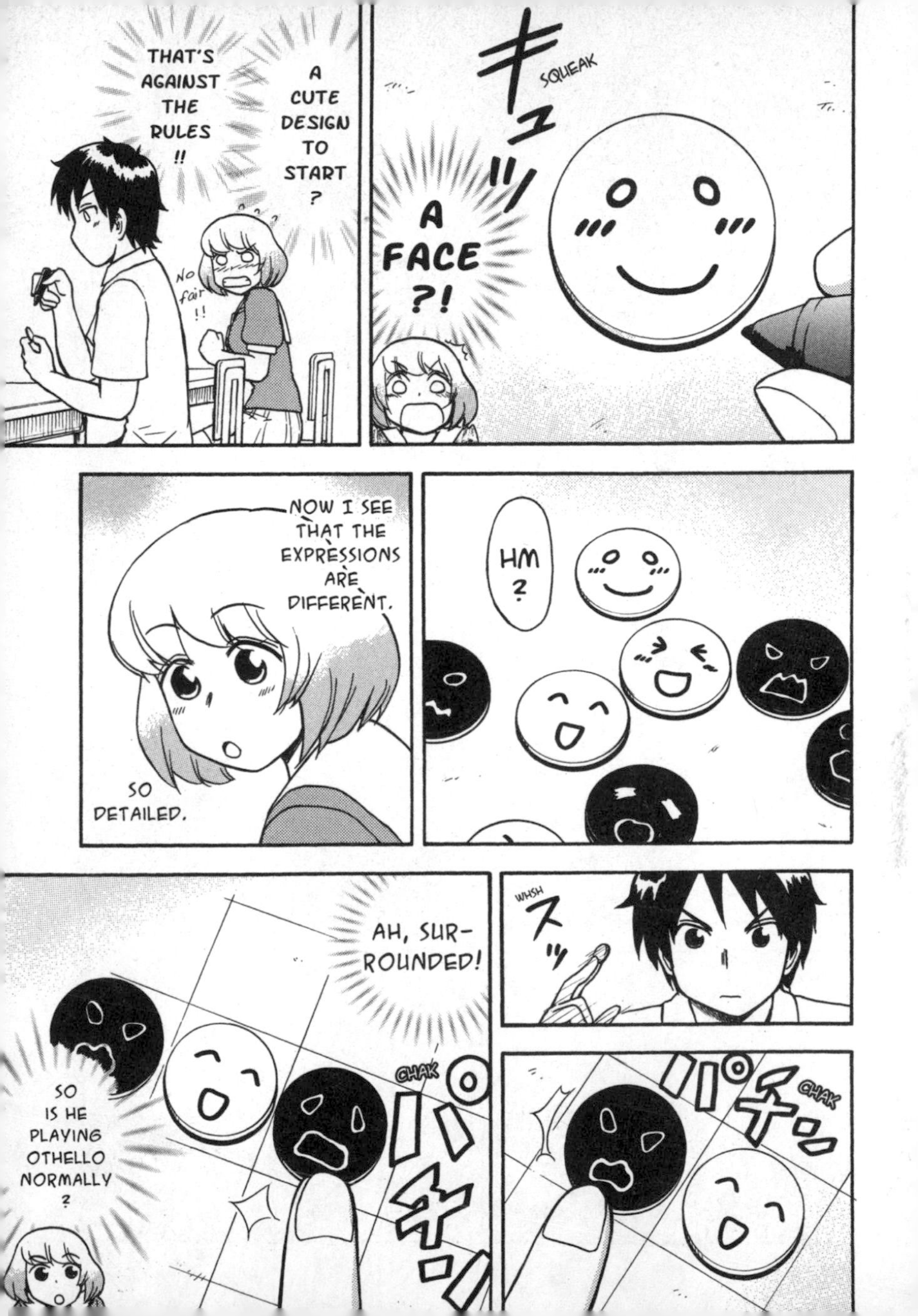
キュッ
SQUEAK
A FACE ?!
A CUTE DESIGN TO START ?
THAT'S AGAINST THE RULES !!
No fair !!
HM ?
NOW I SEE THAT THE EXPRESSIONS ARE DIFFERENT.
SO DETAILED.
スッ
WHSH
パチッ
CHAK
AH, SUR-ROUNDED!
パチッ
CHAK
SO IS HE PLAYING OTHELLO NORMALLY ?

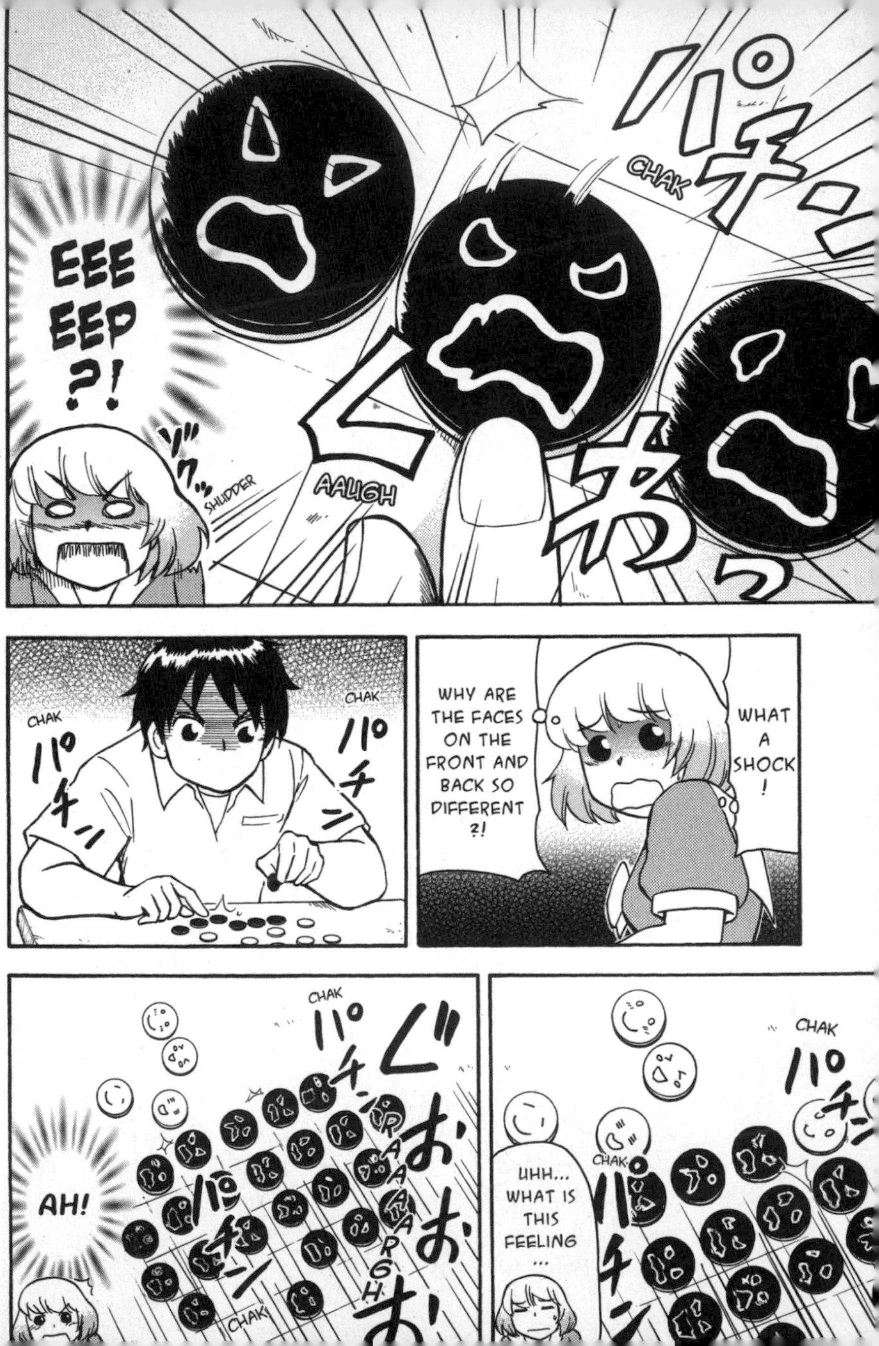
パチッ
CHAK
ぐわっ
AAUGH
EEEEEEP ?!
ゾクッ
SHUDDER
WHAT A SHOCK!
WHY ARE THE FACES ON THE FRONT AND BACK SO DIFFERENT ?!
CHAK
パチン
CHAK
パチン
CHAK
パチン
UHH... WHAT IS THIS FEELING ...
CHAK
パチン
CHAK
パチン
ぐおおお
RAAAARGH
AH!
パチン
CHAK

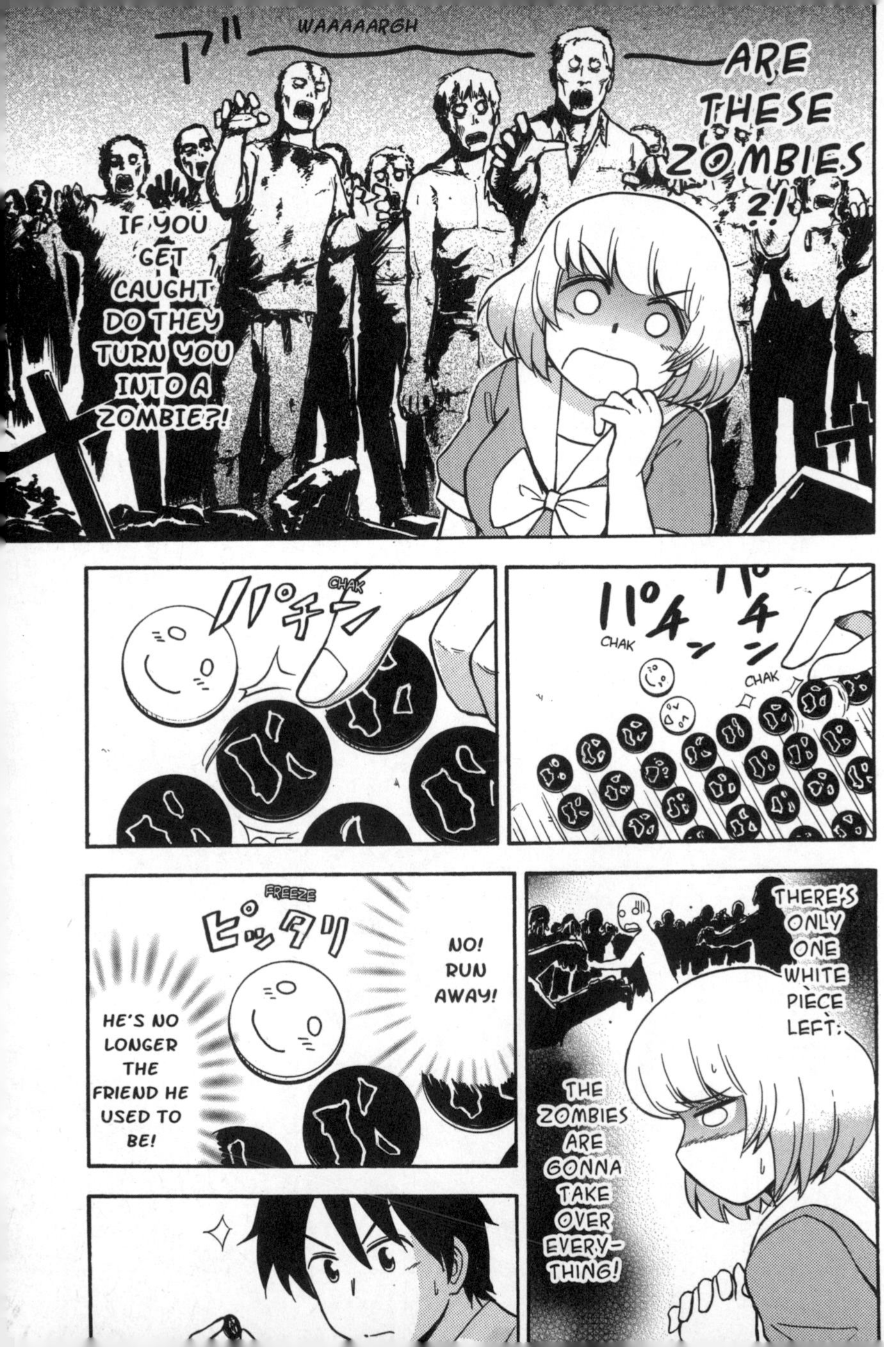
アﾞ
WAAAAARGH
ARE THESE ZOMBIES?!
IF YOU GET CAUGHT DO THEY TURN YOU INTO A ZOMBIE?!
パチン
CHAK
パチン
CHAK
パチーン
CHAK
THERE'S ONLY ONE WHITE PIECE LEFT.
THE ZOMBIES ARE GONNA TAKE OVER EVERYTHING!
ピッタリ
FREEZE
NO! RUN AWAY!
HE'S NO LONGER THE FRIEND HE USED TO BE!

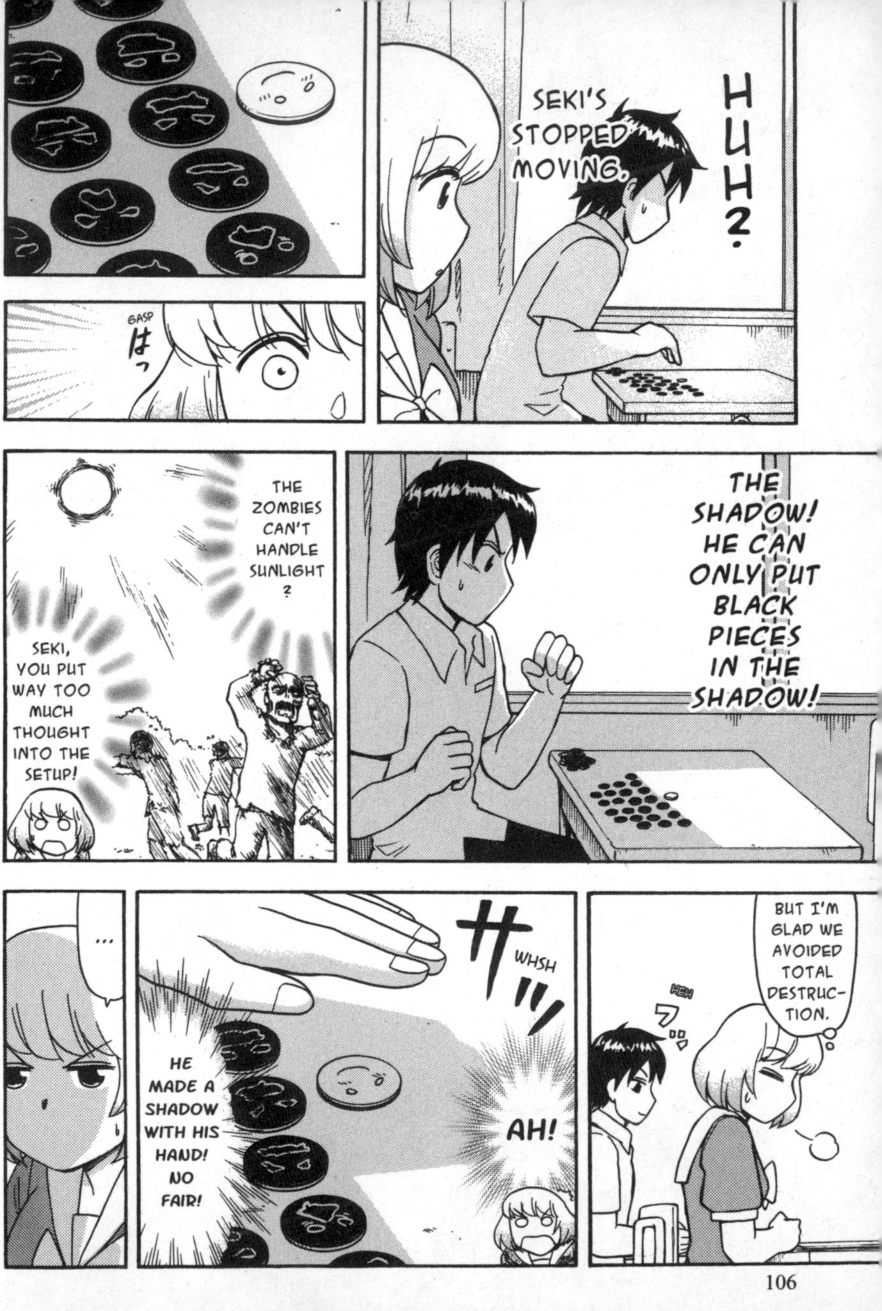
HUH?
SEKI'S STOPPED MOVING.
GASP
はっ
THE SHADOW! HE CAN ONLY PUT BLACK PIECES IN THE SHADOW!
THE ZOMBIES CAN'T HANDLE SUNLIGHT?
SEKI, YOU PUT WAY TOO MUCH THOUGHT INTO THE SETUP!
BUT I'M GLAD WE AVOIDED TOTAL DESTRUCTION.
HEH
フッ
サッ
WHSH
AH!
HE MADE A SHADOW WITH HIS HAND! NO FAIR!
...

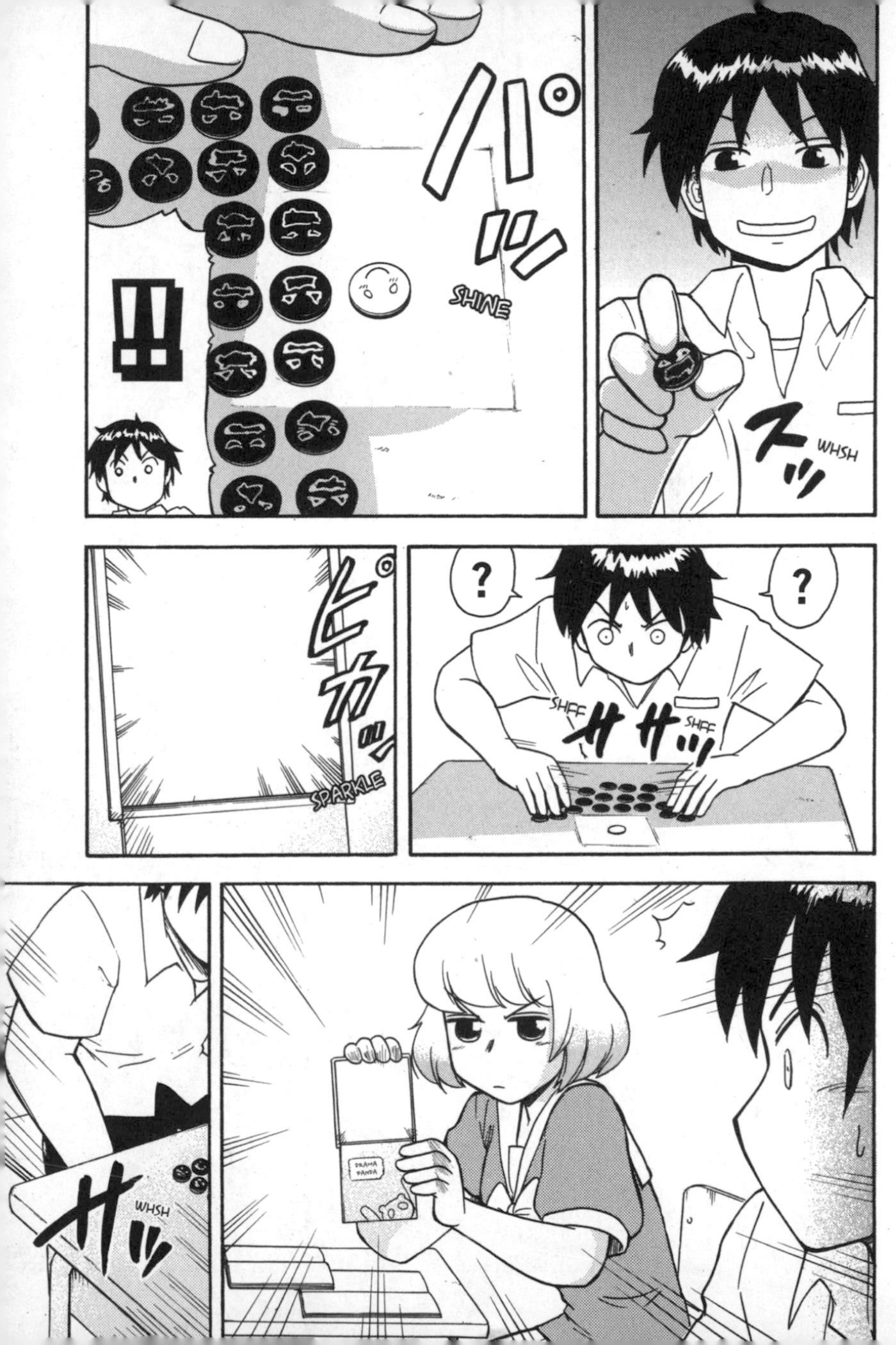
スッ
WHSH
パパッ
SHINE
!!
?
?
ササッ
SHFF
SHFF
ピカッ
SPARKLE
DRAMA PANDA
サッ
WHSH

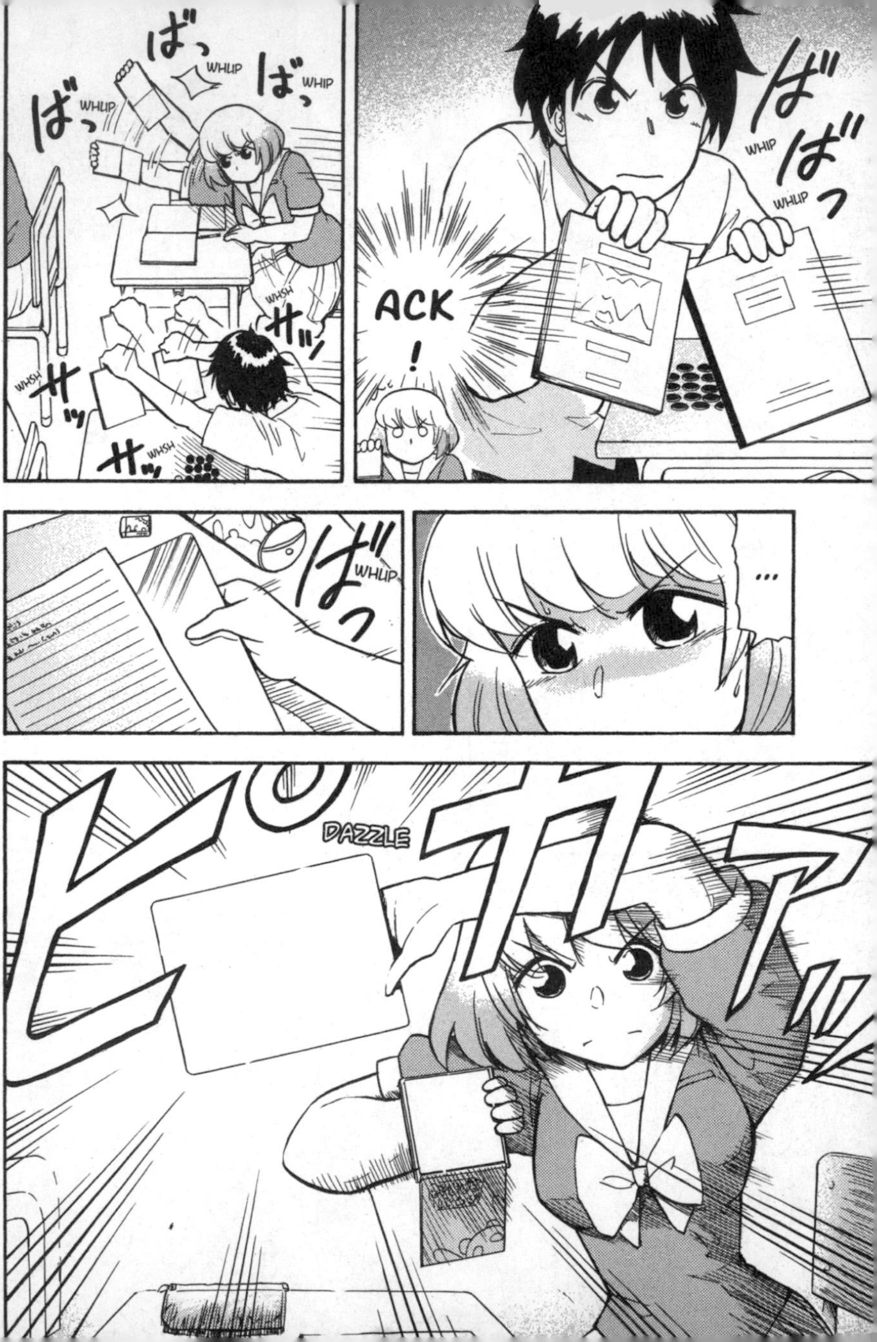
ばっ
WHIP
ばっ
WHUP
ACK
!
ばっ
WHIP
ばっ
WHUP
ばっ
WHUP
ザッ
WHSH
ザッ
WHSH
ザッ
WHSH
...
ばっ
WHUP
DAZZLE

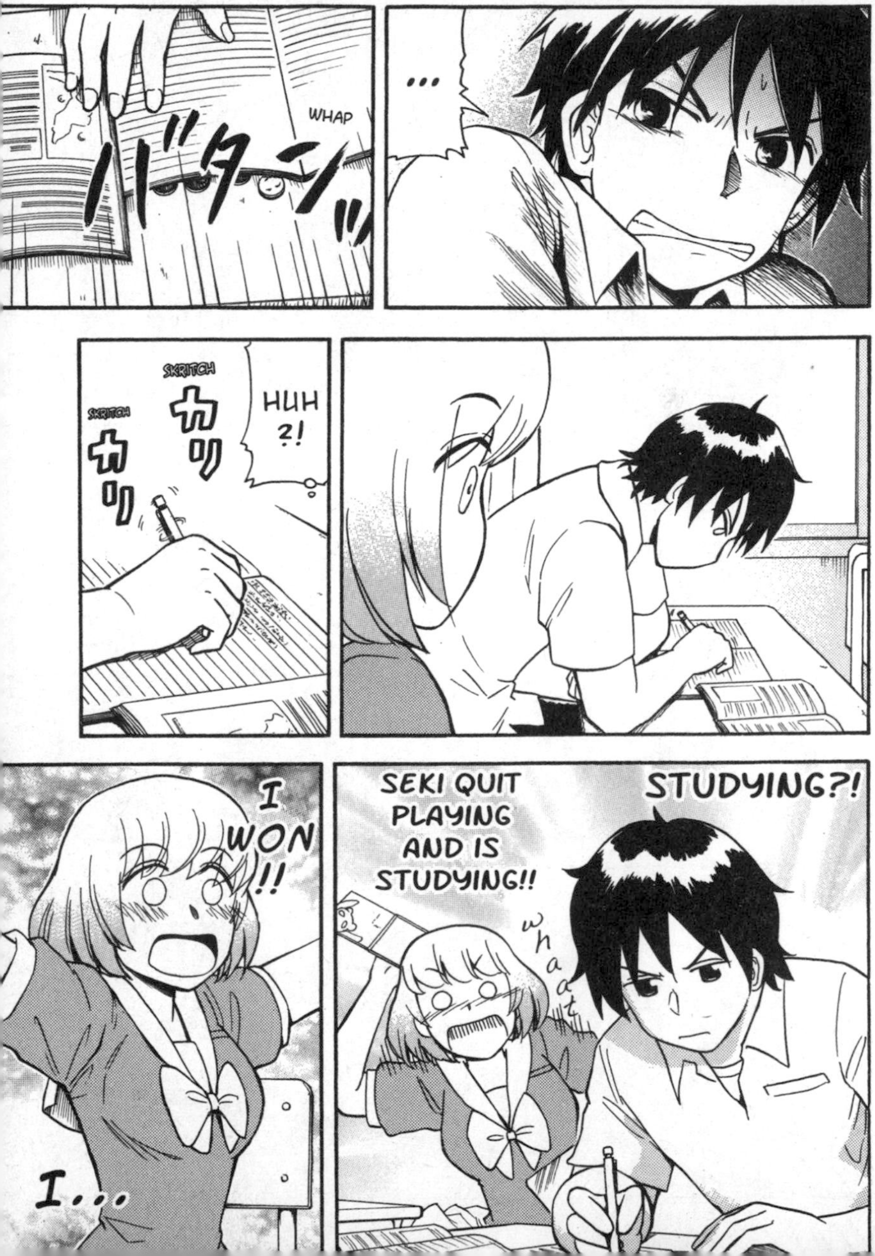
...
WHAP
バタンッ
HUH ?!
SKRITCH
カリ
SKRITCH
カリ
STUDYING?!
SEKI QUIT PLAYING AND IS STUDYING!!
whaat
I WON!!
I...

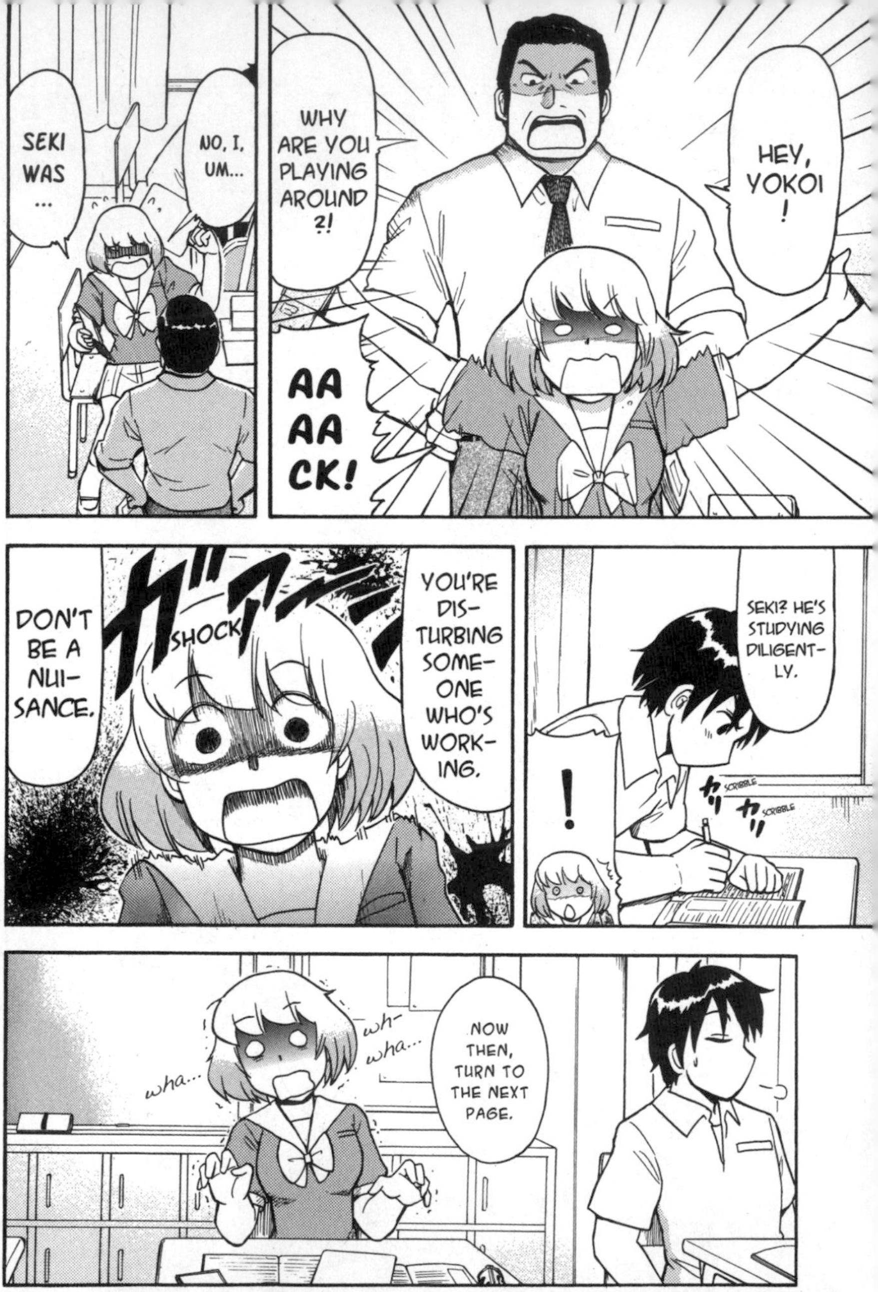
HEY, YOKOI!
WHY ARE YOU PLAYING AROUND?!
AAAACK!
NO, I, UM...
SEKI WAS ...
SEKI? HE'S STUDYING DILIGENT-LY.
SCRIBBLE
SCRIBBLE
!
SHOCK
YOU'RE DIS-TURBING SOME-ONE WHO'S WORK-ING.
DON'T BE A NUI-SANCE.
NOW THEN, TURN TO THE NEXT PAGE.
wh-wha...
wha...

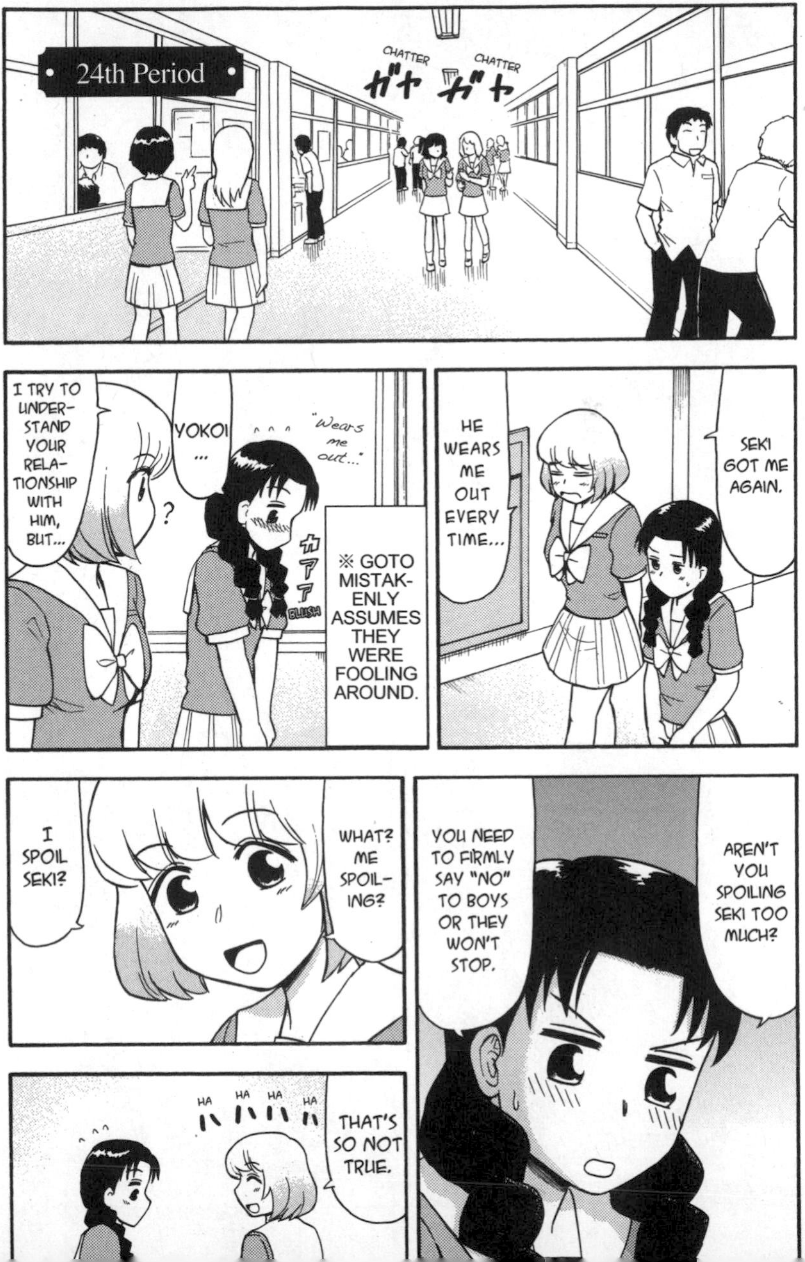
24th Period
CHATTER ガヤ
CHATTER ガヤ
SEKI GOT ME AGAIN.
HE WEARS ME OUT EVERY TIME...
※ GOTO MISTAKENLY ASSUMES THEY WERE FOOLING AROUND.
"Wears me out..."
YOKOI...
I TRY TO UNDERSTAND YOUR RELATIONSHIP WITH HIM, BUT...
カアア BLUSH
AREN'T YOU SPOILING SEKI TOO MUCH?
YOU NEED TO FIRMLY SAY "NO" TO BOYS OR THEY WON'T STOP.
WHAT? ME SPOILING?
I SPOIL SEKI?
HA HA HA HA ハハハハ
THAT'S SO NOT TRUE.

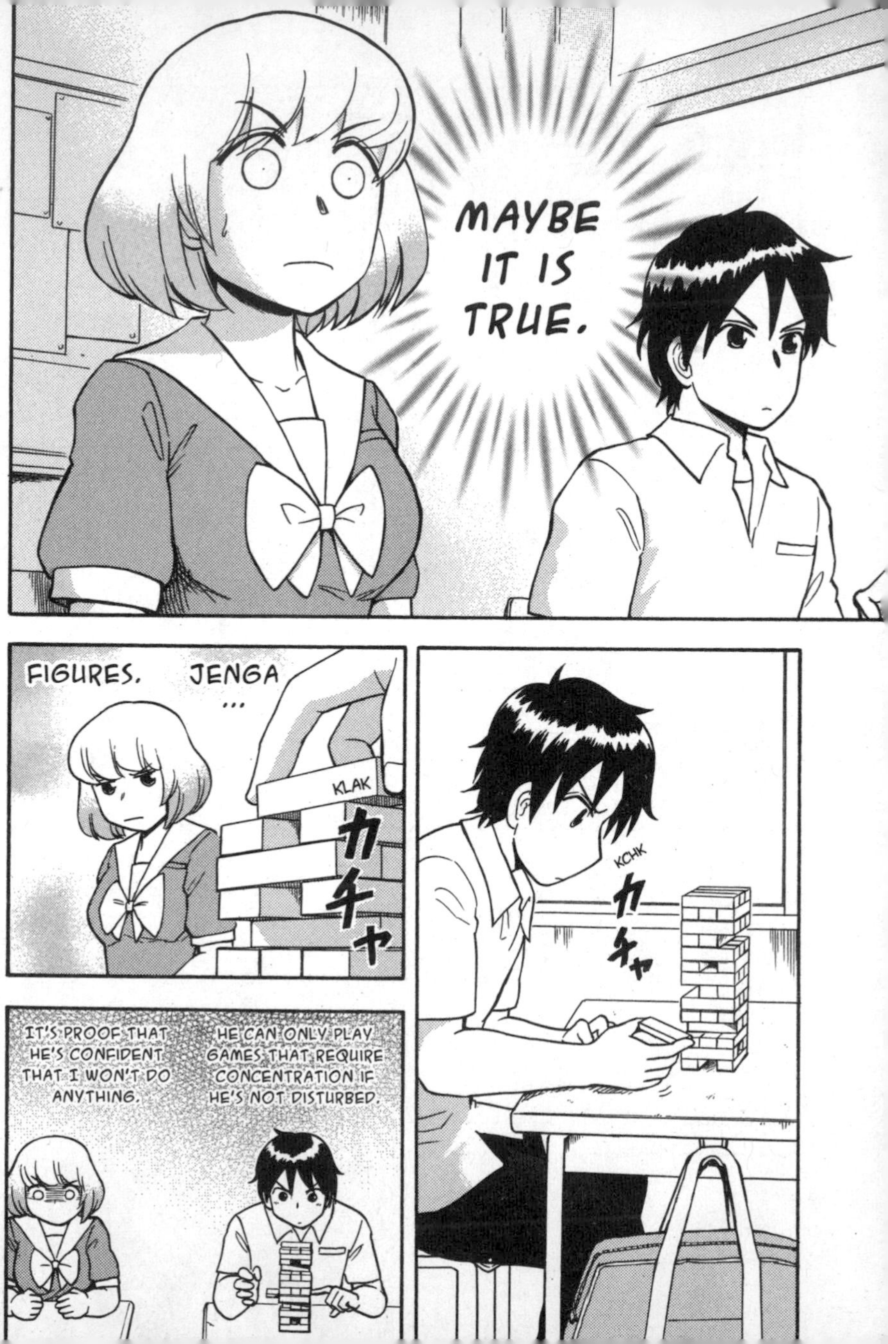
MAYBE IT IS TRUE.
KCHK
カチャ
JENGA ...
KLAK
カチャ
FIGURES.
HE CAN ONLY PLAY GAMES THAT REQUIRE CONCENTRATION IF HE'S NOT DISTURBED.
IT'S PROOF THAT HE'S CONFIDENT THAT I WON'T DO ANYTHING.

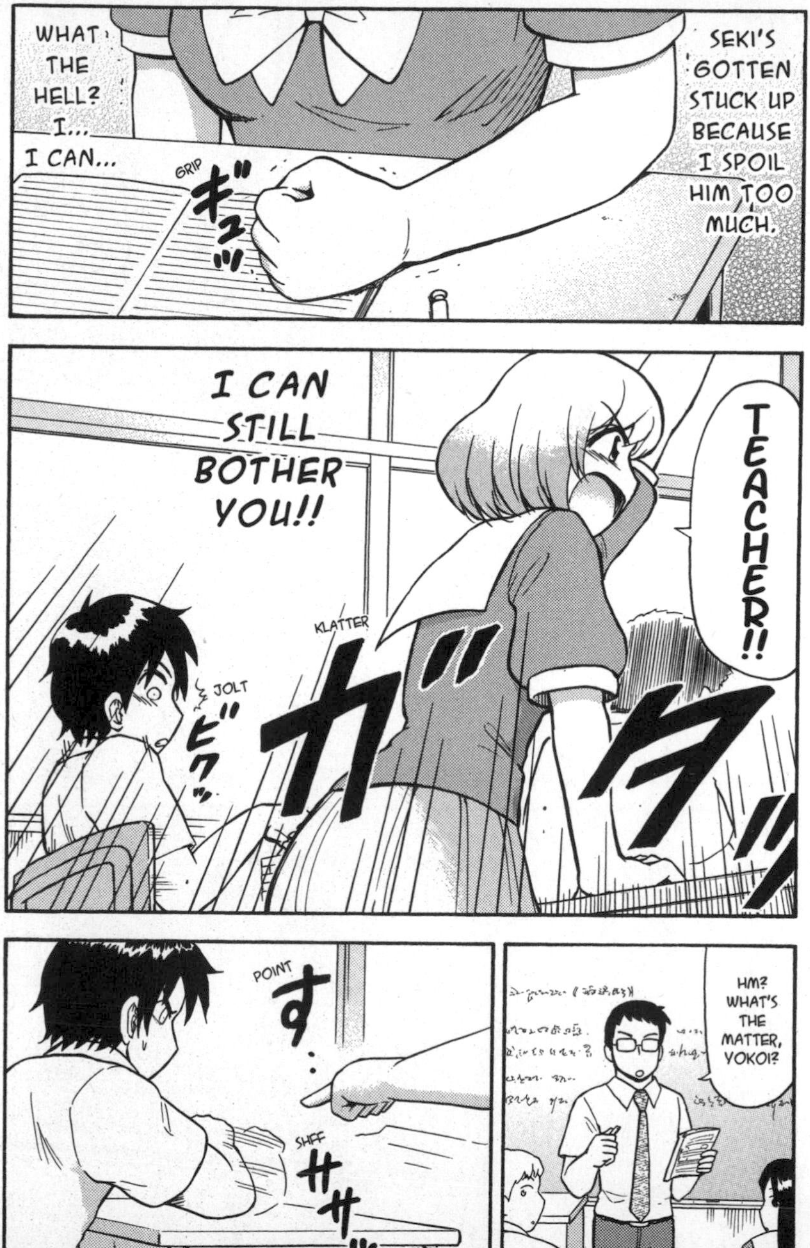
SEKI'S GOTTEN STUCK UP BECAUSE I SPOIL HIM TOO MUCH.
WHAT THE HELL? I... I CAN...
GRIP
ギュッ
TEACHER!!
I CAN STILL BOTHER YOU!!
KLATTER
ガタッ
JOLT
ビクッ
HM? WHAT'S THE MATTER, YOKOI?
POINT
す
SHFF
ササッ

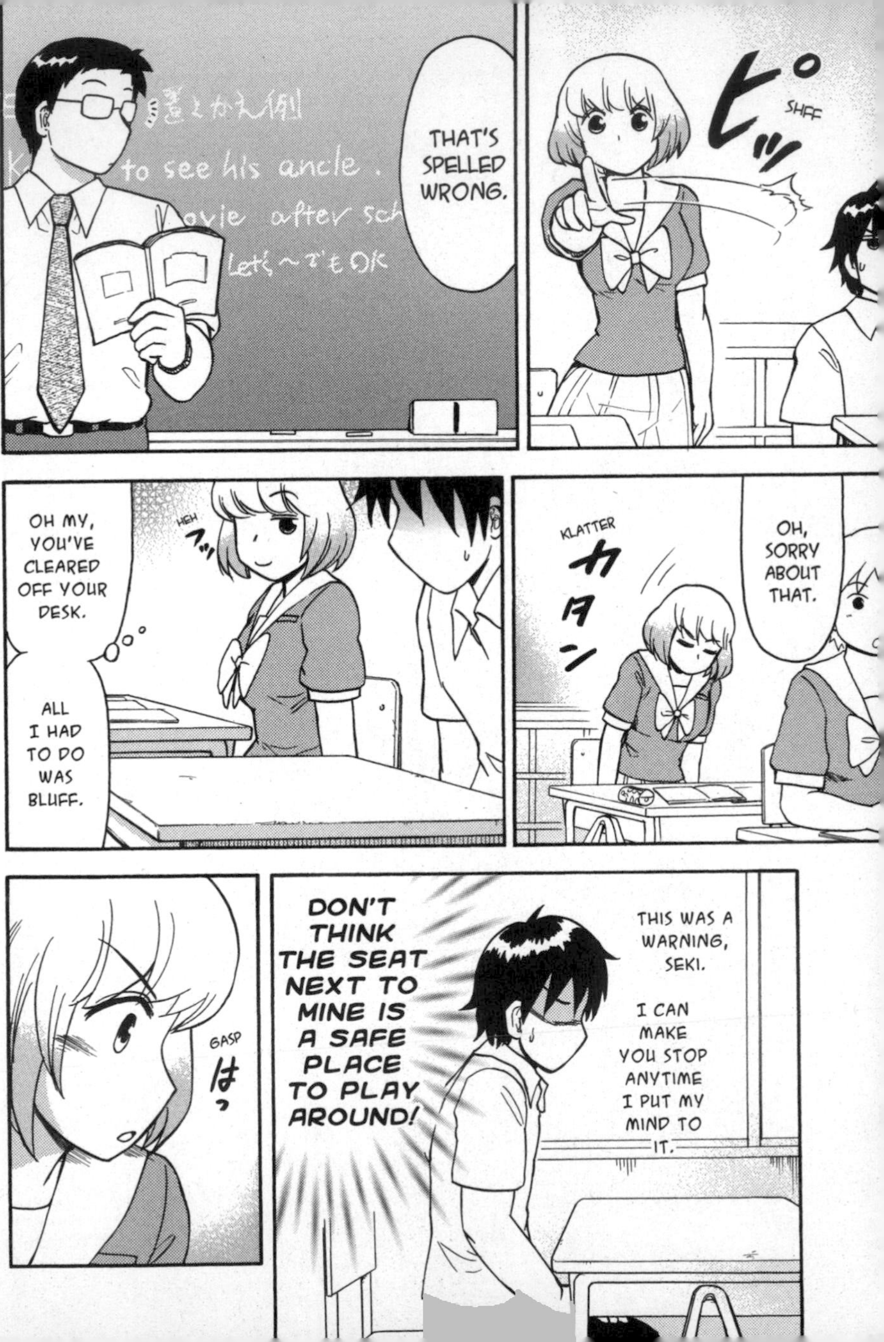
SHFF
ピッ
置きかえ例
to see his ancle.
ovie after sch
Let's ~でもOK
THAT'S SPELLED WRONG.
OH, SORRY ABOUT THAT.
KLATTER
カタン
HEH
フッ
OH MY, YOU'VE CLEARED OFF YOUR DESK.
ALL I HAD TO DO WAS BLUFF.
THIS WAS A WARNING, SEKI.
I CAN MAKE YOU STOP ANYTIME I PUT MY MIND TO IT.
DON'T THINK THE SEAT NEXT TO MINE IS A SAFE PLACE TO PLAY AROUND!
GASP
はっ

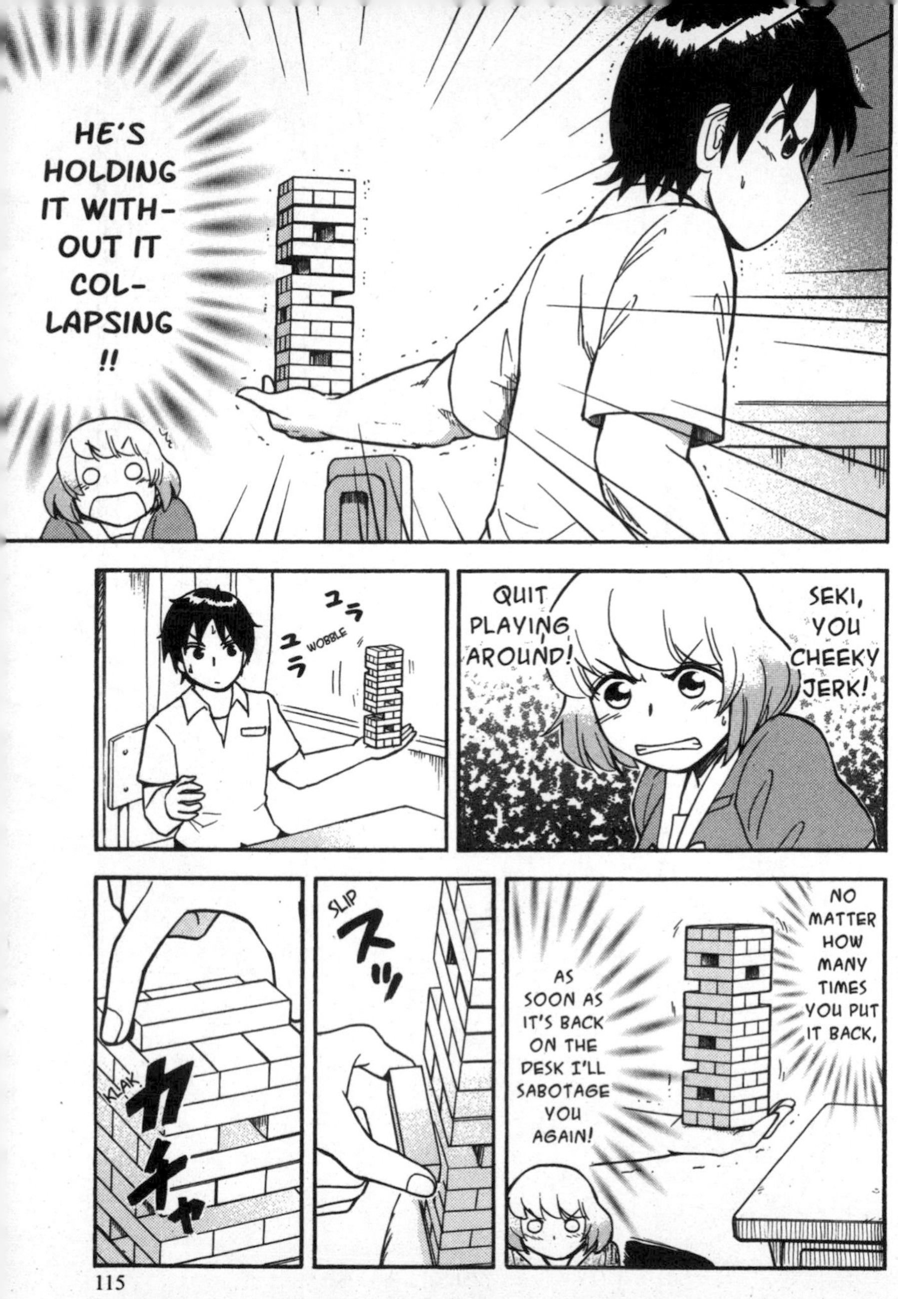

HE'S HOLDING IT WITHOUT IT COLLAPSING!!
SEKI, YOU CHEEKY JERK!
QUIT PLAYING AROUND!
ユラ
ユラ
WOBBLE
NO MATTER HOW MANY TIMES YOU PUT IT BACK,
AS SOON AS IT'S BACK ON THE DESK I'LL SABOTAGE YOU AGAIN!
SLIP
スッ
KLAK
カチャ

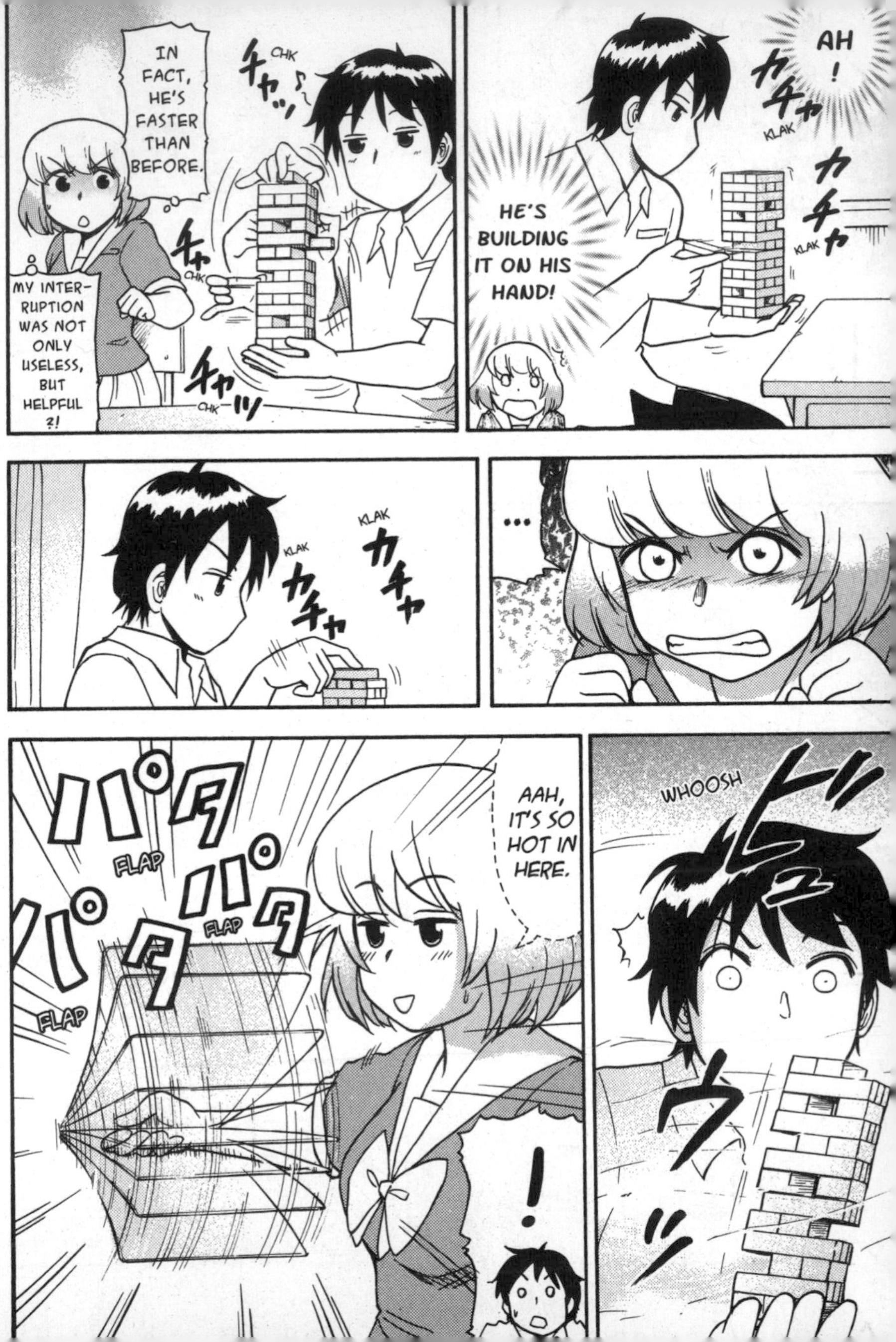
AH!
カチャ
KLAK
カチャ
KLAK
HE'S BUILDING IT ON HIS HAND!
IN FACT, HE'S FASTER THAN BEFORE.
チャッ
CHK
チャ
CHK
MY INTERRUPTION WAS NOT ONLY USELESS, BUT HELPFUL?!
チャッ
CHK
...
KLAK
カチャ
KLAK
カチャ
WHOOSH
AAH, IT'S SO HOT IN HERE.
パタ
FLAP
パタ
FLAP
パタ
FLAP
!

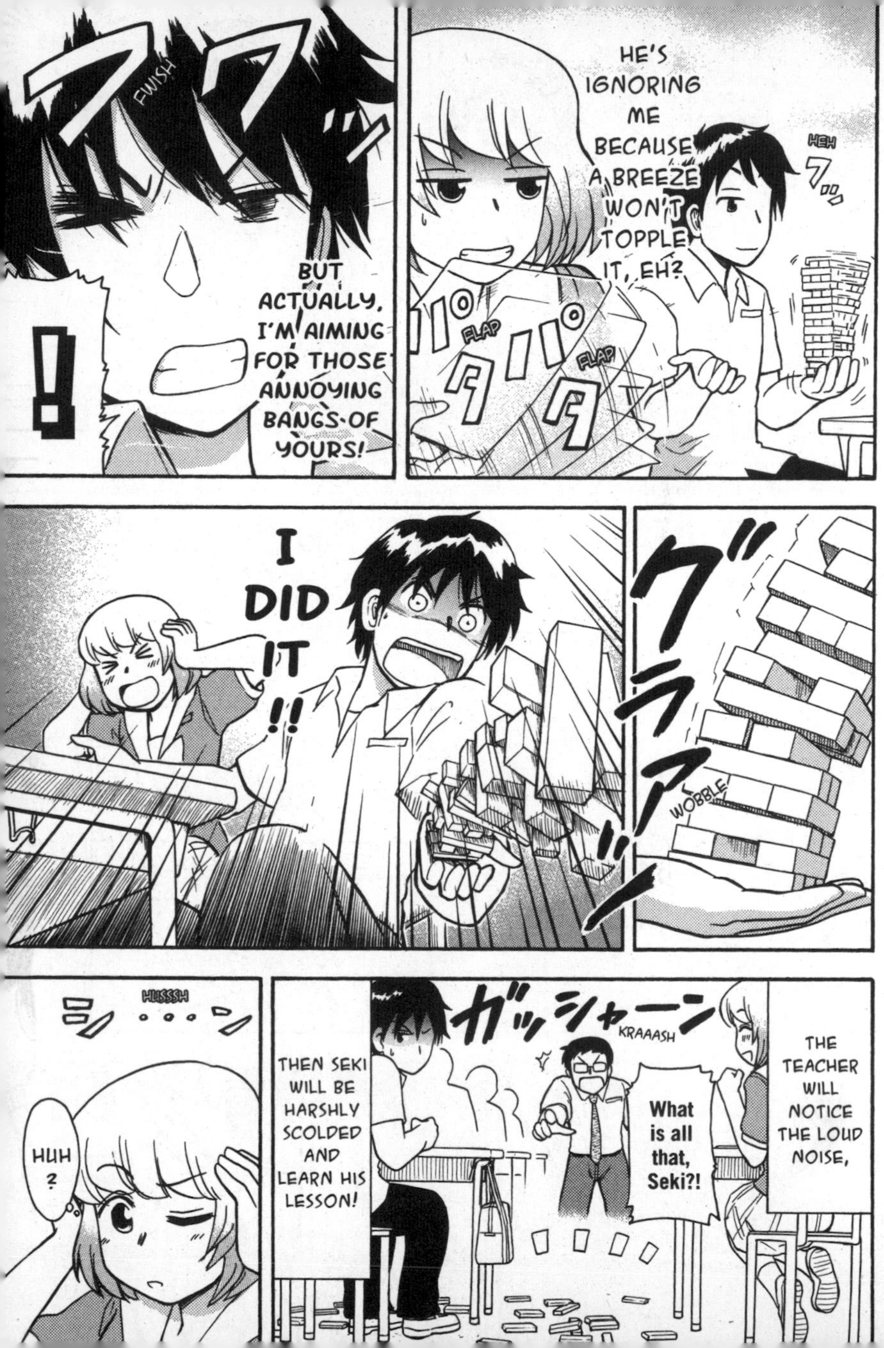
HE'S IGNORING ME BECAUSE A BREEZE WON'T TOPPLE IT, EH?
HEH
FLAP
FLAP
FWISH
BUT ACTUALLY, I'M AIMING FOR THOSE ANNOYING BANGS OF YOURS!
WOBBLE
I DID IT!!
KRAAASH
THE TEACHER WILL NOTICE THE LOUD NOISE,
What is all that, Seki?!
THEN SEKI WILL BE HARSHLY SCOLDED AND LEARN HIS LESSON!
HUSSSH
HUH?

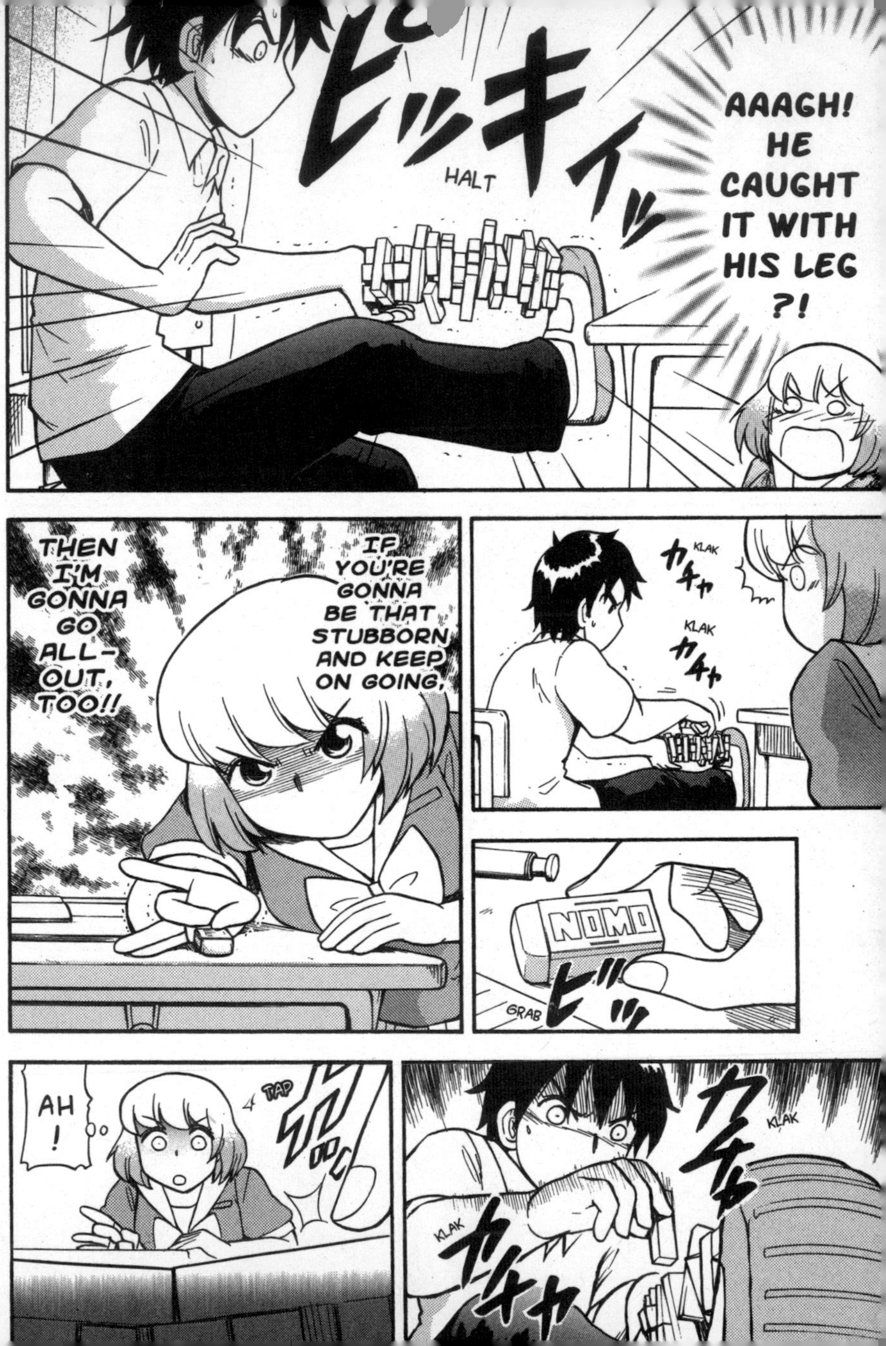
AAAGH! HE CAUGHT IT WITH HIS LEG ?!
HALT
KLAK
KLAK
NOMO
GRAB
IF YOU'RE GONNA BE THAT STUBBORN AND KEEP ON GOING,
THEN I'M GONNA GO ALL-OUT, TOO!!
KLAK
KLAK
TAP
AH!

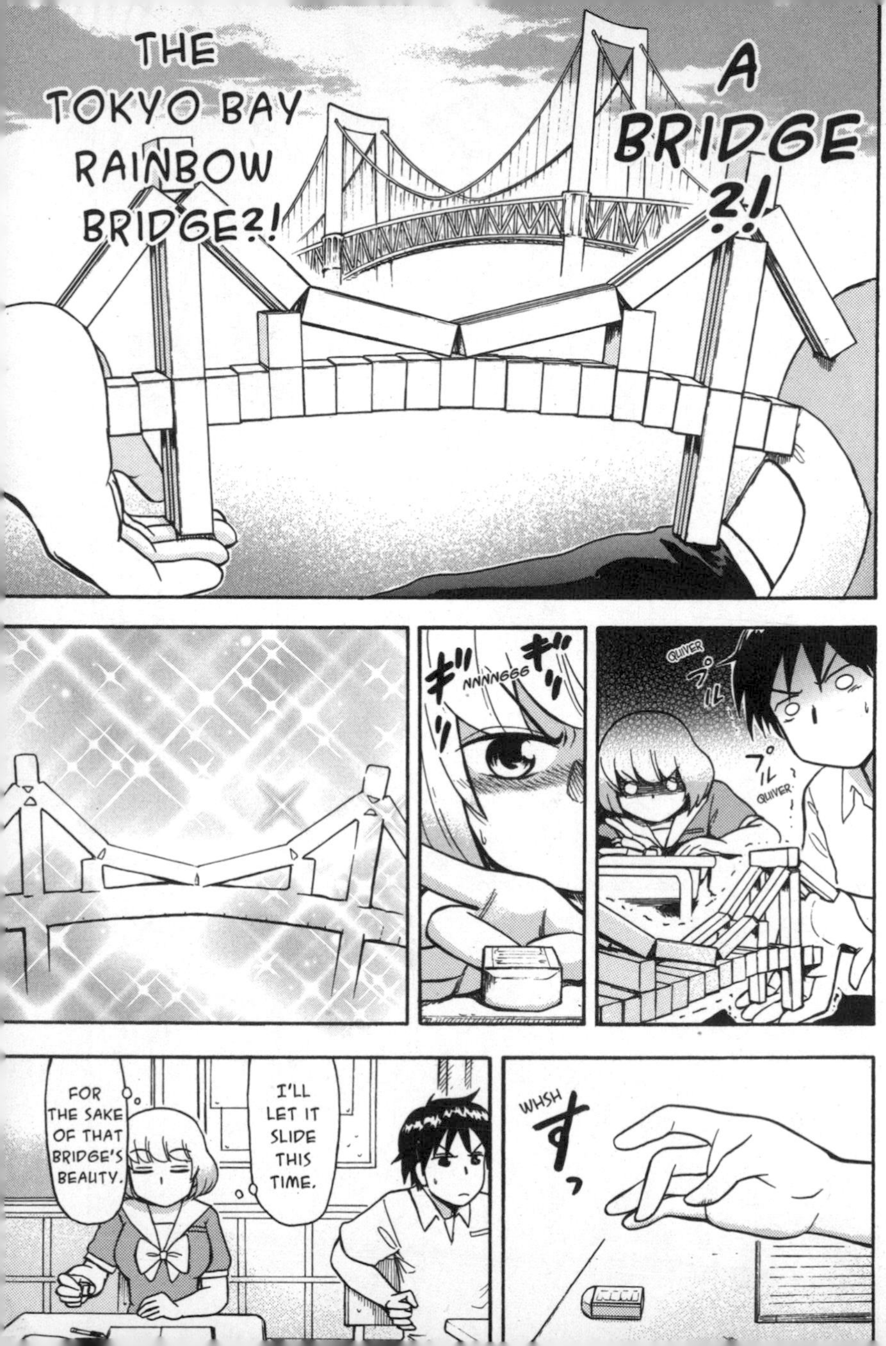
A BRIDGE ?!
THE TOKYO BAY RAINBOW BRIDGE?!
QUIVER
プル
プル
QUIVER
NNNNGGG
WHSH
すっ
I'LL LET IT SLIDE THIS TIME.
FOR THE SAKE OF THAT BRIDGE'S BEAUTY.

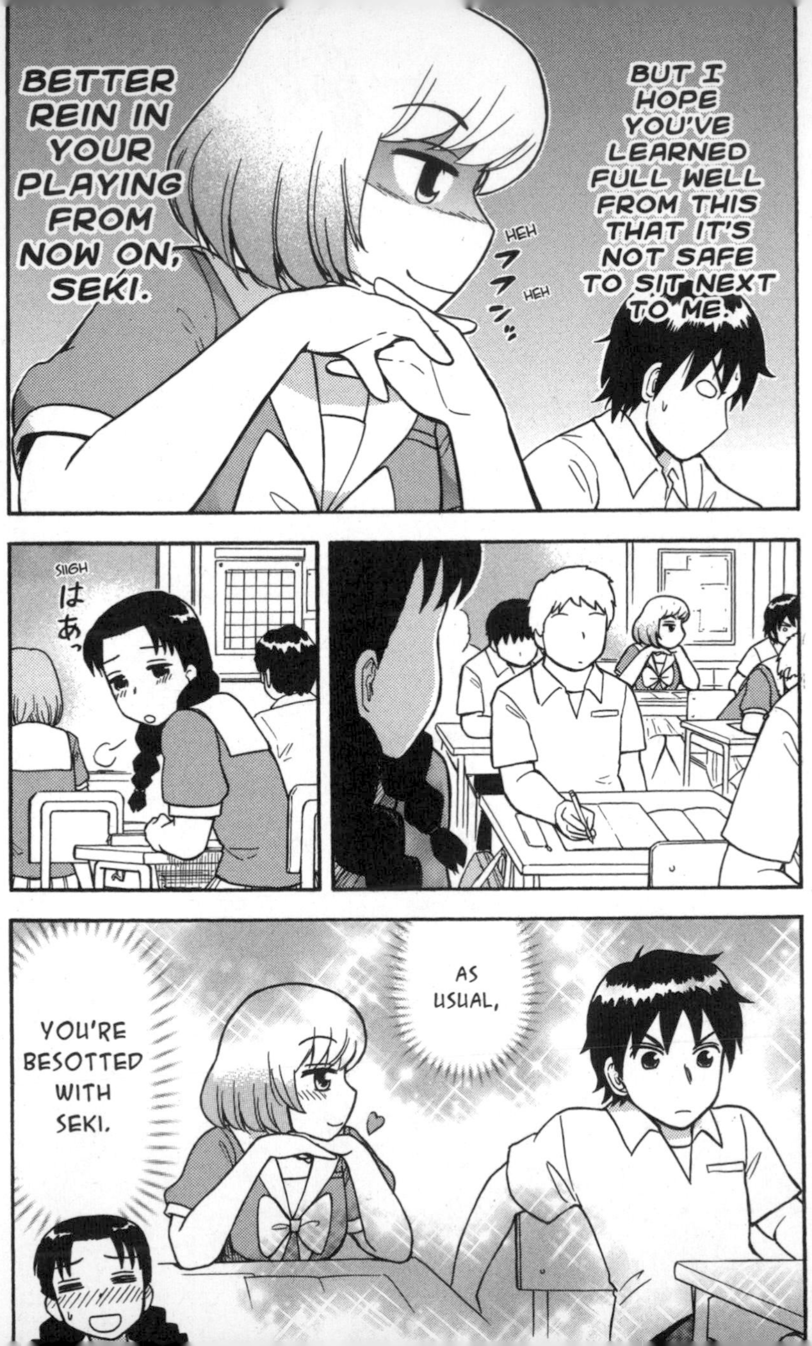
BUT I HOPE YOU'VE LEARNED FULL WELL FROM THIS THAT IT'S NOT SAFE TO SIT NEXT TO ME.
HEH
フフンッ
HEH
BETTER REIN IN YOUR PLAYING FROM NOW ON, SEKI.
SIIGH
はあっ
AS USUAL,
YOU'RE BESOTTED WITH SEKI.

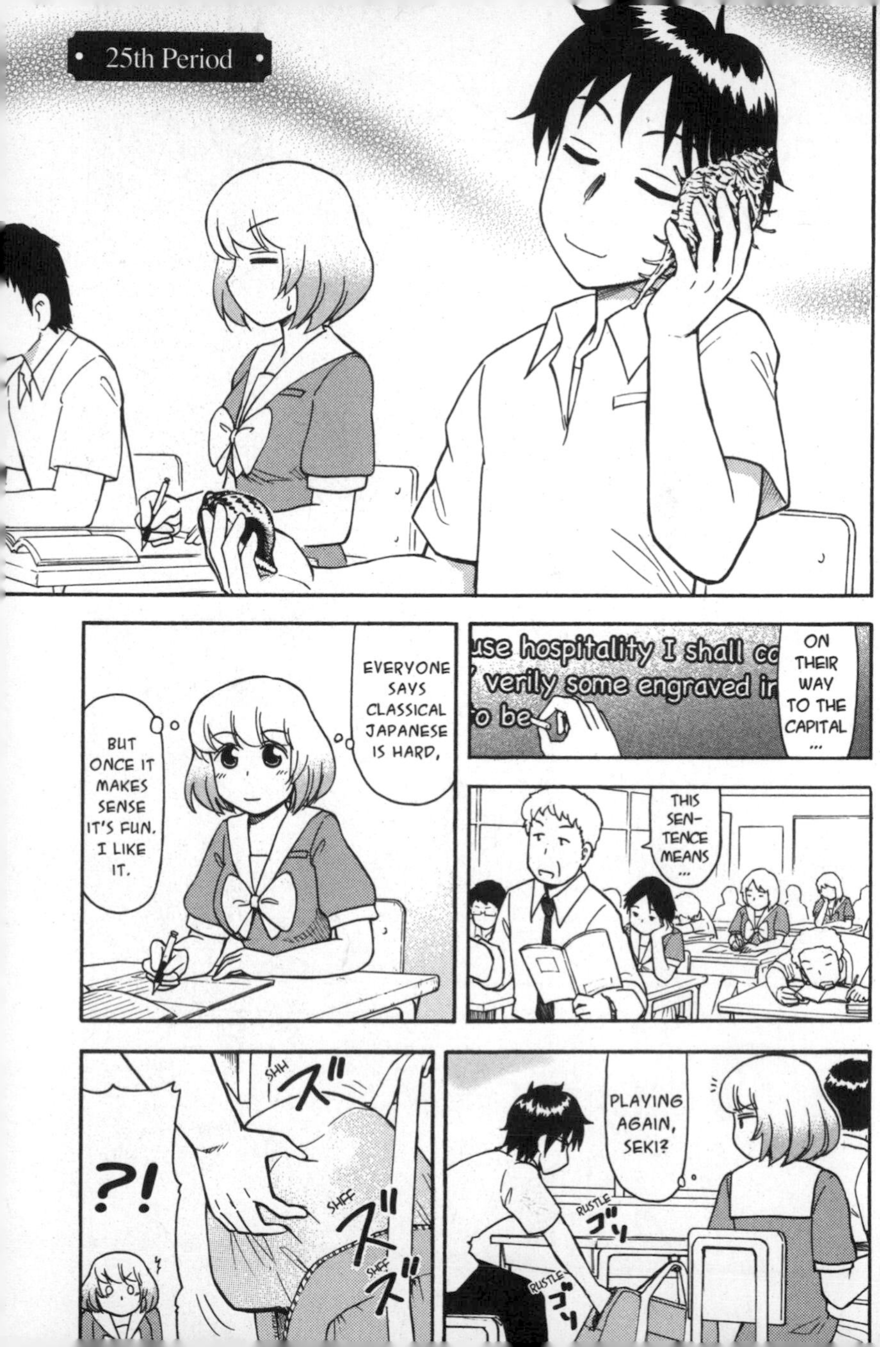
25th Period
use hospitality I shall co
verily some engraved in
o be
ON THEIR WAY TO THE CAPITAL ...
THIS SEN-TENCE MEANS ...
EVERYONE SAYS CLASSICAL JAPANESE IS HARD,
BUT ONCE IT MAKES SENSE IT'S FUN. I LIKE IT.
PLAYING AGAIN, SEKI?
RUSTLE ゴソ
RUSTLE ゴソ
SHH ズ
?!
SHFF ズ
SHFF ズ

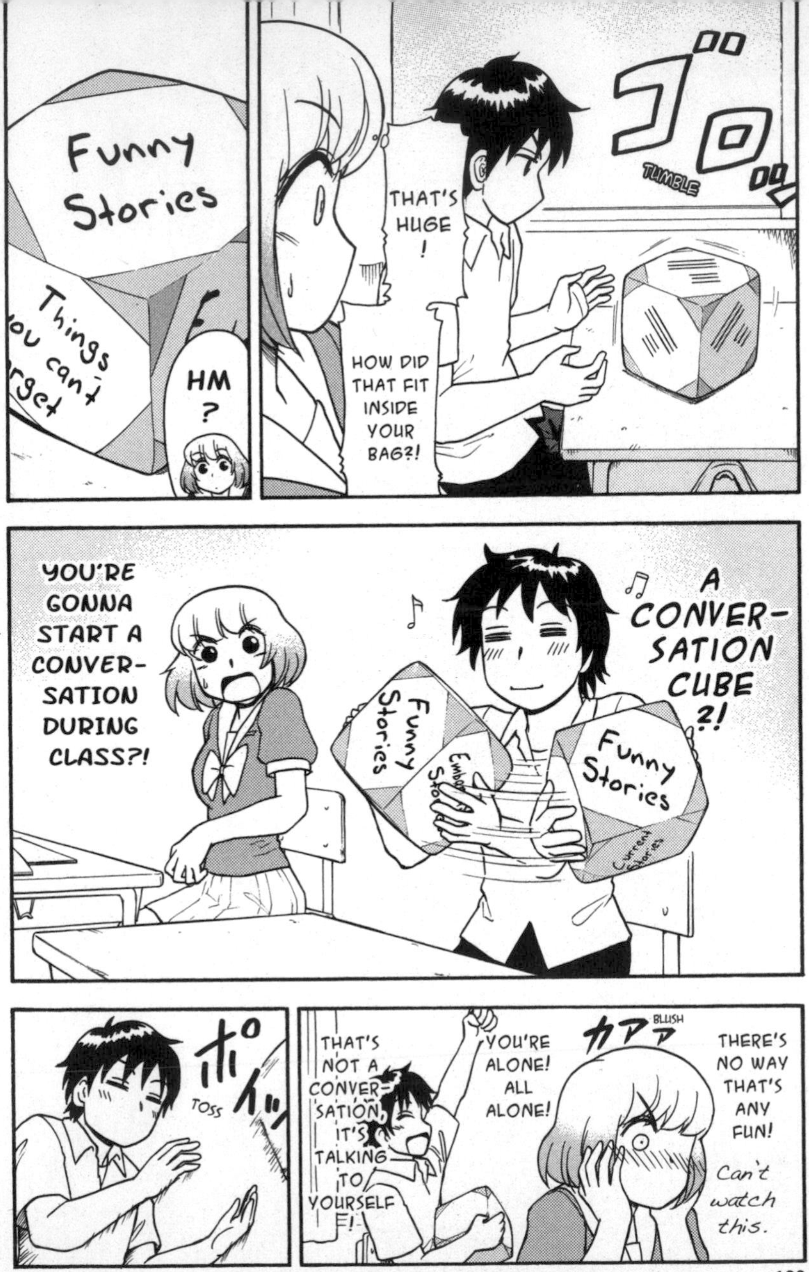

ゴロ
TUMBLE
ロロ
THAT'S HUGE!
HOW DID THAT FIT INSIDE YOUR BAG?!
Funny Stories
Things
HM?
A CONVER-SATION CUBE?!
YOU'RE GONNA START A CONVER-SATION DURING CLASS?!
Funny Stories
Funny Stories
Current Stories
カァァ
BLUSH
THERE'S NO WAY THAT'S ANY FUN!
Can't watch this.
YOU'RE ALONE! ALL ALONE!
THAT'S NOT A CONVER-SATION, IT'S TALKING TO YOURSELF!
ポイッ
TOSS

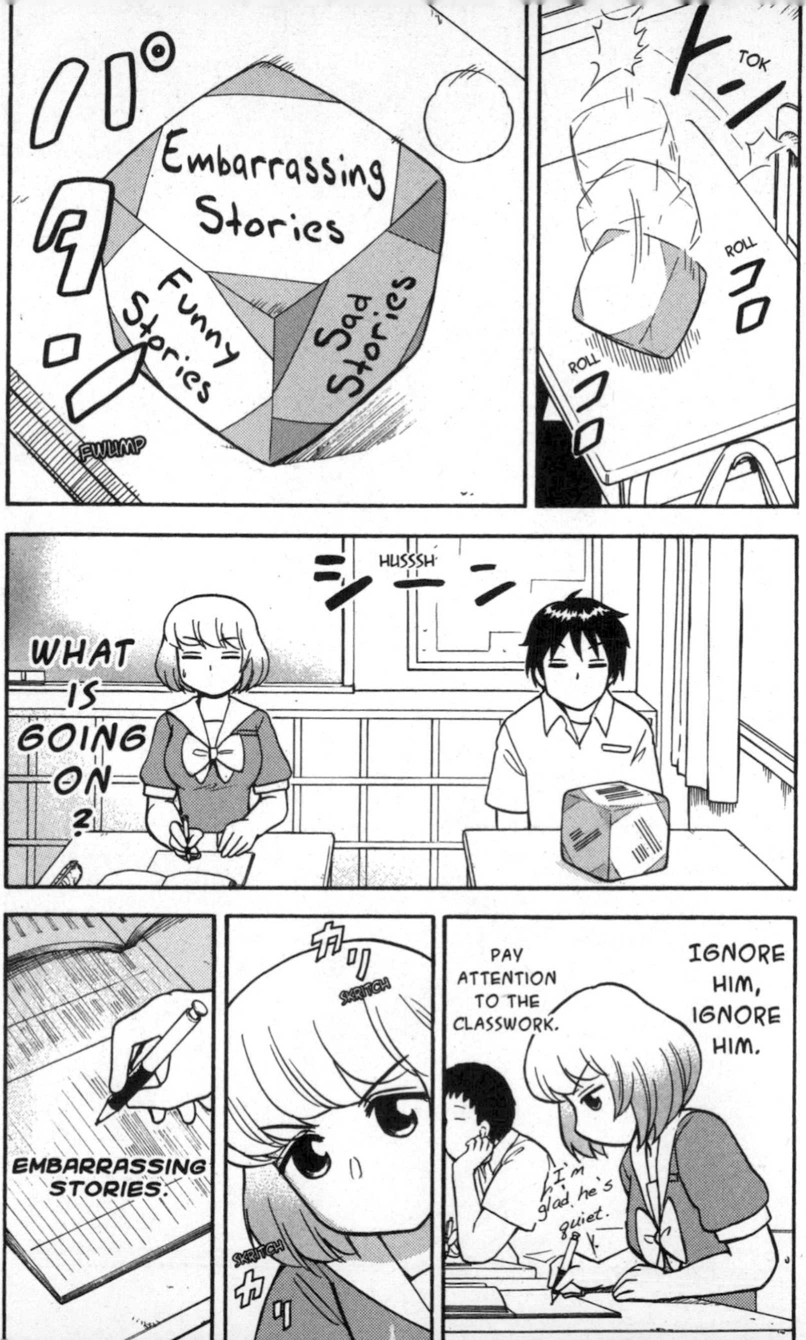
TOK
ROLL
ROLL
Embarrassing Stories
Funny Stories
Sad Stories
FWUMP
HUSSSH
WHAT IS GOING ON?
IGNORE HIM, IGNORE HIM.
PAY ATTENTION TO THE CLASSWORK.
I'm glad he's quiet.
SKRITCH
SKRITCH
EMBARRASSING STORIES.

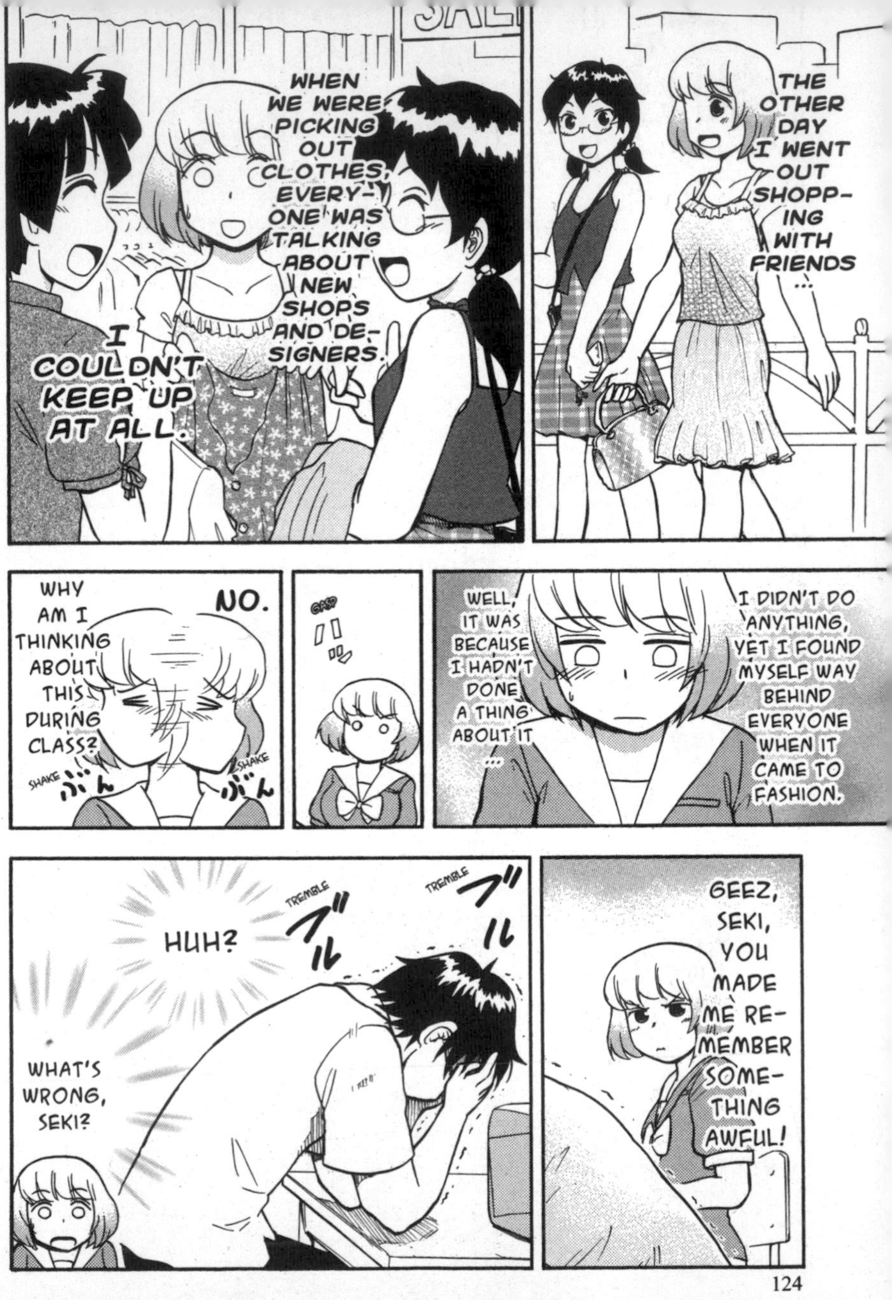
THE OTHER DAY I WENT OUT SHOPP-ING WITH FRIENDS...
WHEN WE WERE PICKING OUT CLOTHES, EVERY-ONE WAS TALKING ABOUT NEW SHOPS AND DE-SIGNERS.
I COULDN'T KEEP UP AT ALL.
I DIDN'T DO ANYTHING, YET I FOUND MYSELF WAY BEHIND EVERYONE WHEN IT CAME TO FASHION.
WELL, IT WAS BECAUSE I HADN'T DONE A THING ABOUT IT...
GASP
NO.
WHY AM I THINKING ABOUT THIS DURING CLASS?
SHAKE ぶん
SHAKE ぶん
GEEZ, SEKI, YOU MADE ME RE-MEMBER SOME-THING AWFUL!
TREMBLE ブル
TREMBLE ブル
HUH?
WHAT'S WRONG, SEKI?

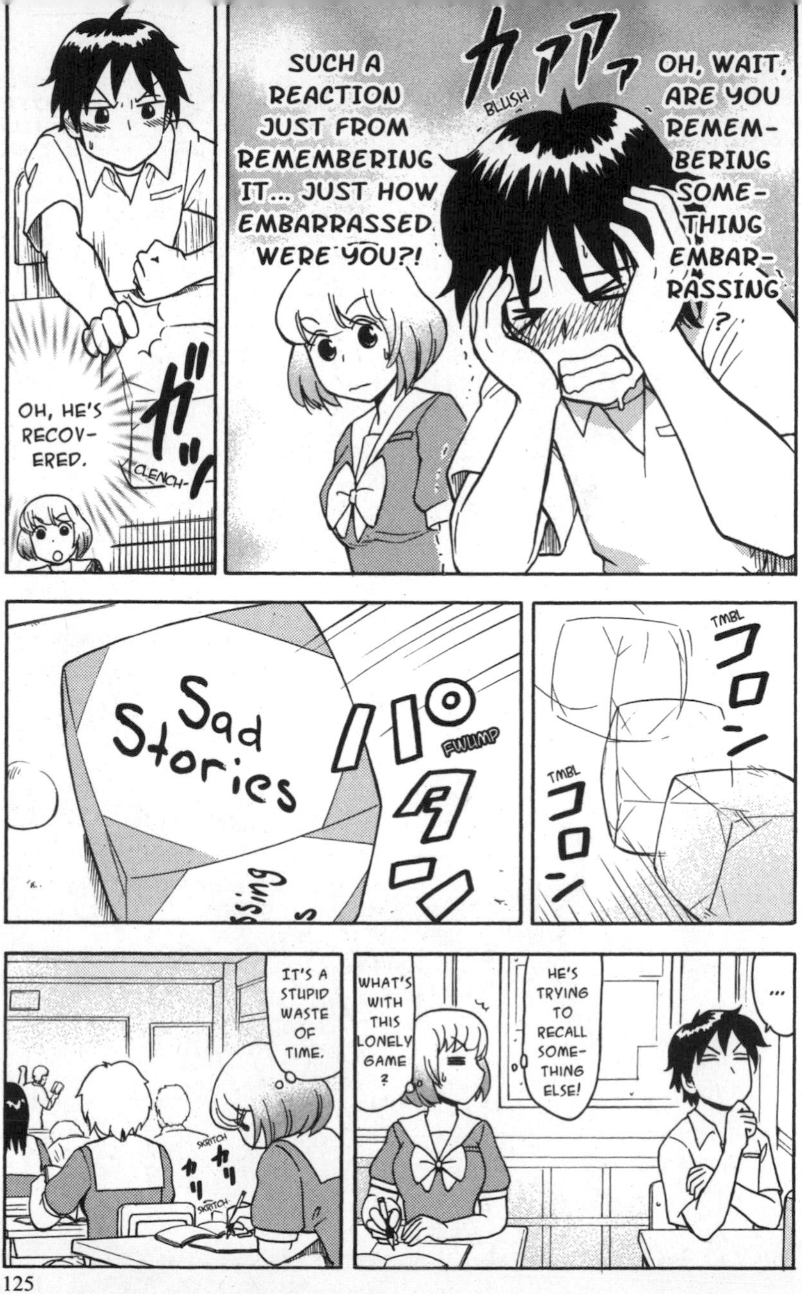
OH, WAIT, ARE YOU REMEMBERING SOMETHING EMBARRASSING?
BLUSH
SUCH A REACTION JUST FROM REMEMBERING IT... JUST HOW EMBARRASSED WERE YOU?!
CLENCH
OH, HE'S RECOVERED.
TMBL
TMBL
FWUMP
Sad Stories
...
HE'S TRYING TO RECALL SOMETHING ELSE!
WHAT'S WITH THIS LONELY GAME?
IT'S A STUPID WASTE OF TIME.
SKRITCH
SKRITCH

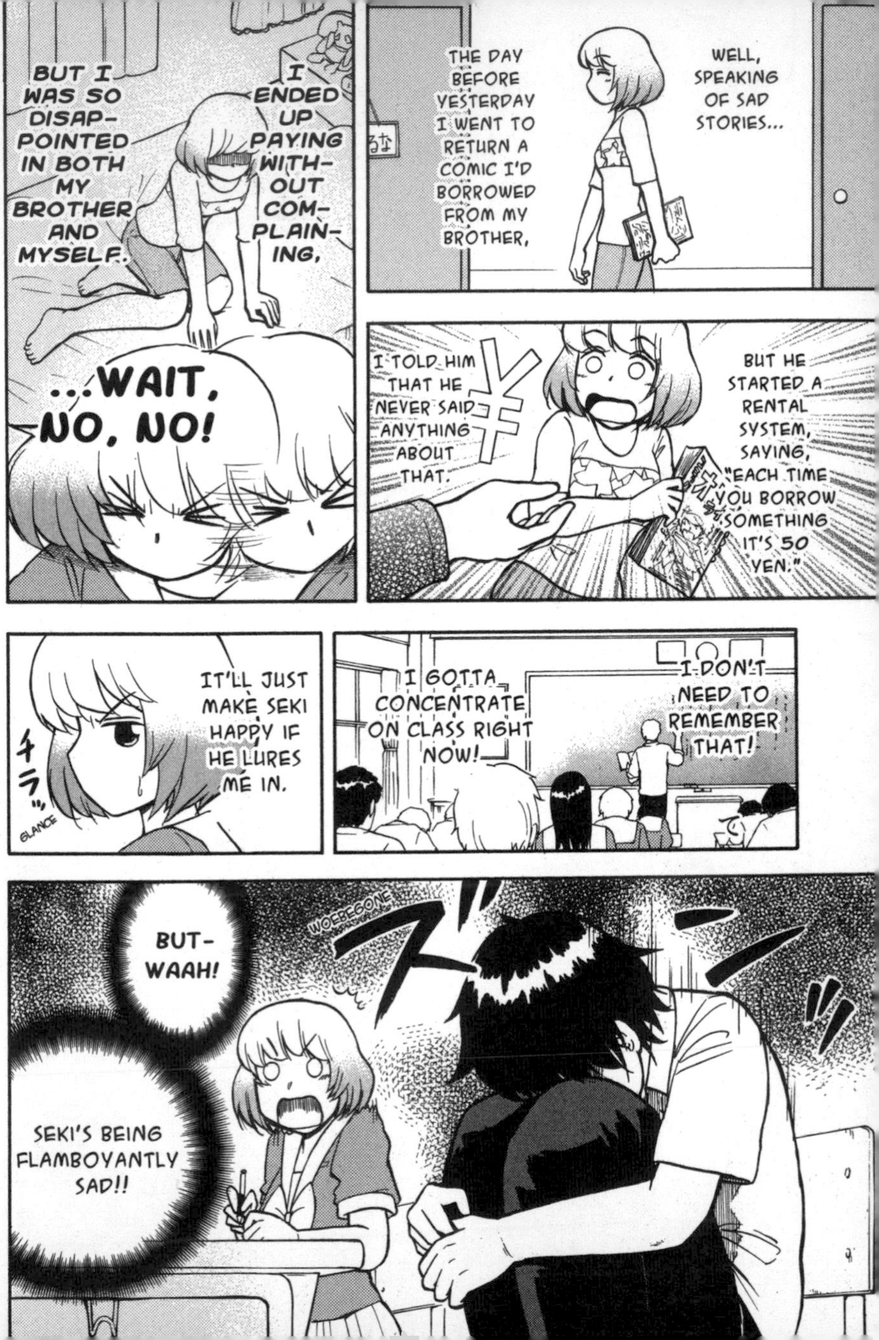
WELL, SPEAKING OF SAD STORIES...
THE DAY BEFORE YESTERDAY I WENT TO RETURN A COMIC I'D BORROWED FROM MY BROTHER,
BUT HE STARTED A RENTAL SYSTEM, SAYING, "EACH TIME YOU BORROW SOMETHING IT'S 50 YEN."
I TOLD HIM THAT HE NEVER SAID ANYTHING ABOUT THAT.
I ENDED UP PAYING WITHOUT COMPLAINING,
BUT I WAS SO DISAPPOINTED IN BOTH MY BROTHER AND MYSELF.
...WAIT, NO, NO!
I DON'T NEED TO REMEMBER THAT!
I GOTTA CONCENTRATE ON CLASS RIGHT NOW!
IT'LL JUST MAKE SEKI HAPPY IF HE LURES ME IN.
GLANCE
WOEBEGONE
BUT-WAAH!
SEKI'S BEING FLAMBOYANTLY SAD!!

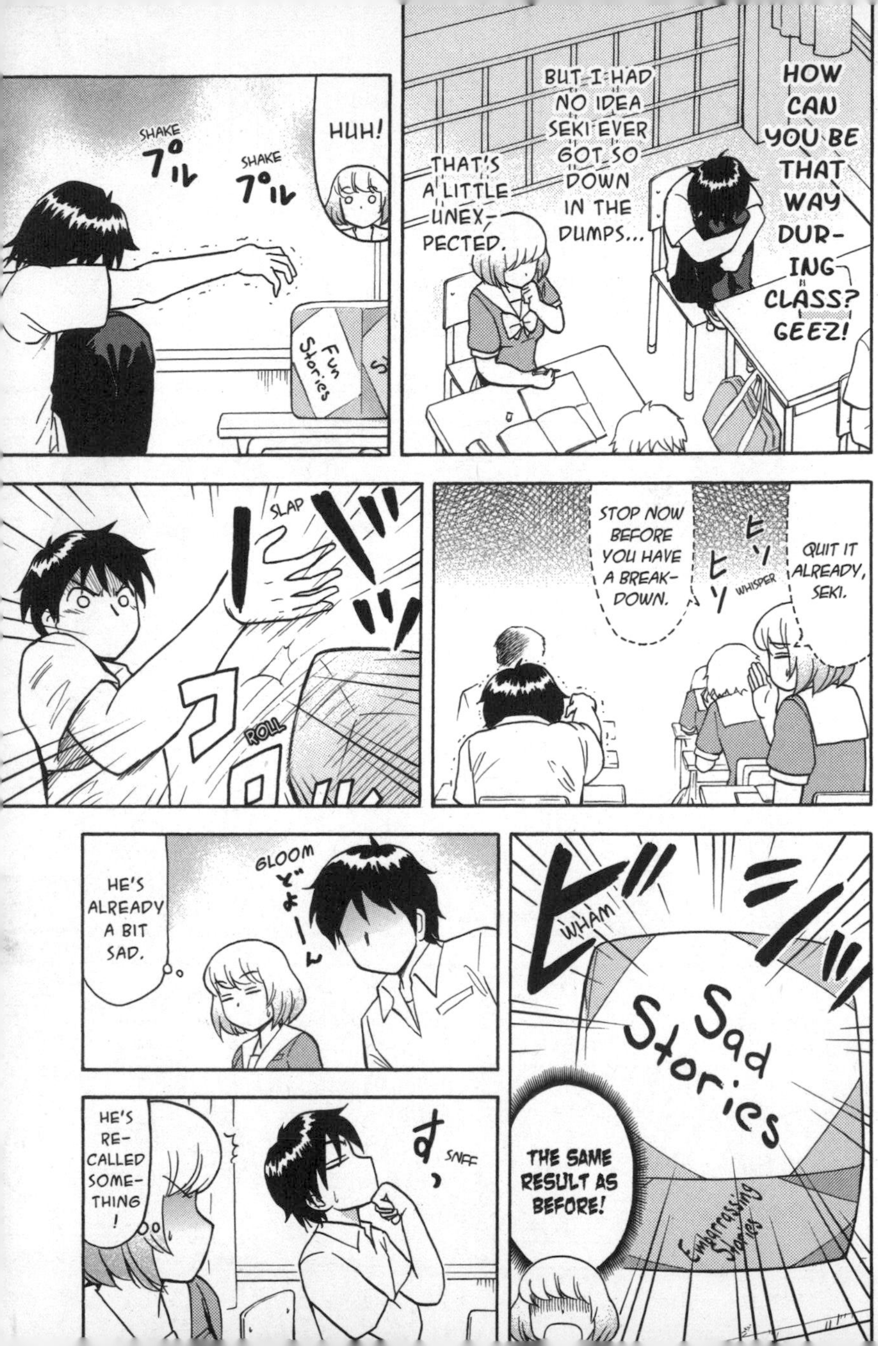
HOW CAN YOU BE THAT WAY DUR-ING CLASS? GEEZ!
BUT I HAD NO IDEA SEKI EVER GOT SO DOWN IN THE DUMPS...
THAT'S A LITTLE UNEX-PECTED.
HUH!
SHAKE プル
SHAKE プル
Fun Stories
QUIT IT ALREADY, SEKI.
ヒソ ヒソ WHISPER
STOP NOW BEFORE YOU HAVE A BREAK-DOWN.
SLAP
ROLL
WHAM
Sad Stories
THE SAME RESULT AS BEFORE!
Embarrassing Stories
GLOOM どよーん
HE'S ALREADY A BIT SAD.
す, SNFF
HE'S RE-CALLED SOME-THING!

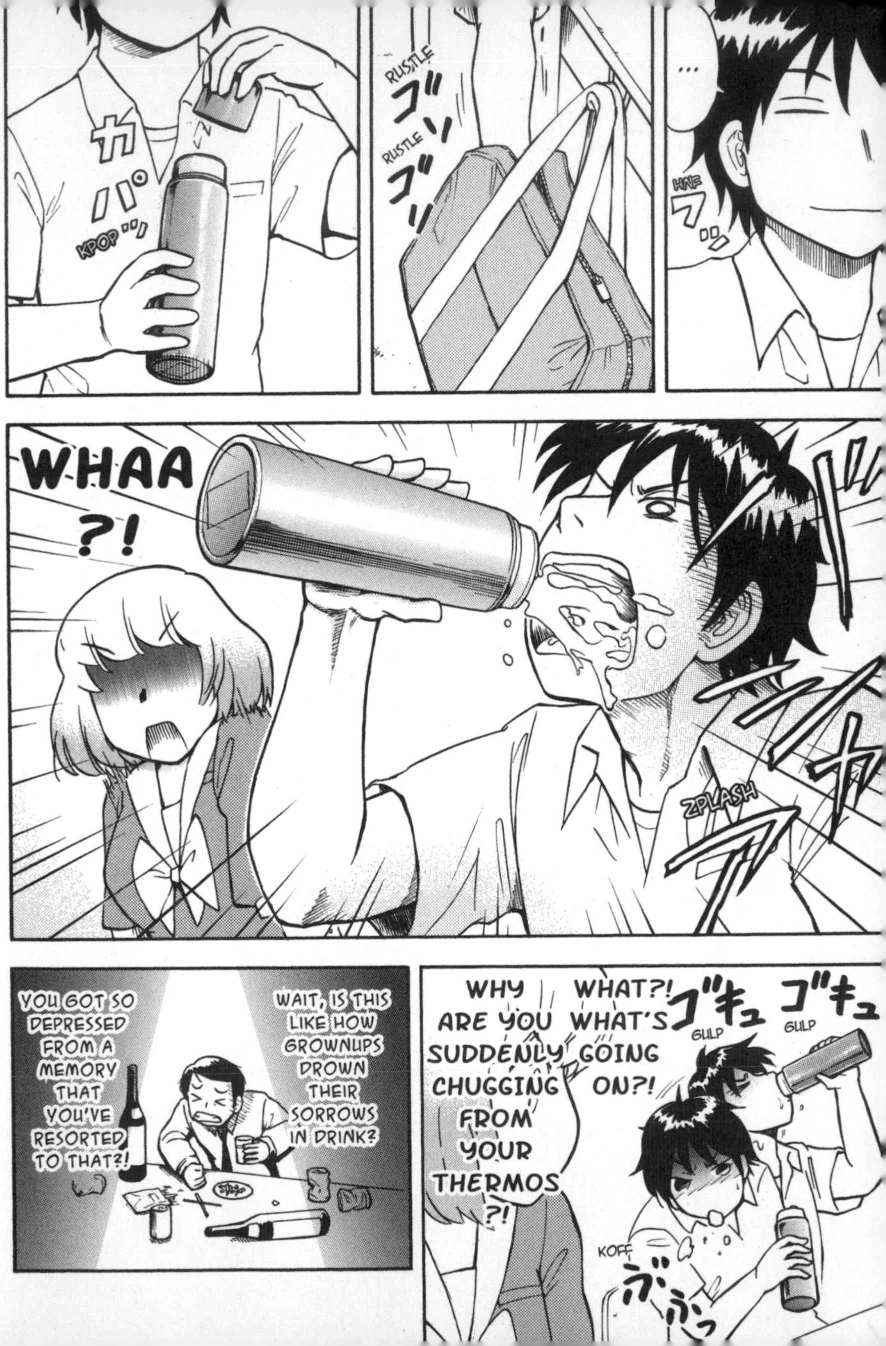
...
HNF
RUSTLE
RUSTLE
KPOP
WHAA ?!
ZPLASH
WHAT?! WHAT'S GOING ON?!
WHY ARE YOU SUDDENLY CHUGGING FROM YOUR THERMOS?!
GULP
GULP
KOFF
WAIT, IS THIS LIKE HOW GROWNUPS DROWN THEIR SORROWS IN DRINK?
YOU GOT SO DEPRESSED FROM A MEMORY THAT YOU'VE RESORTED TO THAT?!

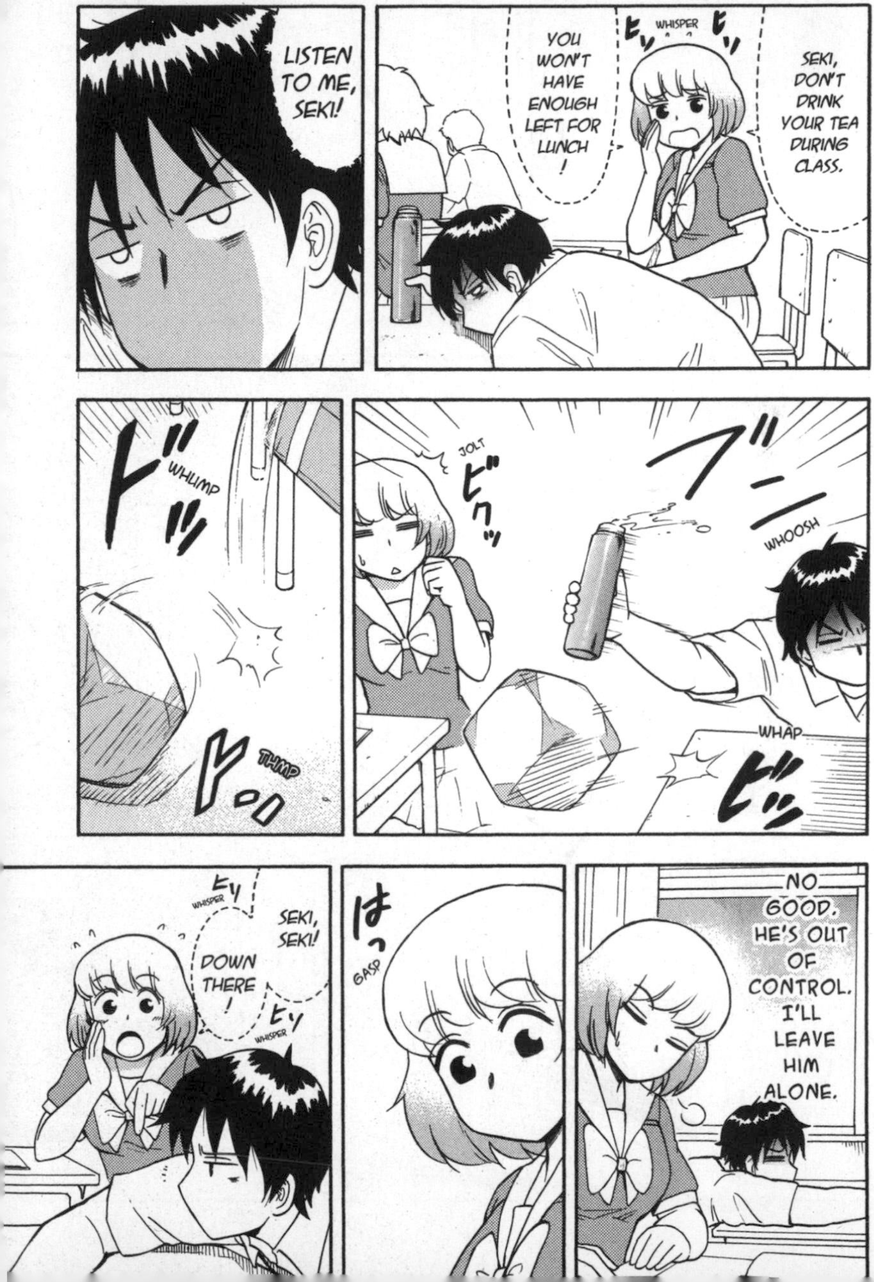

ヒッ WHISPER ヒッ
SEKI, DON'T DRINK YOUR TEA DURING CLASS.
YOU WON'T HAVE ENOUGH LEFT FOR LUNCH!
LISTEN TO ME, SEKI!
ブン WHOOSH
ビクッ JOLT
ビッ WHAP
ドッ WHUMP
ドッ THMP
NO GOOD. HE'S OUT OF CONTROL. I'LL LEAVE HIM ALONE.
はっ GASP
ヒッ WHISPER
SEKI, SEKI!
DOWN THERE!
ヒッ WHISPER

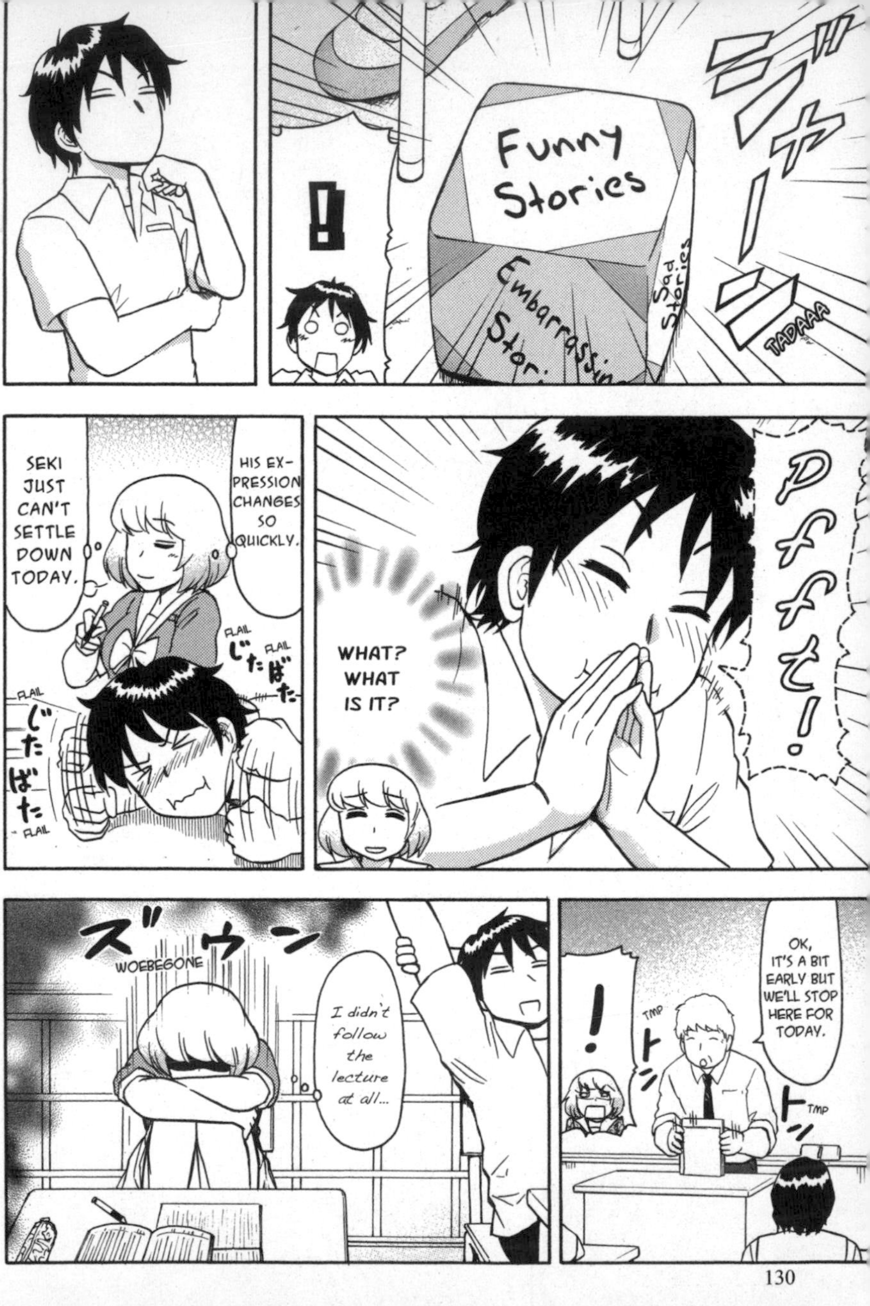

TADAAA
Funny Stories
Sad Stories
!
Pfft!
WHAT? WHAT IS IT?
HIS EX-PRESSION CHANGES SO QUICKLY.
SEKI JUST CAN'T SETTLE DOWN TODAY.
じたばた
FLAIL FLAIL
じたばた
FLAIL FLAIL
OK, IT'S A BIT EARLY BUT WE'LL STOP HERE FOR TODAY.
!
TMP
TMP
I didn't follow the lecture at all...
ズウン
WOEBEGONE

My Neighbor Seki

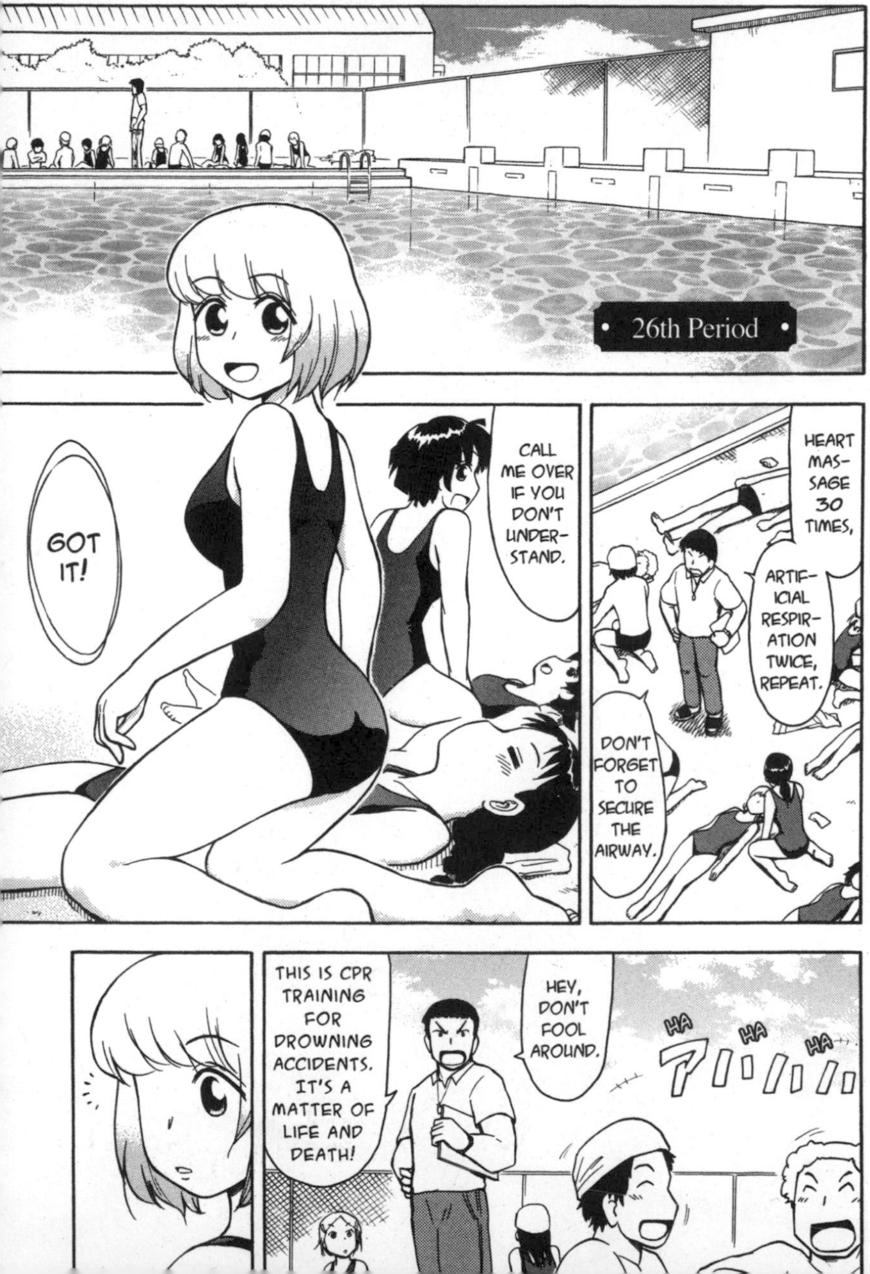
• 26th Period •
HEART MASSAGE 30 TIMES,
ARTIFICIAL RESPIRATION TWICE, REPEAT.
DON'T FORGET TO SECURE THE AIRWAY.
CALL ME OVER IF YOU DON'T UNDERSTAND.
GOT IT!
HA HA HA
HEY, DON'T FOOL AROUND.
THIS IS CPR TRAINING FOR DROWNING ACCIDENTS. IT'S A MATTER OF LIFE AND DEATH!

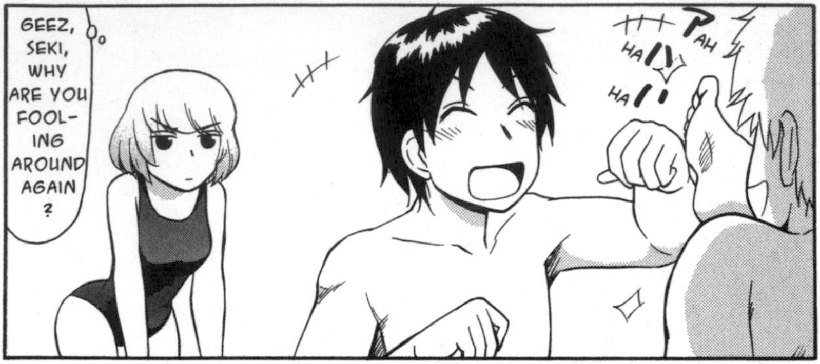
PAH
HA!!
HA!!
GEEZ, SEKI, WHY ARE YOU FOOL-ING AROUND AGAIN?

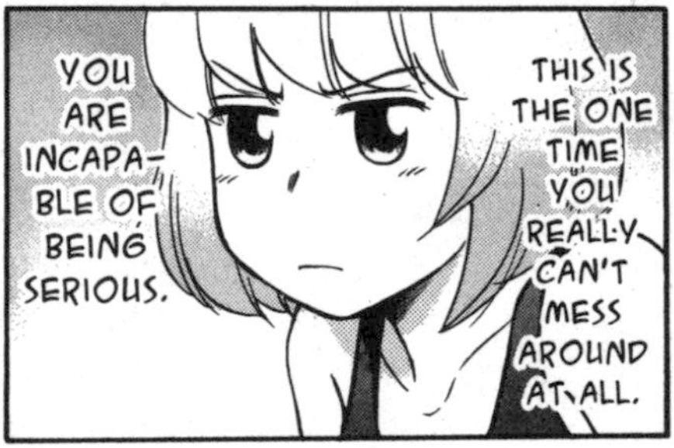
THIS IS THE ONE TIME YOU REALLY CAN'T MESS AROUND AT ALL.
YOU ARE INCAPA-BLE OF BEING SERIOUS.

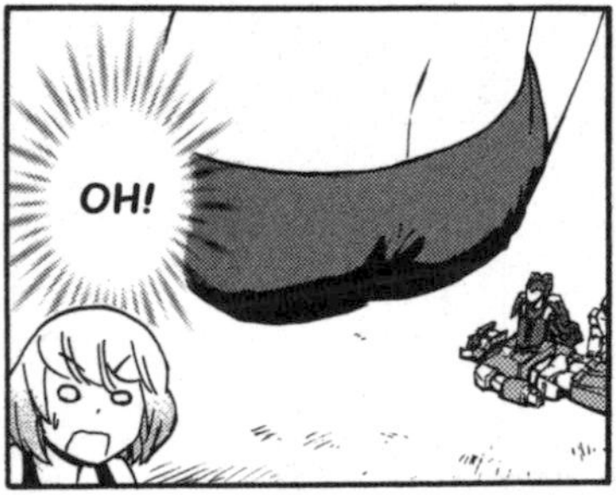
OH!

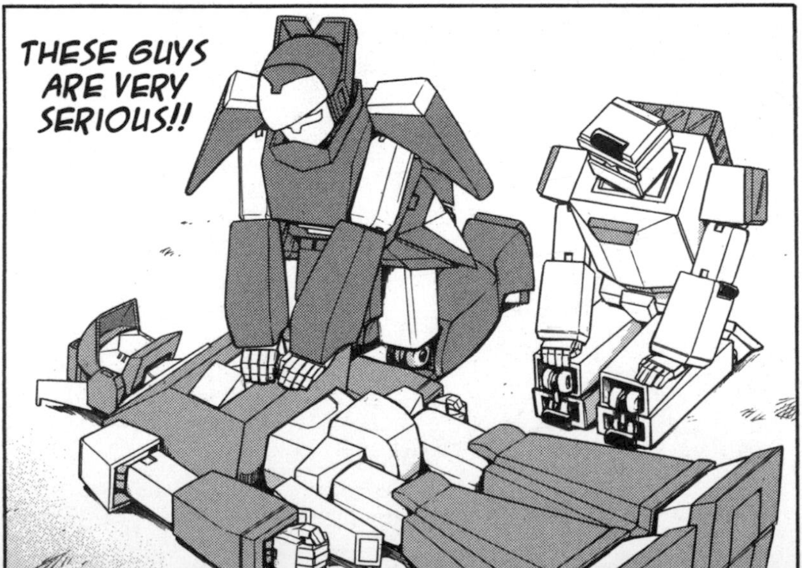
THESE GUYS ARE VERY SERIOUS!!

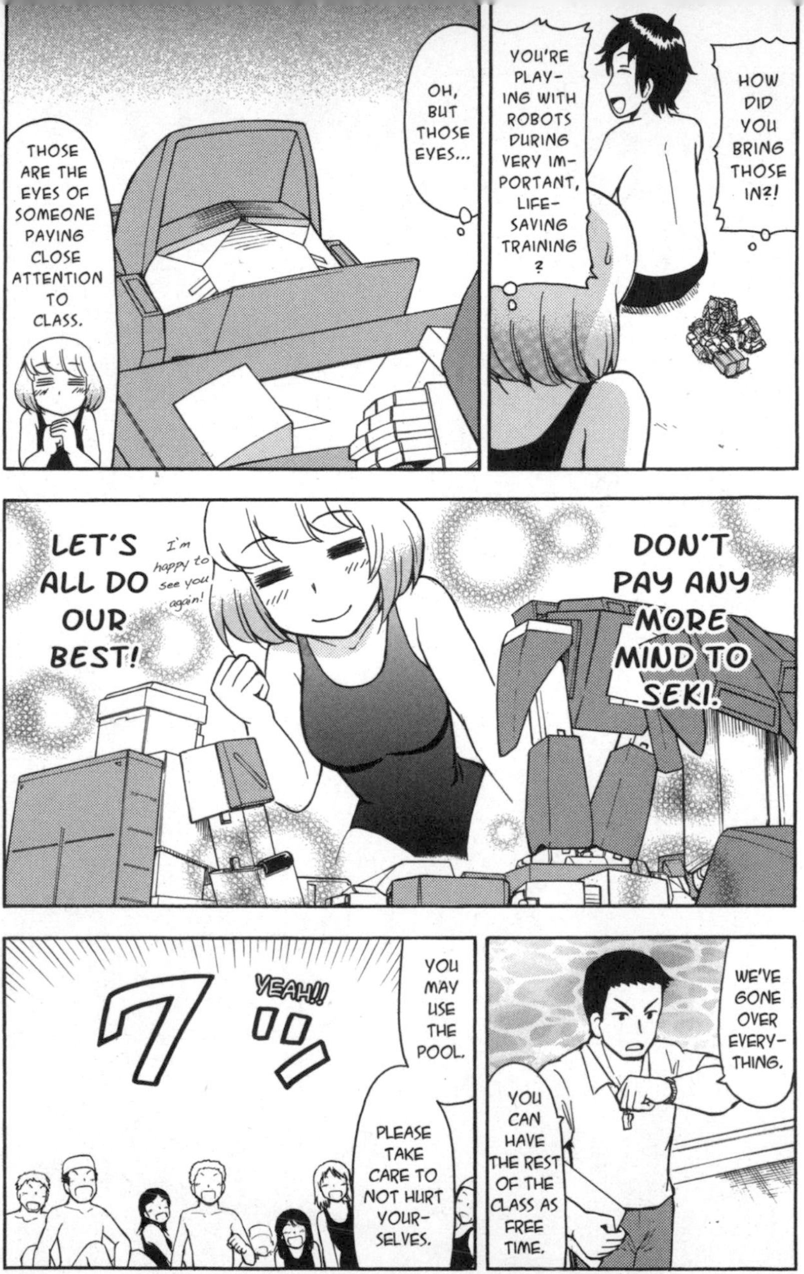

HOW DID YOU BRING THOSE IN?!
YOU'RE PLAYING WITH ROBOTS DURING VERY IMPORTANT, LIFE-SAVING TRAINING?
OH, BUT THOSE EYES...
THOSE ARE THE EYES OF SOMEONE PAYING CLOSE ATTENTION TO CLASS.
DON'T PAY ANY MORE MIND TO SEKI.
I'm happy to see you again!
LET'S ALL DO OUR BEST!
WE'VE GONE OVER EVERYTHING.
YOU CAN HAVE THE REST OF THE CLASS AS FREE TIME.
YOU MAY USE THE POOL.
PLEASE TAKE CARE TO NOT HURT YOURSELVES.
YEAH!!

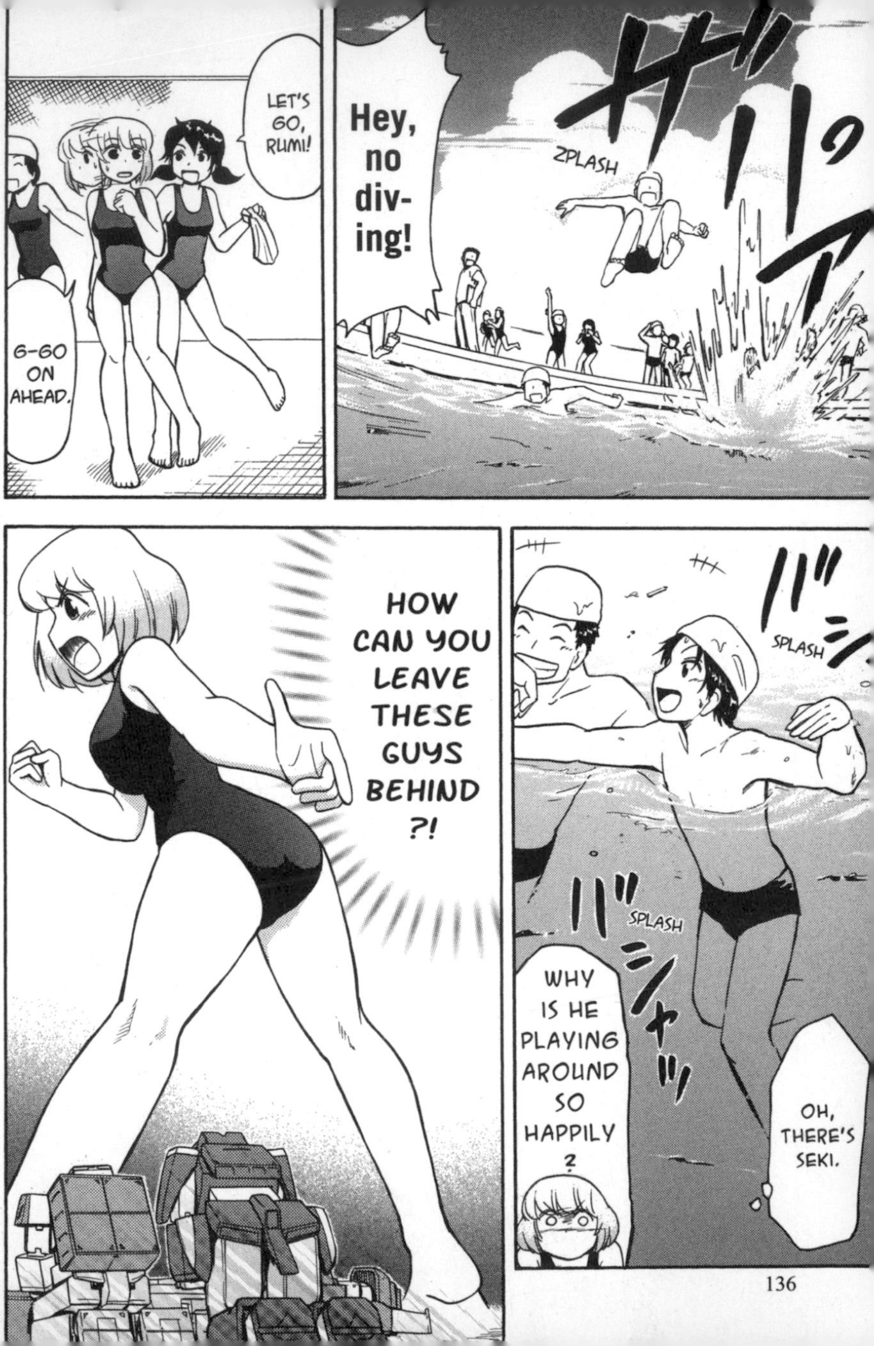
ZPLASH
Hey, no div- ing!
LET'S GO, RUMI!
G-GO ON AHEAD.
SPLASH
SPLASH
OH, THERE'S SEKI.
WHY IS HE PLAYING AROUND SO HAPPILY?
HOW CAN YOU LEAVE THESE GUYS BEHIND?!

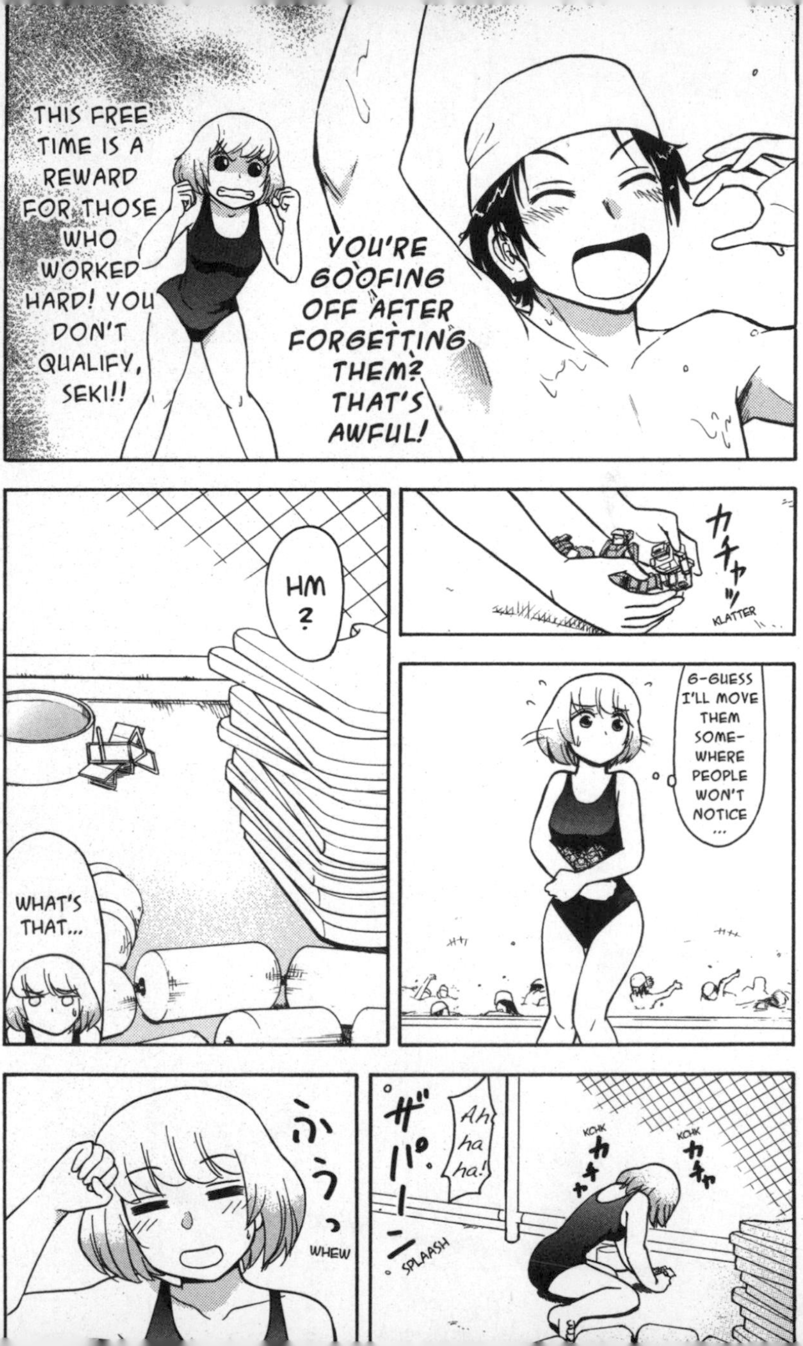
YOU'RE GOOFING OFF AFTER FORGETTING THEM? THAT'S AWFUL!
THIS FREE TIME IS A REWARD FOR THOSE WHO WORKED HARD! YOU DON'T QUALIFY, SEKI!!
カチャッ
KLATTER
G-GUESS I'LL MOVE THEM SOMEWHERE PEOPLE WON'T NOTICE...
HM?
WHAT'S THAT...
カチャ
KCHK
カチャ
KCHK
Ah ha ha!
ザパーン
SPLAASH
ふうっ
WHEW

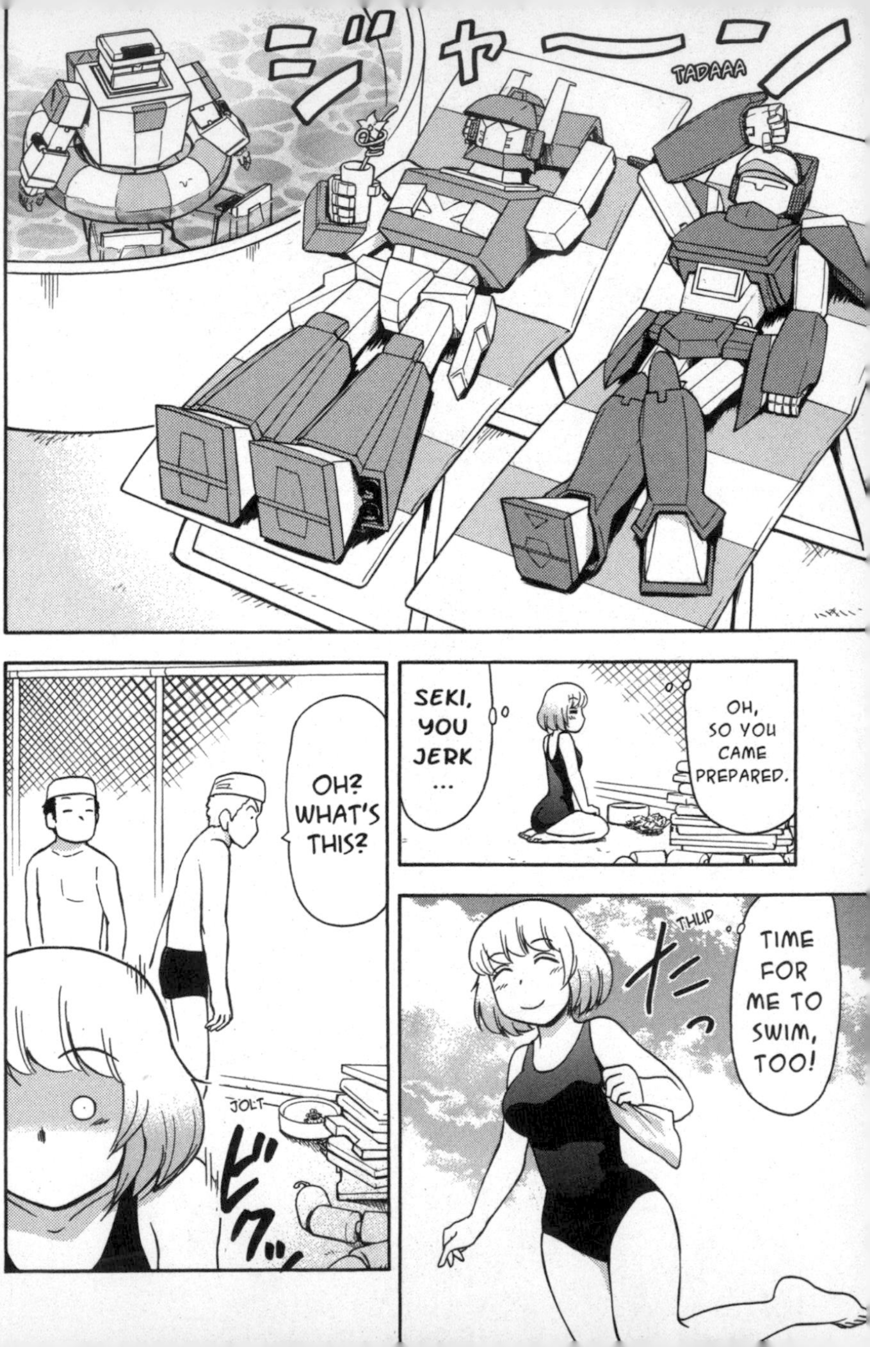
TADAAA
OH, SO YOU CAME PREPARED.
SEKI, YOU JERK ...
THUP
TIME FOR ME TO SWIM, TOO!
OH? WHAT'S THIS?
JOLT

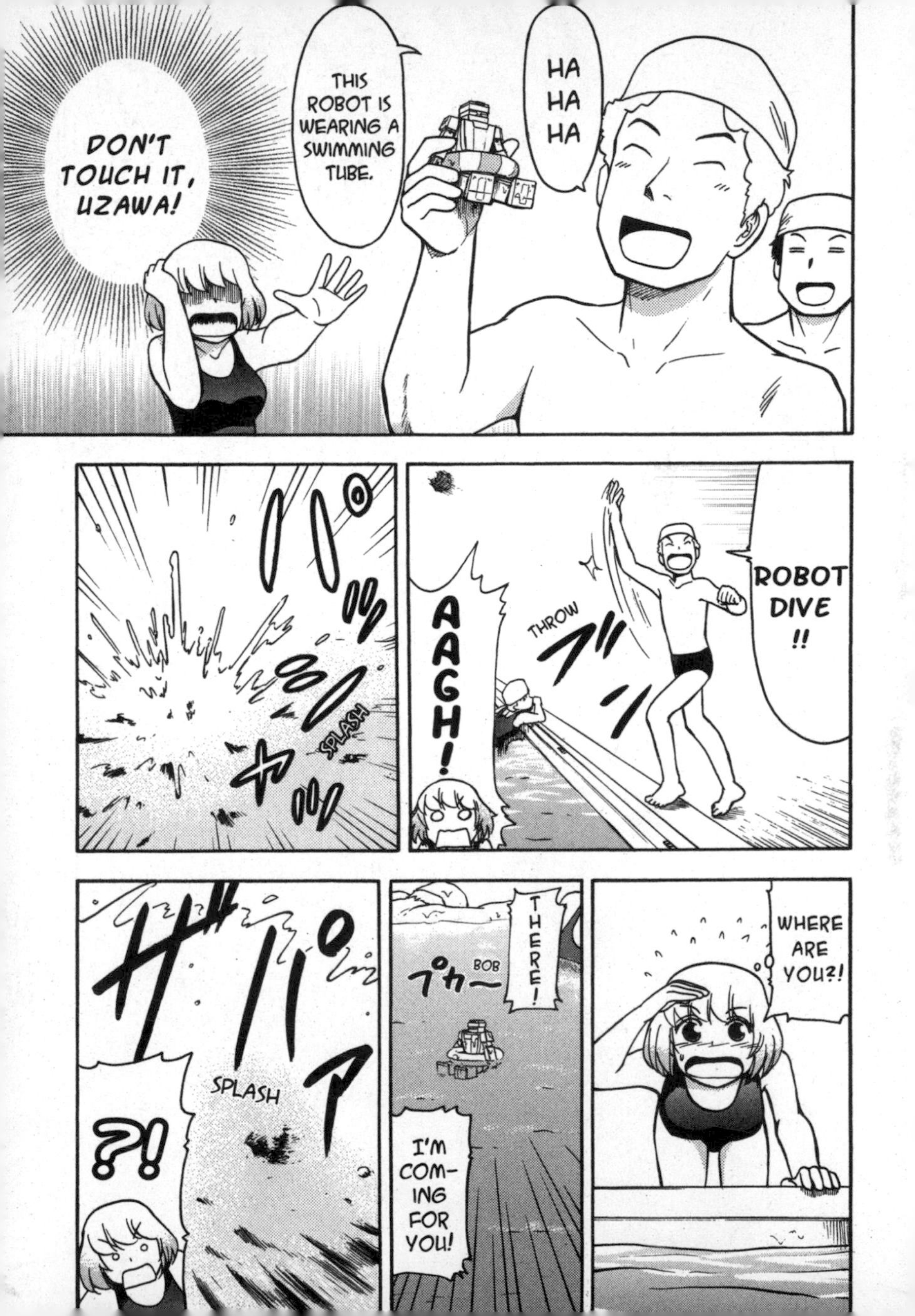
HA HA HA
THIS ROBOT IS WEARING A SWIMMING TUBE.
DON'T TOUCH IT, UZAWA!
ROBOT DIVE !!
THROW
AAGH!
SPLASH
WHERE ARE YOU?!
THERE!
BOB
I'M COMING FOR YOU!
SPLASH
?!

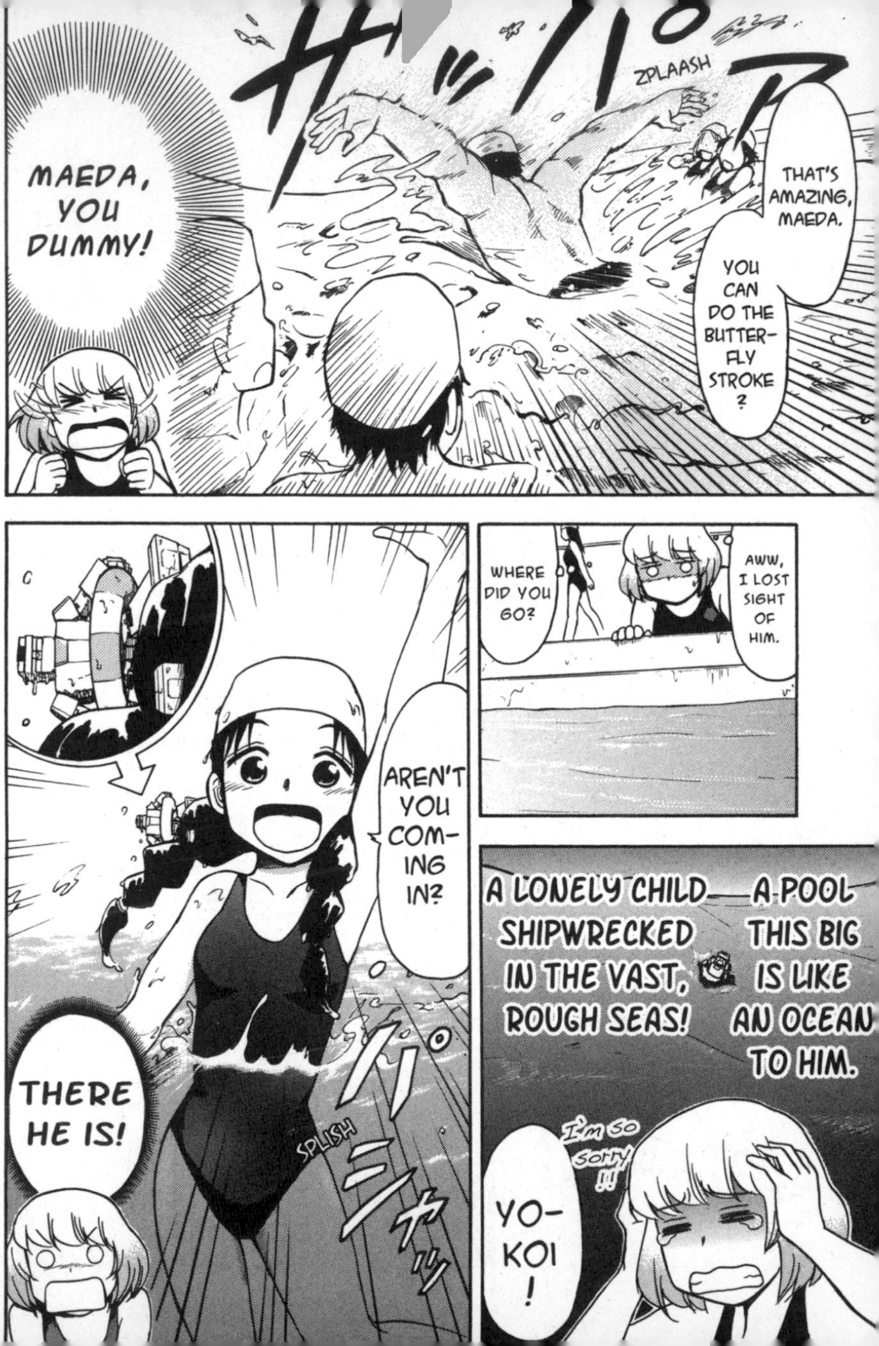
ZPLAASH
THAT'S AMAZING, MAEDA.
YOU CAN DO THE BUTTER-FLY STROKE?
MAEDA, YOU DUMMY!
AWW, I LOST SIGHT OF HIM.
WHERE DID YOU GO?
A POOL THIS BIG IS LIKE AN OCEAN TO HIM.
A LONELY CHILD SHIPWRECKED IN THE VAST, ROUGH SEAS!
I'm so sorry!!
YO-KOI!
AREN'T YOU COM-ING IN?
SPLISH
THERE HE IS!

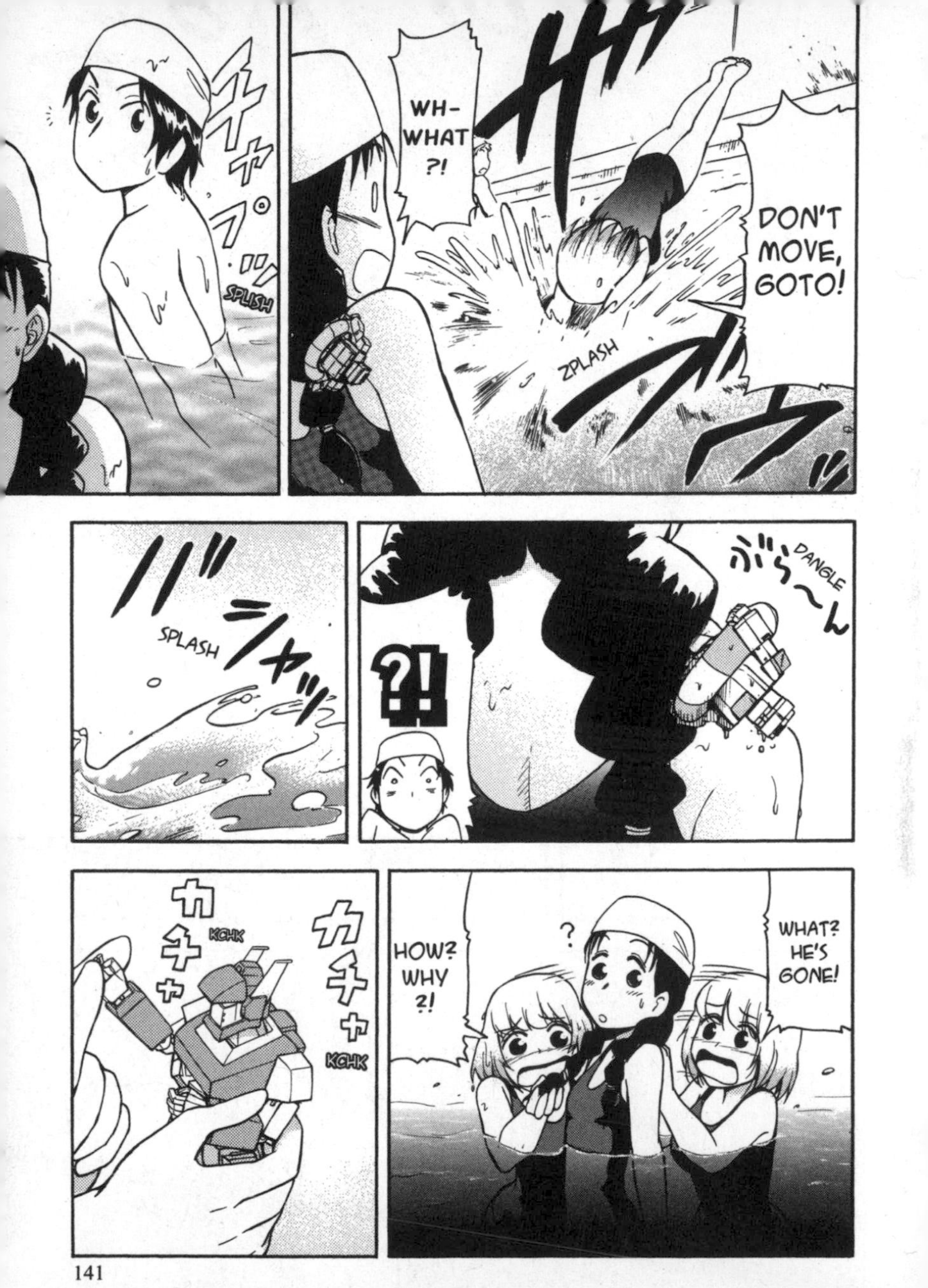
WH-WHAT?!
DON'T MOVE, GOTO!
ZPLASH
SPLISH
ぶら〜ん
DANGLE
?!
バシャッ
SPLASH
WHAT? HE'S GONE!
HOW? WHY?!
カチャ
KCHK
カチャ
KCHK

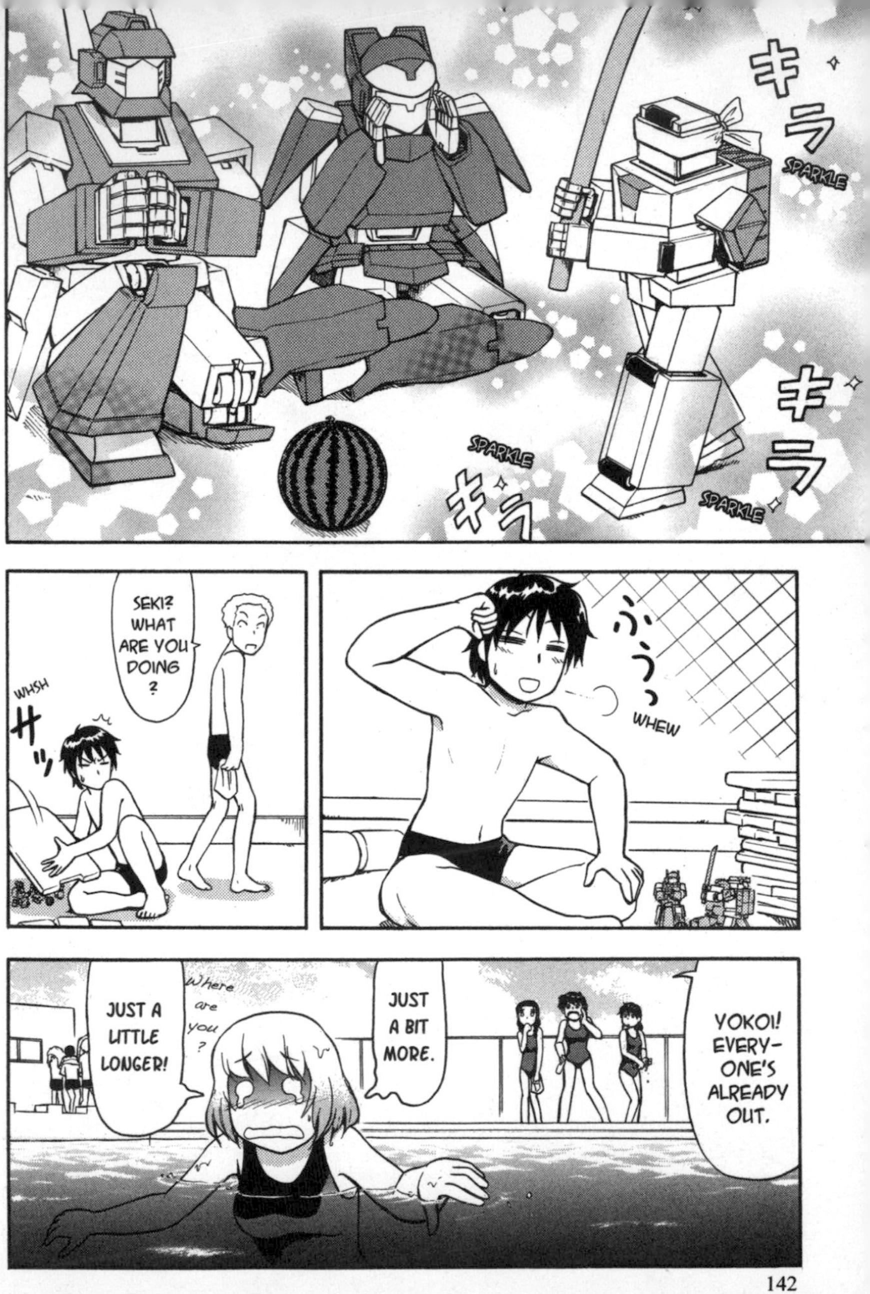
キラ
SPARKLE
キラ
SPARKLE
キラ
SPARKLE
ふうっ
WHEW
SEKI!? WHAT ARE YOU DOING?
WHSH
サッ
YOKOI! EVERY-ONE'S ALREADY OUT.
JUST A BIT MORE.
Where are you?
JUST A LITTLE LONGER!

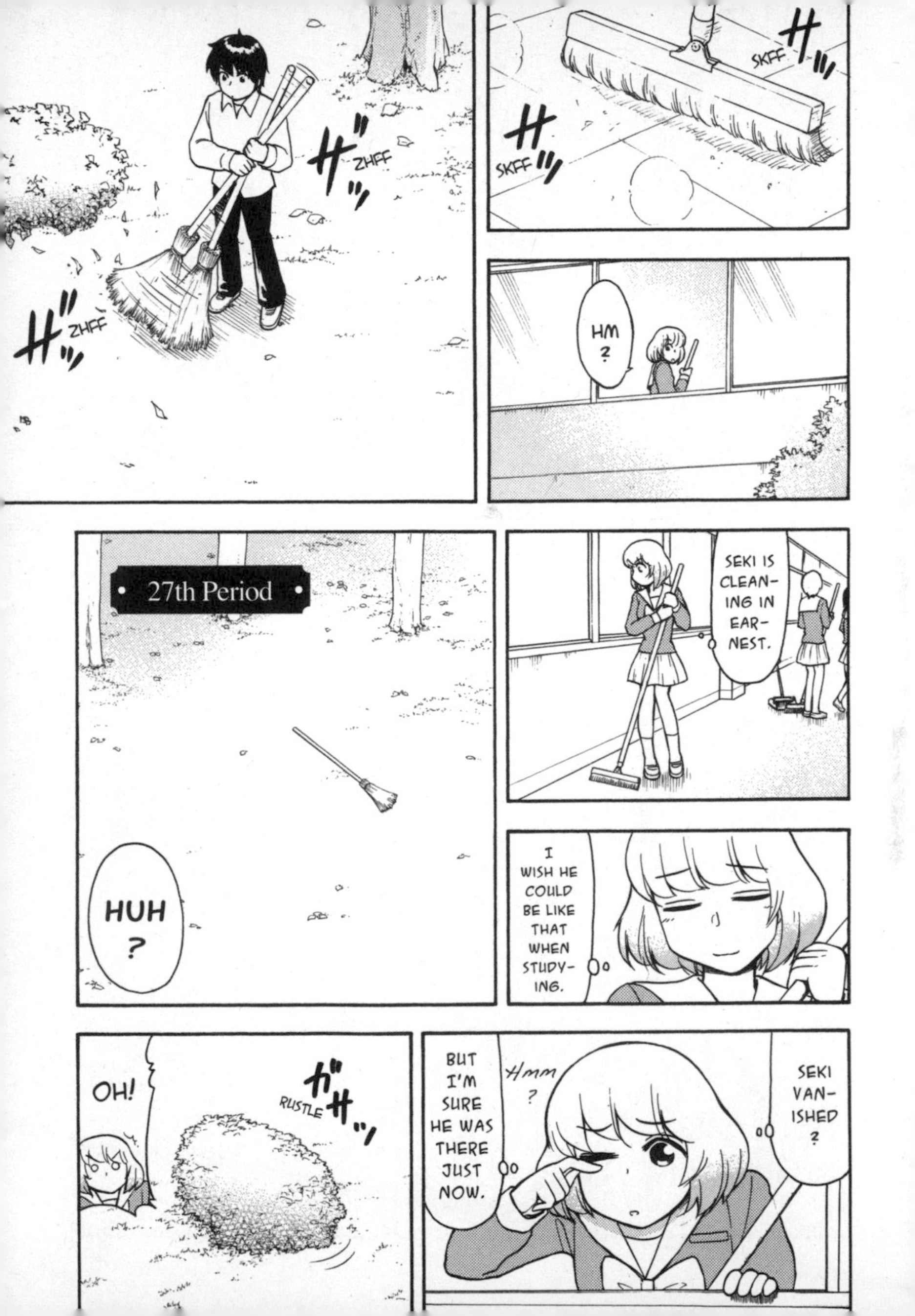

ザッ
SKFF
ザッ
SKFF
HM?
ザッ
ZHFF
ザッ
ZHFF
SEKI IS CLEANING IN EARNEST.
I WISH HE COULD BE LIKE THAT WHEN STUDYING.
27th Period
HUH?
SEKI VANISHED?
Hmm?
BUT I'M SURE HE WAS THERE JUST NOW.
ガサッ
RUSTLE
OH!

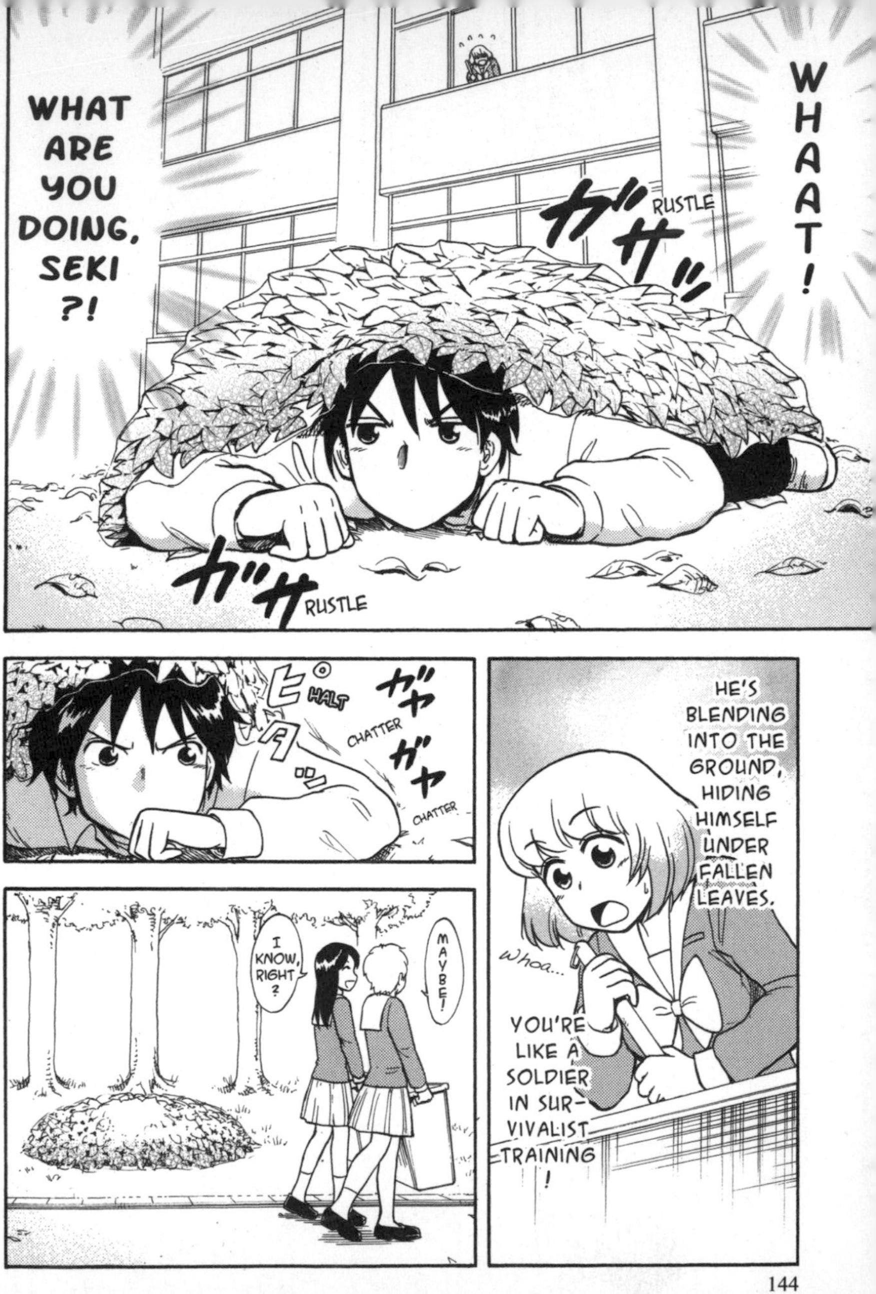
WHAAT!
ガサッ
RUSTLE
WHAT ARE YOU DOING, SEKI?!
ガサ
RUSTLE
HE'S BLENDING INTO THE GROUND, HIDING HIMSELF UNDER FALLEN LEAVES.
Whoa...
YOU'RE LIKE A SOLDIER IN SUR-VIVALIST TRAINING!
ピタッ
HALT
ガヤガヤ
CHATTER
CHATTER
MAYBE!
I KNOW, RIGHT?

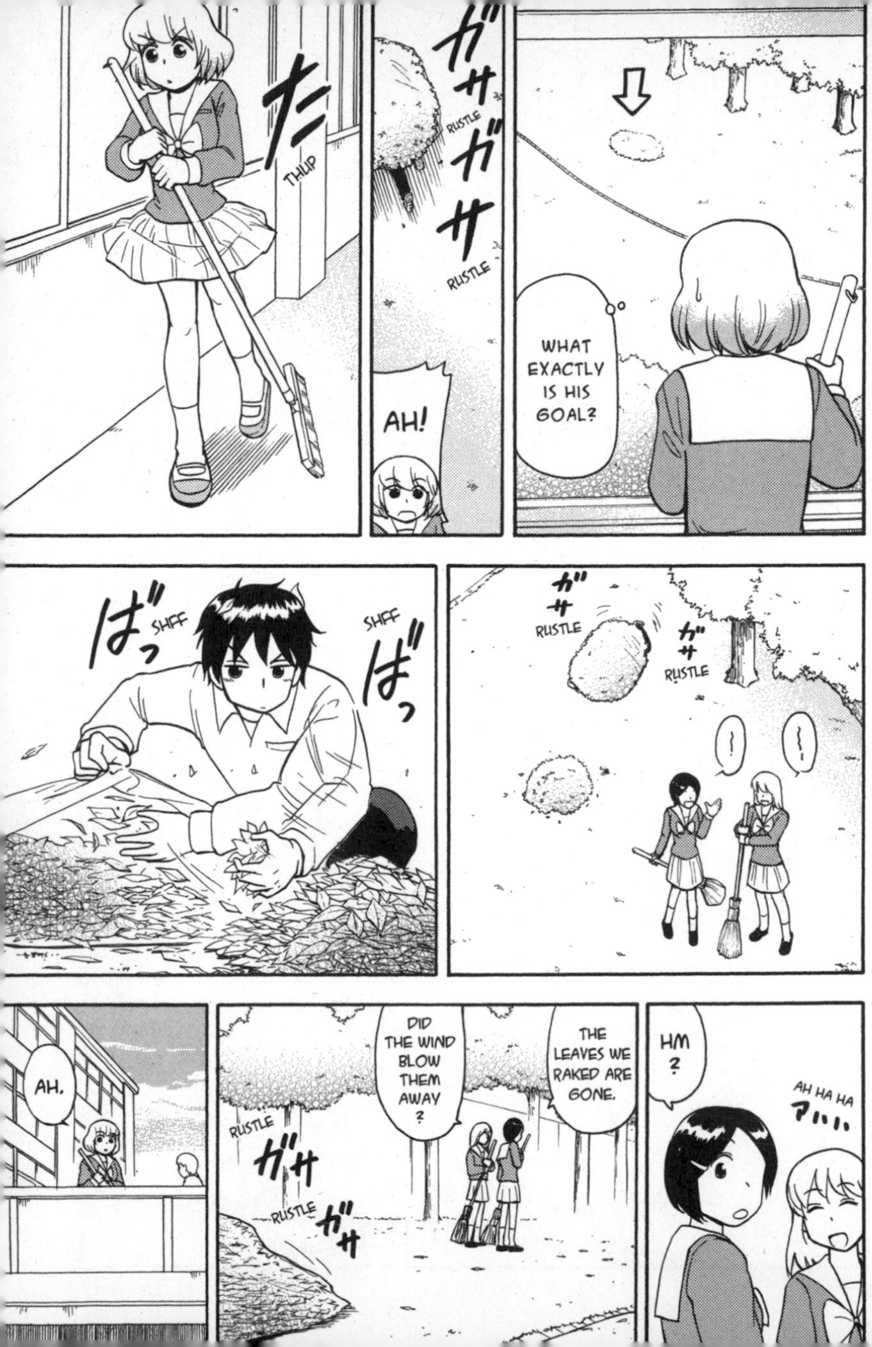
WHAT EXACTLY IS HIS GOAL?
ガサガガサ
RUSTLE
RUSTLE
AH!
た
THUP
ガサ
RUSTLE
ガサ
RUSTLE
!
!
ばっ
SHFF
ばっ
SHFF
HM?
AH HA HA
アハハ
THE LEAVES WE RAKED ARE GONE.
DID THE WIND BLOW THEM AWAY?
RUSTLE
ガサ
RUSTLE
ガサ
AH.

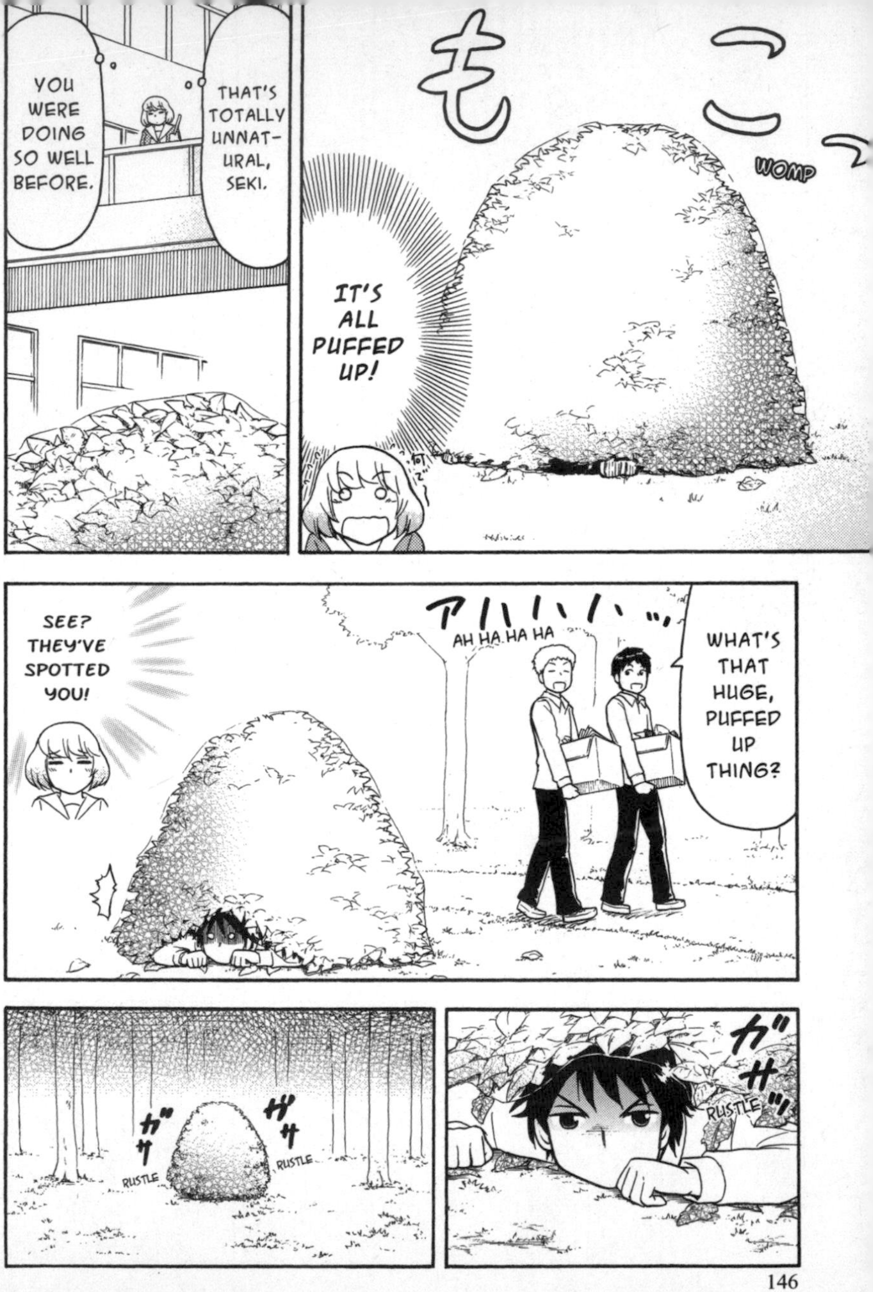
もこっ
WOMP
IT'S ALL PUFFED UP!
何?
THAT'S TOTALLY UNNATURAL, SEKI.
YOU WERE DOING SO WELL BEFORE.
アハハハッ
AH HA HA HA
WHAT'S THAT HUGE, PUFFED UP THING?
SEE? THEY'VE SPOTTED YOU!
ガサッ
RUSTLE
ガサ
RUSTLE
ガサ
RUSTLE

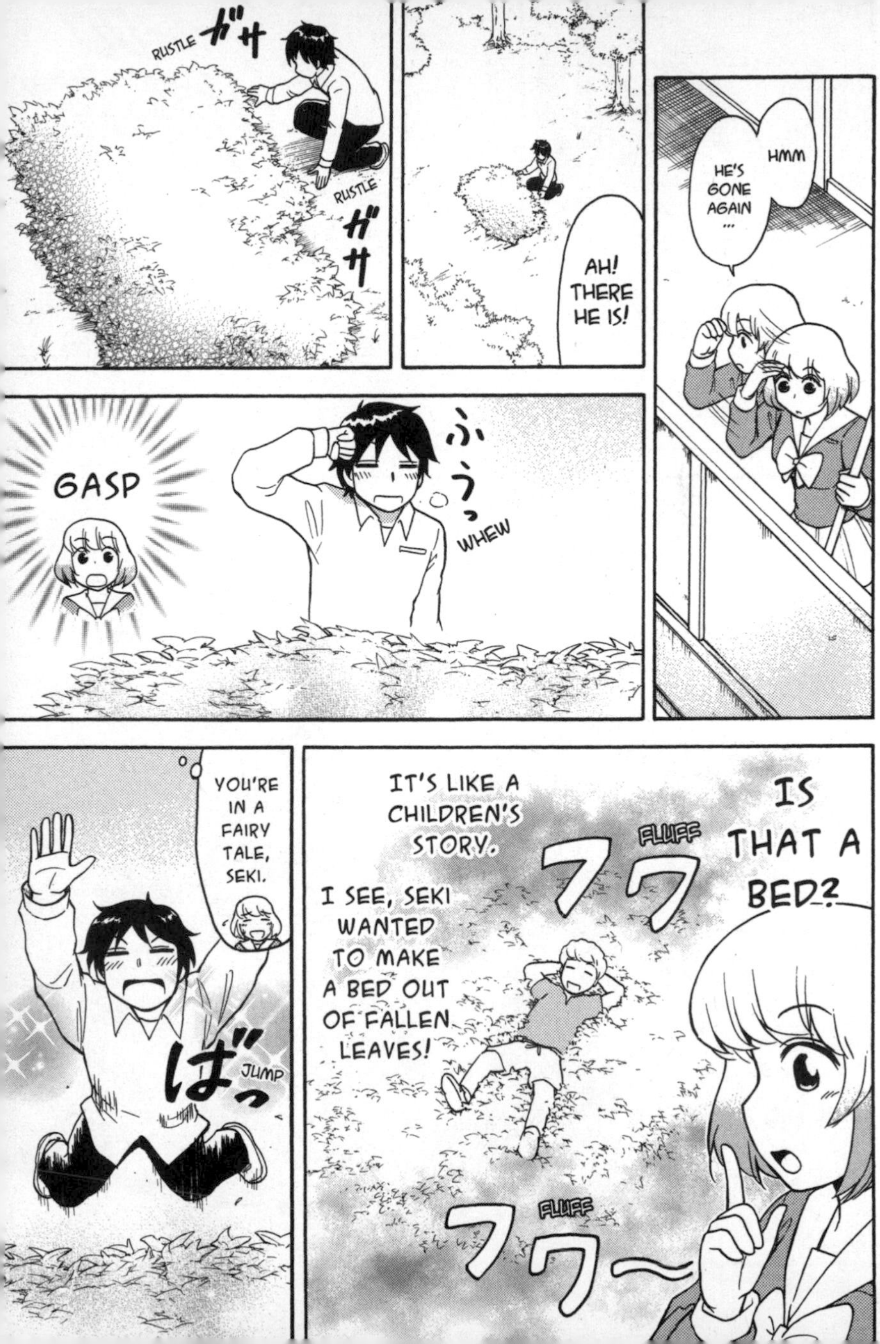

HMM
HE'S GONE AGAIN ...
AH! THERE HE IS!
RUSTLE ガサ
RUSTLE ガサ
ふうっ WHEW
GASP
IS THAT A BED?
FLUFF フワ
IT'S LIKE A CHILDREN'S STORY.
I SEE, SEKI WANTED TO MAKE A BED OUT OF FALLEN LEAVES!
FLUFF フワ〜
YOU'RE IN A FAIRY TALE, SEKI.
ばっ JUMP

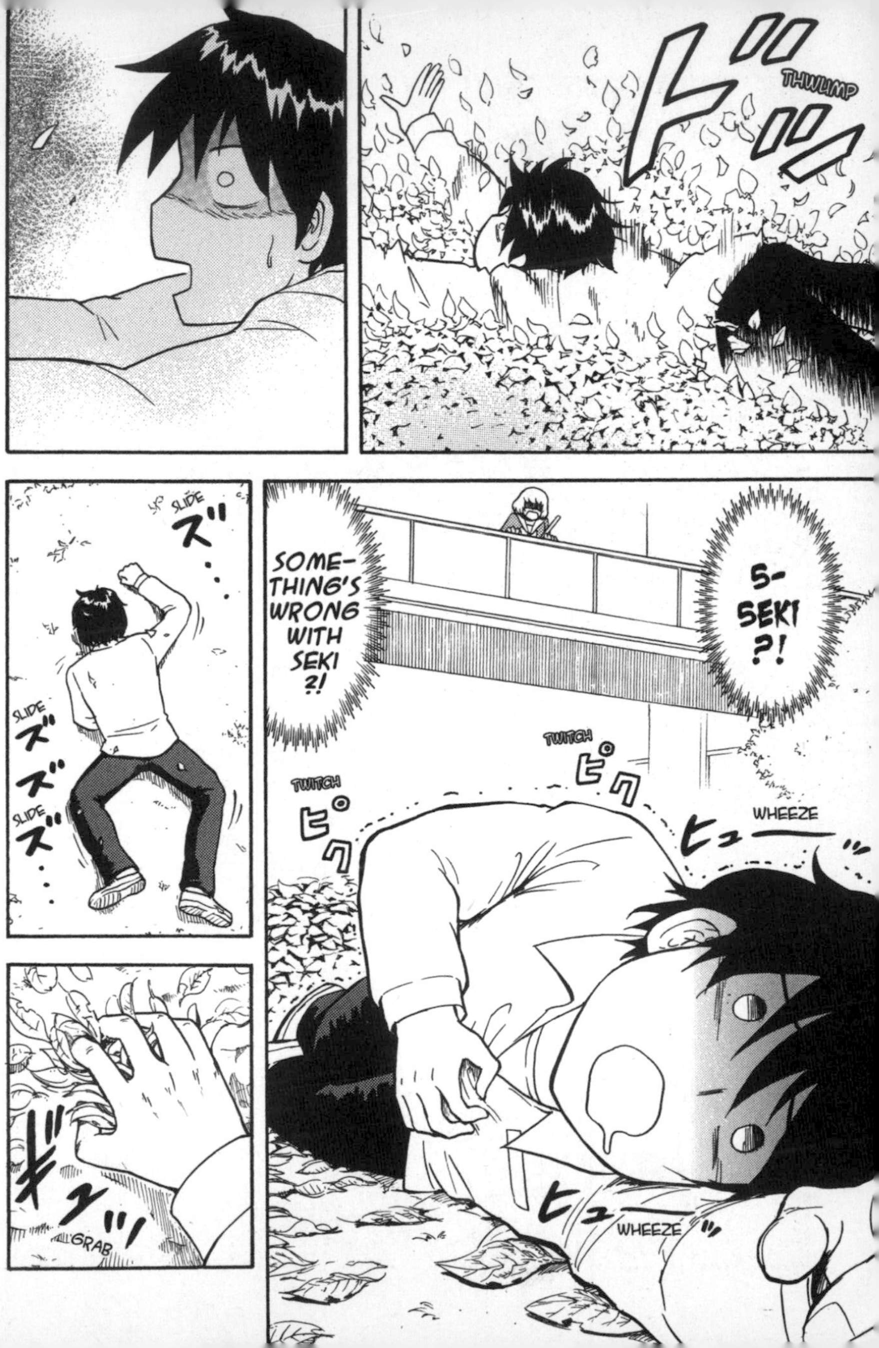
ドッ
THWLUMP
S-SEKI?!
SOME-THING'S WRONG WITH SEKI?!
ピク
TWITCH
ピク
TWITCH
ヒュー
WHEEZE
ヒュー
WHEEZE
ズ...
SLIDE
ズズズ
SLIDE
ズ...
SLIDE
ギュッ
GRAB

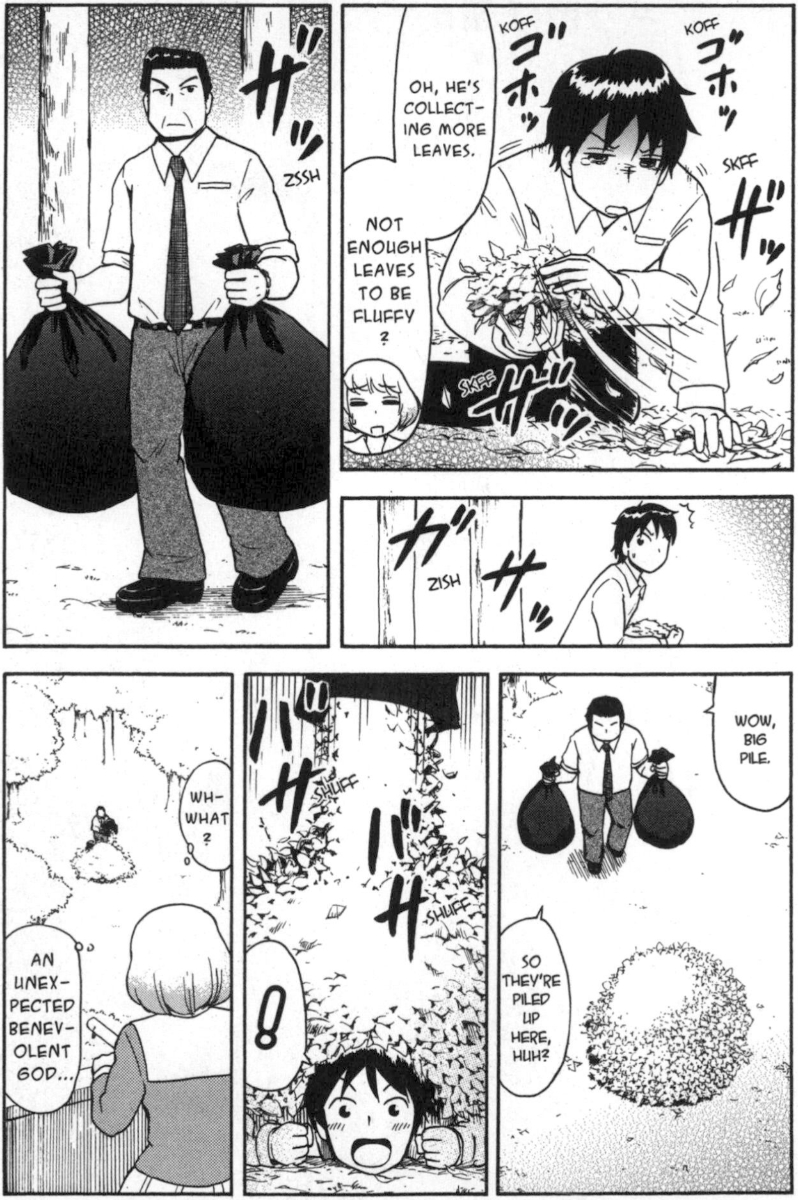
KOFF
KOFF
OH, HE'S COLLECT-ING MORE LEAVES.
NOT ENOUGH LEAVES TO BE FLUFFY?
SKFF
SKFF
ZISH
ZSSH
WOW, BIG PILE.
SO THEY'RE PILED UP HERE, HUH?
SHUFF
SHUFF
!
WH-WHAT?
AN UNEX-PECTED BENEV-OLENT GOD...

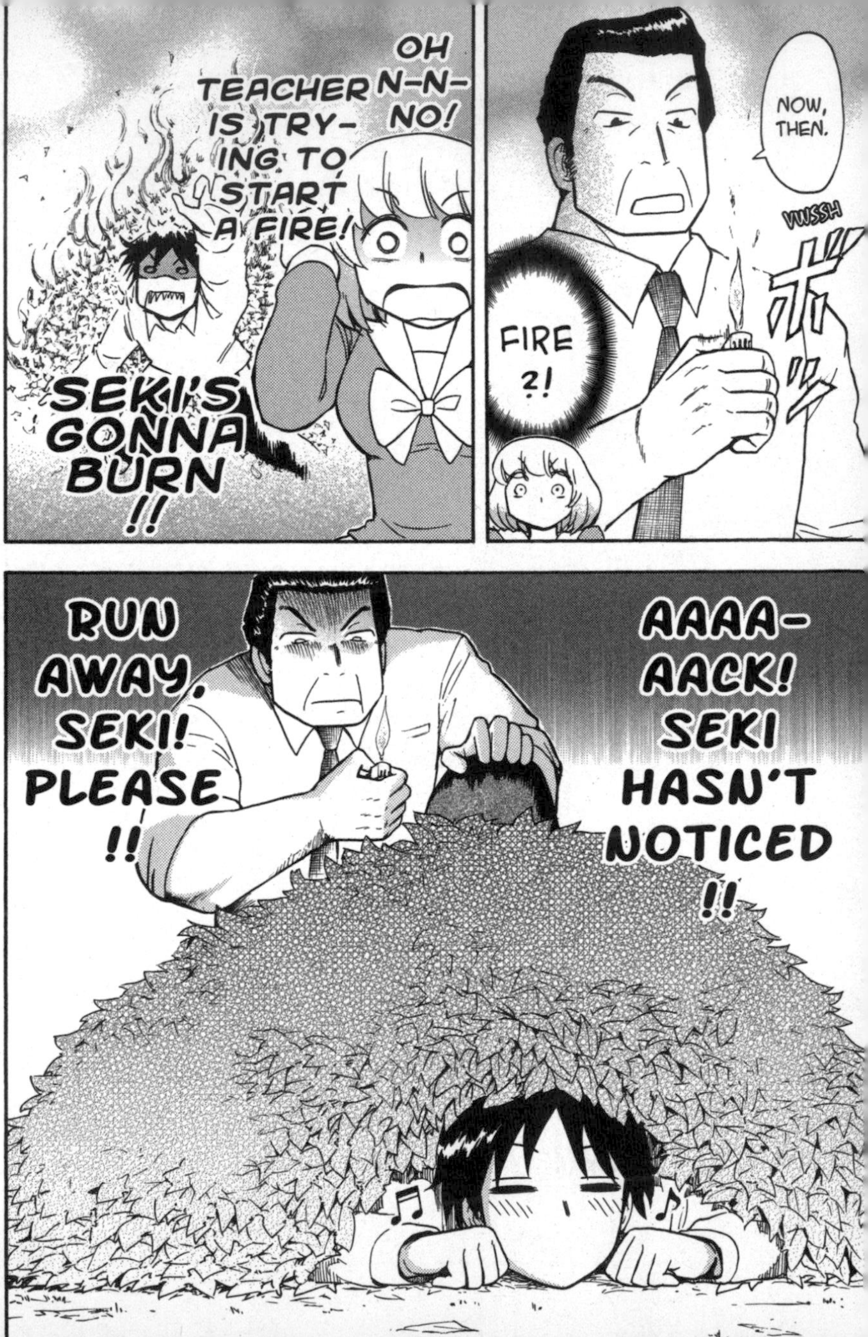
NOW, THEN.
VWSSH
ボッ
FIRE?!
OH N-N-NO!
TEACHER IS TRYING TO START A FIRE!
SEKI'S GONNA BURN!!
AAAA-AACK! SEKI HASN'T NOTICED!!
RUN AWAY, SEKI! PLEASE!!

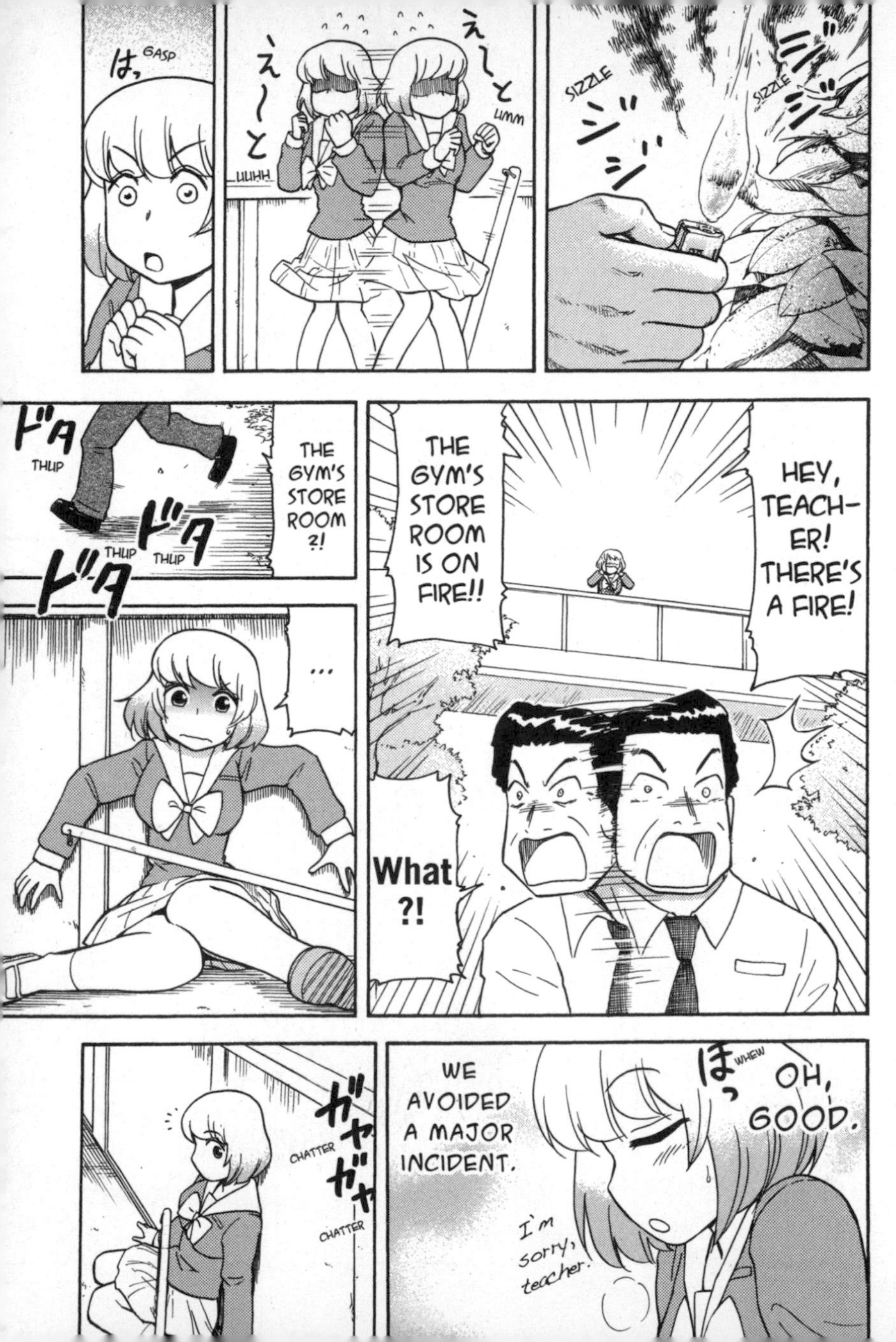
ジジジ
SIZZLE
ジジジ
SIZZLE
えーと
UMM
えーと
UHHH
はっ
GASP
HEY, TEACHER! THERE'S A FIRE!
THE GYM'S STORE ROOM IS ON FIRE!!
What ?!
THE GYM'S STORE ROOM ?!
ドタ
THUP
ドタ
THUP
ドタ
THUP
...
ほっ
WHEW
OH, GOOD.
WE AVOIDED A MAJOR INCIDENT.
I'm sorry, teacher.
ガヤガヤ
CHATTER
ガヤガヤ
CHATTER

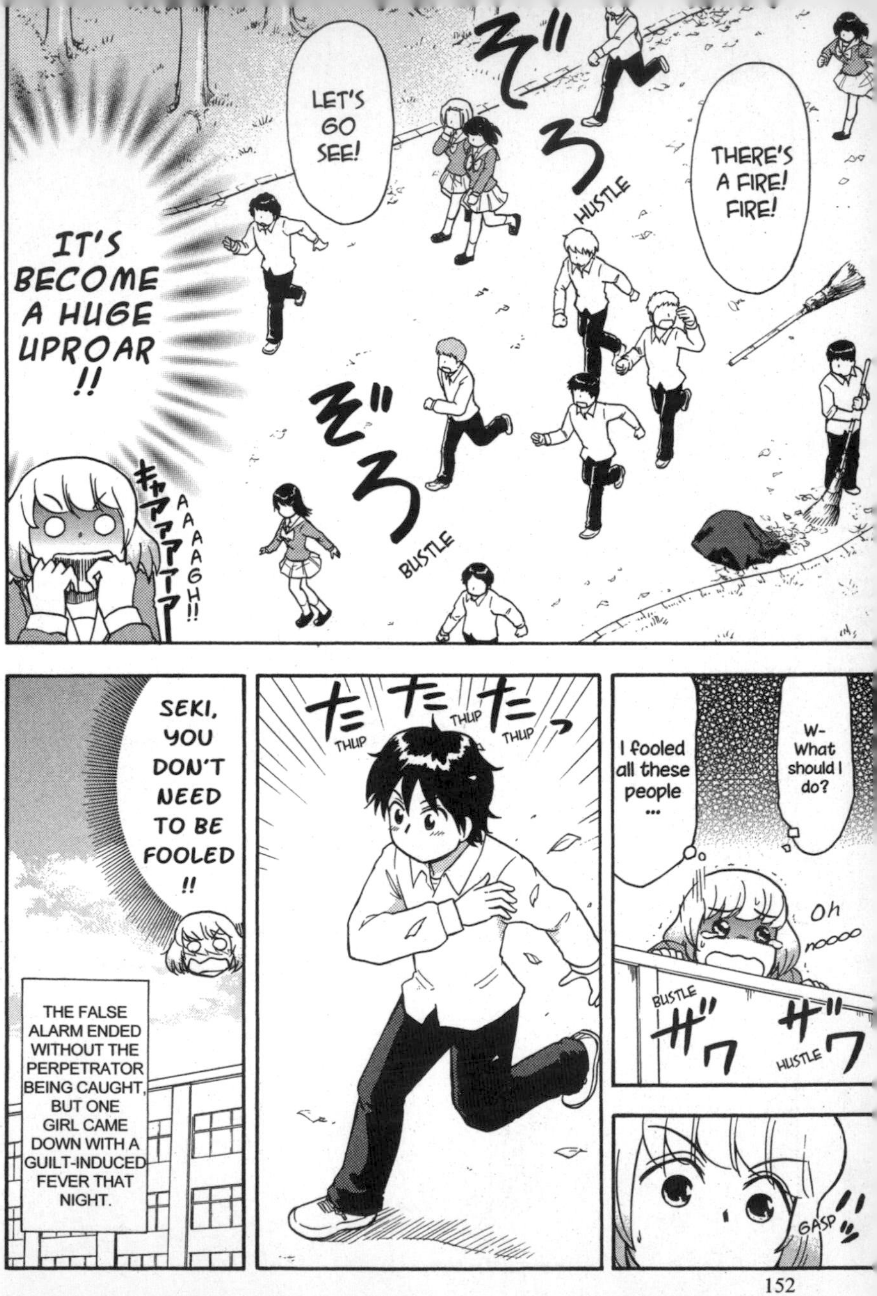
THERE'S A FIRE! FIRE!
ぞろ
HUSTLE
LET'S GO SEE!
IT'S BECOME A HUGE UPROAR!!
ぞろ
BUSTLE
キャアアアーア
AAAAGH!!
W- What should I do?
I fooled all these people...
Oh noooo
BUSTLE
ザワ
ザワ
HUSTLE
GASP
たたたっ
THUP THUP THUP
SEKI, YOU DON'T NEED TO BE FOOLED!!
THE FALSE ALARM ENDED WITHOUT THE PERPETRATOR BEING CAUGHT, BUT ONE GIRL CAME DOWN WITH A GUILT-INDUCED FEVER THAT NIGHT.

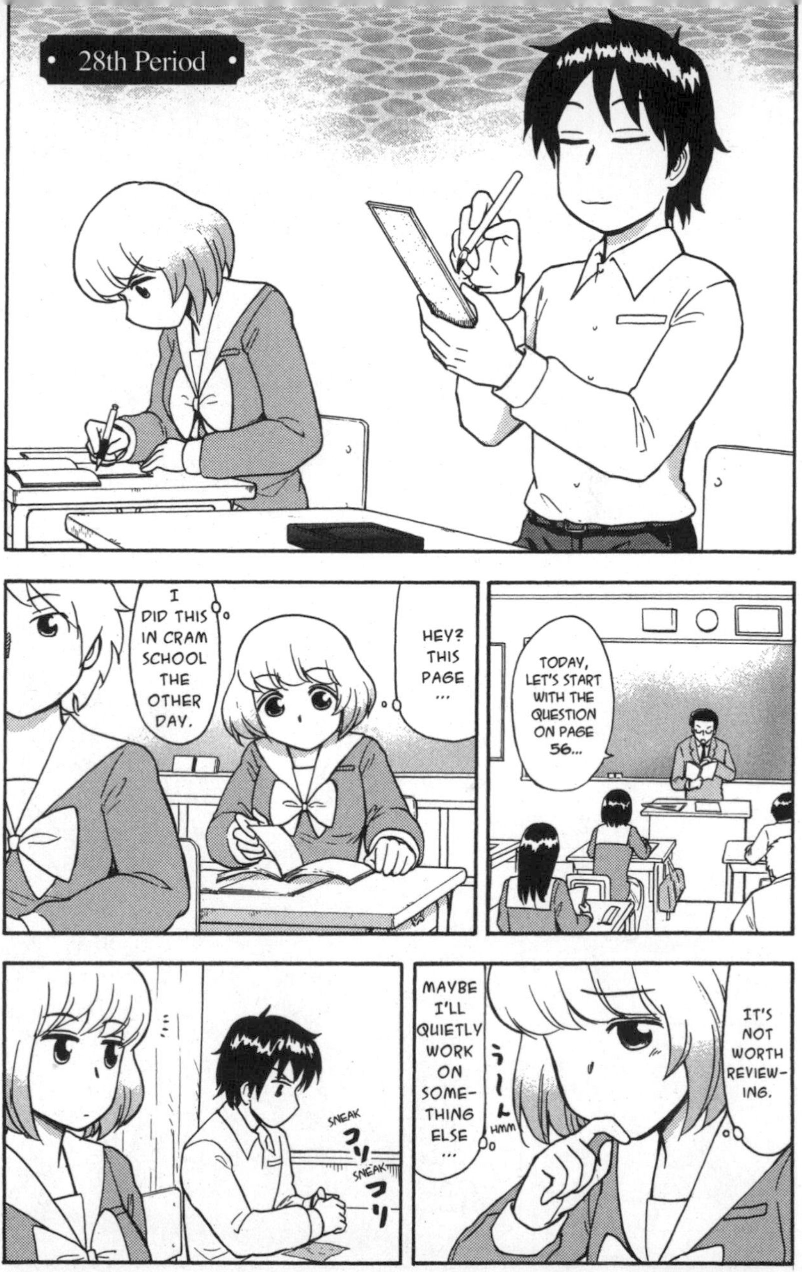
28th Period
TODAY, LET'S START WITH THE QUESTION ON PAGE 56...
HEY? THIS PAGE ...
I DID THIS IN CRAM SCHOOL THE OTHER DAY.
IT'S NOT WORTH REVIEWING.
うーん HMM
MAYBE I'LL QUIETLY WORK ON SOMETHING ELSE ...
SNEAK コソ
SNEAK コソ

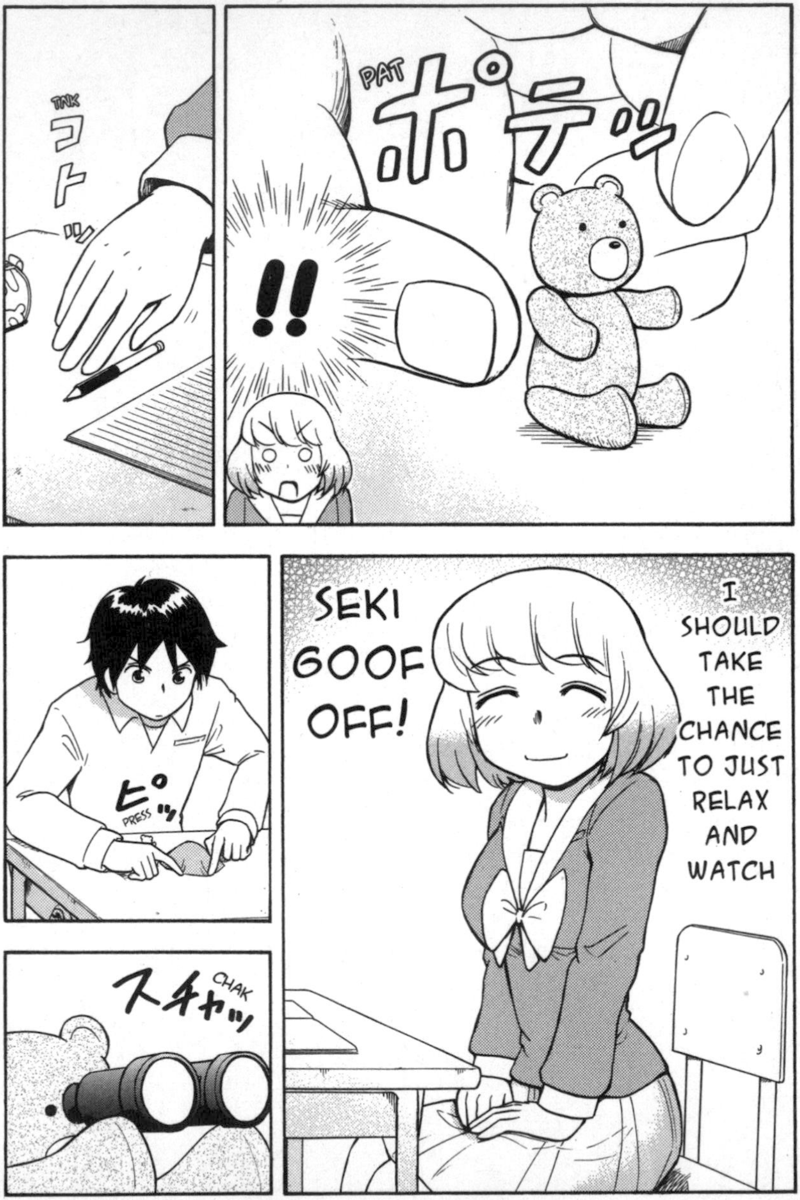
PAT
ポテッ
!!
TNK
コトッ
I SHOULD TAKE THE CHANCE TO JUST RELAX AND WATCH
SEKI GOOF OFF!
ピッ
PRESS
スチャッ
CHAK

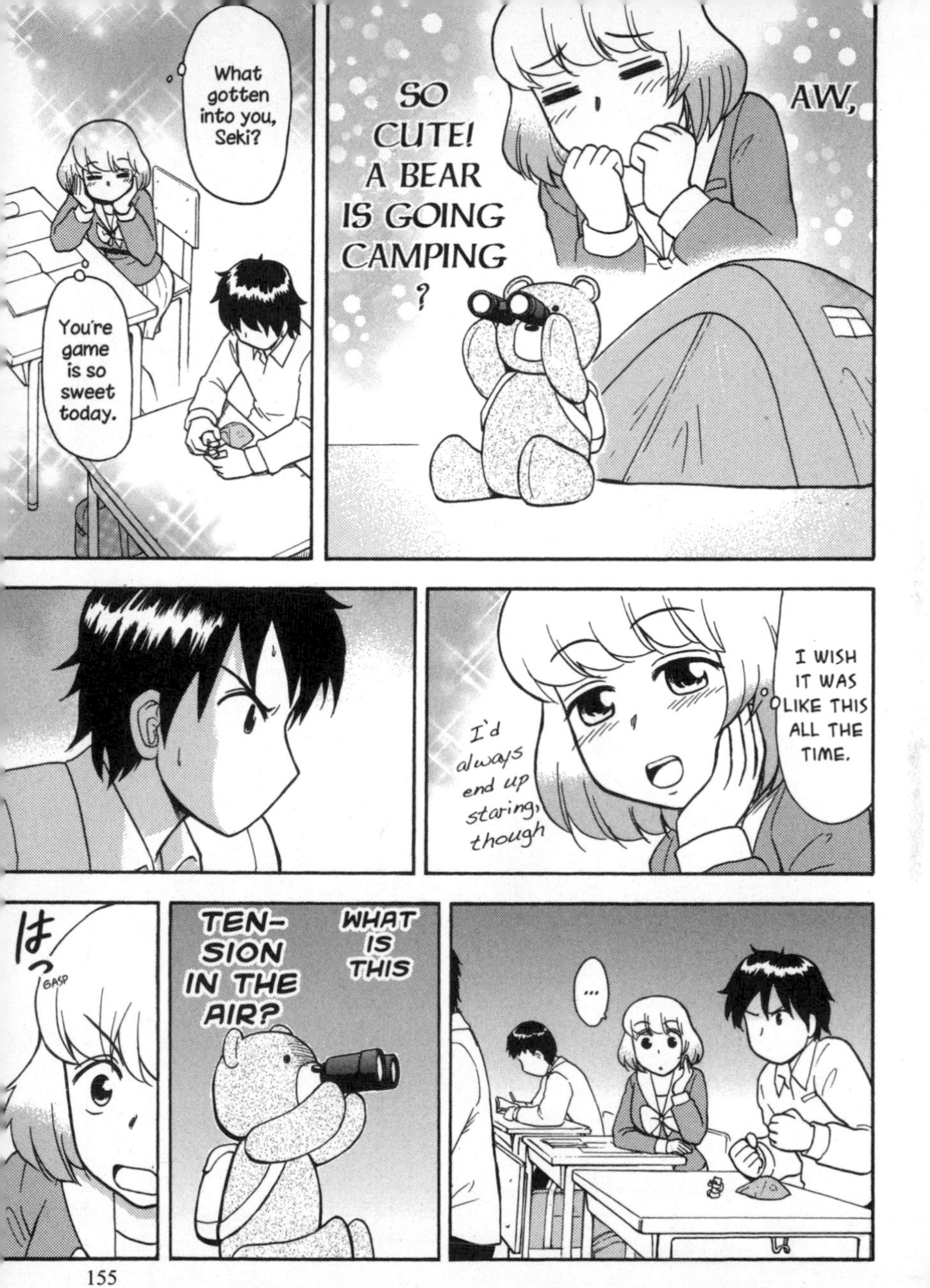
AW,
SO CUTE! A BEAR IS GOING CAMPING?
What gotten into you, Seki?
You're game is so sweet today.
I WISH IT WAS LIKE THIS ALL THE TIME.
I'd always end up staring, though
...
WHAT IS THIS
TEN-SION IN THE AIR?
はっ
GASP

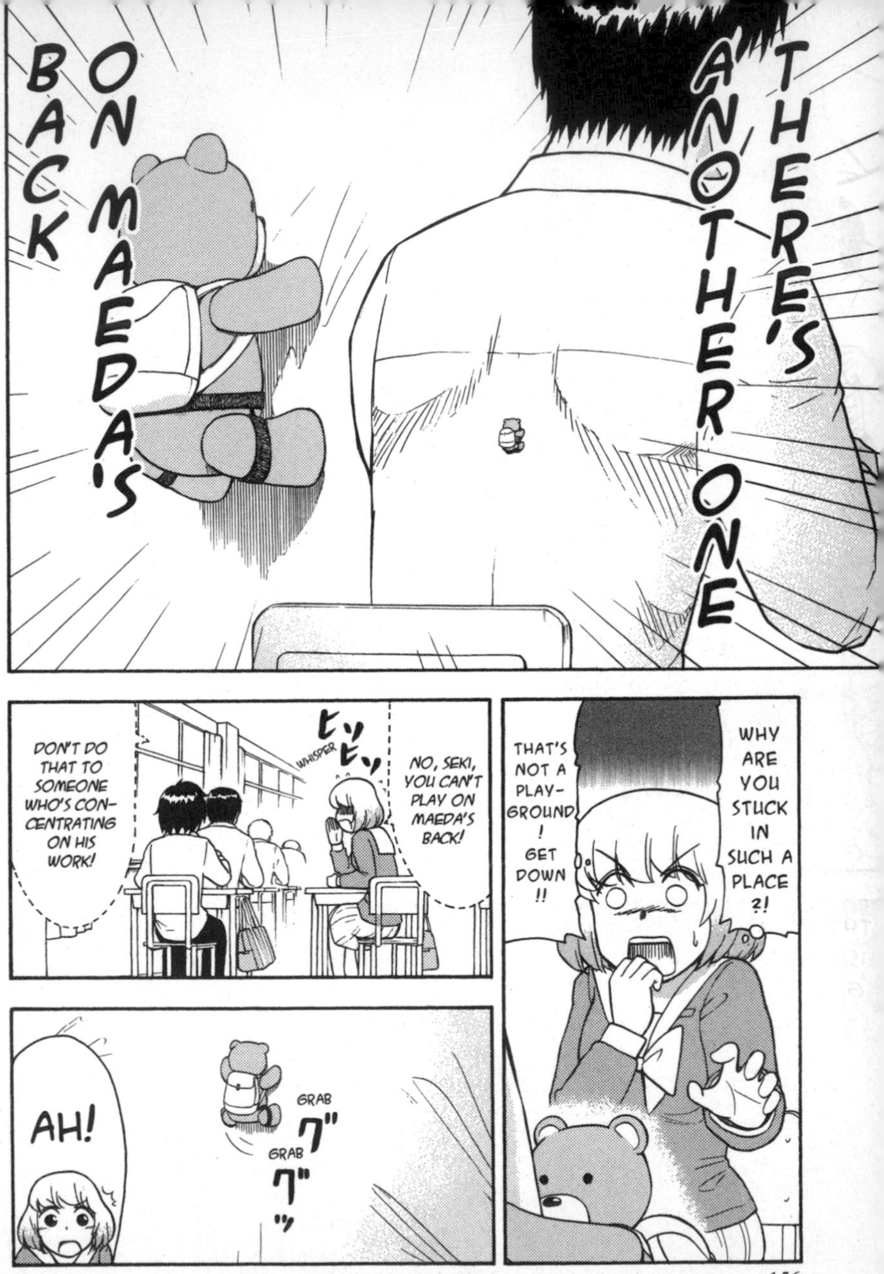
THERE'S ANOTHER ONE
ON MAEDA'S BACK
WHY ARE YOU STUCK IN SUCH A PLACE ?!
THAT'S NOT A PLAY-GROUND! GET DOWN!!
NO, SEKI, YOU CAN'T PLAY ON MAEDA'S BACK!
ヒソヒソ
WHISPER
DON'T DO THAT TO SOMEONE WHO'S CON-CENTRATING ON HIS WORK!
GRAB
グ
GRAB
グッ
AH!

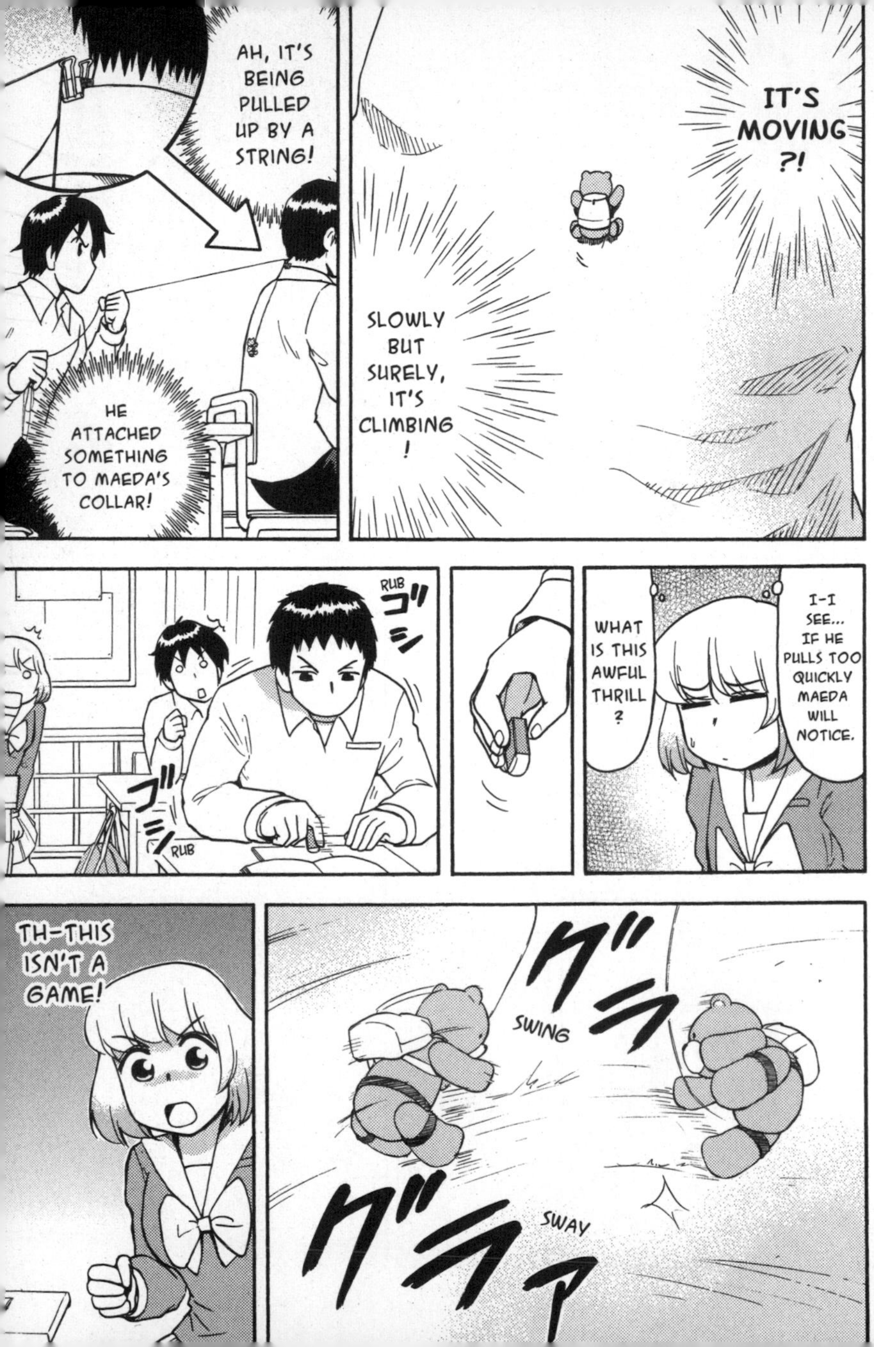
IT'S MOVING ?!
SLOWLY BUT SURELY, IT'S CLIMBING!
AH, IT'S BEING PULLED UP BY A STRING!
HE ATTACHED SOMETHING TO MAEDA'S COLLAR!
I-I SEE... IF HE PULLS TOO QUICKLY MAEDA WILL NOTICE.
WHAT IS THIS AWFUL THRILL?
ゴシ
RUB
ゴシ
RUB
グラ
SWING
グラァ
SWAY
TH-THIS ISN'T A GAME!

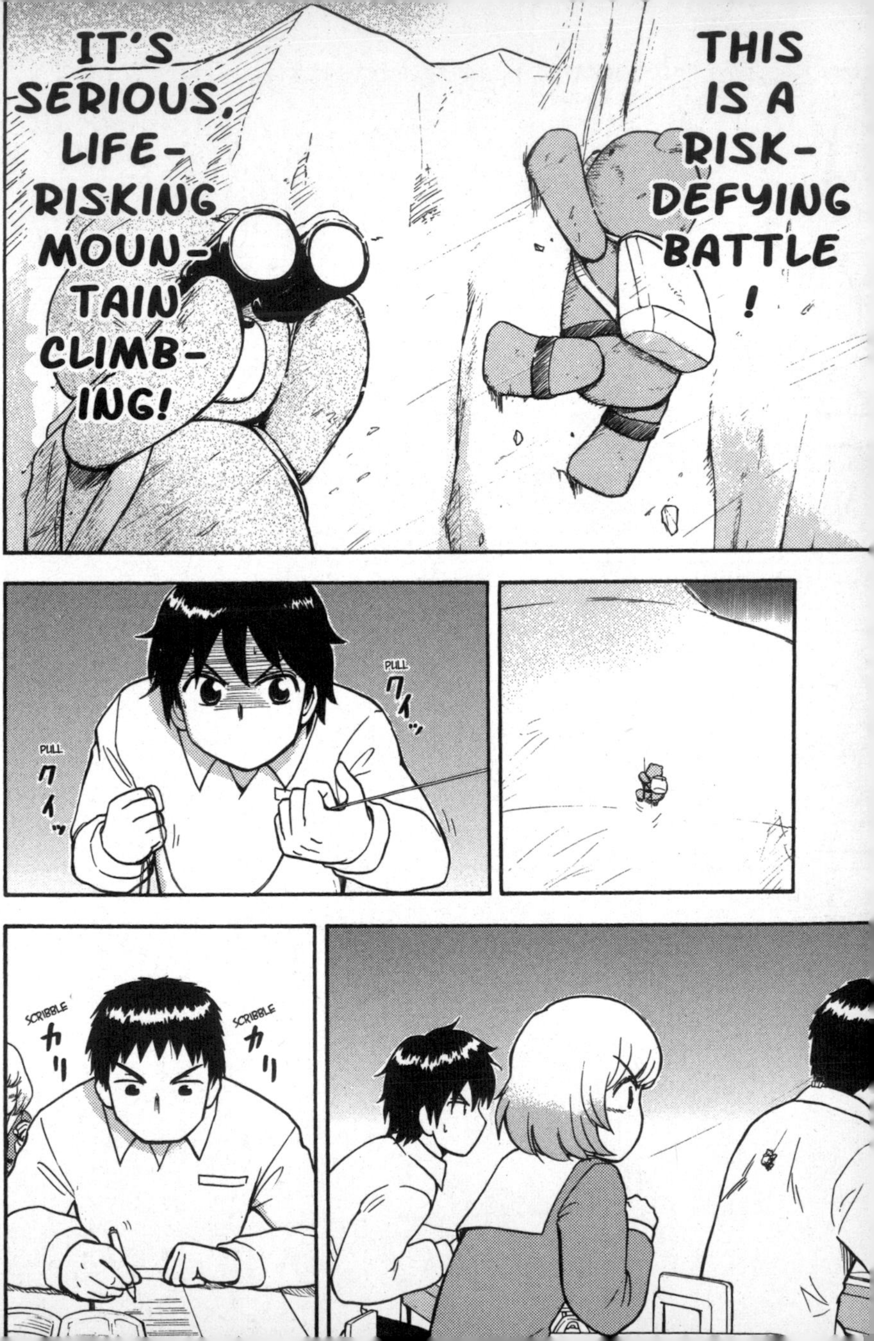
THIS IS A RISK-DEFYING BATTLE!
IT'S SERIOUS, LIFE-RISKING MOUNTAIN-CLIMBING!
PULL
クイッ
PULL
クイッ
SCRIBBLE
カリ
SCRIBBLE
カリ

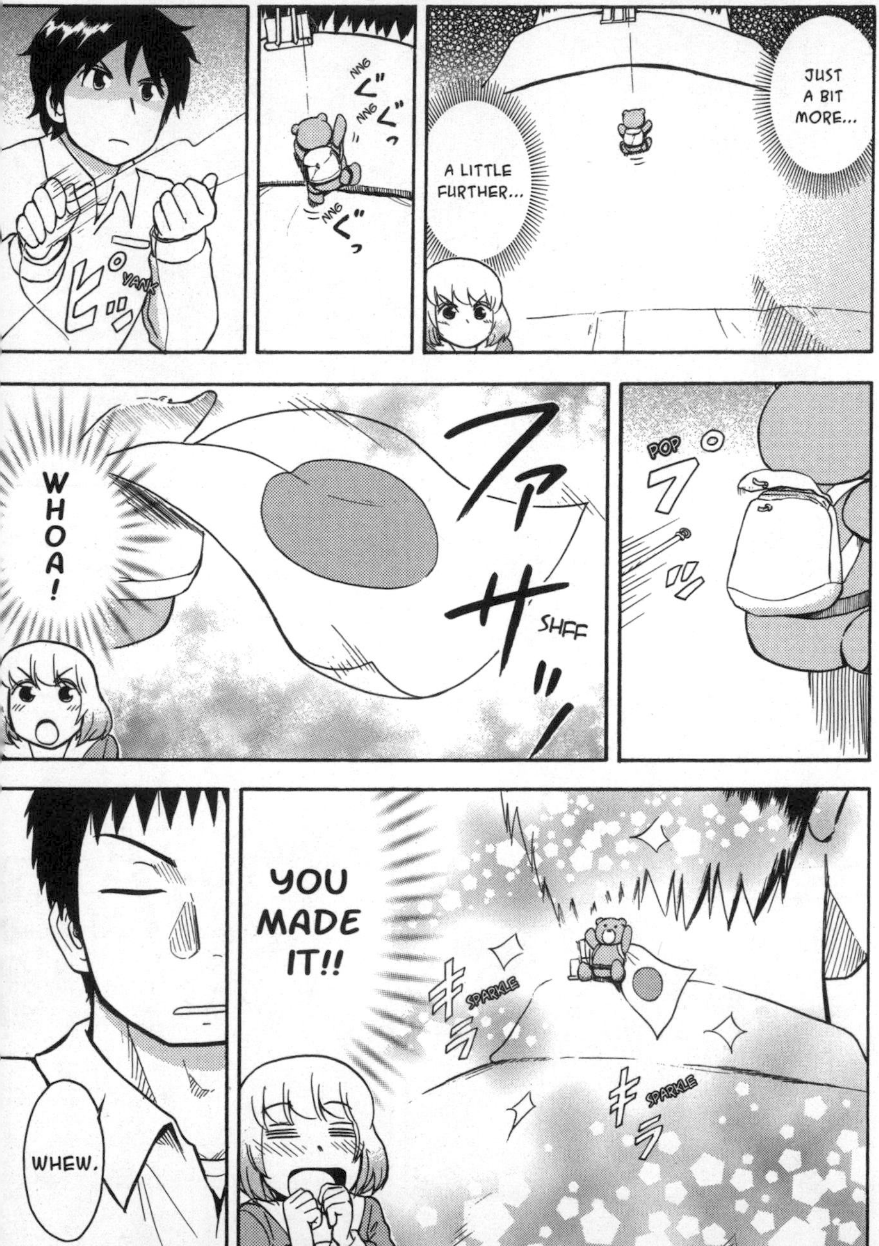
JUST A BIT MORE...
A LITTLE FURTHER...
NNG ぐ
NNG ぐっ
NNG ぐっ
YANK
ピッ
POP
プ
ツ
ファサッ
SHFF
WHOA!
YOU MADE IT!!
SPARKLE
キラ
SPARKLE
キラ
WHEW.

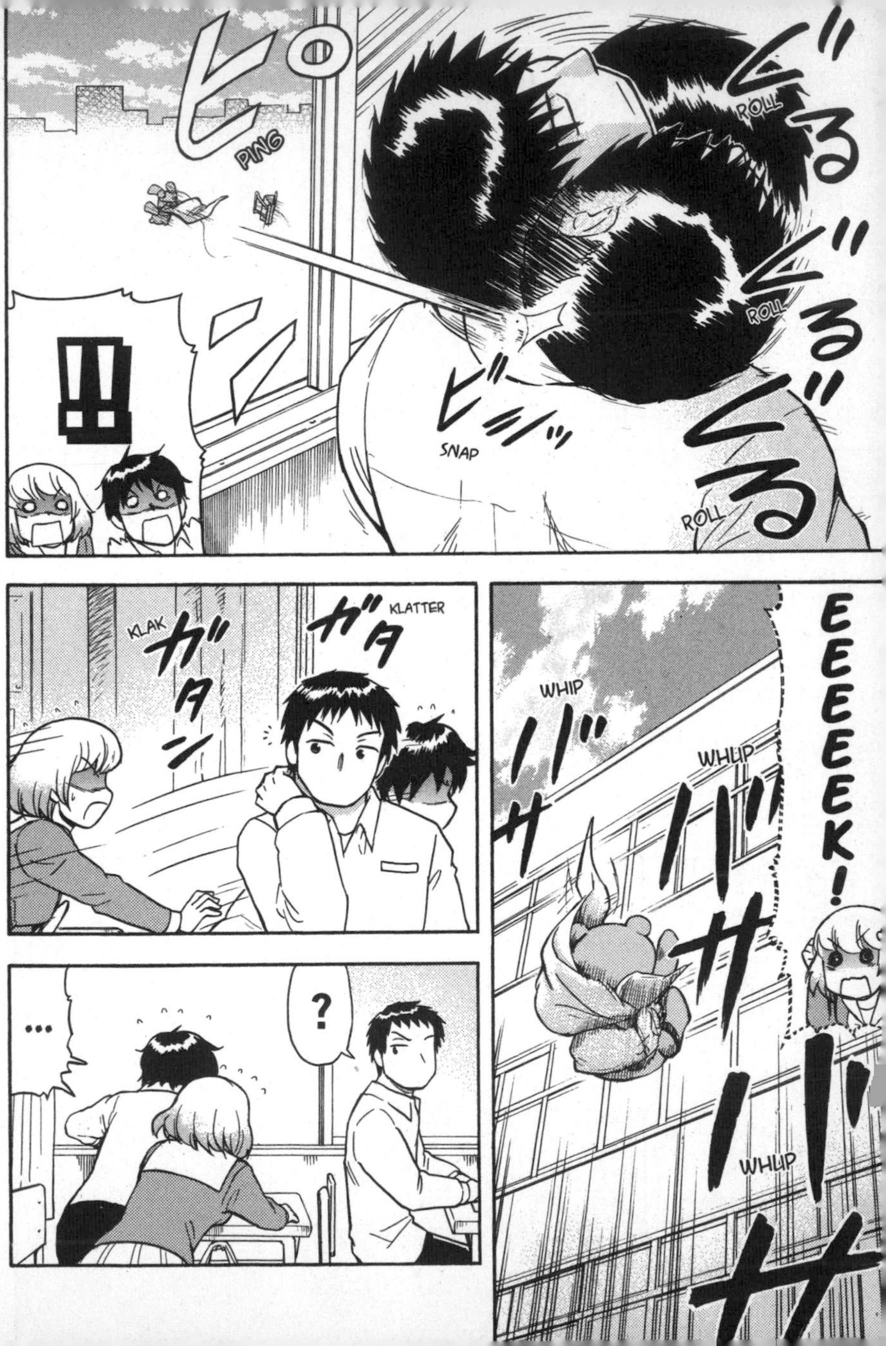

ぐるぐるぐる
ROLL
ROLL
ROLL
ピ
PING
ビシッ
SNAP
!!
EEEEEEK!
バサ
WHIP
バサ
WHUP
バサ
WHUP
ガタ
KLATTER
ガタン
KLAK
?
...

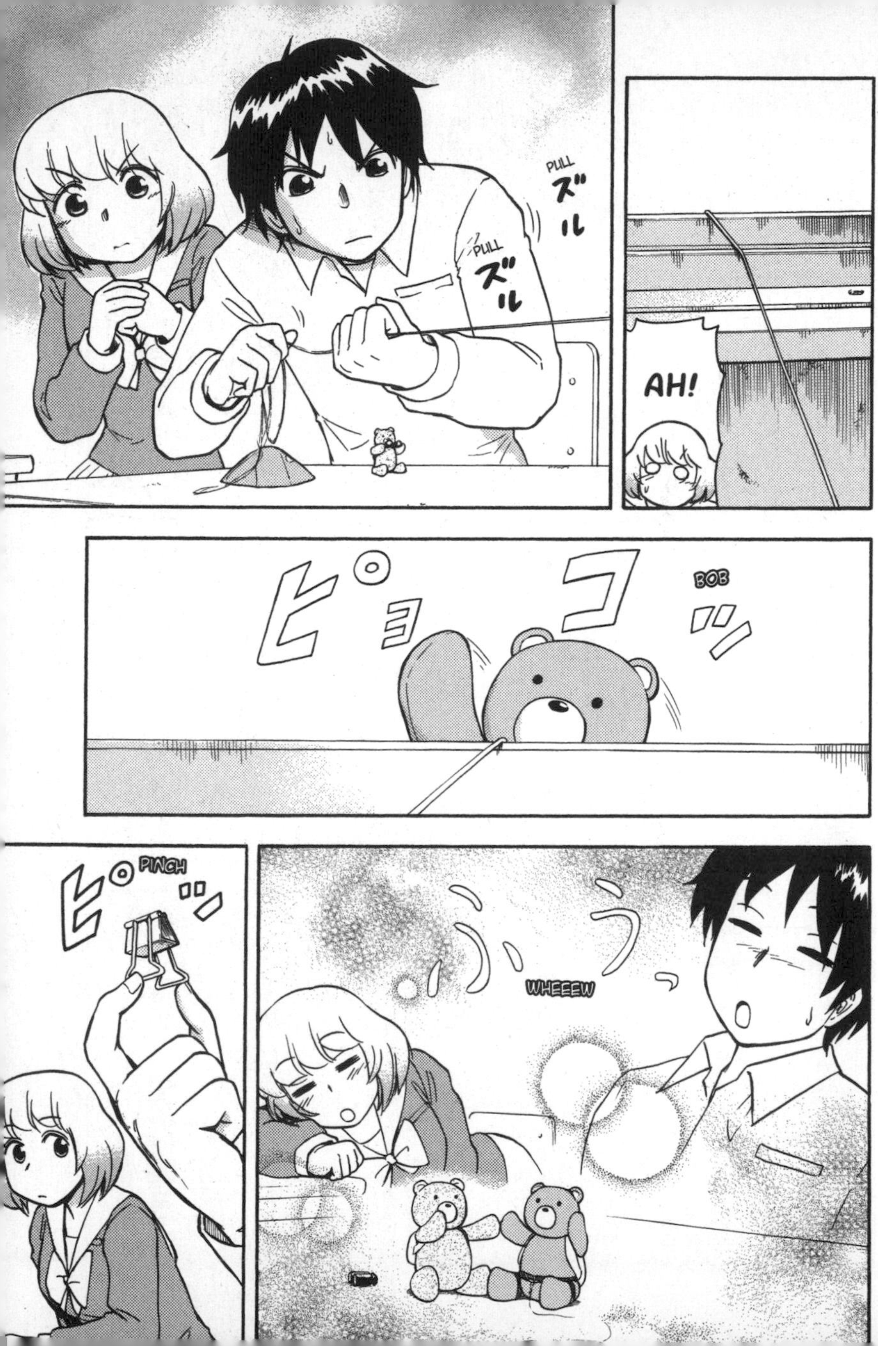
AH!
PULL
ズル
PULL
ズル
ピョコッ
BOB
ふぅ
WHEEEW
ピッ
PINCH

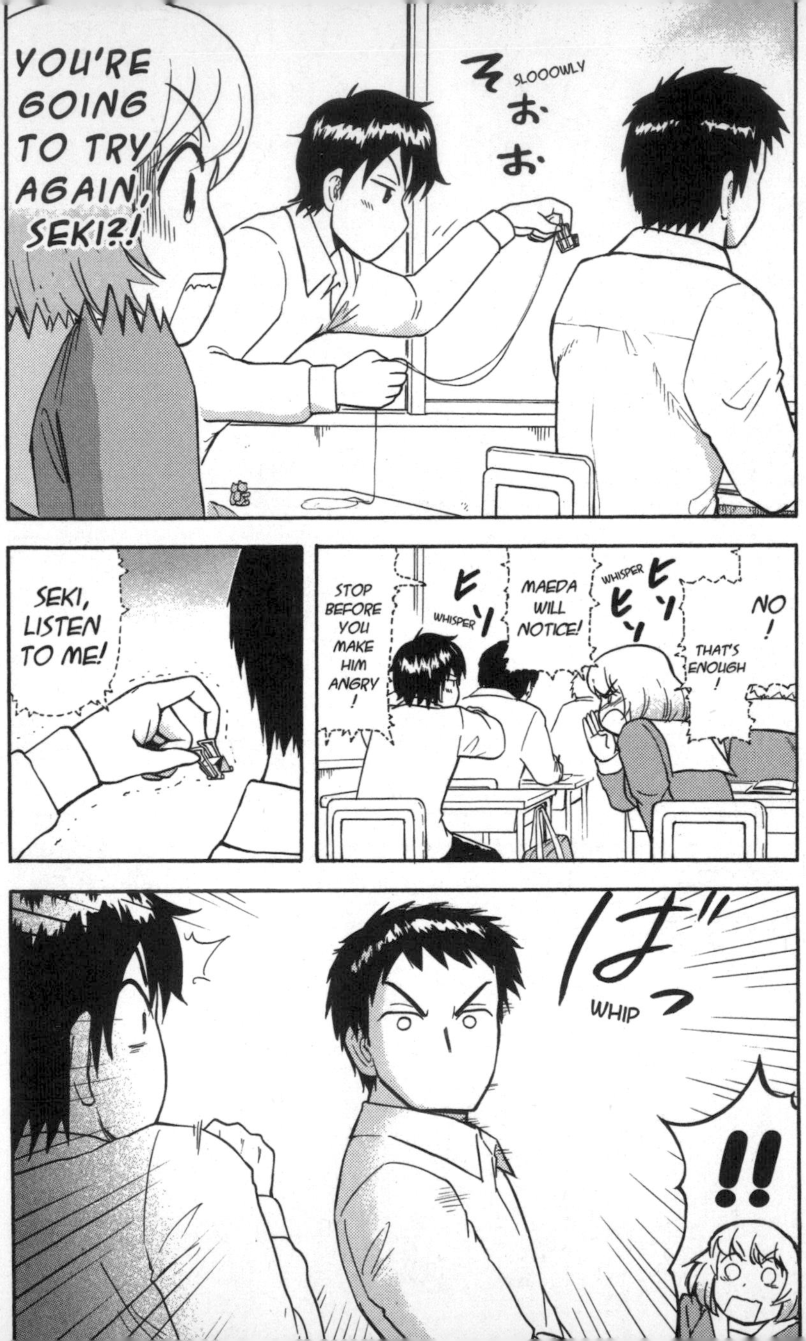
そぉぉ
SLOOOWLY
YOU'RE GOING TO TRY AGAIN, SEKI?!
NO! THAT'S ENOUGH!
ヒソヒソ
WHISPER
MAEDA WILL NOTICE!
ヒソ
WHISPER
STOP BEFORE YOU MAKE HIM ANGRY!
SEKI, LISTEN TO ME!
ばっ
WHIP
!!

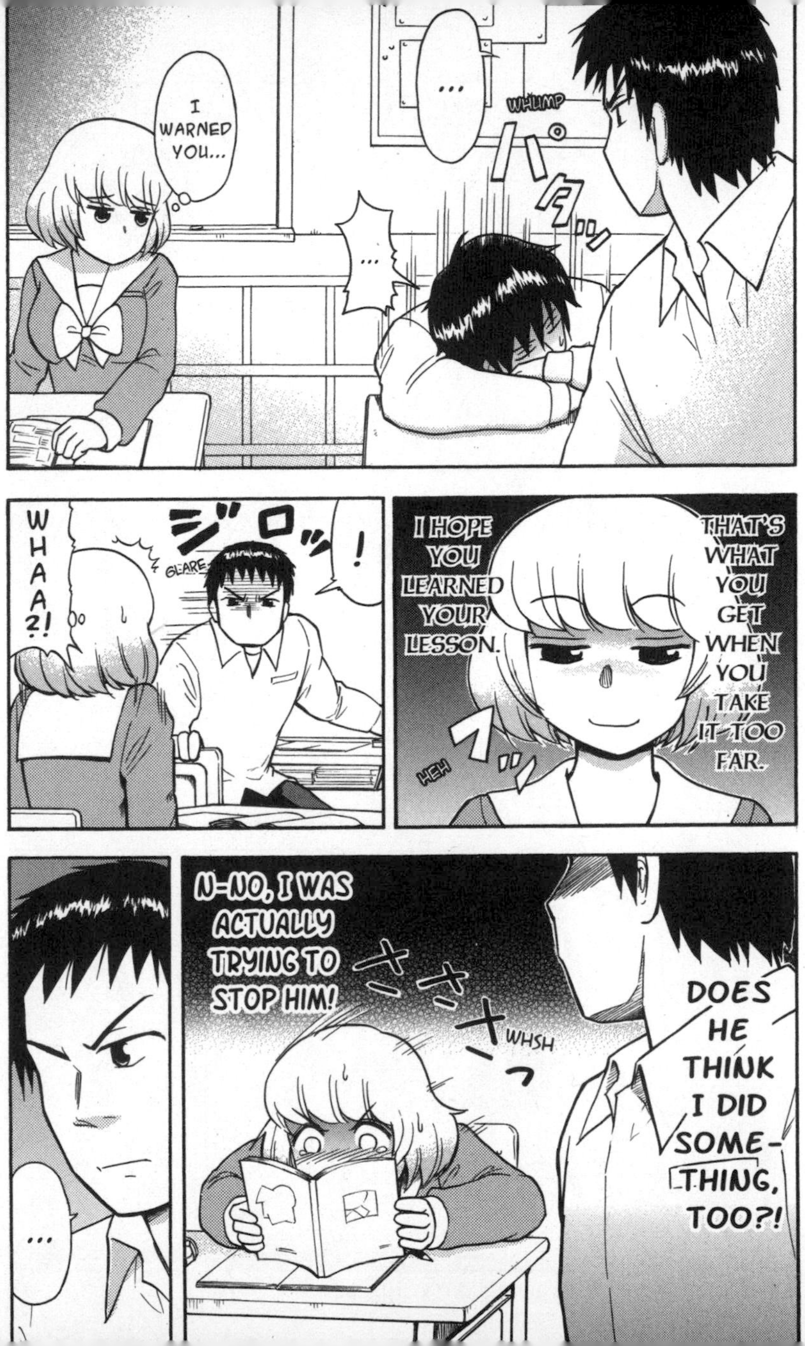
...
WHLUMP
...
I WARNED YOU...
THAT'S WHAT YOU GET WHEN YOU TAKE IT TOO FAR.
I HOPE YOU LEARNED YOUR LESSON.
HEH
!
GLARE
WHAAA?!
DOES HE THINK I DID SOME-THING, TOO?!
WHSH
N-NO, I WAS ACTUALLY TRYING TO STOP HIM!
...

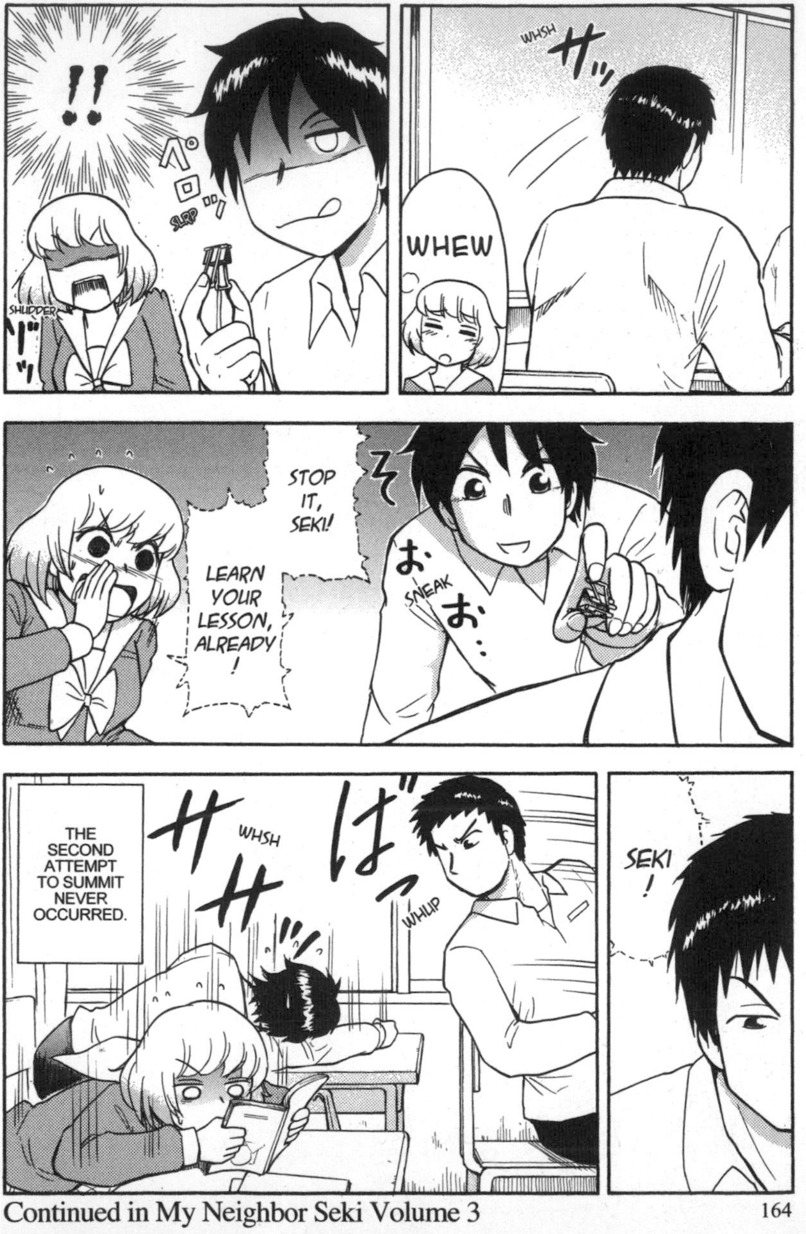
WHSH
WHEW
!!
SLRP
SHUDDER
STOP IT, SEKI!
LEARN YOUR LESSON, ALREADY!
SNEAK
SEKI!
WHUP
WHSH
THE SECOND ATTEMPT TO SUMMIT NEVER OCCURRED.

Continued in My Neighbor Seki Volume 3

My Neighbor Seki

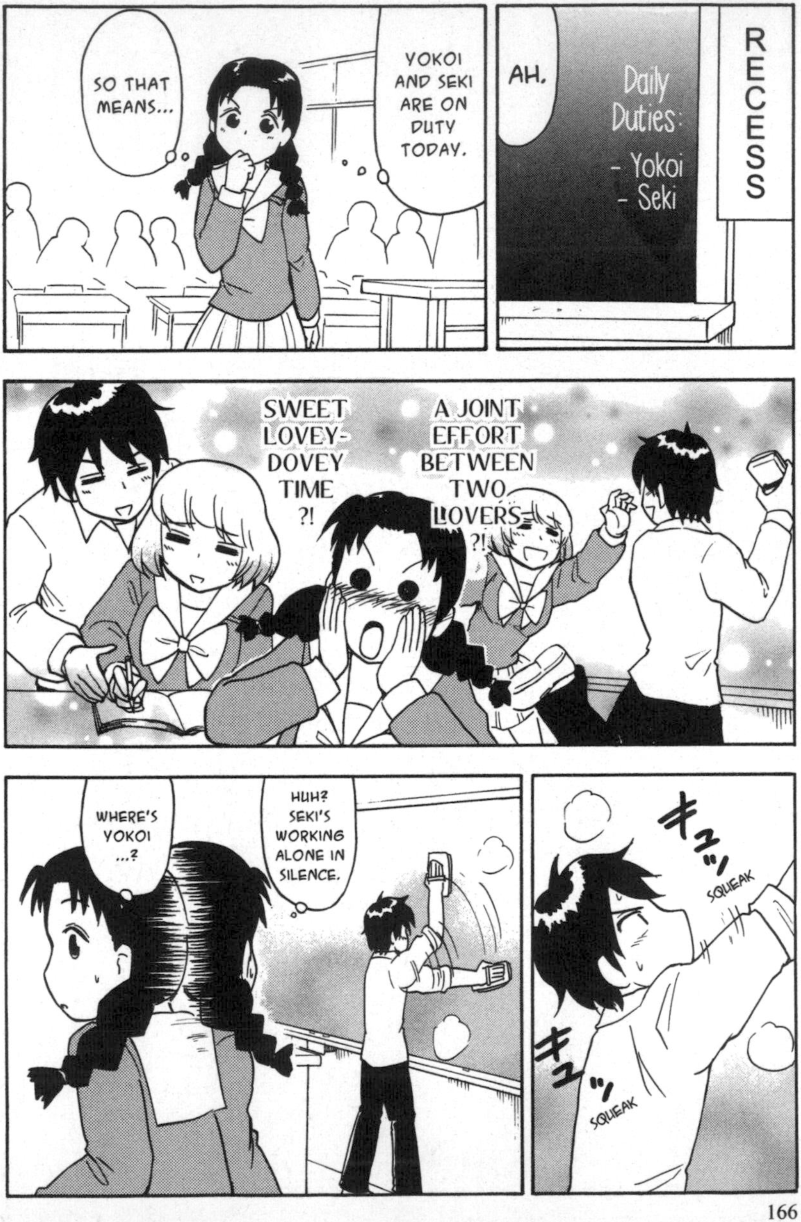
RECESS
Daily Duties:
- Yokoi
- Seki
AH.
YOKOI AND SEKI ARE ON DUTY TODAY.
SO THAT MEANS...
A JOINT EFFORT BETWEEN TWO LOVERS ?!
SWEET LOVEY-DOVEY TIME ?!
SQUEAK
SQUEAK
HUH? SEKI'S WORKING ALONE IN SILENCE.
WHERE'S YOKOI ...?

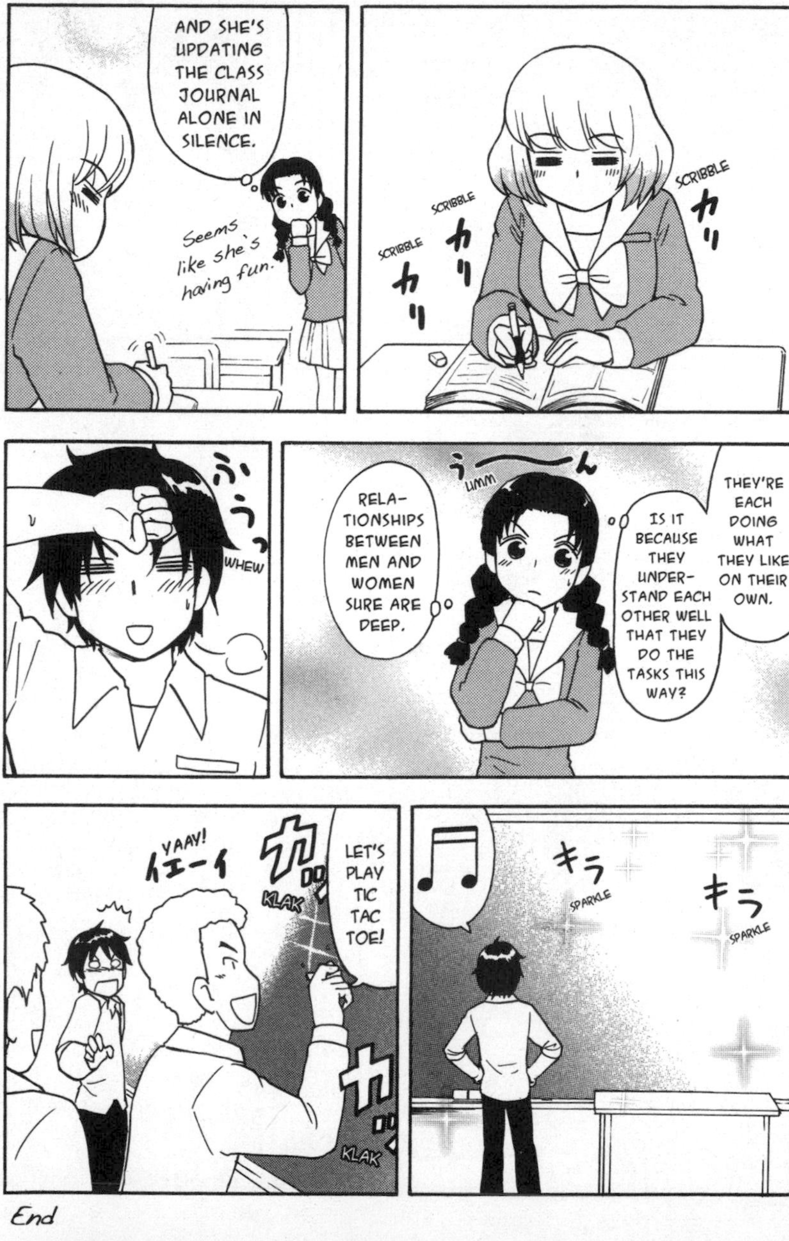
カリ
SCRIBBLE
カリ
SCRIBBLE
カリ
SCRIBBLE
AND SHE'S UPDATING THE CLASS JOURNAL ALONE IN SILENCE.
Seems like she's having fun.
THEY'RE EACH DOING WHAT THEY LIKE ON THEIR OWN.
IS IT BECAUSE THEY UNDER-STAND EACH OTHER WELL THAT THEY DO THE TASKS THIS WAY?
うーーん
UMM
RELA-TIONSHIPS BETWEEN MEN AND WOMEN SURE ARE DEEP.
ふうっ
WHEW
キラ
SPARKLE
キラ
SPARKLE
LET'S PLAY TIC TAC TOE!
カッ
KLAK
イエーイ
YAAY!
カッ
KLAK

End

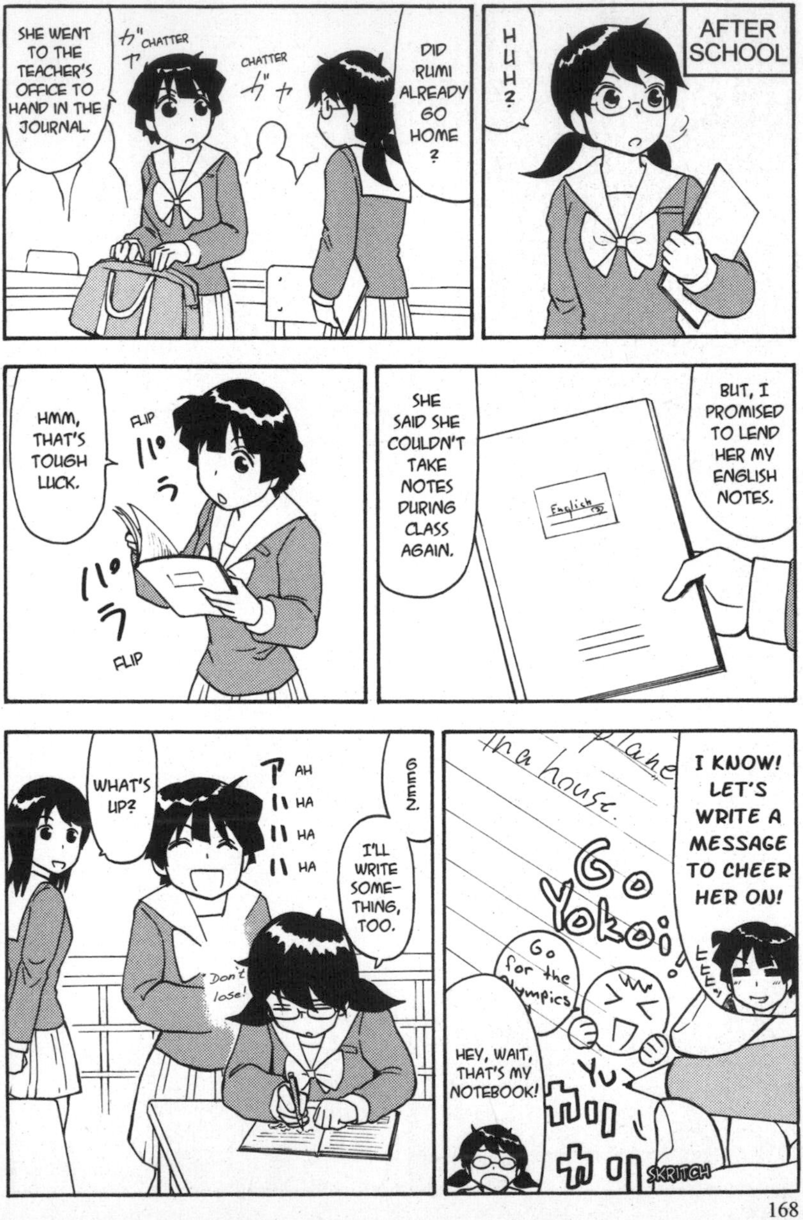
AFTER SCHOOL
HUH?
DID RUMI ALREADY GO HOME?
CHATTER
CHATTER
SHE WENT TO THE TEACHER'S OFFICE TO HAND IN THE JOURNAL.
BUT, I PROMISED TO LEND HER MY ENGLISH NOTES.
SHE SAID SHE COULDN'T TAKE NOTES DURING CLASS AGAIN.
English
HMM, THAT'S TOUGH LUCK.
FLIP
FLIP
I KNOW! LET'S WRITE A MESSAGE TO CHEER HER ON!
plane
in a house.
Go Yokoi!
Go for the Olympics
Yu
HEY, WAIT, THAT'S MY NOTEBOOK!
SKRITCH
GEEZ.
I'LL WRITE SOMETHING, TOO.
AH HA HA HA
WHAT'S UP?
Don't lose!

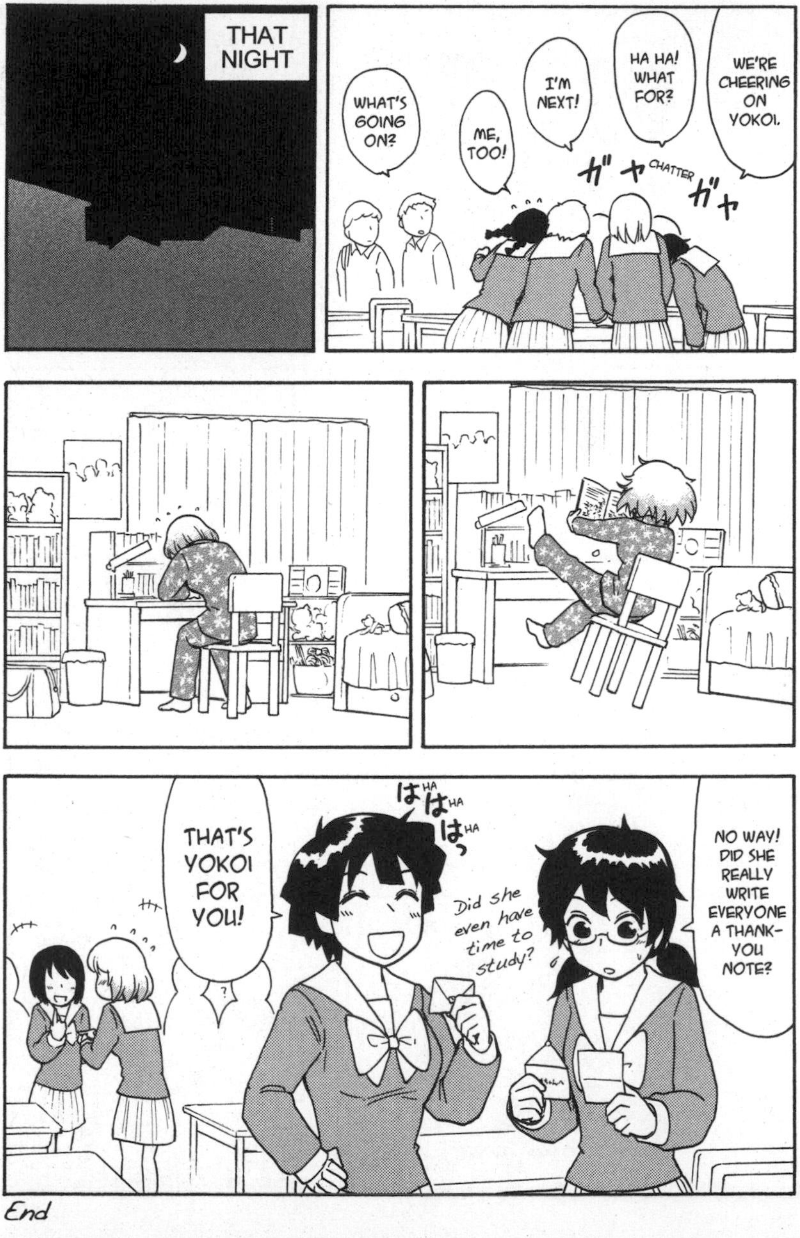
WE'RE CHEERING ON YOKOI.
HA HA! WHAT FOR?
I'M NEXT!
ME, TOO!
WHAT'S GOING ON?
ガヤ CHATTER ガヤ
THAT NIGHT
NO WAY! DID SHE REALLY WRITE EVERYONE A THANK-YOU NOTE?
は HA は HA はっ HA
THAT'S YOKOI FOR YOU!
Did she even have time to study?
?

End

BONUS ②

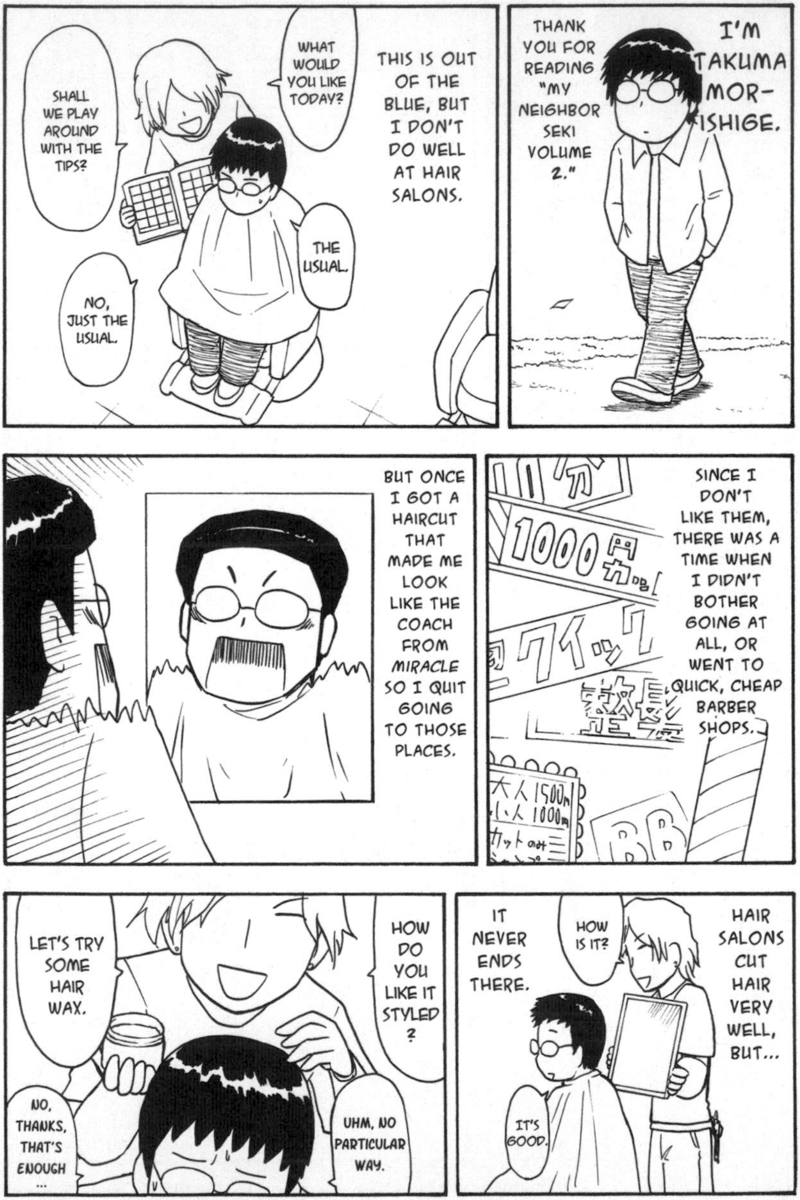
I'M TAKUMA MORISHIGE.
THANK YOU FOR READING "MY NEIGHBOR SEKI VOLUME 2."
THIS IS OUT OF THE BLUE, BUT I DON'T DO WELL AT HAIR SALONS.
WHAT WOULD YOU LIKE TODAY?
SHALL WE PLAY AROUND WITH THE TIPS?
THE USUAL.
NO, JUST THE USUAL.
SINCE I DON'T LIKE THEM, THERE WAS A TIME WHEN I DIDN'T BOTHER GOING AT ALL, OR WENT TO QUICK, CHEAP BARBER SHOPS.
1000円
整髪
大人1500円
小人1000円
カットのみ
BB
BUT ONCE I GOT A HAIRCUT THAT MADE ME LOOK LIKE THE COACH FROM *MIRACLE* SO I QUIT GOING TO THOSE PLACES.
HAIR SALONS CUT HAIR VERY WELL, BUT...
HOW IS IT?
IT NEVER ENDS THERE.
IT'S GOOD.
HOW DO YOU LIKE IT STYLED?
UHM, NO PARTICULAR WAY.
LET'S TRY SOME HAIR WAX.
NO, THANKS, THAT'S ENOUGH...

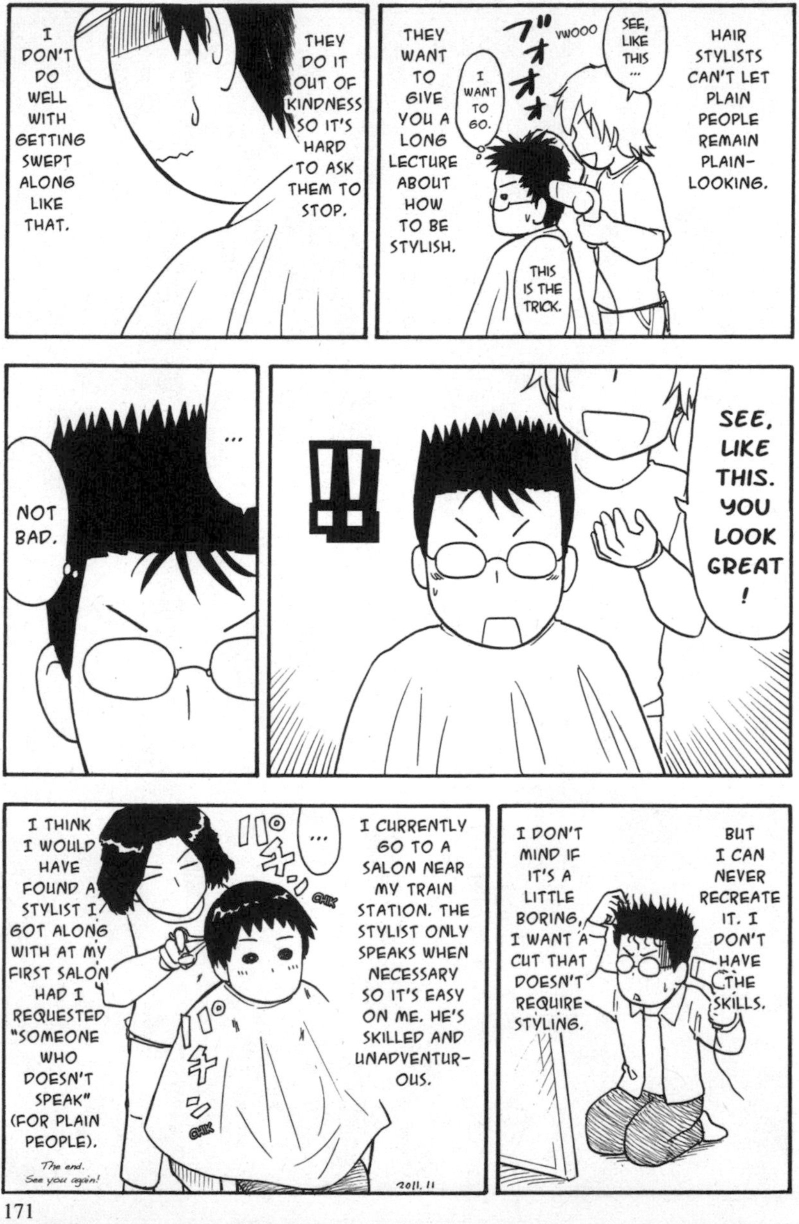
HAIR STYLISTS CAN'T LET PLAIN PEOPLE REMAIN PLAIN-LOOKING.
SEE, LIKE THIS ...
ブォォォ
VWOOO
I WANT TO GO.
THEY WANT TO GIVE YOU A LONG LECTURE ABOUT HOW TO BE STYLISH.
THIS IS THE TRICK.
THEY DO IT OUT OF KINDNESS SO IT'S HARD TO ASK THEM TO STOP.
I DON'T DO WELL WITH GETTING SWEPT ALONG LIKE THAT.
SEE, LIKE THIS. YOU LOOK GREAT!
!!
...
NOT BAD.
BUT I CAN NEVER RECREATE IT. I DON'T HAVE THE SKILLS.
I DON'T MIND IF IT'S A LITTLE BORING, I WANT A CUT THAT DOESN'T REQUIRE STYLING.
I CURRENTLY GO TO A SALON NEAR MY TRAIN STATION. THE STYLIST ONLY SPEAKS WHEN NECESSARY SO IT'S EASY ON ME. HE'S SKILLED AND UNADVENTUR-OUS.
...
パチッ
CHIK
パチン
CHIK
I THINK I WOULD HAVE FOUND A STYLIST I GOT ALONG WITH AT MY FIRST SALON HAD I REQUESTED "SOMEONE WHO DOESN'T SPEAK" (FOR PLAIN PEOPLE).
2011.11
The end. See you again!

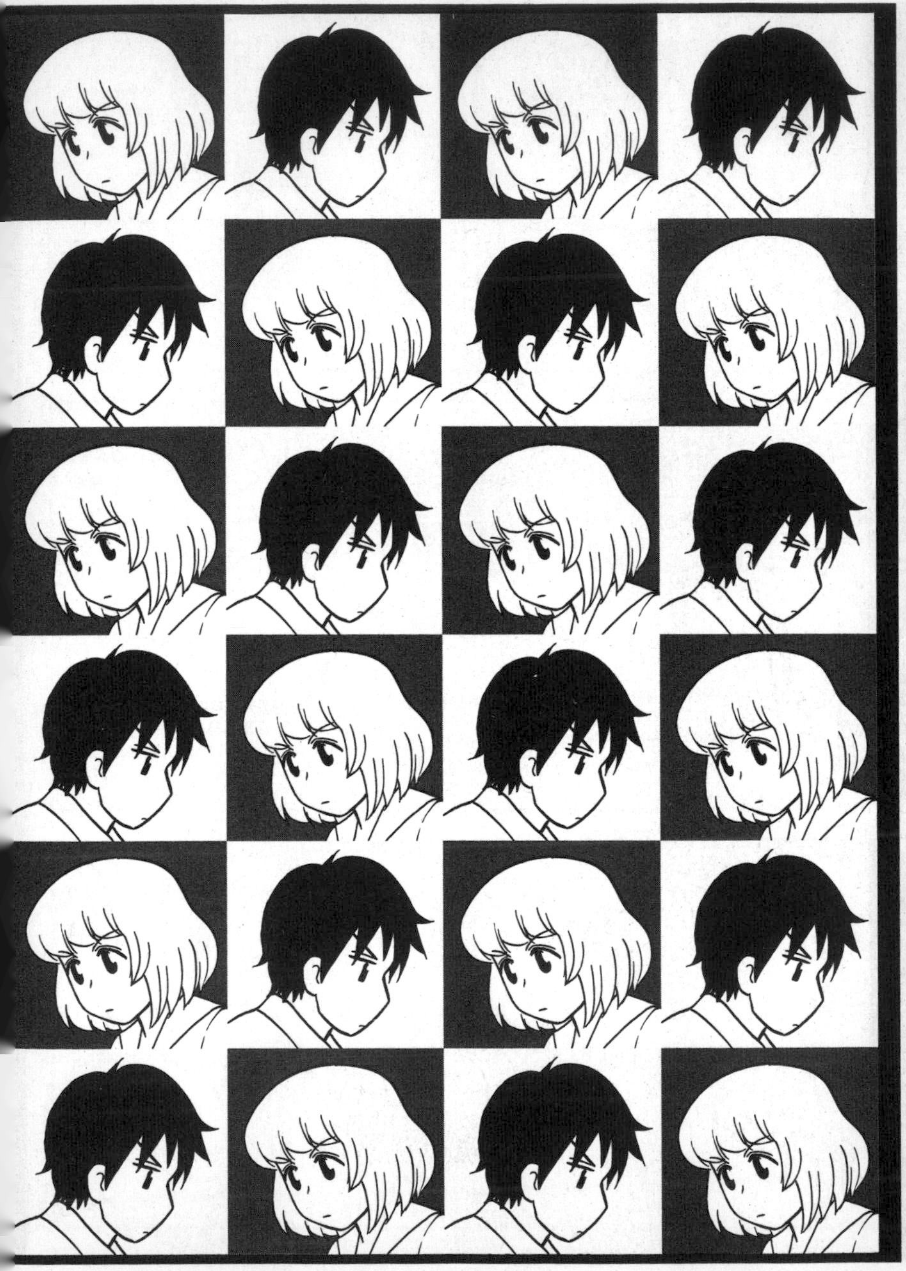

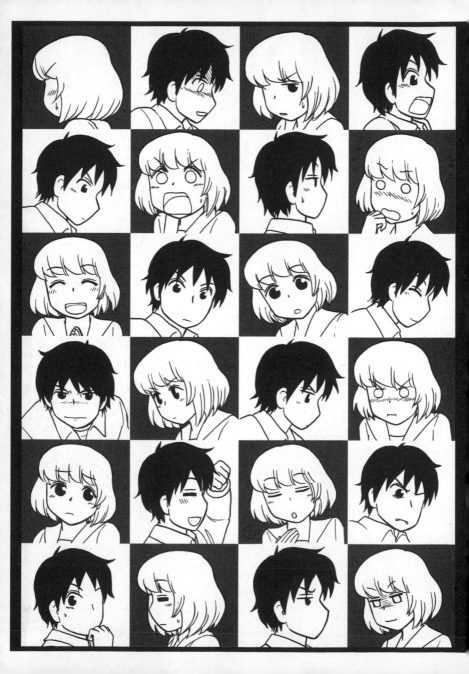